The State of Economic Inclusion Report 2021

The State of Economic Inclusion Report 2021

THE POTENTIAL TO SCALE

Colin Andrews, Aude de Montesquiou,
Inés Arévalo Sánchez, Puja Vasudeva Dutta,
Boban Varghese Paul, Sadna Samaranayake,
Janet Heisey, Timothy Clay, and
Sarang Chaudhary

Contents

FIGURES

TABLES

Foreword

The *State of Economic Inclusion Report 2021: The Potential to Scale* gives voice to one of the most stubborn challenges in development—transforming the economic lives of the extreme poor and vulnerable. At the time of writing, this challenge is being magnified by the fallout of the COVID-19 pandemic. The pandemic affects the poor and vulnerable most strongly, with early evidence suggesting disproportionate gender impacts. Economic inclusion programs face the dual challenge of adapting delivery norms during a pandemic and ensuring readiness to respond as part of the medium- and long-term recovery efforts.

Against a backdrop of much uncertainty, this report provides some hope. A central hypothesis of the report is that people who are poor and vulnerable face multiple constraints when encountering "poverty traps" for which a multidimensional response is required. Economic inclusion programs now under way in over 75 countries demonstrate that this hypothesis and response show signs of success. Defined here as a bundle of coordinated multidimensional interventions that support individuals, households, and communities in increasing incomes and assets, economic inclusion programs show flexibility in a variety of settings. One area with transformative potential is women's economic empowerment. There is now a considerable body of operational work focused on explicit gender-intentional program design to promote empowerment and mitigate unintended household and community risks.

The global landscape for economic inclusion has shifted significantly in recent years. A surge in global operations is driven by the scale-up of government-led programs that build on social protection, livelihoods and jobs, and financial inclusion investments. Continued momentum draws on a wealth of innovation and learning, spanning several technical experiences and domains, including graduation, social safety nets "plus," and community-driven programs as well as local economic development initiatives. A major contribution of this report is to present—for the first time—a systematic review of both government and nongovernment efforts. Evidence gathered in the report provides a unique baseline to benchmark the current global landscape and will enable us to track how it evolves in coming years.

All of this brings to the fore a central question: What is the potential for these multidimensional programs to scale up? The true potential of economic inclusion programs will be unlocked through the scale that is achieved through adoption by government actors. Many countries are at a nascent stage of this journey and wrestling with questions of program feasibility and sustainability. For this reason, the report focuses squarely on the political realities surrounding program scale-up and the manifold trade-offs that governments face in moving this agenda forward. The report highlights opportunities for improved program delivery and fiscal and policy coherence with stronger leadership and collaboration. Of course, successful government-led interventions also require strong partnership at the local level, with community organizations, nongovernmental organizations (NGOs), and the private sector.

The *State of Economic Inclusion Report 2021* emphasizes the possibility of leveraging social protection systems and the cross-sectoral collaboration that this involves. Recent years have seen a strong increase in financing and coverage of social protection programs across the world, with a demonstrated set of impacts reflecting how cash transfers, in particular, can boost the equity and resilience of the poorest. As countries expand the coverage and financing of this form of social protection, the terms *safety nets–plus* and *cash-plus* are gaining prominence, the "plus" indicating the potential to complement cash with additional inputs and service components or link to other sectors (agriculture, environment, financial services, and so forth). Economic inclusion is a key driver of the social safety nets–plus agenda, demonstrating particular promise to strengthen program impacts, but also bringing with it the reality of increased costs and complexity.

For this reason, the report moves forward key debates on program impact and costs, which are central to the sustainability of economic inclusion programs at scale. The report identifies a promising and potentially sustained set of impacts across a wide range of outcomes. A multicountry costing analysis helps to clarify the major cost drivers and cost ranges in different programs. Notably, the discussion brings into focus the need to rebalance debates on impacts and costs to reflect a shift from stand-alone nonprofit-led projects to government-led programs. This will have important operational implications for identifying cost-effective interventions and for cost optimization. Continued learning and evidence generation will be especially important as programs adapt to changing poverty contexts and megatrends, such as fragility, shocks (including climate change), urbanization, digitization, and demography.

As a flagship publication under the Partnership for Economic Inclusion (PEI), the report places a welcome emphasis on joint learning and collaboration. PEI is a dedicated platform to support the adoption and adaptation of national economic inclusion programs working with a variety of stakeholders, including national governments and bilateral, multilateral, NGO, research, and private-sector organizations. The partnership network is critical for contributing to evidence-based good practice, crowding in expertise, and providing a platform to refine and share cutting-edge knowledge on economic inclusion, with a strong emphasis on women's economic inclusion. As an example of this joint learning, the report is launched with an online and open-access PEI Data Portal (www.peiglobal.org), which will facilitate cross-learning and help track the development of the global landscape in years to come.

To this end, we welcome *The State of Economic Inclusion Report 2021* as an important milestone for continued learning in the common mission to support the scale-up of cost-effective and sustainable economic inclusion programs for the poorest in the years to come.

We look forward to continued and successful collaboration.

Michal Rutkowski
Global Director
Social Protection and Jobs, World Bank

Rakesh Rajani
Vice President, Programs
Co-Impact

Shameran Abed
Senior Director
BRAC

Birgit Pickel
Deputy Director General
BMZ (Federal Ministry for Economic Cooperation and Development, Germany)

Acknowledgments

The report was prepared by a team led by Colin Andrews, program manager, and Aude de Montesquiou, social protection specialist and co-task team leader, and coauthors Inés Arévalo Sánchez, Sarang Chaudhary, Timothy Clay, Puja Vasudeva Dutta, Janet Heisey, Boban Varghese Paul, and Sadna Samaranayake.

The team acknowledges inputs from the case study authors who were foundational to informing the key concepts and overall direction of the report. Writing on the Sahel were Edward Archibald (independent consultant), Thomas Bossuroy (World Bank Group, WBG), and Patrick Premand (WBG). Writing on Haku Wiñay was Raúl Asensio (Instituto de Estudios Peruanos). Writing on JEEViKA was Sadna Samaranayake (WBG), with contributions from JEEViKA's Paramveer Singh and Ajit Ranjan and from Kshovan Guha and Gautam Patel of the Abdul Latif Jameel Poverty Action Lab. Writing on BRAC was Isabel Whisson, with contributions from Rozina Haque, Julie Kedroske, and Munshi Sulaiman, all from BRAC, and Imran Matin, Narayan Das, and Syed Hashemi from BRAC University.

The team is grateful for the overall guidance of Ian Walker (WBG). The team further appreciates strategic guidance from Lindsay Coates (BRAC), Margaret Grosh (WBG), Doris King (Co-Impact), Ralf Radermacher (Deutsche Gesellschaft für Internationale Zusammenarbeit, GIZ), Rakesh Rajani (Co-Impact), Dena Ringold (WBG), and Michal Rutkowski (WBG). Throughout the report-drafting process, the team drew on the previous work and early guidance from Katharine McKee (WBG, retired) and Steen Lau Jorgensen (WBG, retired).

This report would not have been possible without the detailed survey contributions from nearly 100 organizations, including government partners, the United Nations, and NGO agencies as well as from World Bank operational staff. The report appendixes document each of these partner's programs in full.

The team benefited from substantive analytical and technical inputs from Edward Archibald (independent consultant) for chapters 1 and 2 and Johanne Buba (WBG) for chapters 3 and 4. Hitoishi Chakma (WBG) provided extensive support to the authors and editors in the research, drafting, and editing stages of the report. Significant research support is also acknowledged from Vasumathi Anandan (WBG), Karen Peffley (WBG), and Kevwe Pela (WBG).

We are grateful for the thorough guidance and direction from peer reviewers and Partnership for Economic Inclusion Interim Advisory Council (PEI IAC) members: William Abrams (Trickle Up), Anush Bezhanyan (WBG), Joanne Carter (Results), Aline Coudouel (WBG), Frank De Giovanni (PEI IAC), Ugo Gentilini (WBG), Nathanael Goldberg (Innovations for Poverty Action), Jakob Lessin (GIZ), Jesse Marsden (Results), Yves Moury (Fundación Capital), Laura Ralston (WBG), Indhira Santos (WBG), Parmesh Shah (WBG), Carolina Trivelli (PEI IAC), and Will Wiseman (WBG).

The following people provided valuable contributions, ideas, and feedback during the report-writing process: Gayatri Acharya (WBG), Jackie Aldrette (AVSI Foundation), Kathleen Beegle (WBG), Christian Bodewig (WBG), Ioana Botea (WBG), Hugo Brousset Chaman (WBG), Laura Campbell (WBG), Eliana Carranza (WBG), Wendy Chamberlin (BOMA Project), Luc Christiaensen (WBG), Tim Conway (Department for International Development, DFID), Louise J. Cord (WBG), February Curry (GIZ), Vidya Diwakar (Overseas Development Institute, ODI), Sara Giannozzi (WBG), Markus Goldstein (WBG), Lisa Hannigan (Department of Foreign Affairs and Trade, DFAT),

Alessandra Heinemann (WBG), Aylin Isik-Dikmelik (WBG), Dean Karlan (Innovations for Poverty Action), Christof Kersting (GIZ), Mattias Lundberg (WBG), Fazley Mahmud (DFAT), Brett Matthews (My Oral Village), Carolina de Miranda (Fundación Capital), Matteo Morgandi (WBG), Edmundo Murrugarra (WBG), Benedetta Musillo (DFID), David Myhre (USAID), Juan Navarrete (Fundación Capital), Aileen O'Donovan (IrishAid), Alreena Renita Pinto (WBG), Nelly Ramirez (Fundación Capital), Tatiana Rincón (Fundación Capital), Keetie Roelen (Institute of Development Studies), Andrew Shepherd (ODI), Anton Simanowitz (consultant), Sandor Sipos (WBG), Cornelia Tesliuc (WBG), Siv Tokle (WBG), and Natalia Winder Rossi (Food and Agriculture Organization).

We are grateful to the team at the World Bank Group Publications Office, in particular for the close guidance and support from Jewel McFadden and Mark McClure and for the additional support provided by Yolaina Montoya (WBG) and Marc DeFrancis (consultant).

About the Authors

Colin Andrews is a program manager in the World Bank's Social Protection and Jobs Global Practice. He has over 15 years of social protection experience in Africa and South Asia and in global policy. Colin leads the Partnership for Economic Inclusion, a multipartner initiative to support the scale-up of national economic inclusion programs. Colin has managed lending operations on safety nets and service delivery in Africa. He has published widely on safety net impacts, crisis response, and financing. Previously, he worked for the Food and Agriculture Organization of the United Nations, the European Commission, and nongovernmental organizations. He received a master's degree in economics from Trinity College, Dublin.

Inés Arévalo Sánchez is a consultant with the Partnership for Economic Inclusion. She is an economist with 15 years of experience in monitoring and evaluation, research, and learning, mostly focused on financial inclusion, agriculture, and social policy. Her experience also includes nearly five years of operational work in China, supporting the development of community-based financing within an environmental and rural development program. Inés has worked as a consultant with private philanthropical organizations and consultancies across many regions, primarily East and Central Asia. She holds a master's degree in development economics from the University of Sussex, England.

Sarang Chaudhary is a consultant in the World Bank's Social Protection and Jobs Global Practice. His work at the World Bank focuses on using data and econometric analysis in operations and research. Prior to that, he led a nonprofit in India working on community-driven development and grassroot program implementation alongside state and city governments. Sarang received a bachelor's degree in electronics and communication engineering from Uttar Pradesh Technical University in India and a master's degree in public policy from the University of California, Berkeley.

Timothy Clay is a consultant with the World Bank's Social Protection and Jobs Global Practice. In his current role, he works with the Partnership for Economic Inclusion to support analytical and operational work on economic inclusion programming. Timothy is experienced in labor market analysis, social security design and financing, and monitoring and evaluation of lending projects. He holds bachelor of science degrees in economics and international affairs and a dual master of science degree in public policy and human development from Maastricht University and the United Nations University Merit in the Netherlands.

Aude de Montesquiou is a social protection specialist in the World Bank's Social Protection and Jobs Global Practice. She co-led the startup of the Partnership for Economic Inclusion and managed the Consultative Group to Assist the Poor (CGAP)–Ford Foundation Graduation Program, a multipartner economic inclusion initiative with 10 pilot projects in eight countries. With over 15 years of experience in poverty reduction, Aude has published widely on social protection, livelihoods, and financial inclusion. Previously, she worked on aid effectiveness, impact, and client value at CGAP and with microfinance providers in Lebanon and Togo. She holds a master's degree in development studies from Sciences-Po Paris and a bachelor's degree in history from the Sorbonne.

Puja Vasudeva Dutta is an economist with expertise in social protection. She worked as a senior economist in the World Bank's Social Protection and Jobs Global Practice in South Asia and East Asia for more than a decade. Before joining the World Bank, she was a researcher in the Poverty Research Unit (Sussex, UK) and the National Council of Applied Economic Research (India), focusing on poverty, inequality, and labor markets. Her recent work spans research, technical assistance, and operational support on social protection policy reform, program design, and delivery systems. Puja holds a doctoral degree in economics at the University of Sussex, England.

Janet Heisey is a senior consultant with the Partnership for Economic Inclusion, supporting the country engagement and global knowledge workstreams. She also consulted for the World Bank's Kenya Social and Economic Inclusion Program. She has more than 20 years of experience developing strategy and designing economic inclusion programs for people living in poverty, with a focus on people with disabilities and displaced populations. Previously, Janet created and led a technical assistance unit at Trickle Up, working in partnership with the UN High Commissioner for Refugees to design economic inclusion programs that foster refugee self-reliance. She has a bachelor's degree from Michigan State University.

Boban Varghese Paul is an economist with the World Bank's Social Protection and Jobs Global Practice and focuses on livelihoods, social safety nets, and delivery systems. His prior experience includes private sector management consulting, NGOs, and government. He has advised governments and the private sector on agriculture value chain development and led the national monitoring and evaluation team of India's largest education NGO. He was part of the chief economic adviser's office for the government of India, working on universal basic income and other policies. He holds a master's degree in public administration in international development from the Kennedy School of Government, Harvard University.

Sadna Samaranayake is a senior consultant with the Partnership for Economic Inclusion. Her work focuses on developing PEI's country engagement strategy, providing technical guidance to governments and World Bank teams on economic inclusion programming and strategies integrated with livelihoods, social protection, and financial inclusion. Previously, Sadna was the founding director of BRAC's Ultra-Poor Graduation Initiative, where she led delivery of technical assistance, program design, implementation oversight, and knowledge products for several government and multilateral clients on BRAC's graduation approach. Sadna earned a master of arts degree with a concentration in international development and social entrepreneurship from New York University, where she was a Catherine Reynolds Social Entrepreneurship Fellow.

Abbreviations

AFD	Agence Française de Développement
ASPIRE	Atlas of Social Protection Indicators of Resilience and Equity
BMZ	Federal Ministry for Economic Cooperation and Development (Germany)
BRLP	Bihar Rural Livelihoods Project (JEEViKA, local acronym)
BRLPS	Bihar Rural Livelihoods Promotion Society
BTDP	Bihar Transformative Development Project
CESAM	Centre de Suivi et d'Assistance en Management
CGAP	Consultative Group to Assist the Poor
CLAR	Local Committee for the Allocation of Resources
CLF	cluster-level federation
CLM	Chemen Lavi Miyò (Haiti)
CSA	climate-smart agriculture
CSO	civil society organization
DFID	Department for International Development (United Kingdom)
FAO	Food and Agriculture Organization of the United Nations
FCV	fragility, conflict, and violence
FI	financial inclusion
FONCODES	Fund for Economic and Social Development (Chile)
FOSIS	El Fondo de Solidaridad e Inversión Social (Chile)
GDP	gross domestic product
GIZ	Deutsche Gesellschaft für Internationale Zusammenarbeit (German Agency for International Cooperation)
G2P	government-to-person
GUP	Graduating the Ultra Poor
ICF	International Community Foundation
IDA	International Development Association (of the World Bank Group)
IDS	Institute of Development Studies
IEF	Ingreso Ético Familiar (Chile)
IFAD	International Fund for Agricultural Development
IGVGD	Income Generation for Vulnerable Group Development
ILO	International Labour Organization
IPA	Innovations for Poverty Action
J-PAL	Abdul Latif Jameel Poverty Action Lab
JEEViKA	local acronym for Bihar Rural Livelihoods Project (BRLP)
L&J	livelihoods and jobs
LIPW	labor-intensive public works
M&E	monitoring and evaluation
MDTF	Multi-Donor Trust Fund
MIDIS	Ministry of Development and Social Inclusion (Peru)
MISFA	Microfinance Investment Support Facility for Afghanistan
MPI	Multidimensional Poverty Index
NEC	Central Executing Nuclei
NGO	nongovernmental organization
NPL	national poverty line
NRLM	National Rural Livelihood Mission (India)
PAD	project appraisal document

PEI	Partnership for Economic Inclusion
PEIMT	Partnership for Economic Inclusion management team
PEJEDEC	Projet d'Urgence de Création d'Emploi Jeunes et de Développement des Compétences
PID	project information document
PIKE	Productive Inclusion Knowledge Exchange
PISEAR	Socio-Economic Inclusion in Rural Areas Project (Argentina)
PO	producer organization
PP	project paper
PPP	purchasing power parity
PRISE	Projet d'Insertion Socio-Economique (Côte d'Ivoire)
Pronamachs	National Program for the Management of Water Basins and Land Conservation (Peru)
PSDS	Project Information and Integrated Safeguards Data Sheet
PSNP	productive safety net program
PSSN	Productive Social Safety Net
PWP	public works–plus
PxMF	Produciendo Por Mi Futuro (Colombia)
RCT	randomized controlled trial
REAP	Rural Entrepreneur Access Program (Kenya)
RLLP	Resilient Landscapes and Livelihoods Project (Ethiopia)
ROSCA	rotating savings and credit association
SASPP	Sahel Adaptive Social Protection Program
SDG	Sustainable Development Goal
SHG	self-help group
SJY	Satat Jeevikoparjan Yojana
SSN	social safety net
TDA	Text and Data Analytics team
THCP	Targeting the Hard-Core Poor
TUP	Targeting the Ultra Poor
UNHCR	United Nations High Commissioner for Refugees
UYEP	Urban Youth Employment Program (Papua New Guinea)
VO	village organization
VSLA	village savings and loan association
VSSC	village social solidarity committee
VUP	Vision 2020 Umurenge Programme (Rwanda)
WASH	water, sanitation, and hygiene
WFP	World Food Programme
WINGS	Women's Income-Generating Support (Uganda)
YOP	Youth Opportunity Program (Uganda)

All dollar amounts in this publication are US dollars unless otherwise indicated.

Executive Summary

In recent years there has been growing global momentum to strengthen and scale up economic inclusion for the poorest. Key actions are being taken in light of the Sustainable Development Goals (SDGs)—to "end poverty in all its forms everywhere by 2030" and to address inclusive and sustainable growth (SDG 8). *The State of Economic Inclusion Report 2021: The Potential to Scale* brings to light a shifting global landscape, as reflected through the experiences of the 75 countries featured in the review. The momentum for this shift is driven by the scale-up of government-led programs that build on social protection, livelihoods and jobs, and financial inclusion investments. This shift is also fueled by a promising evidence base and a groundswell of learning, originating especially from graduation programs within the nonprofit sector.

Efforts to scale up respond to high levels of extreme poverty and most recently the fallout of COVID-19. By 2030, following a business-as-usual scenario, an estimated 479 million people are projected to be living in extreme poverty, and the share of global poor living in fragile and conflict-affected countries is expected to reach 50 percent by 2030.[1] In the final months of 2020, the fallout from the coronavirus pandemic raises the possibility of more than 80 million people being pushed into extreme poverty. Emerging experiences show the potential of economic inclusion programs—as part of integrated policy responses—to mitigate the economywide and sector-specific downturns created by this pandemic and ultimately to facilitate the restoration of livelihoods and the recovery of communities.

Great Expectations and Some Skepticism

As economic inclusion programs for the poorest evolve, a story of great expectations and considerable skepticism emerges. A sustainable and inclusive economy that "leaves no one behind" is more important than ever. While transformative economic growth will be the ultimate driver of poverty reduction, it is not automatically inclusive and does not always penetrate the poorest households. In strengthening economic inclusion for the poorest, it is important to recognize "poverty traps" and to realize that unleashing the productive potential of people living in poverty involves the removal of multiple constraints through a multidimensional response. In practice, household, community, local economy, and institutional constraints may impact specific population cohorts most strongly, such as women, youths, people with disabilities, and those who have been displaced. As a cross-cutting priority, economic inclusion programs tend to strongly emphasize women's economic empowerment as a key driver for change.

Data from this report suggest there are three entry points through which governments are building on existing antipoverty programs to customize specific economic inclusion efforts:

1. Social safety nets (SSNs)
2. Livelihoods and jobs (L&J)
3. Financial inclusion (FI)

While these entry points are not mutually exclusive—or exhaustive—they do serve as a foundation on which investments can be built and broader sectoral collaborations can be achieved. This carries important operational implications. Governments are deliberately integrating economic inclusion programs as part of national strategies and frameworks for poverty reduction. Economic inclusion programs are seen as an important complement to existing antipoverty efforts. For example, as countries expand the coverage and financing of safety nets, the terms *social safety net–plus* (SSN-plus) or *cash-plus* are gaining prominence. Economic inclusion is a key driver of the safety nets–plus agenda, the "plus" indicating the potential to complement cash with additional inputs, service components, or links to external services. Ultimately a trend from stand-alone to more integrated approaches presents opportunities for improved program delivery and fiscal and policy coherence.

Despite much progress, the potential to scale up economic inclusion programs is considered in light of critical debates on feasibility and program sustainability. Economic inclusion programs may be considered too complex or too costly to operate at scale. Governments in many countries, especially in low-income settings, will face capacity constraints to administer and manage multidimensional and cross-sector interventions. As programs scale up, political economy factors become more prominent, and the adoption and scale-up of economic inclusion programs will hinge on political acceptability and involve trade-offs, especially around program objectives and priority target groups. In this context, the report brings fresh perspective on program impacts and costs, with the aim of better understanding the evidence base and fiscal realities that will ultimately determine the question of scale.

Major Contributions of *The State of Economic Inclusion Report 2021*

This report identifies 219 active economic inclusion programs in 75 countries, reaching nearly 92 million individuals, with additional programs in the planning phase. The Partnership for Economic Inclusion (PEI) Landscape Survey 2020 (see appendix A) reveals a variety of program implementers, but government programs are quickly increasing, and government-led programs cover approximately 90 percent of program beneficiaries and half of the projects surveyed (see figure O.1). Note that these figures are a lower-bound baseline, given gaps in the available data, fast-moving project pipe-lines, and challenges in the reporting of coverage. However, these estimates provide an important baseline to track the evolution of programs in the coming years. Many of these programs are approaching an important inflection point, with expansion, and greater refinement to address the needs of the poorest, to follow.

Technical Clarity

There is a need for definitional clarity and a common framework for economic inclusion, and that need underpins this report. The report focuses on economic inclusion programs that reach the extreme poor and the vulnerable. In this report, economic inclusion involves the gradual integration of individuals and households into broader economic and community development processes, with a focus on increasing their incomes and assets and a view to strengthening their resilience and future opportunities. Economic inclusion programs often include a combination of cash or in-kind transfers, skills training, coaching, access to finance, and links to market support. These interventions cover a diverse landscape, including, among other efforts, productive inclusion, graduation, and community-driven development programs. Scaling up is the process by which a program is established, expanded, or adapted under real-world conditions into broader national policy and programming. Scaling up often builds

FIGURE O.1 **Percent Distribution of Economic Inclusion Programs and Beneficiaries by Region, Lead Institution, and Entry Point**

a. By region

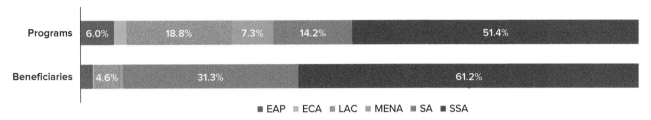

■ EAP   ■ ECA   ■ LAC   ■ MENA   ■ SA   ■ SSA

b. By lead institution

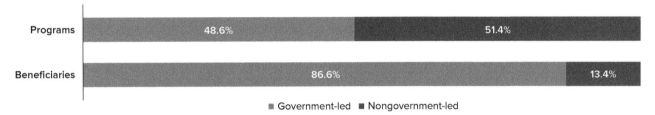

■ Government-led   ■ Nongovernment-led

c. By entry point

■ Social safety nets   ■ Livelihoods and jobs   ■ Financial inclusion

Source: Partnership for Economic Inclusion, World Bank.

Note: EAP = East Asia and Pacific; ECA = Europe and Central Asia; LAC = Latin America and the Caribbean; MENA = Middle East and North Africa; SA = South Asia; SSA = Sub-Saharan Africa. Data on the number of beneficiaries are missing for 18 programs—6 nongovernment and 12 government programs—which when broken down by entry point signify 6 social safety net (SSN) and 12 livelihoods and jobs (L&J) programs. The graph also excludes data from JEEViKA in India (a government-led L&J program), which covers over 50 percent of all beneficiaries in the survey. The total number of programs, excluding JEEViKA, is 218 (112 nongovernment-led and 106 government-led programs or 77 SSN, 137 L&J, and 4 financial inclusion (FI) or 13 in East Asia and Pacific, 5 in Europe and Central Asia, 41 in Latin America and the Caribbean, 16 in the Middle East and North Africa, 31 in South Asia, and 112 in Sub-Saharan Africa. The number of total beneficiaries is 45,319,700, which includes direct and indirect beneficiaries. When JEEViKA is included, the number of programs is 219 (112 nongovernment-led and 107 government-led programs or 77 SSN, 138 L&J, and 4 FI or 13 in East Asia and Pacific, 5 in Europe and Central Asia, 41 in Latin America and the Caribbean, 16 in the Middle East and North Africa, 32 in South Asia, and 112 in Sub-Saharan Africa). The number of total individual beneficiaries equals 91,933,700.

on the success of programs shown to be effective on a small scale or under controlled conditions. It may also be driven without prior piloting and testing, and often in response to a political decision or directive.

An Evidence Base

The need to establish a more comprehensive evidence base around economic inclusion is a hallmark of this report. A central focus is the assimilation of new data and evidence around program design and implementation, impacts, and costs. This is critical to determine the feasibility of program scale-up. Through the PEI Landscape Survey 2020, this report brings together formerly disconnected strands of experiences in government and nongovernment programs and across a range of sectors. The impact review documents experiences across 80 quantitative and qualitative evaluations in 37 countries. The report introduces the PEI Quick Costing Tool 2020 as a starting point to inform debates on cost optimization and cost efficiency. Key data gathered throughout this report are presented and will be updated on the PEI Data Portal available at http://peiglobal.org. This open-access approach to data has been devised to encourage debate and to facilitate new evidence generation over time.

Continued Learning

The report draws attention to the need for continued learning from first-hand country experiences. Adaptation to changing poverty contexts and megatrends is increasingly important. Economic inclusion programs are flexible and can be customized to local settings, and major shocks, such as COVID-19, will fundamentally reshape economic inclusion programs in each country. As the state of economic inclusion evolves, new learning comes to light, and the report provides an in-depth set of case studies highlighting lessons and operational insights from government-led and nongovernment-led projects. The case studies include (1) the Sahel Adaptive Social Protection Program, (2) India's Bihar Rural Livelihoods Promotion Society (BRLPS), locally known as JEEViKA's Satat Jeevikoparjan Yojana, (3) BRAC's Ultra Poor Graduation program in Bangladesh, and (4) Peru's Haku Wiñay program (box O.1).

BOX O.1 **Learning by Doing: Four Case Studies**

This report features four case studies that shed light on emerging lessons in the design and implementation of economic inclusion programs in a variety of contexts. Findings from these case studies, and wider survey data, underpin the key concepts and analysis presented throughout this report.

The Sahel Adaptive Social Protection Program (SASPP), supported by the World Bank and development partners, features productive inclusion programs implemented in tandem with the national safety net programs of four Sahel countries: Burkina Faso, Mauritania, Niger, and Senegal. More than 50,000 households to date, across the four participating countries, have received a comprehensive package of products and services to help them move out of poverty. A multicountry randomized controlled trial (RCT) evaluation is under way to determine the impact of these productive measures on cash transfer beneficiaries and how such measures can be optimized and made more cost-effective. The case study presents insights on the importance of government leadership and institutional coordination, the value of broader investments in the safety net system, and the need for flexibility in delivery arrangements depending on the country context.

The Satat Jeevikoparjan Yojana (SJY) program of JEEViKA, in the state of Bihar, India, is a livelihoods program that utilizes the graduation approach by leveraging self-help groups and village organizations to help with key program functions,

(Box continues next page)

BOX O.1   **Learning by Doing: Four Case Studies** *(continued)*

such as targeting and delivering assets to poor households. SJY identifies and trains large cadres of community members as frontline implementers of the program and demonstrates how large-scale government programs can alleviate implementation-related capacity constraints. Although at an early stage of implementation, SJY is a large-scale effort intended to reach 100,000 households within JEEViKA's larger economic inclusion effort, which currently reaches 10 million rural women.

The BRAC case study reflects the experience of a large nongovernmental organization in pioneering the graduation approach, featuring their experience over the past 20 years and lessons emerging from recent innovations. BRAC's graduation program in Bangladesh has reached over 2 million households, accepting approximately 100,000 women heads of household into the program each year. An RCT evaluation on BRAC's program demonstrated sizeable economic impacts that continue years after the intervention. Other RCTs evaluating global graduation models have produced similar positive impact results, which helped catalyze a global wave of graduation and graduation-like programs. BRAC's approach highlights the importance of long-term investment, constant adaptation, and innovation supported by research.

In Peru, the Haku Wiñay program, implemented by the Ministry of Development and Social Inclusion, through the Social Development Cooperation Fund, is an economic inclusion program introduced to create economic gains among the most disadvantaged rural households. This case study explores how an economic inclusion program can integrate socially accepted community structures with a national program strategy and ultimately replicate this approach. Successful scale-up is being achieved thanks to participatory decision-making and the engagement of community project management systems and community trainers (*yachachiqs*). Replication required significant adaptations, including giving implementers in different parts of the country the freedom to apply locally relevant microstrategies to make the approach successful in varying contexts of rural poverty.

Transforming the Lives of the Extreme Poor and Vulnerable: A Framework

The report is anchored around a simplified framework to consider the pathways for scaling up economic inclusion programs that strengthen resilience and opportunities of the extreme poor and vulnerable. The framework (see figure O.2) illustrates an overall context and response diagnostic linked to a desired set of outcomes at the household and community level and in government systems. The framework was developed iteratively using findings from the underlying report survey, stakeholder consultations, and available literature cited throughout. In presenting this framework, certain limitations are noted: economic inclusion at scale is not a "silver bullet," considerable heterogeneity is masked by a simplified framework, and the engagement of local community and nongovernment structures remain critical to its execution. The framework presents a starting point for ongoing discussion.

FIGURE O.2 **Pathways to Economic Inclusion at Scale: A Framework**

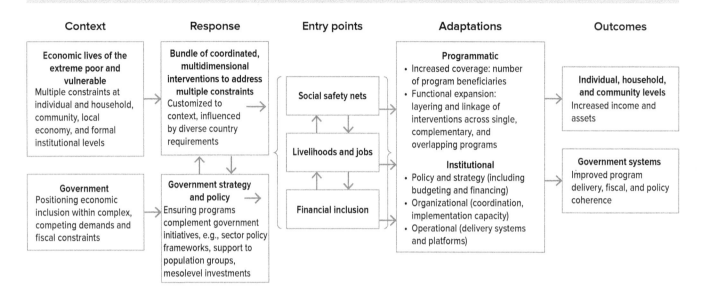

Source: Partnership for Economic Inclusion, World Bank.

The starting point of the framework is the goal of transforming the economic lives of the poor. Unleashing the productive potential of extreme poor and vulnerable people involves the removal of multiple constraints. Addressing both external constraints related to community, local economy, and institutional failures and internal constraints reflecting intrahousehold dynamics and behavior is critical, although internal constraints are less well understood. Improving integrated responses that link the individual and household components of economic inclusion programs to wider community and local economy processes is required. A multidimensional response is proposed, the components of which are likely to evolve over time as learning and adaptation continue to develop.

Importantly, the framework centers on the potential to effect change within a government landscape, requiring clear alignment to national institutions, strategies, and policies. This represents an important shift in popular discourse around economic inclusion programs and leads to a consideration of the incentives, trade-offs, and strategic entry points in scale. Ultimately, the evolution of these programs at the country level will hinge on political acceptability and will be shaped by several political economy considerations, such as historical processes, structural forces, and institutions. The report highlights how governments face strong challenges in determining target groups, often against a backdrop of excess demand and tight fiscal constraints. The success or failure of economic inclusion programs will often rest on three programmatic decisions: program objectives, financing, and institutional arrangements for delivery.

Ten Key Findings

1 *An unprecedented surge in economic inclusion programming is occurring worldwide.* Survey data show inclusion programs are under way in at least 75 countries, reaching approximately 20 million households and benefiting nearly 92 million individuals, either directly or indirectly. This report presents data and evidence from 219 programs and the Partnership for Economic Inclusion Landscape Survey 2020 identified a further 40 programs in the planning stages. Nearly half of all programs worldwide are government led, and these programs cover 93 percent of beneficiaries across all programs featured in this report. Rapid expansion is driven by low-income countries; half of all programs surveyed are in Sub-Saharan Africa.

2 *There is strong potential for economic inclusion programs to build on preexisting government programs, and this may prove critical in the long-term recovery efforts arising from the COVID-19 economic crisis.* Economic inclusion is becoming a critical instrument in many governments' large-scale antipoverty programming. One of the primary means by which governments scale up economic inclusion is through social safety nets, which offer an opportunity to build on cash transfers. The scale-up of government programs has the potential to introduce economies of scale and allow for integrated approaches. The report points to the fact that government programs typically include five or more components, most commonly transfers, skills training, coaching, market links, and access to financial services.

3 *The current scale of economic inclusion interventions is modest, and a sustainable approach to scaling up involves more than expanding program beneficiary numbers.* The Partnership for Economic Inclusion Landscape Survey 2020 shows that more than 50 percent of existing government-led programs have the potential to support between 5 and 10 percent of the extreme poor. Many government-led programs are in the process of expanding coverage. Yet scaling up is not simply about the size of coverage but also about quality: the quality of impact and sustainability of coverage as well as the quality of processes of change and adaptation. Economic inclusion at scale therefore considers the associated programmatic and institutional mechanics, many of which are important prerequisites before introducing new program beneficiaries.

4 *Economic inclusion programs provide considerable flexibility for adaptations. Despite heterogeneity, there is common prioritization on rural development, fragility, and the needs of specific vulnerable groups.* The Partnership for Economic Inclusion Landscape Survey 2020 revealed a strong focus on protecting most vulnerable groups, including children (25 percent of programs surveyed), people with disabilities (27 percent of programs surveyed), and displaced populations (33 percent of programs surveyed). The most frequently cited objectives for economic inclusion programs include self-employment, income diversification, and resilience. This reflects an agenda with a strong rural focus (87 percent of all programs) and an emphasis on fragility (25 percent of programs surveyed) coupled with a focus on climate change mitigation (55 percent of all programs surveyed).

5 *Women's economic empowerment is a key driver of economic inclusion programming, with nearly 90 percent of programs surveyed having a gender focus.* Program design adaptations to promote empowerment and mitigate unintended household and community risks have emerged. There is a considerable body of operational work focused on explicit gender-intentional program design to boost effectiveness. At the same time, there is heightened interest and recognized risks in the unintended consequences of gender-specific program adaptations, such as exacerbated time poverty, reinforced traditional gender roles, and gender-based violence.

6 *Economic inclusion programs look set to increasingly adapt to the realities of informality, especially for youths in urban areas.* Programmatic approaches vary, with some self-employment interventions having broad inclusion objectives and others explicitly seeking high-potential entrepreneurs. Only one-third of programs facilitate access to wage employment opportunities, an agenda pushed by government-led programs. Nearly 70 percent of programs help participants link to existing value chains and markets (local, regional, national, or international), and some even support the creation of new value chains. Almost 40 percent of programs report operations in urban centers, with 64 percent of programs focused on youth, reflecting broader demographic and urbanization megatrends. The adaptation of economic inclusion programs to urban areas impacted by COVID-19 looks set to become an area of particular focus.

7 *Digital innovations will be critical to leapfrog capacity constraints and to strengthen program management.* Many programs are currently utilizing government social registries, beneficiary registries, and other government databases to identify program participants (33 percent of all programs and 45 percent of government-led programs). Digital technology is an important factor across 85 percent of all government-led programs and is prevalent in all regions. Thirty percent of government-led programs provide access to program components through digital platforms.

8 *Economic inclusion programs build on a promising evidence base that will soon grow significantly.* A review of 80 quantitative and qualitative evaluations in 37 countries shows that a bundle of coordinated multidimensional set of interventions demonstrates greater impact on income, assets, and savings relative to stand-alone interventions. The interactions between components likely drive overall program impact. As highlighted in figure O.3, the existing evidence base is dominated by nongovernment programs, which in many cases are stand-alone programs. This is set to change in the coming years. About 80 percent of the surveyed programs have planned research; results

FIGURE O.3 Distribution of Studies Reporting on Specific Outcomes, by Lead Agency

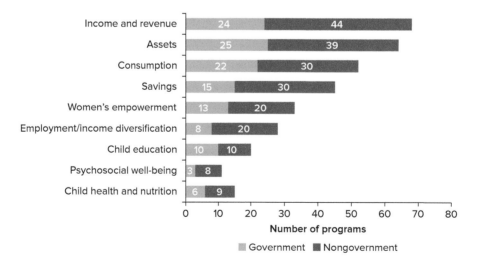

Source: See appendix B for the detailed bibliography of sources.

Note: This summary reflects 97 quantitative impact evaluations for 71 programs for which complete information from the studies could be obtained.

from two-thirds of these studies will be available in 2020–21. The emergence of greater evidence from government-led programs will be important for rebalancing the discussion on program impacts, especially to reframe how long-term impacts are understood within a national system of support.

9 *An improved understanding of basic cost structures is a vital starting point to assessing the cost-effectiveness of economic inclusion programs by more than just "sticker price."* The report breaks new ground in the approach to costing analysis, a topic fraught with complications, including challenges in measurement, heterogeneity of program objectives, and complications in comparability. It provides one of the first multicountry cost disaggregations for government- and nongovernment-led economic inclusion programs globally. The PEI Quick Costing Tool 2020, which facilitated data collection, emerges in the absence of other operational costing tools critical to informing real-time program design and policy dialogue.

The cost of economic inclusion programs tends to be driven by a single intervention, such as cash grants, asset or input transfers, or safety net transfers (figure O.4). Human resource and staff costs are more prominent cost drivers in more complex projects, where costs are driven by multiple components, rather than those driven by one large component provided in conjunction with others. The size of the components varies considerably and depends on the modality of support, for example, strictly time-bound or continuous support. The overall price range of economic inclusion programs sampled varies substantially. The total cost of economic inclusion programs is between $41 and $2,253 (in 2011 purchasing power parity, or PPP) per beneficiary over the duration (3.6 years on average) of each program.[2] This variance continues to exist when the programs are further broken down by entry points: SSN programs range from $77 to $2,253 (2011 PPP) and livelihoods and jobs programs range from $41 to

FIGURE O.4 Largest Cost Component as a Percentage of Total Cost, Selected Programs

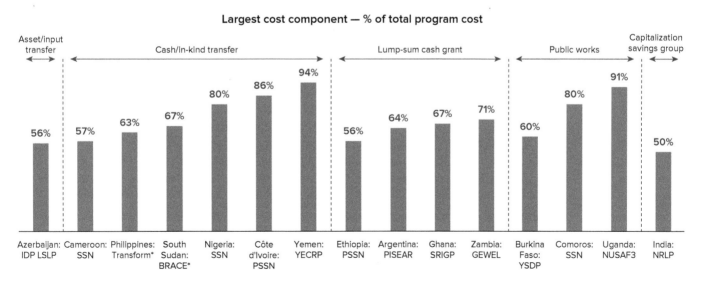

Largest cost component — % of total program cost

Source: PEI Quick Costing Tool 2020, World Bank.

Note: See appendix C, table C.1 for full program names and details.

* NGO-led programs. All other programs are government led.

$2,076 (2011 PPP). However, program sticker prices need to be understood based on their adequacy and impact.

10 *Strong partnership is integral to the success of economic inclusion programs.* The engagement of community mechanisms is a critical driver of program delivery, with most programs leveraging community structures, including informal savings and credit community groups (42 percent), local governance groups (59 percent), and formalized producer organizations (44 percent). Community structures can further expand livelihood opportunities and increase program sustainability, particularly if the community organizations are formally linked to other market actors, including financial service providers and private training providers. Nongovernmental organizations (NGOs) provide technical assistance to 64 percent of government programs, and 67 percent of governments partner with NGOs to deliver their programs. Partnership is also critical at the global level to advance global operational knowledge, best practices, learning, and leveraging financial support.

Future Directions

The report points to a continued and growing learning agenda around economic inclusion for the poorest. Across the world, economic inclusion programs are being customized to local settings, with programs invariably adopting a learning-by-doing approach. The flexibility of economic inclusion programs makes them well suited to adapt to changing poverty contexts and megatrends, such as informality, urbanization, demographic shifts, and technology. This flexibility also points to the potential for the increased importance of economic inclusion programs in response to major shocks, including the medium- to long-term response and recovery effort around COVID-19. As programs evolve, the learning agenda will continue to grow, with the promise of better informing the existing evidence base and bolstering political buy-in for programs and approaches that demonstrate effectiveness. The Partnership for Economic Inclusion will serve as an important platform to meet this demand for knowledge and continued innovation and learning.

Delivery

Refining program delivery systems across diverse contexts will gain in importance. Documentation of effective operational models and delivery systems in different contexts is required to facilitate effective design and coordination of economic inclusion programming. With a wide range of configurations of partners, programs, and structures under way, there are important opportunities to improve program effectiveness. It will be important to gather evidence on the interplay between different government institutions, and between government and partner organizations, such as community networks, NGOs, and private sector firms. This evidence will help to reveal commonalities and key differences across each of the program entry points—a critical gap in this report. Digital solutions can help to leapfrog some delivery constraints and increase cost-effectiveness. These solutions will grow in prominence as social distancing restrictions affect training and coaching activities in the wake of the COVID-19 crisis.

Customization

Increasing customization based on the needs of specific population cohorts—including women, youths, and people with disabilities—is a certainty. As a cross-cutting priority, more economic inclusion programs will likely include specific design features to promote women's economic empowerment. Changes in the aspirations of youths will also provide an important impetus for program expansion. Given high levels of youth underemployment and uncertain pathways to formal jobs, economic inclusion programs will play an important role in providing opportunities for self-employment and microenterprise development. Demographic shifts and increased urbanization are likely to fuel significant demand for these programs, as emerging experiences in Bangladesh, Egypt, Ghana, Indonesia, and Kenya, among other countries, now suggest. For people with disabilities, multidimensional economic inclusion programs can offer a means of increasing their economic opportunities and reaching their full potential. The body of knowledge on how to adapt design and delivery to increase outcomes for people with disabilities to reach their full potential is growing. But nearly all programs, regardless of their target populations, find that their participants' performance trajectories differ, with some "fast climbers" and "slow climbers" in every group. These varying trajectories have important implications for program design.

Shock Sensitivity

Programming for economic inclusion cannot be divorced from the vagaries of external shocks, vulnerability, and fragility. Beyond the current COVID-19 context, the direction and nature of economic inclusion programs will also be shaped by different types of shocks, including economic shocks or shocks caused by conflict or the effects of climate change. As a response, economic inclusion programs in fragile settings are increasing in size and number, and a better understanding of operational models in these contexts is paramount. Good practice in linking economic inclusion to humanitarian interventions and facilitating market links for displaced and host populations will be critical. One strong implication is the need for program adaptability and flexibility to withstand shocks and to adapt program design in the context of dynamic short- and medium-term needs.

Links to Community and Local Economy

As programs develop to address the needs of specific populations or demands of different contexts, the report makes clear the importance of linking traditional economic inclusion responses for individuals and households with the wider community and local economy processes. Economic inclusion programs foster links with existing community structures, productive organizations, and savings networks. Improved market and value chain links can increase the productivity of livelihood activities and bolster program sustainability. Increased mesolevel linkages help alleviate structural barriers and constraints to access to markets, infrastructure, and production inputs and increase the potential of the private sector. Closer integration of these programs with the local economy may also have important community spillover effects. As experience grows, the menu of programmatic responses will likely evolve.

New Wave of Evidence

Given anticipated program innovations and ongoing research, the economic inclusion knowledge base is set to grow. While there is much evidence already, the next wave of evaluations will likely focus on government programs at scale and will help isolate the mechanisms of impact across entry points and for different groups. This will have important operational implications for identifying cost-effective bundles of interventions in each context and lessons on the effectiveness of different operational delivery models. A critical learning agenda is emerging to help address several evidence gaps. First, few studies provide details on the context in which programs operate, and a major gap exists on cost analysis. Second, most evaluations are not designed to isolate channels of impact, that is, to understand key drivers of program outcomes. Third, there is very limited quantitative evidence on resilience and empowerment, with the exception of some experiences from community-driven development programs. Going forward, a new wave of evaluations will shape the state of global evidence significantly. About 80 percent of the surveyed programs in this report have planned research and, as noted, two-thirds of the results will be available by 2021. In moving the evaluation agenda forward, there is a critical need to complement impact evaluations with real-time operational research, program-monitoring assessments, and qualitative fieldwork to identify opportunities to enhance program performance.

Cost Effectiveness

The ability to determine program costs is an essential step in determining the cost-effectiveness of economic inclusion programs and their sustainability. The PEI Quick Costing Tool 2020 developed as part of this report is a practical resource to guide practitioners through the disaggregation of costs in multidimensional programs. Going forward, it is critical that economic inclusion program implementers (both government and nongovernment) and policy makers better scrutinize their cost structures in order to increase program efficiency. Researchers assessing the impact of economic inclusion programs should systematically collect and report on cost data in addition to impact sizes. The systematic understanding of costs will allow governments to make sense of program cost-benefit ratios and guide their policy choices. Having reliable costing data offers considerable scope to further understand cost optimization. Opportunities to optimize costs include variations in size and cost recovery of cash grants and variations in intensity of modality, frequency, and content of training, mentoring, and coaching.

Political Economy

Too often the discussion of economic inclusion and related programs focuses on specific technical solutions for program design and implementation. This report draws close attention to the "political economy" of economic inclusion to consider the local and national considerations that influence the decision to adopt these programs or not. The adoption and scale-up of economic inclusion programs hinges on political acceptability and involves trade-offs in program design and implementation. While economic inclusion programs tend to have support across the political spectrum, governments face strong challenges in the process of scaling up. The success or failure of economic inclusion programs can be shaped by three decisions: program objectives, financing, and institutional arrangements for delivery. Political realities may require that programs cover a broad range of population cohorts, in addition to the poorest, often to ensure popular support. As programs scale up, transparency and accountability measures become important in limiting political bias. Two aspects stand out as critical for scaling up economic inclusion: (1) political leadership and (2) the quality of evidence needed to help shift preferences and bolster political support. These considerations—and the perspectives of historical processes, structural forces, and institutions—underpin the central question of scale-up, and occupy a cross-cutting focus throughout the report.

Notes

1. World Bank, *Poverty and Shared Prosperity 2018: Piecing Together the Poverty Puzzle* (Washington, DC: World Bank, 2018), https://openknowledge.worldbank.org/handle/10986/30418.
2. Note that here we do not divide the total cost by duration of each program. While dividing by duration would help standardize the comparison across programs, it is misleading, as duration of economic inclusion packages is an important aspect of the program's design. Those designed so their beneficiaries receive a set of interventions over a longer duration of time (perhaps because they are slow climbers or highly vulnerable) will likely cost more than those of shorter duration. In discussing adequacy of benefits, however, we standardize by duration.

PART A

Moving to Scale: Concepts, Practice, and Evidence

CHAPTER 1
Economic Inclusion: A Framework

KEY MESSAGES

Economic inclusion programs focused on extreme poor and vulnerable groups are being implemented in at least 75 countries. This report presents data and evidence from 219 programs. Economic inclusion programs are a bundle of coordinated, multidimensional interventions that support individuals, households, and communities in their efforts to increase their incomes and assets.

Governments lead program scale-up. Their efforts cover 93 percent of program beneficiaries surveyed in the report. This carries important implications for design and implementation.

Women's economic empowerment is a key feature of program design. Nearly 90 percent of the programs surveyed in this report have a gender focus. Program design adaptations to promote empowerment and mitigate unintended household and community risks have emerged.

This report proposes a new framework for governments to strengthen the resilience of and opportunities for the extreme poor and vulnerable. The framework envisions the alignment of economic inclusion programs with national institutions, strategies, and policies.

FUTURE DIRECTIONS

Adapting to changing poverty contexts and megatrends is increasingly important. Economic inclusion programs are flexible and can be customized to local settings, and major shocks such as COVID-19 will fundamentally reshape economic inclusion programs in each country.

Unleashing the productive potential of the extreme poor and vulnerable involves the removal of multiple constraints. Addressing both external constraints related to community, local economy, and institutional failures and internal constraints reflecting intrahousehold dynamics and behavior is critical, although internal constraints are less well understood.

Improving integrated responses that link the individual and household components of economic inclusion programs to wider community and local economy processes is required. As a result, the menu of programmatic responses will likely grow over time as learning and adaptation continues.

Introduction

Recent years have witnessed a growing global momentum to strengthen inclusive economic development and "leave no one behind." The first challenge posed by the Sustainable Development Goals (SDG)—to "end poverty in all its forms everywhere by 2030"—is being seized. A key action under the SDG agenda is to address this challenge through *inclusive and sustainable growth* (SDG 8). Economic inclusion initiatives that seek to do this are proliferating today, and they show strong potential to build on preexisting national efforts to develop social protection systems and jobs strategies worldwide.

Emerging evidence, including the experience of the 75 countries reviewed in this report, illustrates both the potential for and challenges to governments to implement economic inclusion initiatives at scale. This report features data and evidence from 219 economic inclusion programs across 75 countries, reaching in excess of 92 million individuals.[1] This estimate of program reach is considered a lower-bound baseline, given gaps in the available data, fast-moving project pipelines, and challenges in the reporting of coverage.

The scale-up of government-led programs is central to the operational surge around economic inclusion. Government-led programs cover 90 percent of estimated beneficiaries in this report and half of the programs surveyed. These interventions represent a diversity of approaches and are sometimes referred to as "productive inclusion," "graduation," or "community-driven" development programs. Common interventions include a combination of cash or in-kind transfers, skills training or coaching, access to finance, and links to market support (see box 1.1). Many of these programs have now reached an important inflection point of expansion and refinement to address the needs of the poorest.[2]

The potential to scale-up builds on a promising evidence base and a groundswell of learning, especially in the nonprofit sector. This report places a spotlight on the role of evidence and cost-effectiveness linked to economic inclusion programs. The report recognizes a growing body of research, including the work of the 2019 Nobel laureates in economics.[3] The rich tapestry of emerging evidence illustrates the capacities—and limitations—of governments across the globe to implement programs at scale. The methodology behind the survey of this tapestry of research is found in appendix A, and details of the review of program impacts are in appendix B. The costing analysis, covered in chapter 6, is detailed in appendix C. By way of illustration, four country case studies supporting this report provide firsthand country experiences spanning a range of contexts from Africa to South Asia to Latin America.

A Story of Great Expectations . . .

Expectations to strengthen economic inclusion recognize the persistence of poverty and "poverty traps" facing the poor. The momentum to scale up occurs in the context of stubbornly high levels of extreme poverty, whereby poverty becomes self-reinforcing and perpetual (Barrett, Carter, and Chavas 2019). By 2030, following a business-as-usual scenario, an estimated 479 million people are projected to be living in extreme poverty, and the share of global poor living in fragile and conflict-affected countries is expected to reach 50 percent by 2030 (World Bank 2018). As of September 2020, the fallout from the coronavirus pandemic raises the possibility of pushing more than 80 million people into extreme poverty (see spotlight 1). Concerted efforts will be required to mitigate the economywide or sector-specific downturns created by this pandemic and ultimately to facilitate the restoration of livelihoods and the recovery of communities.

An effort to foster changes in the aspirations of the poor can provide an important impetus for the expansion of economic inclusion programs. A discrete set of literature considers how poverty lays the foundations for "aspirations failure" among the poor, causing a "behavioral poverty trap" (Dalton, Ghosal, and Mani 2016). In this scenario, internal psychological constraints of the poor perpetuate poverty. More recent events and literature highlight opportunities and challenges related to changing aspirations among certain cohorts. For example, recent events, including the Arab Spring and protest movement of unemployed youths in countries of the Organisation for Economic Co-operation and Development, have contributed to the popular sentiment that access to employment, earnings, and jobs is an important driver of social cohesion (Wietzke and McLeod 2012). Across the Africa region, changing population dynamics and technology diffusion also bring into focus new aspirations of youth populations, particularly in urban areas (Filmer and Fox 2014).

These changing aspirations put underemployment and jobs at the top of the development agenda. Yet labor markets remain, for the most part, informal, and pathways to formal employment for the poorest are very limited. Informal labor is widespread in developing countries, representing 70 percent of the labor force and 30 percent of the gross domestic product (Loayza 2018). Economic inclusion programs provide opportunity to address these concerns, with the potential to create links in the rural economy, across household enterprises, and, increasingly, to modern wage sectors. In this context, economic inclusion programs provide promise to address the needs of the extreme poor and vulnerable who have not yet benefited from broader economic development.

The report focuses deliberately on the economic lives of the extreme poor and vulnerable and the multiple constraints they face in increasing incomes and assets. While transformative economic growth will be the ultimate driver of poverty reduction, it is not automatically inclusive and does not always penetrate the poorest households (Ravallion, Jolliffe, and Margitic 2018). Further, the needs of specific individuals within those households are brought to the forefront. For example, women's economic empowerment is a key driver of economic inclusion programs, and program design and adaptation focuses on the productive role of the woman in a household and community (see spotlight 2). Similarly, efforts to address the needs of youth cohorts are important, for youths increasingly lack pathways to formal employment and will require support as "own account" workers in the labor market (see chapter 3).

To respond to growing expectations around economic inclusion programs, governments must navigate a range of political economy challenges. While economic inclusion programs may garner strong support in principle, in practice competing preferences and incentives shape the policy arena. As programs move to scale, there will be several trade-offs inherent in policy choices, such as how scarce resources are distributed across different population groups (see chapter 2). In this context, a logical starting point for many governments is to customize existing antipoverty programs to address economic inclusion priorities. At the center of this customization is an effort to build on existing systems, policies, and capacities and ultimately to deliver cost-effective interventions at a reasonable level of scale.

In this report, we classify three primary entry points through which governments can customize existing antipoverty programs and scale up economic inclusion:

1. Social safety nets (SSNs)

2. Livelihoods and jobs (L&J)

3. Financial inclusion (FI)

While these entry points are not mutually exclusive, they do provide a foundation on which investments can be built and broader sectoral collaborations can be achieved.

The report draws attention to the strong links between social protection and jobs, building on the considerable expansion of SSNs across the world. SSN programs—especially cash transfers—now reach about one-fifth of all households in low-income countries and represent approximately 26 percent of the income of the poorest. As social protection systems mature, opportunities to strengthen broader sector links become an imperative and critical to supporting mesolevel integration of economic inclusion programs with other sectoral interventions, for example, agriculture, health and sanitation, and environmental health and management.

. . . and Some Skepticism

While country adaptations, evaluations, and analyses provide direction in strengthening economic inclusion for the poor, the absence of a common framework and consistent terminology risks efforts to scale up. This report tackles this challenge by providing a set of definitions, a typology of approaches, and a framework for action. These tools draw from a variety of sector experience and survey data collected for the report, including its four case studies. Some core definitions are explained in box 1.1; these are expanded on throughout the report. A more detailed glossary of key terms is included at the back of the report.

BOX 1.1   Defining Terms: What We Mean by Economic Inclusion and Scale

Economic inclusion: This report considers economic inclusion as the gradual integration of individuals and households into broader economic and community development processes. This integration is achieved by addressing multiple constraints or structural barriers faced by the poor at different levels: the household (for example, human and physical capacity), the community (social norms), the local economy (access to markets and services), and formal institutions (access to political and administrative structures). Throughout the report, these constraints are viewed as simultaneous and often inseparable. They are viewed as impacting extreme poor and vulnerable groups most intensively.

Economic inclusion programs are a bundle of coordinated, multidimensional interventions that support individuals, households, and communities to increase their incomes and assets. Economic inclusion programs therefore aim to facilitate the dual goal of strengthening resilience and opportunities for individuals and households who are poor. These goals are met through strengthening community and local economy links. The term *economic inclusion* is sometimes used interchangeably with the term *productive inclusion*.

Scale: Scaling up is the process by which a program shown to be effective on a small scale or under controlled conditions or both is expanded, replicated, and adapted into broader policy and programming. Scale-up may also be driven without prior piloting and testing, and often in response to a political decision or directive. It is not simply about coverage—the number of beneficiaries served by the program in relation to the total population of the country—but also about quality—of impact and sustainability of coverage as well as processes of change and adaptation. Economic inclusion at scale therefore considers the programmatic and institutional mechanics required to embed programs at the national level through large-scale antipoverty programs, led by governments with clear alignment to national strategies, partnership development, and underlying political economy considerations. In this report, entry points to scaling up are the foundational elements on which other measures are subsequently layered: social safety nets, livelihoods and jobs, and financial inclusion.

Key debates boil down to feasibility. Economic inclusion programs may be considered too complex and too costly to operate at scale. Governments in many countries, especially in low-income settings, will face capacity constraints to administer and manage multidimensional and cross-sector interventions. Across a broad strand of literature, many of these debates have concerned "graduation" programs, implemented largely by nonprofit organizations (see chapters 2 and 3). These programs have generated discussion and controversy regarding their complexity, targeting efficacy, cost-effectiveness, capacity requirements, and conceptual underpinnings (Soares and Orton 2017; Devereux and Sabates-Wheeler 2015; Sulaiman et al. 2016). More broadly, the time-bound nature of many economic inclusion programs may be considered at odds with the notions of social protection as a right and universal social protection across a continuum of needs. These challenges are explored throughout chapters 3 and 4.

There is ongoing debate surrounding the impact and cost-effectiveness of economic inclusion approaches—two topics that take center stage in chapters 5 and 6. A wide range of literature is reviewed in chapter 5, which unpacks the promising evidence base for economic inclusion programs. This evidence base—much of it drawn from nonprofit program implementation—has helped operationalize the agenda on economic inclusion, despite concerns related to the heterogeneity and size of program impacts. Over the next two years, a wave of new impact and process evaluations are anticipated from national programs that will inform this debate. Much debate focuses on the marginal impact of high-cost components and options for effectively customizing the bundle of interventions for different target groups. Chapter 6 explores these debates, highlighting options for improved costing analysis and cost optimization. It is in this context that the report sets out to identify key directions for the next generation of economic inclusion programs, as well as deciphering which expectations of the debate are misplaced or well-founded.

A Framework to Transform Economic Lives

A central contribution of this report is a framework to consider the pathways for scaling up economic inclusion programs that strengthen resilience and opportunities so that beneficiaries can better participate in the local economy. The framework (see figure 1.1) illustrates an overall context and response diagnostic linked to a desired set of outcomes at the household and community level as well as to government systems. The framework was developed iteratively using findings from the underlying report survey, stakeholder consultations, and available literature. This framework represents a baseline designed to inform ongoing discussion. This section introduces the framework applied throughout the report, with the subsequent sections summarizing each aspect of the framework.

The starting point of this framework is the central challenge of transforming the economic lives of the poor. While this report focuses on economic inclusion programs targeted to the extreme poor or vulnerable, it is recognized that economic inclusion programs can be of benefit to a range of population segments across different economic strata. It is also recognized that governments will face competing demands across those population segments. When implemented at scale, adjusting a program approach and weighing trade-offs between serving one group or another are often required. This discussion is carried forward in chapter 2.

The framework centers on the potential to effect change in a government landscape, requiring clear alignment to national institutions, strategies, and policies. This framework is anchored by considerations of the entry points through which

FIGURE 1.1 Pathways to Economic Inclusion at Scale: A Framework

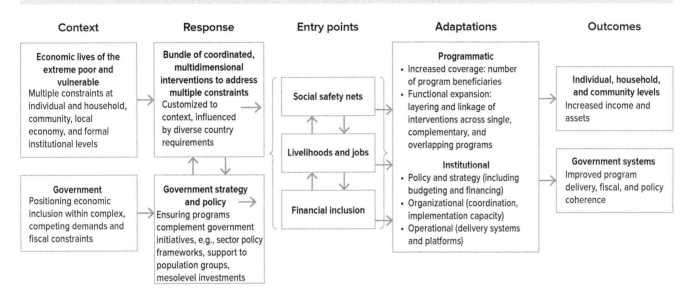

Source: Partnership for Economic Inclusion, World Bank.

governments can customize existing antipoverty programs and the adaptations to scale. The entry points to scale are the foundational elements on which other measures are layered: SSNs, L&J, and FI. Adaptations to scaling up involve the programmatic and institutional means by which programs evolve and grow, all filtered through a political economy lens.

In presenting this framework, certain limitations are worth bearing in mind.

- *First, economic inclusion at scale is not a "silver bullet."* The framework advances a household and local economy perspective best situated in a wider government response to address poverty. Therefore, household- and local-level economic inclusion strategies need to be mindful of, and ideally complement, those national and mid-level investments that greatly influence welfare outcomes.

- *Second, the framework masks the considerable heterogeneity that defines economic inclusion programs across different country settings.* As noted throughout the report, the starting point and trajectory of different population groups, and in different operating contexts, will shape program design and implementation choices. For example, the program objectives and core target populations will vary between a middle-income national context and a low-income fragile one. In the end, program impacts will also vary for different types of programs, for similar programs in different contexts, and for the same program across different population groups. Factors that drive impact will depend on the ecosystem in which programs operate—on both market- and community-level factors—and on the characteristics of participating households and individuals.

- *Third, the engagement of local community and nongovernmental structures is critical in the execution of this framework.* The relative complexity of economic inclusion programs requires the involvement of multiple program partners, including community groups, nongovernmental organizations (NGOs) and private sector organizations. As elaborated in chapter 3, there is a wide range of nongovernment experience in the execution and support of economic inclusion programs. At the same time, several nongovernment-led programs operate outside of national systems, often where capacities are weak, conflict or fragility abound, or political will is absent. In some cases, continued nongovernmental programming may reflect a path dependency or reluctance for adaptation.

Goal and Outcomes

The goal and outcomes of the framework (figure 1.1) must be seen against a backdrop of dynamic poverty, tumultuous economic factors, and political economy constraints. This section considers the broad poverty and economic trends underpinning the framework and previews a broader political economy discussion in chapter 2. Megatrends potentially shaping the direction of economic inclusion programs are highlighted.

Shifting poverty dynamics bring into focus the potential value of tailored economic inclusion programs to improve resilience and opportunities for the poorest. Global poverty has steadily declined for many decades, but that decline is now narrowing, and trends are seeing a reversal for the first time since 1998 (see figure 1.2). Before COVID-19, the world already faced a daunting poverty outlook: continuing with business as usual, an estimated 479 million people were facing extreme poverty by 2030 (World Bank 2018). These estimates mask substantial variations across regions and contexts. Poverty rates remain stubbornly high in low-income countries, particularly those affected by conflict and political upheaval. By 2030, it is predicted that 87 percent of the extreme poor worldwide will be in Sub-Saharan Africa (see figure 1.2). A similar trajectory is likely for countries affected by fragility and conflict, with poverty rates stuck at over 40 percent for the past decade and where up to two-thirds of the world's extreme poor may reside by 2030 (Corral Rodas et al. 2020).

In the new COVID-19 context, the ongoing crisis will erase almost all the progress made in the past five years—thereby compounding existing challenges in rural and fragile settings and raising demand from the "new poor," urban economies, and migrant populations (World Bank 2020). The World Bank estimates that 70 to 100 million more people will fall into extreme poverty (under $1.90 per day) in 2020 compared to 2019 as a result of COVID-19, depending on assumptions on the magnitude of the economic shock. The global extreme poverty rate could rise by 0.3 to 0.7 percentage points, to around 9 percent, in 2020. Additionally, the percentage of people living on less than $3.20 a day could rise by 0.3 to 1.7 percentage points, to 23 percent or higher, an increase of some 40 to 150 million people. Finally, the percentage of people living on less than $5.50 a day could rise by 0.4 to 1.9 percentage points, to 42 percent or higher, an increase of around 70 to 180 million people. It is important to note that these poverty projections are highly volatile and could differ greatly across countries.

High and, in some cases, rising levels of inequality threaten to dilute shared prosperity and reduce opportunities in many countries for the poor to move out of poverty. Although evidence points to a slight recent decline in total global inequality (Revenga and Dooley 2019), inequality *within* the world's economies is greater today than it was 25 years ago, and it is increasing, although at disparate rates. Notwithstanding improved living standards for people in the bottom 40 percent of the income range over recent decades, relatively more income is being captured by the highest quintiles. Between 1980 and 2016, the global share of income held by the top 1 percent grew from 16 percent to more than 20 percent, while the share held by the bottom 50 percent of the world's population remained stagnant at around 9 percent (Alvaredo et al. 2018).

FIGURE 1.2 Global Extreme Poverty by Region (1990–2030) and the Impact of the COVID-19 Crisis

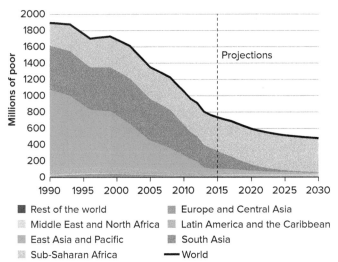

a. Extreme poverty had been projected to steadily decline pre-COVID-19, with most of the extreme poor to live in Sub-Saharan Africa by 2030

■ Rest of the world
▒ Middle East and North Africa
▒ East Asia and Pacific
▒ Sub-Saharan Africa
■ Europe and Central Asia
▒ Latin America and the Caribbean
▒ South Asia
— World

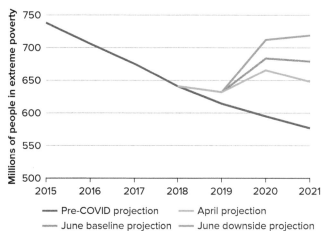

b. Due to COVID-19, estimates show extreme poverty to rise by 70–100 million in 2020

— Pre-COVID projection
— June baseline projection
— April projection
— June downside projection

Source: World Bank 2018.   *Source:* Mahler et al. 2020.

Moreover, countries with high rates of poverty, most of which are in Sub-Saharan Africa, have seen the lowest income growth among the bottom 40 percent, while average incomes have stagnated or even declined in countries affected by fragility or conflict (World Bank 2018). The bottom 40 percent live disproportionally in rural areas, attain less education, and are more likely to be children.

Finally, informal employment and underemployment cast a long shadow on how economic inclusion programs are likely to evolve. Sixty percent of the world's population make their living in the informal economy, including more than 85 percent of the population in Africa (ILO 2018). The agriculture sector accounts for 68 percent of work in low-income countries (Djankov et al. 2018), where the rural landless poor are commonly employed in low-paid, insecure activities. Informality also characterizes urban poverty, a critical concern as urban populations are projected to more than double by 2050—with cities in Africa to double in size faster, over the next 20 years (Djankov et al. 2018; Kharas et al. 2020). In the context of burgeoning youth populations and the search for effective strategies to address underemployment, these forecasts may have serious implications for economic inclusion programs.

The framework focuses on enhancing resilience and opportunity for the poor.

- *Resilience* refers to the strengthened ability of a household to manage risk and respond to and cope with sudden shocks that are likely to overwhelm them. When income and assets increase through economic inclusion, households can maintain consumption and avoid the need to resort to costly and often irreversible coping strategies, such as selling their most productive assets at fire-sale prices or sending children to work rather than to school (Ralston, Andrews, and Hsiao 2017). More resilient households can also generate positive externalities for communities by contributing to local economic recovery in the aftermath of shocks.

- *Opportunity* refers to the capacity of households in economic inclusion programs to capture and capitalize on investments that improve human capital outcomes and that they would otherwise miss (Hernandez 2020; Ralston, Andrews, and

Hsiao 2017). Such investments can help to propel individuals and households out of poverty through improved productivity and access to jobs (World Bank 2012). Capturing better opportunities can also contribute to broader household gains, including for children, such as improved consumption, nutrition, and education.

In this overall context, the framework and broader report focus on two outcomes of interest.

- *First, they focus on increasing incomes and assets of individuals, households, and communities.* The programs surveyed for this report typically use household-level targeting criteria, reflecting the design intent of the initiative and a contextually appropriate means of determining eligibility. Interventions at the individual level are an important feature of economic inclusion programs but are typically devised to account for intrahousehold dynamics (for example, engagement of male household members as well as consideration for care and other work burdens). An additional feature across programs is the engagement of local communities and, increasingly, links to local market structures. Economic inclusion programs by nature leverage community structures and groups, including informal community savings and credit groups, local governance groups, formalized producer organizations, and different group cohorts (for example, youths). A policy implication emerges that suggests that successful economic inclusion at scale will be contingent on effective mesolevel links—a theme that is further assessed in spotlight 3 and later chapters.

- *Second, the framework and report focus on strengthening government systems for improved program delivery as well as fiscal and policy coherence.* The report focuses squarely on the potential to link economic inclusion programs to national policies and strategies such as, for example, social protection and L&J strategies. These different sector entry points are not simply additional features of economic inclusion programs, but rather sine qua nons, essential conditions, without which government programs will not be sustainable. These systems provide a basis on which programs can be scaled and customized. Chapter 2 explores the political economy considerations and the broad set of policy decisions and trade-offs that will help shape the interventions that are devised. This has important institutional implications, since the successful scale-up of economic inclusion programs will require careful coordination across government at different levels: the central, decentralized, and local levels, as discussed further in chapters 3 and 4.

Context and Response: Customizing to Local Settings

The framework is influenced by the *poverty trap hypothesis,* which explains conditions under which poverty becomes self-reinforcing and perpetual. While recent decades have seen hundreds of millions escape dire poverty and premature death (Deaton 2013), extreme poverty continues to persist, alongside increasing inequality both in and between countries. According to the poverty trap hypothesis, the poorest population groups have fundamentally different opportunities than other people as a result of their poverty (Parry, Burgess, and Bandiera 2020; Balboni et al. 2020). The poor face multiple constraints to improving their earning opportunities and assets, such as low levels of human capital and limited access to productive inputs. This is compounded by frequent exposure to uninsured risks, both man-made and natural (Dercon 2008), and a reduction in cognitive bandwidth that impairs decision-making (Mani et al. 2013; Haushofer and Fehr 2014; Mullainathan and Shafir 2013). In combination, these factors can trap individuals, households, communities, and economies in poverty, perpetuating a cycle that limits investments to low-productivity endeavors.

A central argument of the framework is that the poor and vulnerable encountering poverty traps face multiple constraints, around which a multidimensional response is required. The framework proposes that multiple constraints fall on these populations with the greatest force, and often simultaneously. Multiple constraints impede the ability of the poor to improve their earning opportunities not only in the short run—whether through wage employment or self-employment—but also over the longer term. This is an area of extensive research and operational focus (for example, Daidone et al. 2019; Barrientos 2012; FAO 2015). Recent empirical evidence suggests that an intervention that provides an initial amount of capital above a critical threshold ultimately determines whether households can capture higher productivity opportunities and progress out of poverty. These findings suggest that large enough transfers or "big push" approaches have the potential to permanently move individuals to a higher level of wealth (Parry, Burgess, and Bandiera 2020).

This report considers four domains that highlight the external and internal constraints that may limit the economic lives of the poor (figure 1.3).

1. *The first set of constraints that beneficiaries may face is at the individual and household levels, human and physical capacity constraints that limit their income-generating potential.* These include human capital (including cognitive, noncognitive, and technical skills); physical and financial capital (including durable assets, land, savings, and insurance); and social capital. In addition, intrahousehold dynamics that shape aspirations and determine distribution of time use, labor supply, and resources can be a significant constraint for some individuals, especially women and people with disabilities.

2. *A second set of constraints concerns aspects at the community level (such as social norms and gender expectations, as well as local infrastructure, connectivity, and exposure to disaster risk), which may affect some groups or all households in the community.* These constraints may vary significantly across communities and across groups in communities.

3. *A third set of constraints occurs in the local economy.* This includes underlying factors that constrain opportunities for economic growth, such as proximity to physical markets, regional market depth, access to connective infrastructures, and production inputs. Many of the world's extremely poor live in isolated, rural localities where access to local and regional markets is limited.

4. *The fourth constraint involves formal institutions.* It includes institutional and government failures, including lack of access to political and administrative structures as well as civil society organizations and NGO networks. Throughout the report, these constraints are viewed as simultaneous and often inseparable. They are viewed as impacting most intensively the extreme poor and vulnerable, for whom these interlocking deprivations can create poverty traps.

Under this framework, constraints facing women are of special concern and are further discussed in firsthand country experiences cited in the case studies. Experience suggests that economic inclusion efforts have strong potential to strengthen women's economic empowerment through intentionally designed programs and specific adaptations in program delivery, for instance, hiring female community facilitators. However, realizing empowerment opportunities at scale presents operational challenges. Adverse effects of targeting women for economic empowerment programs may include exacerbated time poverty, because women's usual care

FIGURE 1.3 **Overcoming Constraints to Economic Inclusion: Four Domains**

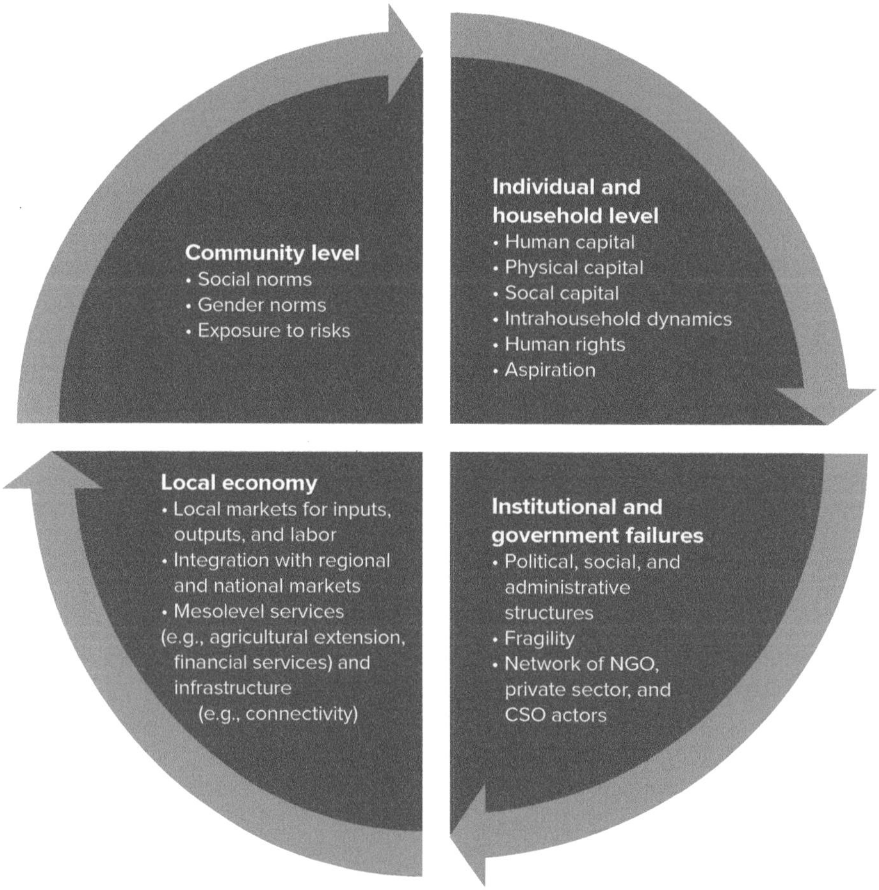

Community level
- Social norms
- Gender norms
- Exposure to risks

Individual and household level
- Human capital
- Physical capital
- Socal capital
- Intrahousehold dynamics
- Human rights
- Aspiration

Local economy
- Local markets for inputs, outputs, and labor
- Integration with regional and national markets
- Mesolevel services (e.g., agricultural extension, financial services) and infrastructure (e.g., connectivity)

Institutional and government failures
- Political, social, and administrative structures
- Fragility
- Network of NGO, private sector, and CSO actors

Source: Partnership for Economic Inclusion, World Bank.

Note: CSO = civil society organization; NGO = nongovernmental organization.

responsibilities are not commensurately reduced. In addition, there may be short-term increases in intimate-partner violence, due to perceived threats to traditional masculinity and gender roles (Laszlo 2019). Considerable innovation is ongoing in this domain, as reflected throughout the report, including in spotlight 2, "Promoting Women's Economic Empowerment through Economic Inclusion."

The framework proposes a bundled package of interventions that supports the poorest and most vulnerable households to tackle multiple constraints. While the measures will vary considerably across countries and contexts—often shaped by specific megatrends (see box 1.2)—the report identifies a common set of multidimensional interventions, which may include some form of cash or in-kind transfer, skills training or coaching, access to finance, and, increasingly, links to market support. These interventions may be delivered in a time-bound capacity and a deliberately sequenced manner. This design response is informed by observed experiences in graduation-focused programs, although economic inclusion extends significantly beyond a graduation framework (see chapter 2). It is also informed by ongoing experiences across broader sectors and program areas, for example, SSNs, community-driven development programs, rural livelihood, and environmental management.

The underlying assumption is that a comprehensive suite of interventions has greater and more sustained impact on income, assets, and well-being relative to stand-alone interventions. For instance, common constraints to setting up a microenterprise

BOX 1.2   **Megatrends Driving the Future Direction of Economic Inclusion at the Country Level**

This report considers megatrends as structural shifts that are long term in nature and have irreversible consequences for economies and societies at large. Two overarching megatrends are patterns in extreme poverty and informality, highlighted throughout this report. The report also acknowledges four other megatrends that will directly impact country-level program design and implementation for economic inclusion programs: human capital formation, demographic trends, shock sensitivity, and technological innovation.

Human capital formation: Shortfalls in health and education among children today have substantial implications for national economies and the productivity of the next generation of workers. A child born in a country at the 25th percentile of the global distribution of education and health will, upon reaching adulthood, be only 43 percent as productive as a child with a full education and good health (Gatti et al. 2018). Evidence shows that economic inclusion and human capital are closely intertwined, with important intergenerational consequences.

Enhanced human capital can strengthen the impact of economic inclusion programs on wages and productivity, because beneficiaries are then better placed to exercise agency, access and process information, and take risks in productive investments. Conversely, participation in economic inclusion can strengthen a beneficiary's human capital through improved skills, agency, and networks, while earnings can be invested in their own as well as their families' human capital. Accrued income can also militate against negative coping mechanisms during times of crisis, for instance, by allowing children to remain in school and for household health and nutrition needs to be met.

Population dynamics with specific impacts on urbanization: The total population in the world will reach almost 10 billion by 2050, compared to around 7.7 billion in 2019 (UNDESA 2019a). Sub-Saharan Africa is projected to double by 2050 due to its higher fertility rate, while Eastern and Southeastern Asia will experience a modest 3 percent increase (Suzuki 2019; UNDESA 2019a). This raises challenges because people living in extreme poverty are disproportionately rural, female, and children. Furthermore, the global population is getting older, with the number of people over 65 expected to double to more than 1.5 billion by 2050. The least developed countries will experience the fastest increase in this regard (UNDESA 2020).[a] Lastly, all the population growth between 2018 and 2050 is projected to take place in urban areas that will inevitably be situated in the poorest economies (UNDESA 2019b). While urbanization has generally been conducive to economic growth, pro-poor policies in the urban context will be needed to harness this trend toward shared prosperity.

Shock sensitivity, fragility, and conflict: As recent events have made clear, programming for economic inclusion cannot be divorced from the vagaries of external shocks and vulnerability. Beyond the current COVID-19 context, the direction and nature of economic inclusion programs will also be shaped by different types of shocks, including economic shocks as well as underlying fragility due to conflict or climate change. In 2015, 54 percent of those living in fragile and conflict affected situations (FCS) were in Sub-Saharan Africa (World Bank 2018). While extreme poverty in FCS economies declined sharply between 2005 and 2011, the poverty rate has since

(Box continues next page)

BOX 1.2   **Megatrends Driving the Future Direction of Economic Inclusion at the Country Level** *(continued)*

stagnated, and the share of the global poor living in FCS has steadily increased since 2010, amounting to 23.2 percent of the world's extreme poor. The report *Financing the End of Extreme Poverty* identifies 30 countries that are most at risk of not meeting the 2030 goal of eradicating extreme poverty (Manuel et al. 2018). Of these countries, 23 with economic inclusion interventions are featured in this report. One strong implication is the need not only for program adaptability and flexibility to withstand shocks but to adapt program design in the context of dynamic, short- and medium-term needs.

Technology adoption: Rapid adoption of technology and the increasing use of mobile phones, which allow people in developing countries to become more connected, is proving to be an enormous opportunity. Today there are more mobile phone subscriptions in the world than people, with over 50 percent of the global population having access to broadband internet (ITU 2018). Additionally, there are now over 1 billion registered mobile money accounts globally, helping increase financial inclusion (GSMA 2019). While such rapid adoption has the potential to bring about positive change, it can also exacerbate existing inequalities and introduce new vulnerabilities. It is important to note that a digital divide persists—half of the world's population is still offline. Most of these people live in developing countries, and increasingly they are women (World Bank 2016; ITU 2019).

a. The group of least developed countries consists of 47 countries. More information can be found on the website of the United Nations Office of the High Representative for the Least Developed Countries, Landlocked Developing Countries and the Small Island Developing States, http://unohrlls.org/about-ldcs/.

include inadequate business knowledge or skills, lack of finance, imperfect insurance, and limited social networks. While stand-alone interventions can also impact incomes, assets, and resilience, a single intervention—such as a regular cash transfer alone, business training alone, or access to finance alone—may not necessarily help those facing multiple constraints or would do so to a lesser extent. Evidence of the marginal impact of these stand-alone interventions as compared with a coordinated package is emerging and is further addressed in chapter 5.

Entry Points and Adaptations: Moving to Scale

The report considers strategic entry points to scale as well as key programmatic and institutional adaptations to ensure the success of programs. These mechanisms are now briefly introduced here and expanded throughout chapters 2, 3, and 4. They also inform the case study summaries presented in the report.

Although economic inclusion programs are multidimensional, they generally include a foundational intervention that acts as the primary entry point, with other measures subsequently layered on top. Drawing on the survey of programs undertaken for this report, three core entry points are identified. These entry points are not mutually exclusive and entail a strong overlap. Chapter 2 considers the following primary entry points in further detail:

- *Leveraging social safety net interventions*: As countries expand the coverage and financing of SSN programs, in particular, cash transfers—the terms *safety nets–plus* or *cash-plus* are gaining prominence. The *plus* indicates the potential to complement cash with additional inputs, service components, or links to external services. Economic inclusion is a key driver of the SSN-plus agenda, showing particular promise to maximize impacts on incomes and productivity. The continuous provision of SSNs and the incorporation of beneficiaries into a social protection system is a potential game changer in the design of economic inclusion programs. It implies a shift from one-off and time-bound interventions to a more regularized system of support with the potential for refresher interventions along the way. This also has the potential to reframe expectations around the sustainability and long-term impacts of such programs.

- *Integrating strategies to promote more and better livelihoods and jobs*: For the poorest and most vulnerable, access to employment tends to be informal, risky, and often limited by constraints to labor supply—human capital, including education, skills, and networks—and labor demand—business environment, including access to finance, infrastructure, technology, and markets. An increasing number of L&J programs focus on removing barriers that keep the extreme poor and vulnerable (for example, poor households in rural or urban areas that include youths, refugees, and women) from participating in the local economy and in higher productivity jobs. Economic inclusion approaches to L&J strategies for the poorest are shaped by thinking about sustainable livelihoods (risk management, community-driven development, and local economic development strategies) and, more recently, on the changing nature of work. Notwithstanding challenges, economic inclusion programs have the potential to leverage both formal and informal wage employment opportunities, including through public works and value chain development.

- *Strengthening financial inclusion and payment systems*: Many poor population segments tend to be excluded from financial services, including credit, savings, insurance, and e-payments or mobile money. Financial inclusion, through the use of savings groups, formal banking services, microcredit, government-to-person payments, and so on, has the potential to improve resilience and opportunities for the extreme poor and the vulnerable, particularly women. An increasing proportion of countries are using mechanisms to deliver social protection transfers directly to bank accounts, electronically or otherwise, creating an entry point to bring people into the formal financial sector and offering a pathway to a broader range of financial services, including savings and credit. More recently, digital services have lowered the cost of connecting excluded groups to the formal financial system, using new technologies and business models such as pay-as-you-go asset finance and fintech.

Because of the multidimensional nature of economic inclusion programs, there may be considerable overlap between the entry points to scale. Most programs have a secondary entry point that balances the emphasis of the focus of an intervention. For instance, an economic inclusion program with an SSN at its core may overlap with an FI intervention—the former being the primary intervention and the latter being the secondary. There tends to be strong overlap across SSN and L&J interventions, often reflecting common objectives around income diversification and productivity. Moving to scale will therefore involve linking and integrating different interventions and programs across the various entry points.

As programs scale up, they will be strongly shaped by each country's political realities and customized along several policy and institutional dimensions (see chapters 2 and 4). Economic inclusion at scale must consider several programmatic and institutional mechanisms required to embed programs at the national level. As noted previously, the report focuses on the scale-up of economic inclusion programs through large-scale antipoverty programs led by governments, with clear alignment to national strategies, partnership development, and underlying political economy considerations.

The concept of scaling up is the process by which a program shown to be effective on a small scale or under controlled conditions or both is expanded, replicated, and adapted into broader policy and programming. Scaling up is about quality of impact, scale, and sustainability, as well as processes of change and adaptation; the concept goes beyond a functional consideration of coverage. Chapter 4 continues this discussion by considering country-level progress on five different dimensions of scale:

- Coverage

- Functional expansion

- Policy and strategy formulation

- Organizational reform

- Operational planning

Future Directions

The flexibility of economic inclusion programs to serve different target groups and contexts is a key feature of this report. Going forward, further emphasis on the adaptive nature of economic inclusion programs reflecting changing poverty contexts and megatrends (such as demographics, urbanization, and technology) is important to enhancing the resilience of and opportunity for the poor. At the time of writing in autumn 2020, living history reminds us that major shocks (COVID-19) have the potential to fundamentally reshape economic inclusion programs at the country level. It is important to recognize the principle that no single blueprint can be wholly replicated in a given setting or during a major shock. Maintaining flexibility can ensure that overall implementation is achieved and regional coherence maintained.

Economic inclusion programs will need to more strongly address external and internal constraints that limit the productive potential of the extreme poor and vulnerable. External constraints tend to focus on issues related to community, local economy, and institutional failures. Internal constraints reflect intrahousehold dynamics as well as behavioral aspects, which are less understood than other factors in program implementation. Addressing both external and internal constraints is critical to strengthening the resilience and opportunity of the extreme poor and vulnerable. The engagement of local community and nongovernmental structures will remain critical in tackling these constraints.

There is strong recognition of the need for integrated responses, linking individual and household components of economic inclusion programs to wider community and local economy processes. In this respect, the menu of interventions may grow over time, as learning and adaptation continues. Over the next several years, a wave of new impact and process evaluations across scaled programs will provide key lessons in scaling. At the same time, the design and implementation of new programs will continue to be informed by ongoing experiences across broader sectors and program areas, among them SSN, community-driven development programs, rural livelihoods, and environmental management.

Notes

1. Note that 201 programs reported beneficiary data; 18 programs are missing beneficiary data.
2. The *poorest* refers to people in a number of economic categories that include several dimensions of poverty and vulnerability. The *poor* are those whose consumption is below the national poverty line, as defined by the government, or those who, because of their personal and/or community characteristics, face barriers in accessing opportunities to earn sustainable livelihoods and have elevated risks of being or staying in poverty and/ or being socially marginalized. The *extreme poor* are those whose consumption is below $1.90 per day (2011 purchasing power parity, PPP), also defined as the bottom 50 percent of the poor population in a country or those unable to meet basic needs. The latter definition captures relative poverty, as well as dynamics in lower-middle-income and upper-middle-income countries. Since 2018 the World Bank has reported poverty rates using two new international poverty lines: the lower-middle-income line is set at $3.20 per day, and the upper-middle-income line is set at $5.50 per day. The *ultrapoor* are those whose consumption is below $0.95 per day (2011 PPP). Also defined as those experiencing the most severe forms of deprivation, for example, persistent hunger, lack of sources of income, and so forth. Finally, the *other vulnerable* are groups who do not meet any of the above criteria, for example, those just above the poverty line and marginalized groups irrespective of their poverty level.
3. The Sveriges Riksbank Prize in Economic Sciences in Memory of Alfred Nobel was awarded in 2019 to Abhijit Banerjee, Esther Duflo, and Michael Kremer "for their experimental approach to alleviating global poverty."

References

Alvaredo, F., Lucas Chancel, Thomas Piketty, Emmanuel Saez, and Gabriel Zucman. 2018. *World Inequality Report 2018*. Paris: World Inequality Lab, Paris School of Economics.

Balboni, Clare, Oriana Bandiera, Robin Burgess, Maitreesh Ghatak, and Anton Heil. 2020. "Why Do People Stay Poor?" STICERD—Economic Organisation and Public Policy Discussion Paper no. 067, Suntory and Toyota International Centres for Economics and Related Disciplines, LSE. http://sticerd.lse.ac.uk/dps/eopp/eopp67.pdf.

Barrett, Christopher B., Michael R. Carter, and Jean-Paul Chavas. 2019. "The Economics of Poverty Traps." Cambridge, MA: National Bureau of Economic Research.

Barrientos, A. 2012. "Social Transfers and Growth: What Do We Know? What Do We Need to Find Out?" *World Development* 40 (1): 11–20.

Corral Rodas, Paul Andres, Alexander Irwin, Nandini Krishnan, Daniel Gerszon Mahler, and Tara Vishwanath. 2020. "Fragility and Conflict: On the Front Lines of the Fight against Poverty." Washington, DC: World Bank. http://documents.worldbank.org/curated/en/375651583211667808 /Fragility-and-Conflict-On-the-Front-Lines-of-the-Fight-against-Poverty.

Daidone, S., B. Davis, S. Handa, and P. Winters. 2019. "The Household and Individual-Level Productive Impacts of Cash Transfer Programs in Sub-Saharan Africa." *American Journal of Agricultural Economics* 101: 1401–31. doi:10.1093/ajae/aay113.

Dalton, Patricio S., Sayantan Ghosal, and Anandi Mani. 2016. "Poverty and Aspirations Failure." *Economic Journal* 126 (590).

Deaton, Angus. 2013. *The Great Escape: Health, Wealth, and the Origins of Inequality*. Princeton, NJ: Princeton University Press.

Dercon, S. 2008. "Fate and Fear: Risk and Its Consequences in Africa." *Journal of African Economies* 17 (suppl. 2): ii97–ii127. https://doi.org/10.1093/jae/ejn019.

Devereux, S., and Rachel Sabates-Wheeler. 2015. "Graduating from Social Protection." *IDS Bulletin* 46 (2): 1–12.

Djankov, S., F. Saliola, C. Avitabile, R. Chen, D. L. Connon, A. P. Cusolito, R. V. Gatti, U. Gentilini, A. M. Islam, A. C. Kraay, S. Sabarwal, I. V. Santos, D. W. Sharrock, C. J. Tan, and Yucheng Zheng. 2018. *World Development Report 2019: The Changing Nature of Work*. Washington, DC: World Bank. http://documents.worldbank.org /curated/en/816281518818814423/Main-Report.

FAO (Food and Agriculture Organization of the United Nations). 2015. *The State of Food and Agriculture: Social Protection and Agriculture; Breaking the Cycle of Rural Poverty*. Rome: FAO.

Filmer, Deon, and Louise Fox. 2014. *Youth Employment in Sub-Saharan Africa*. Africa Development Series. Washington, DC: World Bank.

Gatti, R.V., A. C. Kraay, C. Avitabile, M. E. Collin, R. Dsouza, and N. A. P. Dehnen. 2018. *The Human Capital Project*. Washington, DC: World Bank. http://documents .worldbank.org/curated/en/363661540826242921/The-Human-Capital-Project.

GSMA. 2019. *State of the Industry Report on Mobile Money*. London: GSMA.

Haushofer, Johannes, and Ernst Fehr. 2014. "On the Psychology of Poverty." *Science* 344 (6186): 862–867. doi:10.1126/science.1232491.

Hernandez, E. 2020. "Financial Inclusion for What?" *CGAP Blog*, February 5. https:// www.cgap.org/blog/financial-inclusion-what.

ILO (International Labour Organization). 2018. *Women and Men in the Informal Economy: A Statistical Picture*. 3rd edition. Geneva: ILO.

ITU (International Telecommunication Union). 2018. *Measuring the Information Society Report*. Vol. 1. Geneva: ITU. https://www.itu.int/en/ITU-D/Statistics/Documents /publications/misr2018/MISR-2018-Vol-1-E.pdf.

ITU. 2019. *Measuring Digital Developments: Facts and Figures*. Geneva: ITU. https:// www.itu.int/en/ITU-D/Statistics/Documents/facts/FactsFigures2019.pdf.

Kharas, Homi, Constanza Di Nucci, Kristofer Hamel, and Baldwin Tong. 2020. "To Move the Needle on Ending Extreme Poverty, Focus on Rural Areas." *Future Development* (blog), February 21. https://www.brookings. edu/blog/future-development/2020/02/21/to-move-the-needle-on-ending -extreme-poverty-focus-on-rural-areas/.

Laszlo, Sonia. 2019. "The Gender Transformative Potential of Graduation Programs." Fundación Capital, Bogotá, and IDRC, Ottawa. http://api.web.fundak.io/public /2019-12/file/tCvWBxsTar5dfb16f2bc725.pdf.

Loayza, Norman V. 2018. "Informality: Why Is It So Widespread and How Can It Be Reduced?" (English). *Research & Policy Briefs* no. 20, World Bank, Washington, DC. http://documents.worldbank.org/curated/en/130391545228882358 /Informality-Why-Is-It-So-Widespread-and-How-Can-It-Be-Reduced.

Mahler, Daniel Gerszon, Christoph Laknerr, R. Andres Castaneda Aguilar, and Haoyu Wu. 2020. "Updated Estimates of the Impact of COVID-19 on Global Poverty." *World Bank Blogs*, October 7. https://blogs.worldbank.org/opendata /updated-estimates-impact-covid-19-global-poverty.

Mani, A., S. Mullainathan, E. Shafir, and J. Zhao. 2013. "Poverty Impedes Cognitive Function." *Science* 341: 976–80.

Manuel, Marcus, Harsh Desai, Emma Samman, and Martin Evans. 2018. *Financing the End of Extreme Poverty*. London: Overseas Development Institute. https://www.odi .org/sites/odi.org.uk/files/resource-documents/12411.pdf.

Mullainathan, S., and E. Shafir. 2013. *Scarcity: Why Having Too Little Means So Much*. New York: Times Books/Henry Holt.

Parry, K., R. Burgess, and O. Bandiera. 2020. "Is It Time to Rethink Poverty Policy?" VoxDev, February 14. https://voxdev.org/topic/it-time-rethink-poverty-policy.

Ralston, Laura R., Colin Andrews, and Allan Hsiao. 2017. "The Impacts of Safety Nets in Africa: What Are We Learning?" Policy Research Working Paper WPS 8255, World Bank, Washington, DC.

Ravallion, M., D. Jolliffe, and J. Margitic. 2018. "Social Protection and Economic Development: Are the Poorest Being Lifted-Up or Left-Behind?" NBER Working Paper 24665, National Bureau of Economic Research, Cambridge, MA.

Revenga, A., and M. Dooley. 2019. "Is Inequality Really on the Rise?" *Future Development* (blog), May 28. https://www.brookings.edu/blog/future-development /2019/05/28/is-inequality-really-on-the-rise.

Soares, F., and I. Orton. 2017. "Graduation: An Overview." *Policy in Focus* 14 (2): 7–10. https://ipcig.org/pub/eng/PIF39_Debating_Graduation.pdf.

Sulaiman, M., N. Goldberg, D. Karlan, and A. de Montesquiou. 2016. *Eliminating Extreme Poverty: Comparing the Cost-Effectiveness of Livelihood, Cash Transfer, and Graduation Approaches*. Washington, DC: CGAP.

Suzuki, E. 2019. "World's Population Will Continue to Grow and Will Reach Nearly 10 Billion by 2050." *World Bank Blogs*, July 8. https://blogs.worldbank.org/opendata /worlds-population-will-continue-grow-and-will-reach-nearly-10-billion-2050.

UNDESA (United Nations, Department of Economic and Social Affairs, Population Division). 2019a. *World Population Prospects 2019: Highlights*. ST/ESA/SER.A/423. New York: UNDESA. https://population.un.org/wpp/Publications/Files/WPP2019 _Highlights.pdf.

UNDESA. 2019b. *World Urbanization Prospects: The 2018 Revision*. ST/ESA/SER.A/420. New York: UNDESA. https://population.un.org/wup/Publications/Files/WUP2018 -Report.pdf.

UNDESA. 2020. *World Population Ageing 2019*. ST/ESA/SER.A/444. New York: UNDESA. https://www.un.org/development/desa/pd/sites/www .un.org.development.desa.pd/files/files/documents/2020/Jan/un_2019 _worldpopulationageing_report.pdf.

Wietzke, Frank-Borge, and Catriona McLeod. 2012. *Jobs, Well-Being, and Social Cohesion: Evidence from Value and Perception Surveys*. Background Paper for the *World Development Report 2013*, World Bank, Washington, DC.

World Bank. 2012. *Resilience, Equity, and Opportunity: The World Bank's Social Protection and Labor Strategy 2012–2022*. Washington, DC: World Bank.

World Bank. 2016. *World Development Report 2016: Digital Dividends*. Washington, DC: World Bank. https://openknowledge.worldbank.org/handle/10986/23347.

World Bank. 2018. *Poverty and Shared Prosperity 2018: Piecing Together the Poverty Puzzle*. Washington, DC: World Bank. https://openknowledge.worldbank.org /handle/10986/30418.

World Bank. 2020. "Poverty." World Bank, Washington, DC. https://www.worldbank .org/en/topic/poverty/overview (accessed May 4, 2020).

Economic Inclusion and COVID-19 Recovery

The world is experiencing an unprecedented economic crisis due to the COVID-19 pandemic. Economic inclusion programs for the poorest show strong potential as part of integrated policy responses focused on containing the pandemic, ensuring food security, and supporting medium-term recovery. Beyond the immediate public health crisis, the global economy is projected to shrink by 3 percent in 2020, with only a partial recovery projected for 2021 (IMF 2020). In the most conservative scenario, assuming a 5 percent contraction in per capita incomes, more than 80 million people could be pushed into extreme poverty. Assuming per capita incomes shrink by 10 percent, that number could grow by an estimated additional 180 million people (Sumner, Hoy, and Ortiz-Juarez 2020). The adverse effects on employment, especially in the informal sector, are expected to be far reaching and unprecedented. The International Labour Organization (ILO 2020) estimates that 305 million full-time workers could be unemployed or underemployed as a result of the crisis.

The COVID-19 pandemic is not a great equalizer—the poor and vulnerable are hit much worse. These groups typically face greater health risks compounded by an inability to meet social distancing norms in densely populated informal settlements and inadequate resources to seek testing and treatment. The COVID-19 crisis is likely to exacerbate poverty and destitution, with the accompanying economic downturn depressing demand for labor, goods, and services, severely curtailing income-generation opportunities for the poor and vulnerable (Carranza et al. 2020; World Bank 2020). Furthermore, the pandemic can potentially exacerbate existing gender inequalities and further marginalize people with disabilities.

Adaptation and Early Priorities in a COVID-19 Context

Economic inclusion programs face a dual challenge of adapting delivery norms during a pandemic and ensuring readiness to respond as part of the medium- and longer-term recovery effort. In the short term, ongoing economic inclusion programs can provide an immediate gateway to support existing beneficiaries, their communities, and the local economy. However, significant adaptations are required to avoid pandemic risks. Irrespective of medium-term policy responses, short-term disruption to programs is anticipated, with some operations being put on hold and others facing delays in field-work activities, for example, in-person data collection, beneficiary selection, group meetings, and so on. To mitigate these impacts, economic inclusion programs need to modify the design and delivery of components. In program design, emerging priorities are the following:

1. *Incorporate elements that mitigate health risks.* Economic inclusion programs can serve as a platform for the delivery of reliable and current health messaging. In addition, programs can expand messaging to counter concerns of a possible rise in gender-based violence following containment measures. More generally, the COVID-19 crisis has starkly highlighted the importance of access to affordable finance. Such access can help with hospital bills, medicine, cash to replace lost

income, and capital to restart businesses once containment measures are lifted. Furthermore, economic inclusion programs can layer interventions to mitigate health risks where feasible. To mitigate health risks related to COVID-19, programs can link with existing health insurance programs, waive co-payment requirements, or subsidize the premium for poor and vulnerable groups.

2. *Cope with market disruptions and anticipate possible livelihood opportunities.* As markets continue to falter, economic inclusion programs must adapt to cope with frequent, unpredictable disruptions and anticipate possible livelihood opportunities. Programs need to work with beneficiaries to identify livelihood options that can be run safely and to develop a plan to adapt to the ever-present threat of market disruption. Even during the strictest containment measures, economic inclusion programs have an advantage because microentrepreneur beneficiaries are engaged in highly decentralized production, whether they are individual, group, or community based. Support to these institutions will help sustain productive inclusion, local economic development, and jobs during and after the COVID-19 crisis. Self-help groups, for example, are known to lead to increased business-related spending, resilience, and food security.

3. *Invest in real-time data and evidence generation.* For effective policy response to the poverty consequences of the COVID-19 crisis, the importance of real-time evidence cannot be overemphasized. As an example, the Power and Participation Research Centre (PPRC) and BRAC Institute of Governance and Development (BIGD) teamed up to launch a rapid-response telephone survey utilizing respondent telephone databases from earlier surveys on urban slums and rural poor (PPRC and BIGD 2020). Despite concerns about phone access, literacy, and timing, the team was able to commission a short survey to steer program response.

Economic inclusion programs are already using digital platforms for delivery; these need to be further leveraged and expanded in the aftermath of COVID-19. An emerging priority is to ensure social distancing in the delivery of high-touch components such as training, coaching, savings groups, producer associations, and so on. Adaptations to high-touch activities include shifting to digital platforms. The rapid diffusion of new mobile and internet technologies presents an opportunity to deliver benefits safely, avoid large gatherings, and contain the spread of the virus. Thirty percent of government-led programs already use digital technology to deliver at least one intervention, such as electronic payments, digital financial services, e-coaching, and e-training.

Challenges and Opportunities in Scaling Up Economic Inclusion for COVID-19 Recovery

As economies focus on recovery efforts, it will be important to identify opportunities for economic inclusion in emerging sectors, while being mindful of continued uncertainties. In most developing countries, there will likely be a nonlinear path from response to recovery. With continuously changing epidemiology and transmission patterns, there are frequent changes to containment measures in many developing countries. This generates considerable uncertainty about the resumption of economic activity and, hence, economic inclusion programming that is feasible and likely to have the greatest impact for a post-COVID economic recovery. The mix will depend largely on government priorities in sector support; which sectors are likely to start recovery first and generate labor demand; which sectors may expand in light of changing medium-term needs (for example, frontline sectors like health care will likely expand);

what skills employers would look for in these sectors; and what value chains would look like in these sectors. Lead actors will need to anticipate the implications of possible substantial changes to economic activity, such as continued disruptions, changes in global supply chains, the decline of certain high-touch sectors, and the accelerating pace of automation.

An added dimension to uncertainty is the policy direction on social distancing and suppression that low-income countries are likely to follow. Barnett-Howell and Mobarak (2020) suggest there are fewer benefits to social distancing and social suppression in low-income countries. This conclusion is driven by three factors. First, developing countries have smaller proportions of elderly people to save via social distancing compared to low-fertility rich nations. Second, while social distancing saves lives in rich countries by flattening the curve of infections to reduce pressure on health systems, delaying infections is not as useful in countries where health care systems are already overwhelmed given the limited number of hospital beds and ventilators and the fact that they are not accessible to most. Third, social distancing lowers disease risk while limiting people's economic opportunities. Poorer people are naturally less willing to make those economic sacrifices. They are also likely to have limited options for working from home and may place relatively greater value on their livelihood concerns compared to concerns about contracting coronavirus.

Leveraging Existing Government Programs to Facilitate Livelihood Recovery

A likely consequence of COVID-19 will be the coalescence and persistence of large-scale economic inclusion programs led by governments. Experience from previous global crises suggests that the pathway to scaling is often politically driven, especially when social cohesion is threatened. At present, there is considerable potential to accelerate the scale-up of economic inclusion programming. In doing so, it will be essential for governments to continue working in partnership with nongovernmental organizations and other humanitarian organizations to implement programs on the ground.

Social safety net programs provide a key entry point for governments to scale up economic inclusion efforts. With adaptive social protection systems forming the backbone of the first wave of response, the scale-up of economic inclusion programs is an important complement for households and communities moving forward. Furthermore, the engagement of community mechanisms is a critical driver of program delivery with most programs using community structures. The engagement of community-based organizations will be vital during the recovery period as in-country movement restrictions and the suspension of commercial transport hampers external partners from accessing their programs in some areas. This is especially important in countries affected by fragility, conflict, and violence and other vulnerability hotspots (areas affected by locusts, droughts, and so forth), where the impact from COVID-19 will be especially high.

Scaling up economic inclusion programming will be faster in countries that already have a credible base of economic inclusion programming. Fortunately, almost 80 percent of economic inclusion programs have a foothold in low- or lower-middle-income countries—the vast majority of which are found in Sub-Saharan Africa and South Asia. At present, economic inclusion programming has a strong rural focus, and adaptations to the urban context will need to be introduced for livelihood recovery, as COVID-19 is currently impacting urban areas the hardest. Emerging innovations in urban settings include small-scale municipal infrastructure and slum upgrading projects to rapidly generate short-term employment opportunities for the urban poor through labor-intensive public works. They include as well small grant or microcredit schemes targeted to households for home improvements and informal home-based businesses.

References

Barnett-Howell, Z., and A. M. Mobarak. 2020. *Should Low-Income Countries Impose the Same Social-Distancing Guidelines as Europe and North America to Halt the Spread of COVID-19?* New Haven, CT: Yale School of Management. https://som.yale.edu /should-low-income-countries-impose-the-same-social-distancing-guidelines-as -europe-and-north-america-to-halt-the-spread-of-covid-19.

Carranza, Eliana, Thomas Farole, Ugo Gentilini, Matteo Morgandi, Truman Packard, Indhira Santos, and Michael Weber. 2020. "Managing the Employment Impacts of the COVID-19 Crisis: Policy Options for Relief and Restructuring." Jobs Working Paper 49, World Bank, Washington, DC.

ILO (International Labour Organization). 2020. "ILO Monitor: COVID-19 and the World of Work," 3rd ed., April 29. https://www.ilo.org/wcmsp5/groups/public/--- dgreports/---dcomm/documents/briefingnote/wcms_743146.pdf.

IMF (International Monetary Fund). 2020. *World Economic Outlook, April 2020: The Great Lockdown*. Washington, DC: IMF.

PPRC (Power and Participation Research Centre) and BIGD (BRAC Institute for Governance and Development). 2020. "Livelihoods, Coping, and Support during the COVID-19 Crisis." PPRC and BIGD, Dhaka. https://bigd.bracu.ac.bd/wp-content/ uploads/2020/05/PPRC-BIGD-Final-April-Survey-Report.pdf

Sumner, A., C. Hoy, and E. Ortiz-Juarez. 2020. "Estimates of the Impact of COVID-19 on Global Poverty." United Nations University World Institute for Development Economics Research, Helsinki.

World Bank. 2020. "Protecting People and Economies: Integrated Policy Responses to COVID-19." World Bank, Washington, DC.

CHAPTER 2
Moving to Scale: Political Realities and Entry Points

KEY MESSAGES

The adoption and scale-up of economic inclusion programs hinges on political acceptability. Political leadership and quality of evidence are two critical elements that will determine the drive toward program scale-up.

Governments face strong challenges in determining target groups, often against a backdrop of excess demand and tight fiscal constraints. The prioritization of any target beneficiaries is influenced by policy priorities, poverty levels, economic profiles, and community dynamics.

The success or failure of economic inclusion programs hinges on three programmatic decisions: program objectives, financing, and institutional arrangements for delivery. Design will vary depending on beneficiary income levels, the economic level of the country, and context, such as fragility.

A new generation of economic inclusion programs is emerging building on existing social safety nets (SSNs), livelihoods and jobs (L&J), and financial inclusion (FI) interventions. These programs draw from diverse experiences in productive inclusion, graduation, and community-driven development programs.

FUTURE DIRECTIONS

Testing and refining program objectives, design, and delivery is important in the effort to scale. These help to increase the impact on different population segments and vulnerable groups.

SSN programs can provide a strong foundation from which governments can scale up economic inclusion efforts, especially in light of COVID-19. The first wave of response to the pandemic is strengthening adaptive social protection systems, with scaled-up economic inclusion programs being potentially important as a second wave of response, especially for the informal sector, as governments restart their economies.

The role of political economy in economic inclusion programs is critical, and further learning and research are required. Country experiences with program coordination in and outside of government, transparency and accountability, and beneficiary outreach will be especially relevant.

Introduction

Chapter 2 explores the incentives, trade-offs, and strategic entry points in scaling up economic inclusion programs at the country level. The chapter introduces a political economy perspective considered as the historical processes, structural forces, and institutions shaping the direction of economic inclusion policies and programs. Too often the discussion of economic inclusion and related programs focuses on technical solutions for program design and implementation. This report devotes significant attention to these technical details, which can be described as downstream issues, but this chapter attempts to address upstream issues, such as what influences the demand for inclusion, by drawing attention to the local and national considerations that influence the decision to adopt these programs or not. With these political realities in mind, the chapter discusses the three strategic entry points to scaling up originally set forward in the report framework: social safety nets (SSNs), livelihoods and jobs (L&J), and financial inclusion (FI).

Program Adoption and Scale-Up: Political Realities

The adoption and scale-up of economic inclusion programs hinges on political acceptability and involves trade-offs in program design and implementation because political acceptability depends on how power relations among different groups influence decisions on social policy.[1] Scale-up decisions are influenced by country context (especially as it relates to its institutions), the nature of the actors involved in the policy arena, and their preferences and incentives with respect to economic inclusion policy. There are also particular trade-offs in the distribution of resources across population groups, whether regional or by demographic or wealth categories. However, it is worth remembering that preferences and incentives can evolve over time, and country-specific concerns about jobs, earnings, and opportunities are rapidly changing with each new generation. Political transitions and large, covariate shocks, whether economic, climate linked, or health related (such as the COVID-19 pandemic), can also shift preferences and incentives for action.

Typically, there is strong support for economic inclusion across the political spectrum and among policy makers, with each having different institutional motivations. Redistribution of wealth toward the poor can be seen as either a cost or an investment and is often considered as part of a social contract. Despite divergent outlooks, most policy makers find economic inclusion policies attractive, although for different reasons. For some, these programs are seen to be central to promoting social justice by enabling the poor to participate more actively in economic and social spheres of their communities. For others, concerns about dependency on social protection can also fuel greater support for economic inclusion programs when they are seen, sometimes mistakenly, as a mechanism for program exit.

Given this reality, the potential to scale up economic inclusion will depend on the bargaining strength of the poor relative to the nonpoor, and on the support for such programs among the nonpoor. The poorest households often face the greatest barriers to collective action (and therefore may be less likely to engage in local government or in community networks) and may also face disenfranchisement in the general political system (Desai 2007). Women, in particular, face restrictions to political participation and rarely play senior representation roles, making it difficult for them to shape policy. In this context, political processes become important and a crucial determinant of program adoption.

In all cases, two aspects stand out as critical for scaling up economic inclusion (or any social policy): one, a big idea that has already demonstrated an evidence-based impact in a similar context (even if small scale), and two, a political inflection point, typically accompanied by strong leadership with a vision and strategy for economic inclusion at scale.

- *First, the role of evidence generation is essential in shifting preferences and bolstering political support.* The scale-up of economic inclusion measures owes much to the evidence demonstrated through pilot graduation schemes (Banerjee et al. 2015) as well as schemes that have shown the productive impacts of cash transfers (Alderman and Yemtsov 2013; Argent, Augsburg, and Rasul 2014; Banerjee et al. 2015; Premand and del Ninno 2016) and those that have shown positive impacts from complementary agriculture development and cash transfer programs (FAO 2018; Slater et al. 2016; Soares et al. 2017; Tirivayi, Knowles, and Davis 2013; Maldonado et al. 2016).

  Chapter 5 of this report tackles the question of evidence and program impact in detail and argues that a growing evidence base provides groundwork for considerable optimism. A review of 80 quantitative and qualitative evaluations in 37 countries shows that a broad range of economic inclusion programs have demonstrated the promising—and potentially sustained—impact of a bundled set of interventions relative to stand-alone efforts. The analysis points to a changing landscape, with evidence now unfolding across a variety of government-led programs. This is important as it reflects the integration of inclusion efforts in broader antipoverty strategies and brings into focus the potential to integrate beneficiaries in a wider system of support. A new wave of evaluations looks ready to isolate the impact mechanisms of economic inclusion programming at scale, across entry points, and for different groups. They will also better highlight than previously the magnitude of program impacts.

  Evidence generation also comes in the form of peer-to-peer experience sharing and knowledge exchange. For example, the integration of social protection objectives in a rural development program in Ethiopia partly drew for inspiration on a 1990s study tour by government officials of the Maharashtra Employment Guarantee Scheme in India (Lavers 2016). International development partners now play an active role in providing technical assistance to government counterparts and encouraging such peer-to-peer learning and knowledge exchange, which is important for agenda setting.

- *Second, the decision to scale up an economic inclusion program often stems from a political decision rather than being a purely technical response, especially in the wake of major shocks.* The series of case studies included in this report pinpoint a variety of political inflection points, each of which helped to make the case for scaling up economic inclusion programs. In Peru, the Haku Wiñay program emerged from a window of political opportunity that opened during the first years of President Ollanta Humala's administration. The administration favored a social program that would not carry the perceived risks of promoting dependency. In the Sahel, political economy drivers for the introduction of economic inclusion measures included fiscal constraints, ongoing shocks, high population growth, and persistently deep poverty. In Bihar, India, the Satat Jeevikoparjan Yojana program offered a preelection promise of livelihood support to women affected by the outlawing of liquor selling. As elaborated in chapter 5, the experiences of Ethiopia (through the Productive Safety Net Program, PSNP), Bangladesh, and Indonesia all emerge from crisis contexts in some fashion. This has considerable policy implications for programming in the current COVID-19 context, where economic inclusion programs may be expected to further coalesce as part of medium-term recovery strategies.

Trade-Offs in Shaping Program Design and Implementation

Many trade-offs in designing and implementing economic inclusion measures must be negotiated. These come into play when selecting overall objectives, target groups, and the components of bundled interventions. Chapters 4 to 6 discuss these trade-offs in detail, but the following provides a summary introduction.

The cornerstone in designing any program is the choice of the objective. While the overall goal of economic inclusion programs settles around the increase of income and assets for program beneficiaries, program-specific objectives determine the path through which this will be achieved. For example, there is a diversity of possible desired outcomes for economic inclusion programs, including women's empowerment, income diversification, and resilience, as demonstrated by the 12 program objectives explored in the Partnership for Economic Inclusion (PEI) Landscape Survey 2020, described in chapter 3. Megatrends—such as population growth, shocks, forced displacement, and climate change—are shaping government antipoverty policies and programs, and raise complex decisions in terms of defining objectives for economic inclusion. Also note, the choice of objective has important implications for the engagement of different ministries and implementation partners.

Governments face challenging decisions in identifying target groups, often against a backdrop of tight fiscal constraints. Political realities may require that programs cover a broad range of population cohorts, in addition to (or even beyond) the poorest, often to ensure popular support.

Decisions on program beneficiaries are shaped by several factors, including the poverty and economic profile of the local context.

* *A first set of factors entails a country's extent of poverty.* For instance, programs in low-income countries with vast levels of poverty commonly focus on the extreme poor (see the glossary for definition). In lower-middle or middle-income countries, economic inclusion is sometimes tailored to those with a certain level of assets or incomes, whether poor or not, and at other times it is focused on remaining pockets of the extreme poor. It is also increasingly common for economic inclusion programs in contexts affected by displaced populations to prioritize the most vulnerable refugees, but also include a sizable number of host-community participants to acknowledge endemic poverty and to reduce community tensions. Across many programs, handling excess demand will be a familiar challenge. The Haku Wiñay case study in this report highlights how these challenges can also play to a program's advantage. The program determined that including better-off households in the community would be a driver of successful livelihoods and income-generating activities. Better-off households likely already had some ongoing business, had commercial links, knew about the value chains, and could help shore up a critical volume of economic activity to allow buyers and input providers, such as veterinary support, to come to poor towns.

* *A second relevant factor is the extent to which personal characteristics of an individual shape program eligibility.* For example, some programs prioritize those who demonstrate a perceived "higher potential" to engage in entrepreneurial activities, often through innovative psychometric testing. Yet without a degree of customization, this approach can lead to both inclusion and exclusion errors, giving additional privilege to those who have had prior business experience and inadvertently discriminating against those who lacked such opportunity. It is also worth noting that in most "graduation" programs, potential beneficiary "fast climbers" or "slow climbers" were not easily predicted by program staff, and past experience or inexperience

did not necessarily correlate to future success. Other economic inclusion programs, such as SSN efforts, have adopted the same targeting criteria (and beneficiary lists) as antipoverty programs. Once again, some customization is likely required, particularly in situations where the SSN is targeted to the poor and labor constrained. In many programs, a key consideration is the identification of households with latent and untapped economic potential. In this context, local knowledge and community engagement can be critical to reduce errors and increase community buy-in.

- *A third set of factors used to shape program participation relates to household and community dynamics.* Social norms can restrict the extent to which participants benefit from economic inclusion, and an understanding of household norms and power dynamics could ensure programs are more effective. Programs may consider a variety of factors, including expectations around child labor, the participation of women in the labor market, and different marital structures: for example, polygamous versus monogamous households. At the local level, well-developed community structures can amplify the work of economic inclusion programming—in many cases supporting program implementation. At the same time, several risks are noted. Established norms for sharing wealth in mutual support networks can dilute the expected impact of transfers from economic inclusion programs (Sabates-Wheeler, Lind, and Hoddinott 2013). Similarly, the heavy involvement by some communities in beneficiary selection can result in elite capture in highly stratified communities.

Critical Factors in the Failure or Success of Programs

Poor targeting and weak beneficiary selection mechanisms are one of the key factors that undermine program performance and impact. Even where poor population groups are the target, identifying them can be difficult. A common problem in many countries is the acquisition of reliable and up-to-date data on people's income, which limits the application of administrative targeting measures. Proxy identifiers for income, such as assets, are commonly used, but among the bottom 60 percent of a population, there is often little difference among people in their ownership of basic assets or land or in housing conditions (Booysen et al. 2008). Consequently, this proxy method can lead to misidentification of the very poorest, and here the engagement of the community in targeting may be important. Leveraging existing government systems for beneficiary selection (for example, social registries or community structures) can greatly reduce cost and facilitate links with other programs. The capacity of implementers to actually reach the target group with an intervention is another consideration. For example, reaching nomadic people or people living in conflict-affected areas presents special challenges.

Fine-tuned targeting and effective communication to the public about selection priorities are critical. In some of the classic graduation-style pilots, only about half the beneficiary households had daily per capita consumption below the international extreme-poverty line (Banerjee et al. 2015). Although this was much larger than the national share of the extreme poor in the respective country populations (which averaged about 19 percent), it meant that, in practice, these programs did not necessarily have the sharp focus on the extreme poor that was intended in the program design (Kidd 2019; Kidd, Gelders, and Bailey-Athias 2017). In Sindh, Pakistan, the targeting approach was flawed, as the program relied on local influential leaders to identify participants, an approach that led to elite capture and likely to the exclusion of the poorest (Kabeer et al. 2012). In West Bengal, India, false rumors about religious conversions being effected through the program led to low take-up, particularly among eligible Muslim households (Banerjee and Duflo 2011).

Ensuring financial commitment for a program is paramount and will involve surmounting various fiscal pressures. Chapter 3 highlights a large share of government-led programs that are financed domestically or in combination with development partners. The incorporation of economic inclusion programs with national budget lines is a further indicator of government ownership and commitment. Yet the cost of economic inclusion programs (in isolation and relative terms) is a key debate. As elaborated in chapter 6, program costs will vary depending on context and the number of program components. There is a significant set of knowledge gaps on how to optimize costs, especially as part of a government system of support.

Fiscal pressure may impose design features that ultimately weaken the adequacy of a program. For example, some government-led programs have expanded their coverage but in the process made compromises on the generosity of lump-sum cash transfers. For instance, the scaling-up of a pilot implemented by the Relief Society of Tigray in Ethiopia led to an initial reduction in the cash grant in order to maintain parity among different poverty reduction programs (Sheldon 2016).

The early exit of program beneficiaries from a safety net program is an example of a trade-off between technical and political interests, given fiscal constraints. Under the PSNP, the government of Ethiopia imposed fairly strict exit criteria, which led to the early exit of program beneficiaries. Between 2009 and 2011, intensified political pressure led to 17 percent of registered households being classified as having met the program's graduation criteria. However, in 2010, less than 5 percent of surveyed communities reported graduation rates above 10 percent and nearly half the surveyed communities reported no graduation (Berhane et al. 2011).

Exiting successfully is further complicated by the challenge of capturing household readiness to move to the next stage of policy support. In Bangladesh's Chars Livelihoods Program, a sensitivity analysis found that the share of households considered to have met the criteria for economic inclusion changed dramatically depending on the threshold, ranging from 65 percent having achieved 7 (out of 10) criteria, 37 percent having achieved 8 (out of 10) criteria, and only 2 percent having achieved all 10 criteria (Pritchard, Kenward, and Hannan 2015).

Multidimensional programs require strong intra- and interinstitutional coordination. Achieving interinstitutional cooperation is a challenging task due to the existence of institutional rigidities and inertia, prioritization of individual over collective objectives, and lack of incentives to adequately encourage joint work (World Bank 2020). The challenge is further compounded in low-capacity settings. Typically, this challenge is seen with regard to the engagement of ministries with responsibility for social protection and agriculture. Agricultural and social protection policies originate from different disciplines and are often viewed as parallel policies implemented by different authorities that compete for financial resources (Tirivayi, Knowles, and Davis 2013). While some examples exist regarding effective coordination—for example, in Rwanda, Bangladesh, and Ethiopia—these are the exception rather than the norm, and several other country experiences highlight the political constraints that limit coordination.

There are several opportunities to advance coordination and synergy across government agencies. In some instances, programs have developed political and interagency agreements with a clear definition of the expected value added from this collaboration. In Latin America, for example, countries have opted for fostering collaboration among ministries or agencies, usually under the form of coordination bodies, to facilitate interaction among institutions and levels of governments (for example, in Argentina, Chile, and Mexico). Others have decided to centralize the different components under the same organization (Peru). Experience also suggests that potential synergies could be maximized by sharing knowledge, understanding potential constraints, or developing a systems approach that promotes the cross-sectoral coordination or integration of social protection with agriculture (Tirivayi, Knowles, and Davis 2013).

As programs scale up, careful transparency and accountability measures become paramount to ensuring reduced political bias. To this end, economic inclusion programs at scale can take advantage of established governance mechanisms in a country, as well as actively develop measures to promote accountability and citizen engagement in their own programs; for example:

- In Egypt, economic inclusion services and activities currently under design seek to capitalize on sector mechanisms that are already in place, including social account-ability committees at the village level, performance audits, and security.
- In Malawi, ongoing implementation of the Community Savings and Investment Promotion program is aided by close collaboration with the Anti-Corruption Bureau. Under a new phase of program support in Malawi, new initiatives are being devised, including sensitization and awareness-raising in targeted departments and benefi-ciary communities to prevent misuse of project resources, enhanced engagement of citizens and stakeholders, and enforcement through close supervision.
- In Panama, the Red de Oportunidades program follows the existing laws and proce-dures for consultation and community involvement and outreach of the indigenous territories. The Panamanian government also has a redress and complaint mecha-nism for all its programs, as well as a telephone line for complaints.

Entry Points to Scale

As outlined in chapter 1, the PEI Landscape Survey 2020 revealed three entry points on which economic inclusion programs are built. Figure 2.1 presents the distribution of these entry points, measured as percentages of all programs reviewed in the survey. The dominant entry points for programs overall center on L&J (63 percent), closely followed by SSN (35 percent). Strikingly, among government-led programs the entry points appear to even out, with the proportion of L&J to SSN programs being nearly 1:1 as compared to 3:1 among nongovernment-led programs. The survey results for this report show 45 percent of government-led economic inclusion programs build explicitly on SSN interventions, covering close to 58 percent of total economic inclusion beneficiaries

FIGURE 2.1 **Distribution of Entry Points to Scale: Among Programs Overall, Government-Led Programs, and Nongovernment-Led Programs**

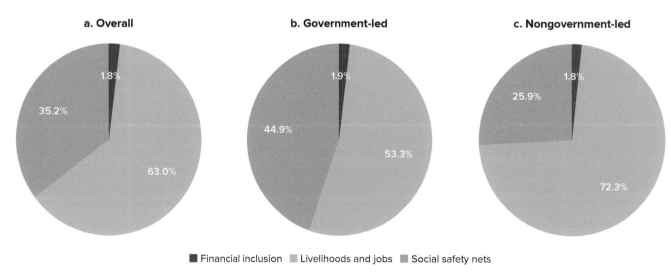

a. Overall | b. Government-led | c. Nongovernment-led

■ Financial inclusion ■ Livelihoods and jobs ■ Social safety nets

Source: Partnership for Economic Inclusion, World Bank.

FIGURE 2.2 **Distribution of Secondary Entry Points, Showing Cross-Cutting Role of Financial Inclusion**

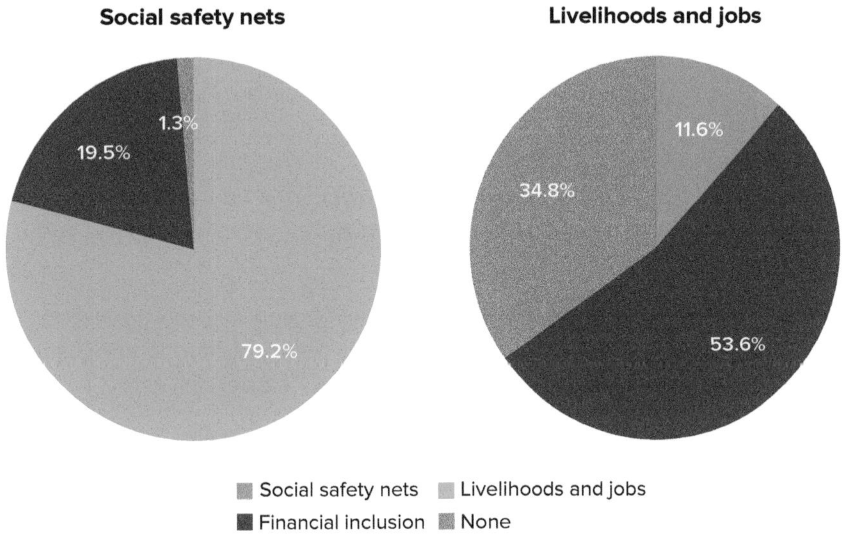

Social safety nets

Livelihoods and jobs

1.3%
19.5%
79.2%

11.6%
34.8%
53.6%

■ Social safety nets ■ Livelihoods and jobs
■ Financial inclusion ■ None

Source: Partnership for Economic Inclusion, World Bank.

featured in the sample.[2] Importantly, most programs also have a secondary entry point that balances the emphasis of the focus of an intervention (figure 2.2).

The entry points reinforce evolving trends in country-level social protection and jobs policy. As social protection coverage for the extreme poor expands globally, there is growing interest in how these investments—especially noncontributory SSNs—can connect with broader development processes and ultimately inform a broader agenda for the poor, especially in the informal sector. While this provides an anchor to much of the analysis in this report, it is important to recognize how experiences related to graduation programs inform this discussion (see box 2.1).

Entry Point 1: Social Safety Nets

SSNs have been found to strengthen equity, resilience, and opportunity, but alone they may be insufficient to transform income and asset levels. A wide body of evidence shows that SSN programs, especially in low-income countries, reach extremely poor populations and reduce household poverty and inequality. While SSN coverage and expenditure may be relatively modest compared to health and education, SSNs reach about one-fifth of all households in low-income countries and represent approximately one quarter of the income of the poorest.

Cash transfers improve cognitive development and human capital and tend to be spent overwhelmingly on improved food consumption, diversified diets, and productive items. Cash transfers are also economic multipliers, including their effect as generators of "effective demand" among low-income beneficiaries, which has the net effect of raising their disposable income by around 26 percent. One study has found that for every dollar transferred this way, between $1.27 and $2.52 is generated in local economies (Handa et al. 2017).

However, an expanding evidence base shows that provision of cash alone may fall short in achieving long-term, second-order impacts (Attah et al. 2016; Bastagli et al. 2016; Roelen et al. 2017; Beegle et al. 2018). As countries expand the coverage and financing of this form of social protection, the terms *social safety net–plus (SSN-plus)* or *cash-plus*

BOX 2.1   **Building on and Graduating from the Graduation Approach**

Economic inclusion programs, as reflected in this report, build on the worldwide experience of graduation-style programs, which were initiated by BRAC in Bangladesh and promoted globally by the Consultative Group to Assist the Poor (CGAP), the Ford Foundation, and others.

> *First,* the report recognizes the demonstration effect of a coordinated and time-bound package of interventions for poor households as evidenced in the literature (Banerjee et al. 2015).
>
> *Second,* it draws on the vast country experiences of graduation programs in more than 40 countries, including the innovations demonstrated in areas such as financial inclusion, livelihoods, coaching, and empowerment.
>
> *Third,* it acknowledges the importance of partnership and collaboration in a carefully sequenced and multisectoral approach.

Graduation as a concept has evolved since the approach was first devised in 2002, leaving it open to varying interpretations as to what programs aspire to achieve. That is, some programs aim for graduation from poverty in general, others aim for graduation from social protection, while still others are designed to graduate households into a social protection program or sustainable livelihoods. These diverse purposes have helped fuel sometimes polarizing discussion among its proponents and detractors. For many, the term *graduation* is itself highly problematic, and the space left for constructive debate is too often very narrow. For others, the term remains a steadfast part of program communications and ethos. Fundamentally, the decisions on how programs are communicated are best brokered at the country level and will be informed by the direction set by government.

Economic inclusion stands as a distinct policy space as part of a broader social policy continuum. It adheres to the core idea of a set of bundled interventions already found in graduation programs. However, it links the household and local-economy aspects of programming with broader sector policies and strategies and seeks to ensure stronger levels of integration across households, communities, and mesolevel interventions. Economic inclusion does not necessarily include any reference to an arbitrary beneficiary cut-off; the implications for beneficiaries after the time-bound interventions conclude are typically defined at the national level.

A defining and distinguishing feature of many economic inclusion programs is the close connection and integration with national SSN systems. The framework in this report illustrates how economic inclusion is integrated in national social protection and antipoverty programs. These approaches are clearly situated at the heart of the government-led development landscape. Embedding economic inclusion in government is a prerequisite for moving to scale and also reflects the value of government leadership, national capacities, and sustainability.

are gaining prominence, the *plus* indicating the potential to complement cash with additional inputs, service components, or links to external services. Economic inclusion is a key driver of the SSN agenda, showing particular promise to strengthen program impacts, but also with the reality of increased costs and complexity.

The first policy arena where SSNs and economic inclusion programs intersect is in rural areas, where a large body of recent programming and associated research shows strong potential synergies between the SSNs and agriculture at both the household and local-economy levels. SSN programs frequently reach a target group of the population engaged in low-productivity employment, particularly in agriculture and household enterprises. Extensive research shows that stronger coherence between social protection measures and agricultural interventions can facilitate productive inclusion, improved risk-management capacities, and increased agricultural productivity (Kagin et al. 2019; Gavrilovic et al. 2016; Pace et al. 2018). Similarly, a meta-analysis of 27 programs in Africa concluded that a multidimensional approach to poverty reduction would better advance productive inclusion than a stand-alone SSN and that integration of complementary interventions would likely boost productive and employment outcomes (Ralston, Andrews, and Hsiao 2017).

Economic inclusion programs have a strong potential to support SSN beneficiaries facing fragility, conflict, or economic reforms. The emerging agenda around "adaptive safety nets" focuses this discussion in stronger terms (Bowen et al. 2020). For example, the Sahel Adaptive Social Protection Program, discussed in the first case study, includes a basic package of time-bound measures, with several design variations being tested through a robust impact evaluation. SSNs also provide a pathway for integrated programming in support of economic reforms. For example, as Egypt undertakes strong economic and social reforms, the government has invested in social mitigation measures to cushion the most vulnerable from adverse impacts. Egypt's Forsa (Opportunity) initiative provides skill development or asset transfers to households enrolled in the government-implemented Takaful and Karama cash transfer program. This program covers 3.1 million households in Egypt, 74 percent of them female. Finally, the intersection between economic inclusion and fragility and conflict-affected situations is also noteworthy. Thirty percent of the SSN programs surveyed for this report operate in fragile and conflict-affected situations. For example, Iraq is considering economic inclusion measures in response to widespread displacement, increased poverty and vulnerability, and high unemployment, especially among youths, women, and host communities.

Where demand for labor is low, public works or cash-for-work programs may feature prominently in an SSN-plus approach. Public works programs are generally viewed as social SSN instruments and are used in diverse contexts across both low- and middle-income countries. Their dual objectives are to provide temporary employment while also generating or maintaining labor-intensive infrastructure projects and social services. Of the SSN programs surveyed for this report, roughly a third include a public works component, of which the considerable majority are in Africa. In Ethiopia, for example, the PSNP provides regular cash or food transfers to 8 million people, with capable beneficiaries undertaking public works, such as landscape restoration, small-scale irrigation, social infrastructures, and agroforestry. Approximately 10 percent of PSNP beneficiaries participate in a combination of training and receipt of a livelihood grant.

Public works programs are also active in fragile and conflict affected situations, where they are increasingly used to serve at-risk populations.

- In Cameroon, for instance, refugees have been integrated into the national SSN program, with 44,500 nationals and 8,500 refugees expected to undertake public works activities that benefit both the host communities and the refugees.

- In the Democratic Republic of Congo, public works are being combined with training and savings to improve the prospects of long-term poverty reduction among populations affected by violent conflict.

There is heightened focus on the capacity of SSN programs to make links and referrals, which has important implications for economic inclusion programs. Referrals to services is increasingly considered an imperative for tackling the various constraints of the poorest and most vulnerable households (Roelen et al. 2017). In Chile, the Chile Solidario scheme included cash transfers, monetary subsidies, psychosocial support, and preferential access to social programs, supported by a system of case management and referrals. Social workers played a crucial intermediary role, providing information and guidance to ensure that beneficiaries had access to programs and services (Roelen et al. 2017). In 2016, Rwanda commenced implementation of the Minimum Package to Support Graduation, a defined package of core social protection services and complementary interventions to strengthen the livelihoods and resilience of extremely poor and vulnerable households. It leveraged social welfare caseworker support to promote social and economic inclusion of the most vulnerable households. Initial piloting in Rwanda shows that caseworkers have usefully served as role models by providing basic advice on key life issues and links to support resources; both are regarded as critical to building households' confidence and motivation. Programs that target people with disabilities also focus more than other programs on wage facilitation to help participants build regular streams of income and also to foster greater self-confidence and challenge societal biases. Further exploration of work with people with disabilities can be found in chapter 3.

There is promising evidence that SSNs can facilitate gender equality and women's empowerment (Peterman et al. 2019). Cash transfers provide immediate and tangible support, are often targeted directly at women, and can help break open traditional power dynamics that prevent women from fulfilling their potential. That said, transformative effects are not ensured, and transferring benefits directly to women does not necessarily lead to changed power dynamics or empowerment. Contextually appropriate program design is critical, and this is discussed at length in this report's spotlight 2, "Promoting Women's Empowerment through Economic Inclusion."

Despite the clear potential for harnessing the links between SSNs and economic inclusion, there are a number of important ongoing debates:

- *Cash transfers alone are a productive investment.* There is a strong political appeal in layering economic inclusion measures over SSN programs, which continue to expand in their coverage. Some stakeholders are uncertain about the financial sustainability of wide-scale SSN programs, for instance, in low-income countries, making more narrowly targeted inclusion programs more politically appealing. However, this should not be perceived as meaning that cash alone is not a productive investment. As noted, there is clear evidence of the multiplier effects of cash.

- *Economic inclusion is not a replacement for cash transfers.* The emerging positive evidence on economic inclusion and the expanding number of corresponding programs should not be viewed as suggesting that there is no longer a role for cash transfers. Cash transfers continue to have a broad range of strong economic and social impacts, including outcomes related to cognitive development, schooling, and health. Cash transfers also play an important role where households are labor constrained, and they have very high coverage in many countries, usually much greater than economic inclusion programs can currently achieve. Furthermore, emerging evidence suggests that large cash transfers produce substantial benefits across a wide range of impacts, including areas traditionally served by other approaches. In Rwanda, for example, the results of an integrated nutrition and water supply, sanitation, and hygiene program were compared with those of a program that transferred an equivalent quantity of unconditional cash. The integrated program improved savings, whereas the cost-equivalent cash transfer boosted productive asset investment and allowed households to pay down debt. A much larger cash transfer (of more than $500 per household) improved savings, assets, and a wide range of consumption measures, including dietary diversity (McIntosh and Zeitlin 2018).

- *Program delivery systems in social protection have a strong potential to amplify the design and implementation of economic inclusion.* Advances in social registry and payment systems present opportunities to improve the impact of economic inclusion programs and are further discussed in chapters 3, 4, and 6. Broad delivery systems (for example, social registries) are considered in chapter 3, although they are also related to elements discussed under "Entry Point 3: Financial Inclusion."

Entry Point 2: Livelihoods and Jobs

L&J strategies for the poorest are shaped by thinking on sustainable livelihoods and, more recently, on the changing nature of work. Chambers and Conway (1992) popularized widespread consideration of the *sustainable livelihoods approach*, defined as a situation where a "livelihood … can cope with and recover from the stresses and shocks and maintain or enhance its capabilities and assets both now and in the future without undermining the natural resource base." Over the years, sustainable livelihood approaches have informed a variety of discussions on risk management (for example, Jorgensen and Siegel 2019), graduation models (Devereux and Sabates-Wheeler 2015), community-driven development (Goldman 2010), and local economic development. In recent years, discussions on sustainable livelihoods have evolved against the backdrop of transforming contexts and aspirations of individuals. The nature of labor market participation and of employment and social protection for the poor have all shifted rapidly, and with that the landscape for economic inclusion is also evolving.

While economic transformation will be the main driver of productivity growth and poverty reduction, it is not automatically inclusive and does not always translate into improvements in household living standards among the poorest (Ravallion, Jolliffe, and Margitic 2018). The expansion of productive and decent work is vital in allowing economies to grow and diversify (World Bank 2019). Productive jobs—in agriculture, in nonfarm household enterprises, and in the modern wage sector—are the key to higher earnings as well as to more stable, less vulnerable livelihoods (Filmer and Fox 2014). An estimated 80 percent of labor productivity growth in low-income countries comes from the reallocation of labor from lower productivity agriculture into relatively higher productivity services and industry. For a considerable cohort of the population, other labor market interventions may be critical in facilitating pathways to better jobs, typically through improved productivity, movement from rural to urban regions, sector and occupational changes, and transitions to waged jobs. However, such pathways may be less available for the poorest populations, especially in rural settings, and the effectiveness of active labor market programs also remains a matter of ongoing debate (McKenzie 2017). The extreme poor and vulnerable (for example, poor households in rural or urban areas, and the poorest youth, refugees, and women) face enormous constraints to climbing out of poverty alone and rely on a broader functioning ecosystem and support, coupled with complementary macro-level policies.

An increasing number of L&J programs focus on removing barriers that keep the extreme poor and vulnerable from participating in the local economy and in higher productivity jobs. An adequate supply of jobs is the foundation of sustained and growing prosperity, inclusion, and social cohesion (ILO n.d.). In many countries, including those in Sub-Saharan Africa, jobs have broader importance than the income they provide. Jobs can convey identity, status, and self-confidence and can contribute to an individual's overall life satisfaction. Furthermore, jobs contribute to social cohesion by shaping identities and the ways individuals relate to one another and by connecting people to one another through networks (Filmer and Fox 2014).

In light of the Arab Spring and other recent events, policy makers, especially in Sub-Saharan Africa, are placing a high priority on the creation of sustainable, productive youth employment. Africa's growing labor force represents an enormous demographic dividend, particularly now, when populations in much of the world are aging rapidly (Banerji et al. 2014). Youth unemployment stems from constraints to labor supply (human capital, such as in education, skills, and networks) and labor demand (business environment, including access to finance, infrastructure, technology, markets, and so forth). Many young people lack the means, skills, knowledge, or connections to translate their education into productive employment. Young women, in particular, may be constrained by occupational segregation, social norms, or the fear of sexual harassment (Scarpari and Clay 2020). L&J interventions can reduce those obstacles to productivity, leading to better employment prospects for youth.

Targeted self-employment programs for youth groups show promise, but they also raise questions as to the appropriate profile for entrepreneurship. Recent years have seen a growing focus on using large cash grants in youth entrepreneurship programs. Whereas traditional SSN interventions typically focus on consumption and human capital, these programs seek to improve employment opportunities for youths. To date they have had differing results. The Youth Opportunities Program in Uganda, which provides a one-time cash grant of approximately $382 per participant, has shown positive outcomes, including a 57 percent increase in business assets and 38 percent higher earnings (Blattman et al. 2013). It is important to highlight, however, that the positive impacts of this program are temporary and largely disappear over time (Blattman, Fiala, and Martinez 2019). Other programs in Uganda have had encouraging results with a focus on young women (Blattman et al. 2013), but similar innovations in Liberia and Sri Lanka have had varying results (Blattman, Jamison, and Sheridan 2016; de Mel, McKenzie, and Woodruff 2013).

In low-income contexts, the availability of wage-paying jobs is often low, leaving many workers relying on informal markets to survive—a situation with stark implications for the extreme poor and vulnerable. Many workers in the informal sector lack the skills, technologies, and access to basic services to effectively undertake productive economic activities. Low-income countries are particularly characterized by a high concentration of employment in low-productivity occupations in agriculture and nonagricultural self-employment, with only a very thin and slow-growing formal sector. Income from informal jobs can be volatile, with limited social protection when circumstances result in a loss of income. In these contexts, then, there is a large population for whom productive work is simply unavailable and who are excluded from formal social protection systems.

As economic inclusion programs typically target poor or developing economies with a sizeable informal sector, there is tremendous potential for economic inclusion programs to unlock opportunities for greater market access and productive work. In Sub-Saharan Africa, almost 80 percent of the workforce work in the informal sector (Filmer and Fox 2014). Informal jobs remain a significant source of employment in low- and lower-middle-income countries (Merotto, Weber, and Aterido 2018). Furthermore, given evidence that formalization has limited effectiveness in increasing incomes, the employment challenge is therefore not just to create jobs in the formal sector but to increase the productivity of those who are in the informal sector (Filmer and Fox 2014). Economic inclusion programs can support informal operators to become more productive and profitable through business training and market access interventions as well as household-level social protection measures that go beyond the poor and include low-income informal workers.

A key question is how to make economic inclusion of the poor—especially the rural poor—a core element of employment approaches and policies. Employment policies often lack a rural-poverty lens, focusing instead on unemployment, on urban areas, or on the formal sectors. Meanwhile, rural poverty reduction efforts have traditionally focused on supporting primary producers, particularly income-generation activities for smallholder farmers, based on the assumption that bottom-up improvements on the supply side will jump-start rural development and eliminate poverty (Mueller and Chan 2015).

Agriculture provides the most immediate means of generating income and employment for the rural poor, especially for large numbers of young people. In Sub-Saharan Africa, agriculture engages more than 70 percent of the labor force in low-income countries (Filmer and Fox 2014). However, the gains from agricultural programs such as those based on microcredit, infrastructure, irrigation, extension, and input technology are often unevenly shared among the poorest populations (Tirivayi, Knowles, and Davis 2013). Relatively little attention has been paid to raising productivity in agricultural and nonagricultural self-employment where the poor work, although recent efforts to link agriculture and social protection for the poorest have shown promise to address a variety of production and consumption constraints (Kagin et al. 2019; Gavrilovic et al. 2016; Pace et al. 2018). L&J programs can help farmworkers increase their productivity through the provision of modern agricultural inputs, improvements in infrastructure (transport, electricity, and irrigation), access to regional markets, and sector-specific training. If workers can gain access to these resources and use them in conjunction with strategies to make agriculture more productive, the results could be transformative for livelihoods and economic growth.

An emerging opportunity is creating links with value chain development, an approach that addresses the constraints of different actors in a value chain (input providers, producers, processors, and distributors) to reduce transaction costs and boost efficiency. In Côte d'Ivoire, a pilot program to integrate economic inclusion into the rice value chain is applying an explicit jobs lens by contracting buyers to purchase rice from smallholder farmers (the program's beneficiaries). Integrating value chain development with economic inclusion may help achieve sustainability, cost-effectiveness, and scalability while improving employment for the most vulnerable. However, connecting vulnerable groups to growing markets also requires sufficient demand for labor, goods, and/or services in a mature and well-functioning value chain. Making this succeed requires a tailored support package designed with an in-depth understanding of the value chain and the specific constraints that vulnerable groups face in accessing jobs and earning opportunities.

Despite a strong set of opportunities to leverage L&J interventions, several challenges persist:

- *A key challenge, as shown by emerging evidence, is that program beneficiaries—or any own-account worker—may not have the appropriate profile to become successful entrepreneurs.* While this may indicate the need for improved selection criteria based on personality traits, it also suggests many youths would be better off in wage employment rather than self-employment. With high population growth creating a huge youth bulge in the coming decades, the implications for cost-effective programming are substantial.

- *Successful approaches may require the combination of jobs, livelihood, and safety net expertise.* One such intervention is through public works programs. Increasingly, public works are designed to enhance employability by combining work experience with other activation measures, such as training. For the workers, these programs establish a minimum income and give them work experience that improves their future employability. Existing public works programs are focused mainly on public infrastructure, such as the construction and maintenance of water and waste management systems, electricity and gas systems, roads, schools, and hospitals. Better community infrastructure can increase market output, lower transaction costs, and improve market access, thereby raising the profitability of small producers and enterprises. It is important to note that the impacts of public works programs are heavily debated and require a great deal of capacity. While public works programs deliver critical economic benefits for the communities in the short term, there is little evidence of sustained impact of economic welfare outcomes in the long run (Mvukiyehe 2018). Economic inclusion programs offer potential to redesign these programs through a bundling of additional interventions, such as capital infusion, training, and coaching.

- *Limited labor demand often spurs urbanization and migration, which require adaptation of economic inclusion interventions.* In many countries, jobs are simply not available where most people live, triggering temporary or permanent migration. There is often a tension between economic inclusion programs that try to create work in the same location as poor households and programs that seek to reduce barriers to safe migration. For many vulnerable people, internal migration may be a preferable alternative for boosting their income and earnings compared to participating in economic inclusion practices, much less remaining self-employed in agriculture. Moreover, the growth of financial services and mobile telecommunications has facilitated the remittance of income to rural areas. The growth of internal migration, particularly to urban areas, will likely continue as an important strategy to stabilize household incomes. However, the broader impacts of young people migrating to urban settings require further research and analysis, given anecdotal evidence that they may often end up in exploitive conditions.

Entry Point 3: Financial Inclusion

Financial inclusion can amplify the movement of economic inclusion to scale. An important entry point for improving economic inclusion is through direct access to financial services, including credit, savings, insurance, and e-payments or mobile money. Methods for expanding financial inclusion have evolved considerably over recent decades, starting with microfinance institutions in the 1990s that began offering small loans to families and microbusinesses as pathways out of poverty. That approach has been followed by a proliferation of financial services that demonstrate how products beyond loans can empower poor people. More recently, digital services have lowered the cost of connecting excluded groups to the formal financial system, and emerging themes include technologies and business models such as pay-as-you-go asset finance and fintech. The scope of available services is much greater than in the past.

Having access to formal banking services and other financial institutions enables women to invest in the growth and development of their businesses and to manage their earnings and savings. As their personal store of funds grows, women can become less dependent on a husband's earnings and less subject to their control, able to make decisions for themselves about where and how to spend their money. This autonomy can also extend beyond finances to decision-making in other domains, such as marriage, leisure time, and contraceptive use (Aker et al. 2016; Bandiera et al. 2013; de Brauw et al. 2014; Field et al. 2016; Holloway, Niazi, and Rouse 2017; Pitt, Khandker, and Cartwright 2006; Schuler and Hashemi 1994; Suri and Jack 2016). For example, in Kenya the BOMA Project supports ultrapoor women through business and savings groups and a digital financial product. Participants saw substantial increases in their income and savings, leading to increased household decision-making power and increased expenditures on education and nutrition. However, BOMA also observed that illiteracy, innumeracy, and unfamiliarity with technology were barriers to full uptake of the digital product. BOMA's experience highlights the need for simpler tools designed thoughtfully for the target population, as well as time for participants to learn to use them.

The spread of government-to-person (G2P) payments has the potential to improve the effectiveness of core cash transfer payments as well as improve financial services such as microloans, savings, and local market information. A shift to electronic payments, for example, can facilitate the link to FI for those previously unbanked. In many countries, policy makers and donors are exploring the case for drawing people into the formal banking system using social protection payments as the "on ramp," especially when the payments are made to bank accounts or electronically. The Better Than Cash Alliance promotes links between social protection and financial inclusion by advocating that G2P payments shift from cash to electronic payments. Electronic payment can provide a pathway to a broader range of financial services, is generally safer (especially for women and girls), and is more efficient for low-income people.

The literature suggests several critical elements that need to be in place for effective digital G2P transfers, including (1) institutional arrangements and coordination between government agencies and the financial sector, (2) a finance and banking regulatory framework to enable secure digital payments and mobile money options, (3) mobile and broadband infrastructure, (4) identification and robust know-your-customer criteria, and (5) payment system interoperability.

Despite considerable potential in the scale-up of FI responses, several challenges remain:

- *Low-income and vulnerable target population groups still tend to be the most excluded from financial services.* This exclusion is due to several underlying constraints, including social norms and cognitive and noncognitive skills. The increasing recognition of this exclusion has led to renewed attention on the potential for financial services to improve resilience and opportunities (El-Zoghbi, Holle, and Soursourian 2019; Ruiz 2013; Schaner and Das 2016). There has also been a realization that financial inclusion alone will not achieve the desired outcomes, and that additional interventions for the poorest need to be included (Escudero et al. 2019; Khandker, Khalily, and Samad 2016; Soares et al. 2017).

- *Inconsistent access to different financial services is an ongoing challenge facing the poor, particularly specific cohorts such as women and youth.* Having access to low-cost credit is vitally important for poor households to reduce their debt-servicing costs and for microentrepreneurs to grow their businesses. Simple design tweaks may promote improved access and outcomes for credit. Research suggests that borrowers who had started a business before gaining access to microcredit are more likely to see significant benefits from taking out loans, whereas those who went into business only after the introduction of microcredit are less likely to see any benefits (Banerjee et al. 2017; Meager 2019). The policy implication is one that naturally favors high-potential entrepreneurs. Meanwhile, other financial products, such as index, crop, or livestock insurance, while important, may be out of reach to the poorest and challenging to scale. A key policy implication is to ensure better customization of financial services, including program tweaks to make products more beneficial to population segments.

- *Experiences in a range of countries suggest that apart from improving account ownership, G2P transfers are not leading to higher account usage or increased uptake of formal financial products.* Evaluations and focus group discussions among SSN beneficiaries in Kenya, Colombia, and Pakistan have found little evidence of beneficiaries using bank accounts or financial services (Weingärtner et al. 2019; Stuart 2016). A 2014 study of the experience of digital transfers in Haiti, Kenya, the Philippines, and Uganda found that insufficient knowledge about program rules and payment methods, inconsistent and delayed payments, and unclear communication about ways to redress grievances reduced trust among beneficiaries and undermined financial inclusion objectives (Zimmerman, Bohling, and Parker 2014). It is also possible that G2P payments could actively undermine the welfare of beneficiaries. In South Africa, the firm delivering social cash transfers digitally marketed loans to beneficiaries using the payments as collateral, contributing to overindebtedness and rapidly declining account balances due to automatic premium payments (Torkelson 2020).

Future Directions

The refinement of program objectives and definition of target groups remain key issues in scaling up economic inclusion programs. While the overall goal of economic inclusion programs settles around the increase of income and assets for program beneficiaries, program-specific objectives determine the direction through which this will be achieved. In moving to scale, economic inclusion programs show considerable flexibility in accommodating diverse needs and priorities. Decisions on program beneficiaries take into account poverty levels, economic profiles, and dynamics at the community and local economy levels. Moving forward, it will be important to test and refine economic inclusion program design and delivery to increase programs' impact on specific population segments and vulnerable groups.

SSN programs provide a premier backbone for governments to scale economic inclusion efforts—especially in the COVID-19 context. With adaptive social protection systems forming the foundation of the first wave of COVID-19 response, the scale-up of economic inclusion programs is an important feature of the medium-to-longer-term response as governments seek to restart their economies, especially in the informal sector. The role of economic inclusion building on SSNs will be critical in strengthening equity, resilience, and opportunity for households and communities.

Greater attention and resources are needed to support learning on the political economy of economic inclusion. The adoption and scale-up of economic inclusion programs hinges on political acceptability and involves trade-offs in program design and implementation. The sharing of evidence, peer-to-peer learning, and cross-country information will be important factors in the scale-up of programs. Country experiences linked to program coordination in and outside of government, transparency and accountability, and beneficiary outreach will be especially relevant across this learning agenda. Furthermore, a new wave of evaluations looks set to help isolate the mechanisms of the impact of economic inclusion programming at scale across entry points and for different groups.

Notes

1. We draw on a political settlements approach to examine the political economy of economic inclusion policy and programming. See the *World Development Report 2017* (World Bank 2017) for a framework. This framework has been used to examine the political economy of social protection in Africa (Hickey et al. 2019) and Asia and the Pacific (O'Keefe et al. forthcoming).
2. Consistent with the approach in chapter 3, this excludes data from JEEViKA, in Bihar, India, which is an outlier program in the overall sample.

References

Aker, Jenny C., Rachid Boumnijel, Amanda McClelland, and Niall Tierney. 2016. "Payment Mechanisms and Antipoverty Programs: Evidence from a Mobile Money Cash Transfer Experiment in Niger." *Economic Development and Cultural Change* 65 (1): 1–37.

Alderman, Harold, and Ruslan Yemtsov. 2013. "How Can Safety Nets Contribute to Economic Growth." Policy Research Working Paper WPS 6437, World Bank, Washington, DC.

Argent, Jonathan, Britta Augsburg, and Imran Rasul. 2014. "Livestock Asset Transfers with and without Training: Evidence from Rwanda." *Journal of Economic Behavior & Organization* 108 (C): 19–39.

Attah, R., V. Barca, A. Kardan, I. MacAuslan, F. Merttens, and L. Pellerano. 2016. "Can Social Protection Affect Psychosocial Well-Being and Why Does This Matter? Lessons from Cash Transfers in Sub-Saharan Africa." *Journal of Development Studies* 52 (8): 1115–31.

Bandiera, O., R. Burgess, N. Das, S. Gulesci, I. Rasul, and M. Sulaiman. 2013. "Can Basic Entrepreneurship Transform the Economic Lives of the Poor?" IZA Discussion Paper 386, Institute of Labor Economics, Bonn.

Banerjee, A., Rukmini Banerji, James Berry, Esther Duflo, Harini Kannan, Shobhini Mukerji, Marc Shotland, and Michael Walton. 2017. "From Proof of Concept to Scalable Policies: Challenges and Solutions, with an Application." *Journal of Economic Perspectives* 31 (4): 73–102.

Banerjee, A. V., and E. Duflo. 2011. *Poor Economics: A Radical Rethinking of the Way to Fight Global Poverty*. New York: Public Affairs.

Banerjee, Abhijit, Esther Duflo, Nathaneal Goldberg, Dean Karlan, Robert Osei, William Parienté, Jeremy Shapiro, Bram Thuysbaert, and Christopher Udry. 2015. "A Multifaceted Program Causes Lasting Progress for the Very Poor: Evidence from Six Countries." *Science* 348 (6236): 1260799.

Banerji, Arup, David Newhouse, Pierella Paci, and David Robalino. 2014. *Working through the Crisis: Jobs and Policies in Developing Countries during the Great Recession*. Directions in Development. Washington, DC: World Bank.

Bastagli, F., J. Hagen-Zanker, L. Harman, V. Barca, G. Sturge, T. Schmidt, and L. Pellerano. 2016. *Cash Transfers: What Does the Evidence Say? A Rigorous Review of Programme Impact and of the Role of Design and Implementation Features*. London: Overseas Development Institute. doi:10.13140/RG.2.2.29336.39687.

Beegle, Kathleen G., Aline Coudouel, Montiel Monsalve, and Mercedes Emma. 2018. *Realizing the Full Potential of Social Safety Nets in Africa*. Washington, DC: World Bank. http://documents.worldbank.org/curated/en/657581531930611436 /Realizing-the-Full-Potential-of-Social-Safety-Nets-in-Africa.

Berhane, Guush, John Hoddinott, Neha Kumar, and Alemayehu Seyoum Taffesse. 2011. *The Impact of Ethiopia's Productive Safety Nets and Household Asset Building Programme: 2006–2010*. Washington, DC: International Food Policy research Institute.

Blattman, Christopher, Nathan Fiala, and Sebastian Martinez. 2019. "The Long-Term Impacts of Grants on Poverty: 9-Year Evidence from Uganda's Youth Opportunities Program." NBER Working Papers 24999, National Bureau of Economic Research, Cambridge, MA.

Blattman, Christopher, Eric Green, Jeannie Annan, and Julian Jamison. 2013. "Building Women's Economic and Social Empowerment through Enterprise an Experimental Assessment of the Women's Income Generating Support (WINGS) Program in Uganda." LOGiCA Study Series 1, San Francisco.

Blattman, Christopher, Julian C. Jamison, and Margaret Sheridan. 2016. "Reducing Crime and Violence: Experimental Evidence on Adult Noncognitive Investments in Liberia." GLMLIC Working Paper 21. Bonn.

Booysen, F., S. Van der Berg, R. Burger, M. von Maltitz, and G. Du Rand. 2008. "Using an Asset Index to Assess Trend in Poverty in Seven Sub-Saharan African Countries." *World Development* 36 (6): 1113–30.

Bowen, Thomas, Carol del Ninno, Colin Andrews, Sarah Coll-Black, Ugo Gentilini, Kelly Johnson, Yasuhiro Kawasoe, Adea Kryeziu, Barry Maher, and Asha Williams. 2020. *Adaptive Social Protection: Building Resilience to Shocks.* International Development in Focus. Washington, DC: World Bank.

Chambers, R., and G. R. Conway. 1992. "Sustainable Rural Livelihoods: Practical Concepts for the 21st Century." Discussion paper 296, Institute of Development Studies, Brighton, UK.

de Brauw, A., Daniel O. Gilligan, John Hoddinott, and Shalini Roy. 2014. "The Impact of *Bolsa Família* on Women's Decision-Making Power." *World Development* 59. doi:10.2139/ssrn.1999073.

de Mel, Suresh De, David McKenzie, and Christopher Woodruff. 2013. "One-time Transfers of Cash or Capital Have Long-Lasting Effects on Microenterprises in Sri Lanka." enGender Impact: The World Bank's Gender Impact Evaluation Database. Washington, DC: World Bank. http://documents.worldbank.org/curated /en/632991468335537284/One-time-transfers-of-cash-or-capital-have-long-lasting -effects-on-microenterprises-in-Sri-Lanka.

Desai, Raj M. 2007. *The Political Economy of Poverty Reduction: Scaling Up Antipoverty Programs in the Developing World.* Wolfensohn Center for Development Working Paper 2, Brookings Institution, Washington, DC.

Devereux, S., and Rachel Sabates-Wheeler. 2015. "Graduating from Social Protection." *IDS Bulletin* 46 (2):1–12.

El-Zoghbi, Mayada, Nina Holle, and Matthew Soursourian. 2019. "Emerging Evidence on Financial Inclusion: Moving from Black and White to Color." Focus Note, CGAP, Washington, DC. https://www.cgap.org/sites/default/files/publications/2019_07 _FocusNote_Emerging_Evidence.pdf.

Escudero, Verónica, Jochen Kluve, Elva López Mourelo, and Clemente Pignatti. 2019. "Active Labour Market Programmes in Latin America and the Caribbean: Evidence from a Meta-Analysis." *Journal of Development Studies* 55 (12): 2644–61, doi:10.108 0/00220388.2018.1546843.

FAO (Food and Agriculture Organization of the United Nations). 2018. *FAO and Cash +: How to Maximize the Impacts of Cash Transfers.* Rome: FAO.

Field, Erica, Rohini Pande, Natalia Rigol, Simone Schaner, and Charity Troyer Moore. 2016. "On Her Account: Can Strengthening Women's Financial Control Boost Female Labor Supply?" Working paper. https://bfi.uchicago.edu/wp-content /uploads/on_her_account.can_strengthening_womens_financial_control_boost _female_labor_supply.pdf.

Filmer, Deon, and Louise Fox. 2014. *Youth Employment in Sub-Saharan Africa.* Africa Development Series. Washington, DC: World Bank.

Gavrilovic, M., M. Knowles, B. Davis, P. Pozarny, G. Calcagnini, and R. Sabates-Wheeler. 2016. *Strengthening Coherence between Agriculture and Social Protection in Africa: Framework for Analysis and Action.* Rome: FAO.

Goldman, I. 2010. "Applying Sustainable Livelihood Approaches to Improve Rural People's Quality of Life." Paper presented at conference on Dynamics of Rural Transformation in Emerging Economies, New Delhi, March 11. http://www.rimisp .org/wp-content/uploads/2010/05/9.pdf.

Handa, S., S. Daidone, A. Peterman, B. Davis, A. Pereira, T. Palermo, and J. Yablonski. 2017. "Myth Busting? Confronting Six Common Perceptions about Unconditional

Cash Transfers as a Poverty Reduction Strategy in Africa." Office of Research–Innocenti Working Paper 2017-11, UNICEF, Geneva. https://www.unicef-irc.org/publications/pdf/IWP-2017-06.pdf.

Hickey, S, T. Lavers, M. Niño-Zarazúa, and J. Seekings, eds. 2019. *The Politics of Social Protection in Eastern and Southern Africa.* Oxford: Oxford University Press.

Holloway, K., Z. Niazi, and R. Rouse. 2017. *Women's Economic Empowerment through Financial Inclusion: A Review of Existing Evidence and Remaining Knowledge Gaps.* New Haven: Innovations for Poverty Action.

ILO (International Labour Organization). n.d. "Jobs and Livelihoods at the Heart of the Post-2015 Development Agenda." ILO Concept Note on the post-2015 Development Agenda. Geneva: ILO. https://www.ilo.org/global/topics/sdg-2030/documents/WCMS_193483/lang--en/index.htm.

Jorgensen, Steen Lau, and Paul Bennett Siegel. 2019. "Social Protection in an Era of Increasing Uncertainty and Disruption: Social Risk Management 2.0." Social Protection and Jobs Discussion Paper 1930, World Bank, Washington, DC. http://documents.worldbank.org/curated/en/263761559643240069/Social-Protection-in-an-Era-of-Increasing-Uncertainty-and-Disruption-Social-Risk-Management-2-0.

Kabeer, Naila, Karishma Huda, Sandeep Kaur, and Nicolina Lamhauge. 2012. "Productive Safety Nets for Women in Extreme Poverty: Lessons from Pilot Projects in India and Pakistan." Discussion Paper 28/12, Centre for Development Policy and Research, School of Oriental and African Studies, London.

Kagin, J., J. E. Taylor, L. Pellerano, S. Daidone, F. Juergens, N. Pace, and M. Knowles. 2019. *Local Economy Impacts and Cost-Benefit Analysis of Social Protection and Agricultural Interventions in Malawi.* Rome and Geneva: FAO and UNICEF.

Khandker, Kazem Adnan, Baqui M. A. Khalily, and Hussain A. Samad. 2016. *Beyond Ending Poverty: The Dynamics of Microfinance in Bangladesh.* Directions in Development. Washington, DC: World Bank. http://documents.worldbank.org/curated/en/366431468508832455/Beyond-ending-poverty-the-dynamics-of-microfinance-in-Bangladesh.

Kidd, Stephen. 2019. "The Effectiveness of the Graduation Approach: What Does the Evidence Tell Us?" *Development Pathways* 27. https://www.developmentpathways.co.uk/publications/the-effectiveness-of-the-graduation-approach-what-does-the-evidence-tell-us-2/.

Kidd, Stephen, Bjorn Gelders, and Diloá Bailey-Athias. 2017. "Exclusion by Design: An Assessment of the Effectiveness of the Proxy Means Test Poverty Targeting Mechanism." ESS Working Paper 56, ILO, Geneva. doi:10.13140/RG.2.2.36802.68805.

Lavers, T. 2016. "Understanding Elite Commitment to Social Protection: Rwanda's Vision 2020 Umurenge Programme." WIDER Working Paper 2016/93, United Nations University World Institute for Development Economics Research, Helsinki.

Maldonado, J. H., R. D. P Moreno Sánchez, J. A. Gómez, and Jurado León Jurado. 2016. *Protection, Production, Promotion: Exploring Synergies between Social Protection and Rural Productive Development in Latin America: Executive Summary.* Bogotá: Universidad de los Andes.

McIntosh, C., and A. Zeitlin. 2018. "Benchmarking a Child Nutrition Program against Cash: Experimental Evidence from Rwanda." Working paper, Innovations for Poverty Action, Washington, DC.

McKenzie, David J. 2017. "How Effective Are Active Labor Market Policies in Developing Countries? A Critical Review of Recent Evidence." Policy Research Working Paper WPS 8011, Impact Evaluation Series, World Bank, Washington, DC. http://documents.worldbank.org/curated/en/256001490191438119/How-effective-are-active-labor-market-policies-in-developing-countries-a-critical-review-of-recent-evidence.

Meager, Rachael. 2019. "Understanding the Average Impact of Microcredit Expansions: A Bayesian Hierarchical Analysis of Seven Randomized Experiments." *American Economic Journal: Applied Economics* 11 (1): 57–91.

Merotto, Dino, Michael Weber, and Reyes Aterido. 2018. "Pathways to Better Jobs in IDA Countries: Findings from Jobs Diagnostics." Jobs Series 14. World Bank, Washington, DC.

Mueller, B., and M. K. Chan. 2015. *Wage Labor, Agriculture-Based Economies, and Pathways Out of Poverty: Taking Stock of the Evidence.* Washington, DC: USAID.

Mvukiyehe, Eric. 2018. "What Are We Learning about the Impacts of Public Works Programs on Employment and Violence? Early Findings from Ongoing Evaluations in Fragile States." *World Bank Blogs*, April 16. https://blogs.worldbank .org/impactevaluations/what-are-we-learning-about-impacts-public-works -programs-employment-and-violence-early-findings.

O'Keefe, Philip, Puja Dutta, Harry Moroz, and Robert Palacios. Forthcoming. *Diverse Paths: The Dynamism of Social Protection in Asia and the Pacific.* Washington, DC, and Barton: World Bank and Australian Department of Foreign Affairs and Trade.

Pace, N., Silvio Daidone, Benjamin Davis, Sudhanshu Handa, Marco Knowles, and Robert Pickmans. 2018. "One Plus One Can Be Greater than Two: Evaluating Synergies of Development Programmes in Malawi." *Journal of Development Studies* 54 (11): 2023–60. doi:10.1080/00220388.2017.1380794.

Peterman, Amber, Neha Kumar, Audrey Pereira, and Daniel O. Gilligan. 2019. "Toward Gender Equality: A Critical Assessment of Evidence on Social Safety Nets in Africa." In *Gender Equality in Rural Africa: From Commitments to Outcomes— ReSAKSS 2019 Annual Trends and Outlook Report,* edited by Agnes Quisumbing, Ruth Meinzen-Dick, and Jemimah Njuki, 140–48. Washington, DC: IFPRI.

Pitt, Mark M., Shahidur R. Khandker, and Jennifer Cartwright. 2006. "Empowering Women with Micro Finance: Evidence from Bangladesh." *Economic Development and Cultural Change* 54 (4): 791–831. doi:10.1086/503580.

Premand, Patrick, and Carlo del Ninno. 2016. "Cash Transfers, Behavioral Accompanying Measures, and Child Development in Niger." Working paper, World Bank, Washington, DC.

Pritchard, M., S. Kenward, and M. Hannan. 2015. "The Chars Livelihoods Programme in Bangladesh: Factors That Enable, Constrain and Sustain Graduation." *IDS Bulletin* 46 (2): 35–47.

Ralston, Laura R., Colin Andrews, and Allan Jer-Yu Hsiao. 2017. "The Impacts of Safety Nets in Africa: What Are We Learning?" Policy Research Working Paper WPS 8255, World Bank, Washington, DC.

Ravallion, M., D. Jolliffe, and J. Margitic. 2018. "Social Protection and Economic Development: Are the Poorest Being Lifted-Up or Left-Behind?" NBER Working Paper 24665. Cambridge, MA: National Bureau of Economic Research.

Roelen, K., Stephen Devereux, Abdul-Gafaru Abdulai, Bruno Martorano, Tia Palermo, and Luigi Peter Ragno. 2017. "How to Make 'Cash Plus' Work: Linking Cash Transfers to Services and Sectors." Innocenti Working Paper 2017-10, UNICEF Office of Research, Florence.

Ruiz, Claudia. 2013. "From Pawn Shops to Banks: The Impact of Formal Credit on Informal Households." Policy Research Working Paper WPS 6634, World Bank, Washington, DC. http://documents.worldbank.org/curated/en/465221468286796985 /From-pawn-shops-to-banks-the-impact-of-formal-credit-on-informal-households.

Sabates-Wheeler, Rachel, Jeremy Lind, and John Hoddinott. 2013. "Implementing Social Protection in Agro-pastoralist and Pastoralist Areas: How Local Distribution Structures Moderate PSNP Outcomes in Ethiopia." *World Development* 50: 1–12.

Scarpari, Raquel, and Timothy Joseph Peter Clay. 2020. "Gender in Jobs Diagnostics: A Guidance Note." Jobs Guide 5, World Bank, Washington, DC.

Schaner, S., and S. Das. 2016. "Female Labor Force Participation in Asia: Indonesia Country Study." ADB Economics Working Paper 474, Asian Development Bank, Manila.

Schuler, Sidney Ruth, and Syed M. Hashemi. 1994. "Credit Programs, Women's Empowerment, and Contraceptive Use in Rural Bangladesh." *Studies in Family Planning* 25 (2): 65–76.

Sheldon, Tony, ed. 2016. *Preserving the Essence, Adapting for Reach: Early Lessons from Large-Scale Implementations of the Graduation Approach.* New York: Ford Foundation.

Slater, R., S. Wiggins, L. Harman, M. Ulrichs, L. Scott, K. Marco, P. Pozarny, and G. Calcagnini. 2016. *Strengthening Coherence between Agriculture and Social Protection: Synthesis of Seven Country Case Studies.* Rome: FAO.

Soares, F. V., M. Knowles, S. Daidone, and N. Tirivayi. 2017. *Combined Effects and Synergies between Agricultural and Social Protection Interventions: What Is the Evidence So Far?* Rome: FAO.

Stuart, G. 2016. *Government to Person Payments: On Ramp to Financial Inclusion?* Washington, DC: Center for Financial Inclusion.

Suri, Tavneet, and William Jack. 2016. "The Long-Run Poverty and Gender Impacts of Mobile Money." *Science* 354 (6317): 1288–92.

Tirivayi, N., M. Knowles, and B. Davis. 2013. *The Interaction between Social Protection and Agriculture: A Review of Evidence.* Rome: FAO.

Torkelson, Erin. 2020. "Collateral Damages: Cash Transfer and Debt Transfer in South Africa." *World Development* 126. doi:10.1016/j.worlddev.2019.104711.

Weingärtner, Lena, Martina Ulrichs, Cecilia Costella, Sarah Kohnstamm, and Elvin Nyukuri. 2019. "Linking Financial Services and Social Protection for Resilience in Kenya." Working and Discussion Papers, Overseas Development Institute, London. https://www.odi.org/publications /11345-linking-financial-services-and-social-protection-resilience-kenya.

World Bank. 2017. *World Development Report 2017: Governance and the Law.* Washington, DC: World Bank. https://www.worldbank.org/en/publication /wdr2017.

World Bank. 2019. *World Development Report 2019: The Changing Nature of Work.* Washington, DC: World Bank.

World Bank. 2020. "Productive Inclusion in Latin America: Policy and Operational Lessons." World Bank, Washington, DC. https://openknowledge.worldbank.org /handle/10986/34199.

Zimmerman, Jamie M., Kristy Bohling, and Sarah Rotman Parker. 2014. "Electronic G2P Payments: Evidence from Four Lower-Income Countries." CGAP Focus Note 93, Consultative Group to Assist the Poor, Washington, DC. http://documents .worldbank.org/curated/en/989941468108546036.

CHAPTER 3
A Surge in Economic Inclusion Programming Worldwide

KEY MESSAGES

The Partnership for Economic Inclusion (PEI) Landscape Survey 2020 provides a snapshot of economic inclusion programs around the world based on 219 programs reaching over 90 million beneficiaries. Economic growth is driven by governments in low-income countries in Sub-Saharan Africa and South Asia. These estimates are conservative and represent an initial baseline.

Economic inclusion programs are implemented in a variety of contexts and geographies and among different target groups. Rural residents, women, and specific vulnerable groups are clear priorities.

Economic inclusion programs provide an integrated package of interventions. They typically include five or more components and most commonly feature transfers, skills training, coaching, market links, and access to financial services.

Existing cash transfer programs show strong potential to support program scale-up. Cash transfers are a driving component across programs. There is growing attention on the structure of cash payments, for example, continuous, less regular, or one-off grant transfers.

Data presented in this chapter are available at www.peiglobal.org, **which allows programs to upload, update, and use data as a global public good.**

FUTURE DIRECTIONS

A strong focus on youth is emerging. Because of young peoples' high levels of underemployment and uncertain pathways to formal jobs, economic inclusion programs will play an important development role, but programs need to adapt to ensure effective links to complementary services.

Coaching and entrepreneurial support need to be strengthened and streamlined. Innovations in program delivery are emerging, including digital options, self-help groups, and peer-to-peer learning networks.

Economic inclusion programs in fragile settings are poised to grow further, necessitating a better understanding of operational models. Good practices in linking economic inclusion to humanitarian interventions and facilitating market links in fragile settings need to be documented.

Multidimensional economic inclusion programs are well placed to help people with disabilities overcome some of the challenges they face in increasing their economic opportunities. The body of knowledge on adapting program design and delivery to increase outcomes for people with disabilities is growing.

A Snapshot in Time

An unprecedented surge in economic inclusion programming is occurring worldwide. The Partnership for Economic Inclusion (PEI) Landscape Survey 2020 features data and information covering approximately 20 million households, benefiting nearly 92 million individuals, either directly or indirectly. Forty-one new programs are in the planning stages in 12 countries. Nearly half of all programs worldwide (49 percent) are government led, as governments have been adopting and expanding them to reach the poorest populations. Moreover, the existing government-led programs are far larger than the nongovernment-led programs, covering nearly 90 percent of beneficiaries across all the programs featured in this report. All of this strongly suggests that there is considerable potential for beneficiary numbers to grow.

This chapter presents a snapshot of current economic inclusion programming under way and establishes a baseline with data from a survey conducted by PEI between November 2019 and May 2020. Although it is difficult to capture the universe of economic inclusion programming, this survey was comprehensive in scope: the data come from 219 programs in 75 countries. Forty-two percent of the programs surveyed are being supported by the World Bank in 53 countries. The full 2020 sample is analyzed in this chapter, and chapter 4 focuses on government-led programs only. The data collected through PEI's Landscape Survey 2020 is publicly available through an online dashboard at http://peiglobal.org, which provides easy access to, and encourages further engagement with, the data. Box 3.1 provides more detail on the survey's scope and methods.

BOX 3.1   Partnership for Economic Inclusion Landscape Survey 2020

To map the universe of economic inclusion programs, the study underlying this report used an online survey tool to gather information from a range of government and technical partners. For World Bank programs, using both manual and text analysis techniques, the survey team reviewed approximately 1,200 programs in all geographic regions and involving six of the World Bank's Global Practices: Urban Resilience and Land; Social Development; Social Protection and Jobs; Finance, Competitiveness, and Innovation; Agriculture; Environment and Natural Resources; and Blue Economy. To map projects outside of World Bank operations, the survey team used PEI's 2017 survey dataset, the database of productive inclusion programs from the Economic Commission for Latin America and the Caribbean, and other sources to identify ongoing projects and key partners, including governments, nongovernmental organizations (NGOs), regional organizations, multilateral organizations, and other development partners involved in economic inclusion programming.

The survey questionnaire was developed through broad consultation and consisted of 44 questions in eight sections, including objectives, target beneficiaries, beneficiary coverage, design and implementation features, institutional arrangements, budgets, financing, and research and evaluation. The survey was completed by staff from the lead implementing agency, implementing partner, or other organization providing support to each program. A detailed overview of the survey methodology can be found in appendix A.

(Box continues next page)

BOX 3.1   **Partnership for Economic Inclusion Landscape Survey 2020 (*continued*)**

During survey preparation, the survey team identified 312 programs (166 supported by the World Bank Group and 146 by others). After reviewing these and discounting for overlaps, closed operations, and pipeline projects, the final survey was undertaken for 246 programs. The overall response rate to the survey was 89 percent, resulting in 219 programs for which data were obtained. One major challenge is the fact that the data is self-reported, and information and interpretation may vary across survey respondents. The survey authors factored in time for a thorough quality review of each survey response and followed up with respondents for queries and clarifications. The online survey provided detailed guidance and was translated into French and Spanish to ensure clarity.

The Current Reach of Economic Inclusion Programs

The 20 million households—consisting of more than 90 million individuals—served by economic inclusion programs today, either directly or indirectly, are heavily concentrated in Sub-Saharan Africa and South Asia. More than half of the programs are in Sub-Saharan Africa, which hosts 30 percent of individuals served, through a proliferation of smaller programs. South Asia is home to 66 percent of people served. The large number of beneficiaries in this latter region is notable given that it is host to only 15 percent of economic inclusion programs, reflecting the scale these programs have achieved, particularly in India and Bangladesh. A single program accounts for 51 percent of total coverage: the Bihar (India) Rural Livelihoods Project (JEEViKA).

Figure 3.1 displays the percentage of total program beneficiaries, excluding JEEViKA, in relation to total programs by region. Just 3 percent of programs are led by multinational organizations, including United Nations agencies such as the Food and Agriculture Organization (FAO), the High Commissioner for Refugees (UNHCR), and the World Food Programme (WFP). (See table D.1 in appendix D for the list of programs and appendix E for the types of components included in them.)

Almost 70 percent of surveyed programs are in low-income countries (categorized by the World Bank as eligible for International Development Association financing).[1] Nevertheless, economic inclusion programs of various kinds are represented across the geographic and income spectrum, in low-, lower-middle-, upper-middle-, and even high-income countries. This suggests applicability both in contexts with extensive poverty and in contexts where poverty occurs in pockets. The Latin America and the Caribbean region hosts all the programs implemented in high-income countries as well as 67 percent of those hosted in upper-middle-income countries, and the region represents 19 percent of all programs identified in the survey.

Close to half (49 percent) of the programs are led by government. The five largest economic inclusion programs are all government led and build on large-scale and mature social protection programs. (See table 3.1 for basic program details on these five.)

FIGURE 3.1 **Percent Distribution of Economic Inclusion Programs and Beneficiaries by Region, Lead Institution, and Entry Point**

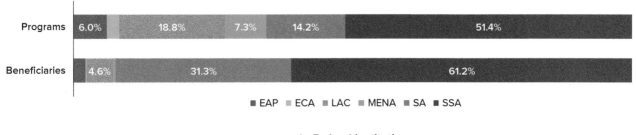

a. By region

Programs: EAP 6.0% | ECA 18.8% | LAC 7.3% | MENA 14.2% | SSA 51.4%

Beneficiaries: 4.6% | 31.3% | 61.2%

■ EAP ■ ECA ■ LAC ■ MENA ■ SA ■ SSA

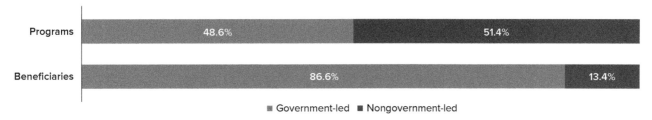

b. By lead institution

Programs: 48.6% | 51.4%

Beneficiaries: 86.6% | 13.4%

■ Government-led ■ Nongovernment-led

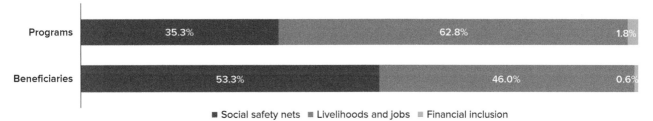

c. By entry point

Programs: 35.3% | 62.8% | 1.8%

Beneficiaries: 53.3% | 46.0% | 0.6%

■ Social safety nets ■ Livelihoods and jobs ■ Financial inclusion

Source: Partnership for Economic Inclusion, World Bank.

Note: EAP = East Asia and Pacific; ECA = Europe and Central Asia; LAC = Latin America and the Caribbean; MENA = Middle East and North Africa; SA = South Asia; SSA = Sub-Saharan Africa. Data on the number of beneficiaries are missing for 18 programs—6 nongovernment and 12 government programs—which when broken down by entry point signify 6 social safety net (SSN) and 12 livelihoods and jobs (L&J) programs. The figure also excludes data from JEEViKA (a government-led L&J program in India), which covers over 50 percent of all beneficiaries in the survey. The total number of programs excluding JEEViKA is 218 (112 nongovernment-led and 106 government-led programs or 77 SSN, 137 L&J, and 4 financial inclusion [FI] or 13 in East Asia and Pacific, 5 in Europe and Central Asia, 41 in Latin America and the Caribbean, 16 in the Middle East and North Africa, 31 in South Asia, and 112 in Sub-Saharan Africa. The number of total beneficiaries is 45,319,700, which includes direct and indirect beneficiaries. When JEEViKA is included, the results are as follows: the number of programs is 219 (112 nongovernment-led and 107 government-led programs or 77 SSN, 138 L&J, and 4 FI or 13 in East Asia and Pacific, 5 in Europe and Central Asia, 41 in Latin America and the Caribbean, 16 in the Middle East and North Africa, 32 in South Asia, and 112 in Sub-Saharan Africa). The number of total individual beneficiaries equals 91,933,700.

Diversity in Programs: Objectives and Contexts

Given the range of institutions implementing economic inclusion programs and the variety of contexts in which they are established, the result is a wide diversity of programming. Whether from governments or nongovernment institutions, program planners are driven by their organizations' priorities. They must account for country or regional context, the services and institutions serving as partners and their institutional cultures, and the unique challenges confronted by people living in extreme poverty and vulnerability in that locality. While many factors account for the variations, programs

TABLE 3.1   **The Five Largest Programs: Lead Organizations, Number of Beneficiaries Served, and Year Started**

Country	Program	Lead organization	Beneficiaries served	Year started
India	JEEViKA	Bihar Rural Livelihoods Promotion Society, Rural Development Department, Government of Bihar	46,614,000	2007
Tanzania	Tanzania Productive Social Safety Nets 2	Tanzania Social Action Fund	5,010,000	2019
Bangladesh	Nuton Jibon Livelihood Improvement Project	Social Development Foundation, an organization under the Ministry of Finance	4,470,000	2015
Ethiopia	Livelihood component of Rural Productive Safety Net Program	Ministry of Agriculture	3,918,306	2017
Sudan	Social Safety Net	Ministry of Labor and Social Development and Ministry of Finance	2,795,000	2016

Source: Partnership for Economic Inclusion, World Bank.

Note: Beneficiaries served represent direct and indirect beneficiaries active at the time of data collection.

broadly define how they will work, what components they will include, and what support they can offer based on program objectives, context, and target populations active at the time of data collection.

Program Objectives

The PEI Landscape Survey 2020 revealed that there are 12 objectives that are most common and help shape economic inclusion programming for respondent programs. As described in chapter 1, megatrends and national policy priorities, such as population growth, forced displacement, and climate change, are challenges reflected in the considerable range of desired outcomes for these programs.

The most common priorities among surveyed programs include building self-employment opportunities (52 percent), income diversification (37 percent), and resilience (32 percent) (Figure 3.2). When viewed in relation to the entry points to scale outlined in chapter 2, differences are limited, but livelihoods and jobs (L&J) programs focus more on women's empowerment (23 percent), while social safety net (SSN) programs focus more on resilience (42 percent).[2]

Priority objectives also vary by region. In an effort to deal with high levels of unemployment, particularly among youths, programs in the Middle East and North Africa and Latin America and the Caribbean overwhelmingly seek to increase employment opportunities (wage or self-employment) (81 percent and 71 percent of the regions, respectively). By contrast, programs in South Asia and Sub-Saharan Africa predominantly seek to support income diversification (50 percent and 40 percent, respectively). In South Asia, a high percentage of programs also focus on social inclusion (44 percent) to reduce the social marginalization of indigenous populations and other vulnerable groups.

Governments are more likely than nongovernmental programs to focus on increasing access to wage employment (24 percent versus 13 percent) and on increased productivity (34 percent versus 19 percent). Conversely, nongovernment-led programs focus more heavily than government-led programs on women's empowerment (22 percent versus 11 percent), resilience (38 percent versus 26 percent), and food security (31 percent versus 19 percent). The six multilateral programs included in the

FIGURE 3.2 Main Program Objectives Overall and by Their Entry Points to Scale

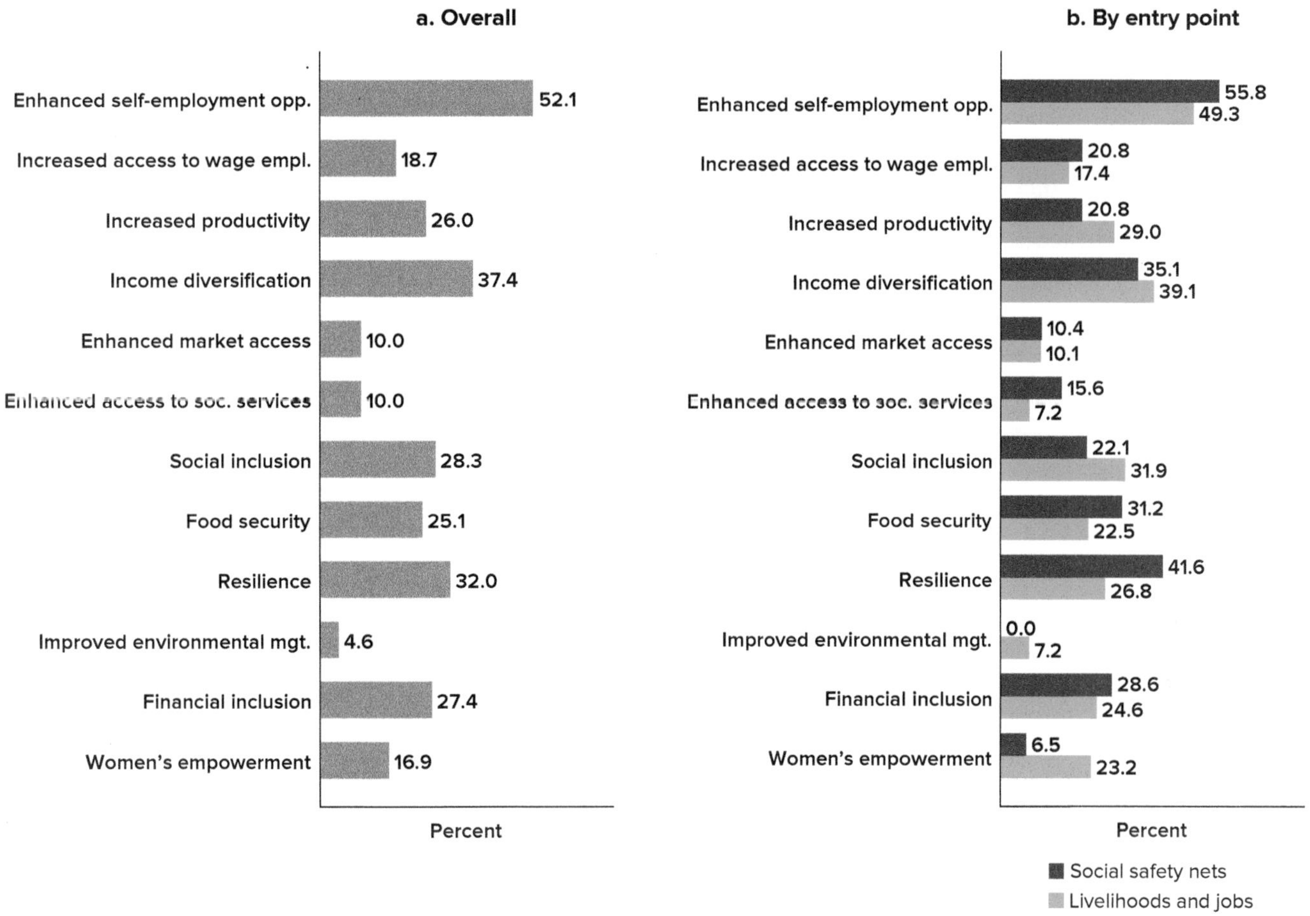

a. Overall

	Percent
Enhanced self-employment opp.	52.1
Increased access to wage empl.	18.7
Increased productivity	26.0
Income diversification	37.4
Enhanced market access	10.0
Enhanced access to soc. services	10.0
Social inclusion	28.3
Food security	25.1
Resilience	32.0
Improved environmental mgt.	4.6
Financial inclusion	27.4
Women's empowerment	16.9

b. By entry point

	Social safety nets	Livelihoods and jobs
Enhanced self-employment opp.	55.8	49.3
Increased access to wage empl.	20.8	17.4
Increased productivity	20.8	29.0
Income diversification	35.1	39.1
Enhanced market access	10.4	10.1
Enhanced access to soc. services	15.6	7.2
Social inclusion	22.1	31.9
Food security	31.2	22.5
Resilience	41.6	26.8
Improved environmental mgt.	0.0	7.2
Financial inclusion	28.6	24.6
Women's empowerment	6.5	23.2

■ Social safety nets
■ Livelihoods and jobs

Source: Partnership for Economic Inclusion, World Bank.

Note: Panel a provides percentage of all programs (N = 219) and panel b percentage of social safety net (SSN) and livelihoods and jobs (L&J) programs (N1 = 77 and N2 = 138, respectively). Respondents were asked to report a maximum of three objectives. Financial inclusion programs are excluded due to the small subsample (four programs).

survey have a distinct focus on resilience (two-thirds of them), food security (half of them), and self-employment opportunities (half of them), likely linked to their emergency or humanitarian mandates.

Contexts

National priorities, political context, and global trends can all shape economic inclusion programs, offering both opportunities and limitations that influence program development and imbue programs with distinct characteristics.

Most economic inclusion programs surveyed, 88 percent of all programs, operate in rural settings, while 46 percent operate exclusively in rural areas. This partly corresponds to the fact that extreme poverty is disproportionately concentrated in rural settings, with about two-thirds of extremely poor people living in rural areas (Kharas et al. 2020). As shown in Figure 3.3, 36 percent of programs are in urban areas, 40 percent in peri-urban areas, and 42 percent operate across

FIGURE 3.3 **Percentage of All Programs with a Presence in Rural, Urban, and Peri-Urban Areas**

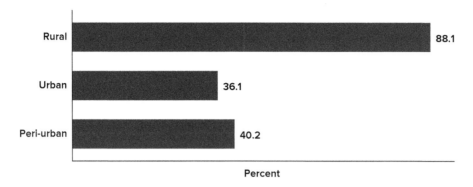

Source: Partnership for Economic Inclusion, World Bank.

Note: Percentage of all programs (N = 219). Respondents could select more than one context.

rural and urban/peri-urban settings. Twelve percent of programs operate exclusively in urban/peri-urban areas.

More than a quarter (26 percent) of all economic inclusion programs surveyed operate in contexts of high fragility, conflict, and violence (FCV). This is based on the World Bank's classification of countries with high institutional and social fragility and countries affected by violent conflict, which is in part a reflection of the preponderance of people living in extreme poverty and vulnerability in these areas (World Bank Group 2020). Economic inclusion programs in FCV contexts are located primarily in Sub-Saharan Africa (75 percent of programs) and the Middle East and North Africa region (11 percent). Many programs operating in FCV contexts are led by NGOs or multilateral organizations (59 percent), highlighting the key role these organizations play when government systems are weak or absent. (See box 3.2 for further detail on the special challenges of programming in FCV contexts.)

A majority of economic inclusion programs seek to mitigate climate change. Climate change mitigation strategies are increasingly important for developing sustainable livelihoods, particularly in rural areas, where climate change impacts can be exacerbated by farm practices. Climate change can cause a loss of income due to a lack of access to suitable financial products to buffer the shocks, in particular savings and insurance. This not only affects the poorest but can also affect better-off members of the community, potentially resulting in the latter households falling below the poverty line. Such shocks typically have long-lasting negative impacts on the poor, since they are the least able to adapt to more frequent and more severe storms, droughts, and floods.

Fifty-seven percent of programs include interventions designed to mitigate climate change, for example, through sustainable natural resource management or climate change adaptation. Of these programs, 38 percent have resilience as a main objective. Across regions, climate change mitigation efforts are more prevalent in South Asia (75 percent) and Sub-Saharan Africa (66 percent) than elsewhere. These regions are severely affected by rising sea levels and drought (figure 3.4).

BOX 3.2 Economic Inclusion in Fragile and Displacement Contexts

The proportion of poor people living in contexts of fragility, conflict, and violence (FCV) has constantly increased since 2010, and it is projected that as many as two-thirds of people living in extreme poverty globally may be living in FCV contexts by 2030 (Corral et al. 2020). Recent analysis paints a stark picture of the implications of FCV on individuals: a person living in an economy facing chronic fragility and conflict is 10 times more likely to be poor than a person living in a country that has not been fragile or in conflict in the past 20 years.

The data show that economic inclusion programs are more likely to target displacement-affected populations, particularly internally displaced populations, in FCV contexts than in non-FCV contexts (34 percent versus 8 percent) and focus more on increasing resilience (43 percent versus 28 percent), social inclusion (38 percent versus 25 percent), and food security (32 percent versus 23 percent). Economic inclusion in these contexts can help build resilience and develop economic opportunities that may enable people to better cope with the economic and social stress while building income and assets. But a lack of government systems and structures, and the presence of corruption and insecurity, make it challenging to link these efforts to government or other programs for ongoing support. Programs in FCV contexts are less likely than programs in non-FCV settings to be government led (41 percent versus 52 percent) or funded by government (16 percent versus 36 percent). They are also less likely than programs in non-FCV settings to be integrated with government programs (43 percent versus 67 percent) and delivered by linking existing programs (7 percent versus 26 percent).

FIGURE 3.4 Climate Change Mitigation and Resilience: Percentage of Programs That Have Either of These as a Main Objective, by Geographic Region

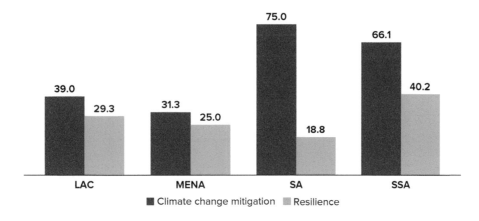

Source: Partnership for Economic Inclusion, World Bank.

Note: LAC = Latin America and the Caribbean; MENA = Middle East and North Africa; SA = South Asia; SSA = Sub-Saharan Africa. Number of programs by region: 41 in Latin America and the Caribbean, 16 in the Middle East and North Africa, 32 in South Asia, and 112 in Sub-Saharan Africa. East Asia and Pacific and Europe and Central Asia are excluded due to small subsamples.

Target Populations

Typically, programs target specific population groups or poverty segments, including the poor, extreme poor, and ultrapoor (figure 3.5).[3] In Sub-Saharan Africa and South Asia, where the rates of extreme poverty are the highest, there are correspondingly higher proportions of programs that target extreme poor populations than in other regions. Many programs have eligibility criteria that participants must meet in order to join the programs, with 78 percent of all programs using some combination of attributes that may include age, sex, or having dependents.

Some economic inclusion programs seek to serve people in specific demographic categories, particularly women, either because of their institutional mission or because of program goals (figure 3.6). Eighty-eight percent of all programs target women as a priority segment and, in 64 percent of programs that reported the number of beneficiaries, women constitute the majority of all program participants.[4] Fifteen percent of all programs (and about a fifth of those that reported the number of female beneficiaries) serve only women.

Programs that predominantly serve women focus on building the skills and confidence of female participants through training and coaching. As compared to other programs, those primarily serving women typically place a strong emphasis on life skills training (72 percent of women-focused programs versus 40 percent of other programs) and financial training (82 percent versus 60 percent). Coaching more often includes health and nutrition guidance (63 percent versus 27 percent) and discussions around social issues affecting the family, such as child marriage, and intrahousehold dynamics (68 percent versus 33 percent), as compared to other programs. Programs

FIGURE 3.5 **Targeting of the Ultrapoor, Extreme Poor, Poor, and Others: Percentage of Programs Overall and by Lead Institution Type**

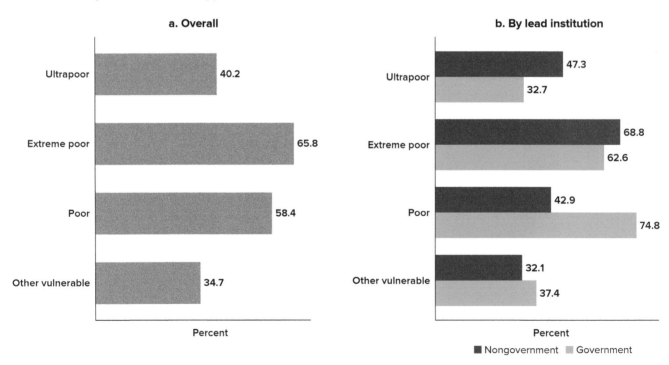

Source: Partnership for Economic Inclusion, World Bank.

Note: Panel a shows percentage of all programs (N = 219). Panel b shows percentage of all nongovernment- and government-led programs (N1 = 112 and N2 = 107, respectively). Programs may target more than one segment.

FIGURE 3.6 **Population Groups Targeted: Percentage of Programs Overall and by Lead Institution**

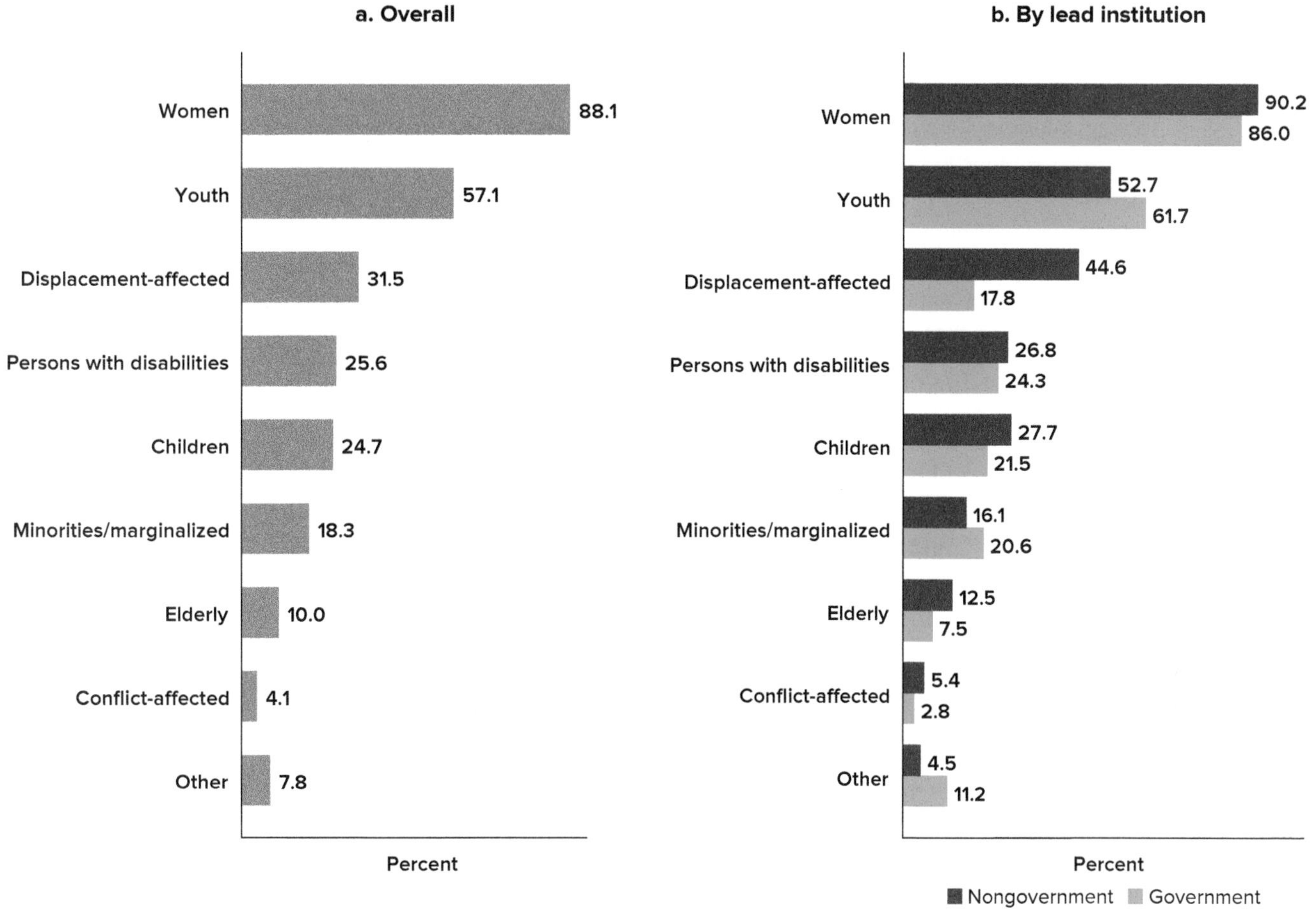

a. Overall

Population group	Percent
Women	88.1
Youth	57.1
Displacement-affected	31.5
Persons with disabilities	25.6
Children	24.7
Minorities/marginalized	18.3
Elderly	10.0
Conflict-affected	4.1
Other	7.8

b. By lead institution

Population group	Nongovernment	Government
Women	90.2	86.0
Youth	52.7	61.7
Displacement-affected	44.6	17.8
Persons with disabilities	26.8	24.3
Children	27.7	21.5
Minorities/marginalized	16.1	20.6
Elderly	12.5	7.5
Conflict-affected	5.4	2.8
Other	4.5	11.2

Source: Partnership for Economic Inclusion, World Bank.

Note: Panel a provides percentage of all programs (N = 219) and panel b percentage by nongovernment- and government-led programs (N1 = 112 and N2 = 107, respectively). Programs may target more than one segment.

that predominantly serve women also focus more on access to financial services (74 percent versus 59 percent in other programs) (see spotlight 2).

Young people are given priority by most economic inclusion programs (57 percent of all programs), particularly those that are built around an employment or livelihood development intervention (62 percent). Youth employment is an area of focus for many programs, given that young people are more likely to be excluded economically than adults: since 1995, youth unemployment rates have been persistently about three times higher than adult unemployment rates (ILO 2020). Youths represent roughly a fourth of the global working population, but the rate of job creation is not keeping up with the increase in the number of young people who will enter the job market in the coming years, particularly in the Middle East and North Africa, South Asia, and Sub-Saharan Africa (UNDP 2015, 64).

Achieving better employment outcomes, in terms of enhanced wage or self-employment opportunities, is more prevalent as a core objective among programs that target youths than in other programs (64 percent versus 51 percent), with government and nongovernment programs equally committed to this area. Among government-led programs, all seven programs in the Middle East and North Africa region and four out of five programs in the East Asia and Pacific region are

BOX 3.3 **Identifying and Customizing Entrepreneurship Support**

Most economic inclusion programs target the poor, but this is not a homogenous group. While some self-employed poor people are entrepreneurs by choice (so-called transformational entrepreneurs), a majority are self-employed by necessity (reluctant or subsistence entrepreneurs) (Schoar 2010; Banerjee and Duflo 2011). For most economic inclusion programs, the majority of participants are likely to be subsistence entrepreneurs, people who operate at low levels of profitability, with little differentiation from other local businesses and few opportunities for growth. These entrepreneurs manage to increase their earnings, but they function more as own-account workers rather than microenterprises that create jobs. They may also transition into wage employment if an opportunity arises (Bandiera et al. 2017; de Mel, McKenzie, and Woodruff 2010).

However, some participants have the necessary entrepreneurial skills to start a business and even transition to become small firms, as economic inclusion programs relax the barriers to their entry and growth. This group requires more customized support in adopting expansion strategies and market links. This distinction between types of entrepreneurs raises two questions for program design.

What characteristics are associated with entry into and success in self-employment? Competency, a combination of knowledge, skills, and attitudes, is an important determinant of success. Specific personality traits are good predictors of entrepreneurial behavior, including risk taking, self-efficacy, and stress tolerance, among others (Arco-Tirado et al. 2019). Many communities attribute entrepreneurial success to hard work and perseverance (see, for example, Poulin and Bomuhangi 2018; Bossuroy, Koussoubé, and Premand 2019). In particular, grit—a combination of passion and perseverance for long-term goals—may be a key determinant of long-term success (Duckworth et al. 2007). Grit is related to self-employment, particularly for risk takers, women, and younger adults (Wolfe and Patel 2016) and with the creation of new businesses (Mooradian et al. 2016; Mueller, Wolfe, and Syed 2017). Socioeconomic status is also important; among youths with high levels of grit, those with higher income levels or with lower satisfaction with their financial status are more likely to become entrepreneurs relative to those with low income or those satisfied with their status (Arco-Tirado et al. 2019). However, further research is required in this area.

What approaches can be used to identify these two types of entrepreneurs and to customize the bundle of interventions? Through training and coaching, many economic inclusion programs seek to equip both "reluctant" and "transformational" entrepreneurs to think creatively, take measured risks, improve problem-solving capabilities, and persevere in the face of failure. Participants often highlight their increased self-confidence as a result of this support; these programs can be an important mechanism to build grit. However, differences in trajectories reveal a set of fast climbers who benefit most and acquire self-confidence through experiential learning during the program. Slow climbers may require additional support and personalized coaching.

Some economic inclusion programs use business plan competitions to select participants with innovative ideas and the competence and personality traits associated with success. These are often targeted at groups to benefit from the complementarity of skills. Successful groups may or may not be provided with coaching. For instance, Uganda's Youth Opportunity Program asked youths to form groups and prepare

(Box continues next page)

BOX 3.3 **Identifying and Customizing Entrepreneurship Support (*continued*)**

business proposals (with some coaching support). Successful applicants each received a cash grant with some training, but no supervision or individualized coaching was provided after the grant. The program had significant positive impacts on earnings, capital stock, and business practices that persisted for at least four years (Blattman, Fiala, and Martinez 2014). Peru's Haku Wiñay program also supports the creation of group-based microbusinesses, but in addition to providing some coaching to develop a viable business proposal, it continues to provide training and support links to markets.

Other economic inclusion programs, especially those targeting the poorest, focus on income-generation activities for both the reluctant and transformational types of entrepreneurs. But given differences in trajectories, some programs introduced mid-term assessments to identify the slow and fast climbers. In India (West Bengal) and Haiti, this assessment builds on the targeting tool (used to identify beneficiaries) to track progress and reconfigure the bundle of interventions for these groups during the program (Huda and Simanowitz 2010; Huda 2009). However, these assessments do not typically include measures of grit or other personality traits, which might be challenging for field staff to capture without sufficient training. In addition, trade-offs exist: standardized case management may be easier to scale up and replicate compared to a highly customized approach (Huda and Simanowitz 2010; Jawahar and Sengupta 2012).

---

youth employment programs. Eighty-two percent of the 125 programs serving youth populations promote employment opportunities by combining training and coaching with wage employment facilitation or business capital. Box 3.3 provides further details on how programs that are focused on enhancing self-employment opportunities adapt their approaches to the particular needs of young populations.

About a third of programs serve populations affected by displacement, particularly refugees (two-thirds of programs serving displacement-affected people). Between 2012 and 2018, the number of forcibly displaced people worldwide more than doubled, to 70.8 million (UNHCR 2019). While forced displacements are mostly a result of conflict, violence, or human rights violations, climate change is expected to significantly add to the numbers of forcibly displaced people in the coming years, particularly in South Asia and Sub-Saharan Africa (Rigaud et al. 2018).

Roughly 40 percent of all forcibly displaced people are refugees. Many refugees have limited or no right to work and are therefore compelled into informal employment without regular earnings or social protection, and many are hosted in developing countries suffering social and economic strain (UNHCR 2018). The 2018 United Nations Global Compact on Refugees commits to reducing the pressure of displacement by helping displaced people benefit from national programs with support from the international community and by enhancing refugee self-reliance.

A significant number of economic inclusion programs target refugees (21 percent), in response to the tremendous challenges host governments face with the influx or displacement of increasing numbers of people (Ayoubi et al. 2017). Economic inclusion programs targeting refugees, internally displaced people, or host communities often build on the humanitarian assistance available to them through organizations such as UNHCR and WFP, assistance that acts as a social safety net on which economic inclusion components are built. Economic inclusion programs can also utilize humanitarian cash transfers, in particular if they are digitized, helping beneficiaries increase household resilience and build human capital (El-Zoghbi et al. 2017).

Most programs working with refugee populations are led by NGOs or multilateral organizations (71 percent of the 21 percent prioritizing refugees). UNHCR is involved in 36 percent of programs working with refugees, either as lead agency, as funder, or as the implementing partner. Programs serving refugees are more likely than other programs to facilitate access to markets (84 percent versus 68 percent) and to work with the private sector to create wage employment opportunities (74 percent versus 47 percent). This is because displaced populations often arrive in new living contexts lacking familiarity with local markets and sometimes having skill sets and experience that do not match local demand.

People with disabilities are represented in 26 percent of programs in the PEI Landscape Survey 2020, among both government-led and nongovernment-led programs equally. Early experience from program implementers suggests that economic inclusion

---

BOX 3.4   **People with Disabilities**

An estimated 15 percent of the global population live with some form of disability (World Bank 2011), and people with disabilities are more likely to experience poverty than others due to a lack of employment and education opportunities, lower wages, and the increased cost of living with a disability. Barriers to full social and economic inclusion of people with disabilities include inaccessible physical environments and transportation, the unavailability of assistive devices and technologies, nonadapted means of communication, gaps in service delivery, and discriminatory prejudice and stigma in society. The employment-to-population ratio of people with disabilities ages 15 and older is almost half that of people without disabilities (UNDESA 2018).

Programs that target people with disabilities also focus more than other programs on wage facilitation (46 percent versus 31 percent) to help participants build regular streams of income and also to foster greater self-confidence and to challenge societal biases. For example, the Chilean government's program, Fórmate para el Trabajo: Línea para Personas en Situación de Discapacidad, links people with disabilities to accessible wage employment opportunities. Finally, programs like Humanity and Inclusion's Alliance for Community Resilience in West Africa (with a consortium of seven NGOs) are also trying to facilitate links to complementary services, such as rehabilitation, health care, and psychosocial support, which can improve the long-term chances of obtaining successful livelihoods.

As COVID-19 continues to have wide-reaching impacts across the globe, people with disabilities are uniquely affected. In particular, many people with disabilities have additional underlying health needs that make them particularly vulnerable to severe symptoms of COVID-19 if they contract it. People with disabilities may also be at increased risk of contracting COVID-19 because information about the disease, including the symptoms and prevention, are not provided in accessible formats, such as print materials in Braille, sign language interpretation, captions, audio provision, and graphics. The social distancing measures imposed by COVID-19 may create greater barriers to full social and economic inclusion of people with disabilities due to inaccessible physical environments and transportation, the unavailability of assistive devices and technologies, nonadapted means of communication, and gaps in service delivery.[a]

a. For more information, see the World Bank web resource "Disability Inclusion," https://www.worldbank.org/en /topic/disability.

programs should, as needed and feasible, support care providers as well as enable people with disabilities to engage in economic activities themselves. While some smaller programs work exclusively with people with disabilities, others also include other community members and work on reducing stigma and isolation. Some NGO programs, like Trickle Up's Desde El Poder Local in Guatemala, also work with participants to consider livelihood options beyond traditional home-based activities and explore higher-return livelihood options outside the home. (See box 3.4 for more information.)

Program Components

Most economic inclusion programs provide an integrated package of interventions, rather than one or two stand-alone interventions, because their design is based on the recognition that the poorest and most vulnerable people face multiple constraints. Most commonly, these packages comprise five or more broad components. This is true of 83 percent of all programs. As depicted in figure 3.7, a higher concentration of government-led programs than nongovernment-led programs provide two to four components, but the majority of both programs provide at least five components (75 percent of government-led and 91 percent of nongovernment-led). Programs most commonly include transfers, skills training, coaching, and financial services facilitation (see figure 3.9).

It is also common for program components to be provided in sequence and in a time-bound period, which may last from one to three years. Figure 3.8 shows that in 84 percent of programs, beneficiaries access components in a specific order, a design intended to address barriers participants face during the course of program implementation. This sequencing may also influence the duration of the intervention, which is from 1 year to more than 3 years in 84 percent of programs (figure 3.8). Budget or other resource limitations or technical considerations, such as the duration of the production cycle for livelihoods supported by the program, may also influence why different programs choose different program durations. Ninety-six percent of programs provide all or some of their program components over a time-bound period. Economic inclusion programs that build on existing government programs are more likely than

FIGURE 3.7 **Distribution of Nongovernment- and Government-Led Programs, by Number of Components**

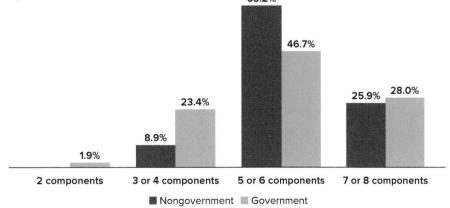

Source: Partnership for Economic Inclusion, World Bank.

Note: Percentage of all nongovernment- and government-led programs (N1 = 112 and N2 = 107, respectively).

FIGURE 3.8 **Economic Inclusion Components Provided in Sequence and for up to Three Years**

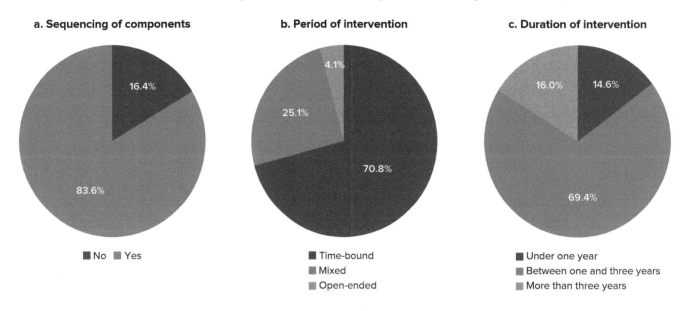

a. Sequencing of components

16.4%
83.6%

■ No ■ Yes

b. Period of intervention

4.1%
25.1%
70.8%

■ Time-bound
■ Mixed
■ Open-ended

c. Duration of intervention

16.0% 14.6%
69.4%

■ Under one year
■ Between one and three years
■ More than three years

Source: Partnership for Economic Inclusion, World Bank.

Note: Percentage of all programs (N = 219).

FIGURE 3.9 **Various Program Components of Economic Inclusion Programs**

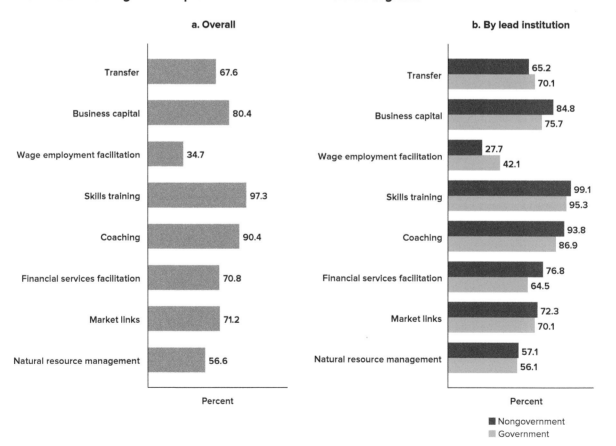

a. Overall

Transfer	67.6
Business capital	80.4
Wage employment facilitation	34.7
Skills training	97.3
Coaching	90.4
Financial services facilitation	70.8
Market links	71.2
Natural resource management	56.6

Percent

b. By lead institution

	Nongovernment	Government
Transfer	65.2	70.1
Business capital	84.8	75.7
Wage employment facilitation	27.7	42.1
Skills training	99.1	95.3
Coaching	93.8	86.9
Financial services facilitation	76.8	64.5
Market links	72.3	70.1
Natural resource management	57.1	56.1

Percent

■ Nongovernment
■ Government

Source: Partnership for Economic Inclusion, World Bank.

Note: Panel a provides percentages of all programs (N = 219) and panel b percentages by nongovernment- and government-led programs (N1 = 112 and N2 = 107, respectively). Programs provide at least two types of components.

other programs to include open-ended interventions (35 percent versus 21 percent), as participation in many government programs is not time bound. For example, in many SSN programs, the social assistance is open-ended while the additional economic inclusion components are time bound.

Figure 3.9 illustrates how eight of the most common components are distributed among programs. Whether they are led by governments or NGOs, programs most commonly include transfers (68 percent), business capital (80 percent), skills training (97 percent), coaching (90 percent), and financial services facilitation (71 percent).

Ninety-five percent of programs sampled provide some form of transfer, which could be the basis for both consumption-smoothing (68 percent of all programs) as well as business development (80 percent of all programs). A noncontributory transfer is the single component that typically drives program costs. This is in line with the costing analysis in chapter 6, which shows that programs allocate between 50 and 86 percent of their overall cost to this component. It is likely that most economic inclusion programs seek to jump-start economic activities with business capital while increasing the chances of their success through training, coaching, and access to finance. Of the programs that include a transfer for consumption support, 48 percent represent existing government cash transfer programs and 25 percent link support to participation in a government public works program. About half of the programs that provide a transfer for business development are linked to a government enterprise development program.

Regardless of the type of program, most interventions provide cash for the transfer (95 percent of programs that include some form of transfer), but differences emerge in the modality used for different purposes by entry point (figure 3.10). Cash transfers, especially when made digitally, are preferred to in-kind assistance because they

FIGURE 3.10 **Distribution of Modalities Used by Programs for Transfers, by Point of Entry**

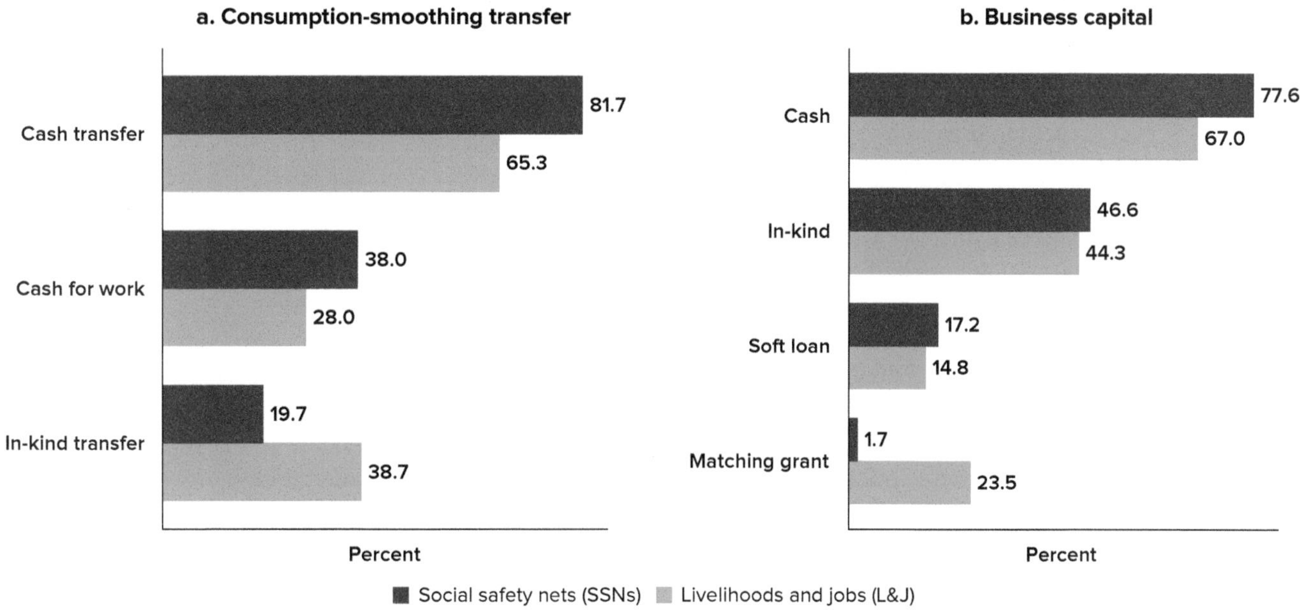

a. Consumption-smoothing transfer

	Percent
Cash transfer	81.7 / 65.3
Cash for work	38.0 / 28.0
In-kind transfer	19.7 / 38.7

b. Business capital

	Percent
Cash	77.6 / 67.0
In-kind	46.6 / 44.3
Soft loan	17.2 / 14.8
Matching grant	1.7 / 23.5

■ Social safety nets (SSNs)   ■ Livelihoods and jobs (L&J)

Source: Partnership for Economic Inclusion, World Bank.

Note: Percentage of SSN and L&J programs, in panel a providing a transfer for consumption smoothing (N1 = 71 and N2 = 75, respectively) and in panel b business capital (N1 = 58 and N2 = 115, respectively). Financial inclusion programs providing transfers and business capital are excluded due to the small subsamples (two and three programs, respectively).

significantly ease the logistical demands on those implementing the program while giving participants more choice in their use of funds. Cash transfers also provide an opportunity to acquire cash management skills and to save formally, especially if a digital transfer is made to an account where recipients can save.

Most programs focus on facilitating self-employment, particularly in rural areas and low-income countries, where wage employment opportunities tend to be more limited than elsewhere. In supporting self-employment, most economic inclusion programs seek to jump-start economic activities with business capital while increasing the chances of success through training, coaching, and access to finance. Sixty-one percent of programs combine these four components to jointly address financial and human capital constraints (68 percent in rural areas versus 42 percent in urban areas and 65 percent in lower-income countries versus 44 percent in upper- and high-income countries).

Governments typically have infrastructure in place that supports employment programs, so government economic inclusion interventions focus more than nongovernment interventions on wage employment (42 percent versus 28 percent). Nongovernment programs focus more on providing business finance (85 percent versus 76 percent) to facilitate self-employment opportunities. Of the 42 percent of government programs that facilitate access to wage employment, 40 percent are linked to an existing government labor intermediation program and 27 percent are linked to an active labor market policy.

The biggest constraint to wage employment through economic inclusion programs is the absence of job opportunities. Most programs that support access to wage employment foster links with employers, particularly L&J programs (64 percent versus 39 percent for SSN programs). For example, 79 percent of programs that facilitate access to wage employment assist participants in accessing job placements or internships, while 55 percent engage with the private sector to create wage employment opportunities.

Most programs are time bound, but interventions that can bring about long-term changes in attitudes and investment behavior can help achieve sustained impact. Toward this end, 97 percent of surveyed programs include training, which for the purpose of the survey was defined as structured teaching with the aim of transferring specific skills and knowledge. Another common component, coaching, is provided by 90 percent of programs. Defined as informal guidance provided in an informal way, coaching is used by programs to build soft skills, support self-confidence, provide emotional support, and foster changes in attitudes and social norms. It may be particularly important for achieving behavioral changes, including changes in the habit of saving formally (Huda and Simanowitz 2010). Eighty-nine percent of programs provide both training and coaching, which highlights the value of effective skill-building by facilitating regular learning activities using different formats.[5] (See box 3.5 for details on new directions in coaching.)

Promoting financial inclusion (FI) is core to economic inclusion programs. Facilitating access to financial services is a critical means of ensuring the sustainability of economic gains for the household. Links to appropriate financial services, in particular savings and microinsurance services, can help poor households build their resilience and livelihoods. Seventy-one percent of surveyed programs facilitate access to financial services, including 88 percent of those in South Asia and 72 percent of those in Sub-Saharan Africa. Forty-seven percent of programs facilitating access to financial services build on a government's FI program.

Formal financial services are more often fostered by governments than nongovernmental programs, either by partnering with formal financial service providers

BOX 3.5   **Coaching at Scale**

Coaching, also known as mentoring, is one of the main components of many economic inclusion programs. It usually consists of regular face-to-face visits from a field worker or community member to help beneficiaries overcome social and emotional barriers, track progress in income-generating activities, reinforce training concepts, boost self-confidence, and introduce additional topics that help improve participants' overall well-being, such as health, nutrition, and legal rights. This component may create a capacity challenge, in particular for governments, as it requires additional training for frontline workers and supervisors and adjustments to human resource rules and incentives. Coaching provides a vital mechanism for monitoring how participants are responding to program elements. Coaches are not experts but individuals equipped with general skills and knowledge on a range of topics and with an ability to link participants to other resources. This may also require recruiting resource persons who are community based and receive specialized training, support, tools, and compensation, as elaborated in the JEEViKA case study (case study 2). Programs may also tap existing community trainers, such as through the use of *yachachiq*, community leaders utilized as trainers in the Haku Wiñay case study (case study 4).

Group coaching. Many economic inclusion programs are exploring options to enhance impact and reduce costs by shifting from individual to group-based coaching. This can reduce program delivery costs as well as administrative burden. Well-designed group-based interventions can promote social interactions in the community and help the poor build social capital (Blattman et al. 2016; Macours and Vakis 2014).

Customized coaching topics. Individual coaching and customized advice may be necessary, for example, to help some types of microentrepreneurs grow their businesses (Kabeer et al. 2012). The United Nations High Commissioner for Refugees (UNHCR) is adapting its economic inclusion programs in Costa Rica, Ecuador, Zambia, and Zimbabwe for refugees by systematically adding psychosocial and legal counseling to the bundle of interventions (UNHCR 2019). UNHCR's challenge in these places is to reduce delivery costs. (See chapter 6 for a discussion of cost issues.)

Digital tools. Some programs, including those supported by Fundación Capital in a variety of locations, are experimenting with the provision of coaching through a mix of in-person interactions and tablet-based videos or training modules designed for very poor and nonliterate participants (MacLennan 2017). Equipping coaches with digital tools can allow them to gather real-time data, facilitating the collection of participant information for program oversight and performance management. To break through the cognitive traps that poor people face (Mullainathan and Shafir 2013), digital coaching content needs to focus on their priority areas with relevant, engaging, and practical content.

(40 percent versus 20 percent) or leveraging formal community groups (29 percent versus 23 percent). Nongovernment-led programs tend to favor facilitating access to financial services through informal community groups, such as rotating savings and credit associations and village savings and loan associations, more than government-led programs do (59 percent versus 38 percent). In some countries, including Peru,

the economic inclusion program is designed to foster "last mile" financial inclusion of the poorest and most vulnerable rural population, with program transfers delivered to financially inclusive bank accounts and with tailored financial literacy training.

Economic inclusion programs also seek to enhance market access and strengthen links among producers, buyers, and other value chain actors. Poor and vulnerable households face many barriers to market access, such as remoteness from the nearest market and prices that leave them with very small profit margins. Challenges like these limit their ability to develop their businesses into profitable enterprises.

Seventy-one percent of all surveyed programs reported that they assist participants with integration into markets, and this was true of 80 percent of programs that operate exclusively in rural areas. Programs help participants link to existing value chains and markets, and some even support the creation of new value chains (local, regional, national, or international). Sixty-three percent of government-led programs (or 51 percent of all programs facilitating market access) link participants to existing cooperatives, such as producer or marketing cooperatives, to help participants sell their products and increase their margins.

Developing community platforms, such as producer organizations or federated self-help groups, can further expand livelihood opportunities and increase program sustainability. This is particularly true if these community organizations are formally linked to other market actors, including financial service providers and private training providers. Economic inclusion programs can work with market players in key sectors where informal workers, producers, and entrepreneurs can have better interaction and negotiation with market players. In India, the National Rural Livelihood Mission has invested in economic organizations like farmer- and women-owned producer companies and thousands of farmer organizations around agriculture, livestock, and nonfarm opportunities through which participants build partnerships through value chains with many market players (see spotlight 3).

More than half of programs support natural resource management, climate change adaptation, or both (57 percent of all programs). Sustainable natural resource management and climate change mitigation strategies are often coupled with programs that build households' resilience and/or income diversification to increase households' ability to cope with climate-related disasters and environmental shocks.[6] In the Sahel, for example, key challenges to the management of renewable resources include increasing conflict between pastoralists and farmers due to competition for land and water, coupled with poor soils and soil erosion, which impact agricultural productivity and crop yields. The problem is not necessarily one of absolute water scarcity but rather a lack of infrastructure to ensure an adequate supply of water in dry seasons or years (USAID 2017).

Future Directions

The PEI Landscape Survey 2020 provides a snapshot of economic inclusion programs implemented globally, with 219 programs reaching over 90 million beneficiaries. Growth is driven by governments in low-income countries in Sub-Saharan Africa and South Asia. The true universe of economic inclusion programs is almost certainly larger. The survey results reveal that half of programs are government led, and many build on existing SSNs and other government interventions. The data presented are lower-bound estimates and reflect information reported by country teams. Data presented in this chapter are available at http://www.peiglobal.org, a site that allows programs to upload, update, and use data as a global public good.

Economic inclusion programs are implemented in a variety of contexts, and geographies and among a variety of target groups. Rural residents, women, and specific vulnerable groups are clear priorities. Governments are adapting existing antipoverty programs to strengthen economic inclusion outcomes for improved resilience and opportunity. The dominant entry point to scaling up is likely to be SSN programs— especially as these programs mature.

Economic inclusion programs provide an integrated package of interventions. They typically include five or more components, and most commonly feature cash transfers, skills training, coaching, market links, and access to financial services. The most frequently cited objectives of economic inclusion programs are self-employment, income diversification, and resilience. This coheres to an agenda with a strong rural focus (88 percent of all programs) and an increasing emphasis on fragility (one in four programs), with one in three programs focusing on displaced populations.

Cash transfers are a leading component, as they provide flexible spending options to the poorest people. Different programs are testing the benefits of regular payments versus lump-sum payments, or a mix of both.

A strong focus is emerging on youths. Over half the programs in the PEI Landscape Survey 2020 focus on youth, reflecting broader demographic and urbanization megatrends. Youths experience high levels of underemployment and uncertain pathways to formal jobs, and economic inclusion programs will play an important role in addressing them, but programs will need to adapt to ensure effectivelinks to complementary services. Close to three quarters of programs help participants link to existing value chains and markets, with some even supporting the creation of new value chains (local, regional, national, and international).

Coaching and entrepreneurial support need to be strengthened and streamlined. Innovations in program delivery are emerging, including digital options and through self-help groups and peer-to-peer learning networks. Going forward, it is critical to identify the design features required to address the constraints of people in specific population subgroups or in certain contexts. This requires testing innovations to correctly size the individual components, the package overall, and how it is delivered, based on an assessment of the needs and potential of target populations in each context.

Economic inclusion programs in fragile settings are poised to continue to grow, requiring a better understanding of operational models. Good practices in linking economic inclusion to humanitarian interventions and facilitating market links in fragile settings need to be documented. Guidance is also needed on best operational models and delivery systems in other contexts, including on how much of the package should be delivered directly by the central government; when and how to partner with other public sectoral agencies, local governments, or local NGOs; how to develop effective links to bring in complementary services; and how to develop appropriate incentive systems for program managers and frontline workers.

Economic inclusion programs are well placed to overcome some of the challenges faced by people with disabilities in increasing their economic opportunities. The body of knowledge on how to adapt design and delivery of programs to increase outcomes for people with disabilities is growing.

Finally, with economic inclusion programs already being used as a flexible response to varied realities, they are well poised to be a medium- and long-term response to the COVID-19 crisis. With adaptive social protection systems forming the backbone of the first wave of response, the scale-up of economic inclusion programs is an important complement for households and communities moving forward.

Notes

1. International Development Association (IDA) funds are allocated to the recipient countries in relation to their income levels and record of success in managing their economies and their ongoing IDA projects. IDA's lending terms are highly concessional, meaning that IDA credits carry no or low interest charges. See IDA, "Financing," https://ida.worldbank.org/financing /ida-financing.
2. The survey identified each program's priority objectives by asking respondents to name their three main program objectives.
3. The survey conducted by PEI between November 2019 and May 2020 used the following definitions: The *poor* are those whose consumption is below the national poverty line as defined by government or those who, because of their personal and/or community characteristics, face barriers in accessing opportunities to earn sustainable livelihoods and have elevated risks of being or staying in poverty and/or being socially marginalized. The *extreme poor* are those whose consumption is below $1.90 per day (2011 purchasing power parity, PPP), also defined as the bottom 50 percent of the poor population in a country or those unable to meet basic needs. The latter definition captures relative poverty as well as dynamics in lower-middle-income and upper-middle-income countries. The *ultrapoor* are those whose consumption is below $0.95 per day (2011 PPP). Also defined as those experiencing the most severe forms of deprivation, for example, persistent hunger, lack of sources of income, and so forth. Finally, the *other vulnerable* are groups that do not meet any of the above criteria, for example, those just above the poverty line, and marginalized groups irrespective of their poverty level.
4. Data on female coverage are based on data from 164 programs (the number of programs reporting on the number of beneficiaries). Among those programs for which data on the number female beneficiaries are missing (55 programs), the majority (52 programs) target or prioritize women, so it is possible that the figure reported here is biased downward—that the percentage of programs where most beneficiaries are female is higher.
5. Many studies suggest that the duration of training matters, with short courses having much less positive impact than longer ones (Kluve 2016). The PEI Landscape Survey 2020, however, did not capture information on duration, intensity, or other quality aspects that may affect the impact of training activities on participants.
6. Programs that have resilience as one of their main objectives (70 programs, or 32 percent of all surveyed programs) are more likely to include natural resource management or climate change adaptation interventions than programs that do not seek to build resilience (67 percent versus 52 percent). The same holds true for programs seeking to support income diversification (81 percent versus 42 percent). Both correlations are statistically significant, at 5 percent and 1 percent, respectively.

References

Arco-Tirado, Jose L., Ana Bojica, Francisco Fernández-Martín, and Rick H. Hoyle. 2019. "Grit as Predictor of Entrepreneurship and Self-Employment in Spain." *Frontiers in Psychology* 10 (389). doi:10.3389/fpsyg.2019.00389.

Ayoubi, Z., S. Hashemi, J. Heisey, and A. de Montesquiou. 2017. "Economic Inclusion of the Poorest Refugees: Building Resilience through the Graduation Approach." UNHCR, Trickle Up, and CGAP, Washington, DC.

Bandiera, Oriana, Robin Burgess, Narayan Das, Selim Gulesci, Imran Rasul, and Munshi Sulaiman. 2017. "Labor Markets and Poverty in Village Economies." *Quarterly Journal of Economics* 132 (2): 811–70.

Banerjee, Abhijit, and Esther Duflo. 2011. *Poor Economics: A Radical Rethinking of the Way to Fight Global Poverty*. New York: Public Affairs.

Blattman, Christopher, Eric P. Green, Julian Jamison, M. Christian Lehmann, and Jeannie Annan. 2016. "The Returns to Microenterprise Support among the Ultrapoor: A Field Experiment in Postwar Uganda." *American Economic Journal: Applied Economics* 8 (2): 35–64.

Blattman, Christopher, Nathan Fiala, and Sebastian Martinez. 2014. "Generating Skilled Self-Employment in Developing Countries: Experimental Evidence from Uganda." *Quarterly Journal of Economics* 129: 697–752. doi:10.1093/qje/qjt057.

Bossuroy, Thomas, Estelle Koussoubé, and Patrick Premand. 2019. *Constraints to Productive Employment Faced by Safety Nets Beneficiaries in the Sahel: Results of a Multi-Country Qualitative Assessment.* Washington, DC: World Bank.

Corral, Paul, Alexander Irwin, Nandini Krishnan, Daniel Gerszon Mahler, and Tara Vishwanath. 2020. *Fragility and Conflict: On the Front Lines of the Fight against Poverty.* Washington, DC: World Bank. https://openknowledge.worldbank.org /handle/10986/33324.

de Mel, Suresh, David McKenzie, and Christopher Woodruff. 2010. "Who Are the Microenterprise Owners? Evidence from Sri Lanka on Tokman versus De Soto." In *International Differences in Entrepreneurship,* edited by Josh Lerner and Antoinette Schoar, 63–87. Chicago: University of Chicago Press.

Duckworth, A. L., C. Peterson, M. D. Matthews, and D. R. Kelly. 2007. "Grit: Perseverance and Passion for Long-Term Goals." *Journal of Personality and Social Psychology* 92 (6):1087–1101. doi:10.1037/0022-3514.92.6.1087.

El-Zoghbi, Mayada, Nadine Chehade, Peter McConaghy, and Matthew Soursourian. 2017. "The Role of Financial Services in Humanitarian Crises." *Forum* 12. Washington, DC: CGAP, SPF, and World Bank.

Huda, Karishma. 2009. "Mid-term (12 Month) Trickle Up India TUP Process Evaluation: CGAP-Ford Foundation Graduation Pilot." BRAC Development Institute, Dhaka.

Huda, Karishma, and Anton Simanowitz. 2010. "Chemin Lavi Miyo: Final Evaluation (24 months)." Concern Worldwide and CGAP, Washington, DC.

ILO (International Labour Organization). 2020. *Global Employment Trends for Youth 2020: Technology and the Future of Jobs.* Geneva: ILO.

Jawahar, V., and A. Sengupta. 2012. *SKS Ultra Poor Programme: Qualitative Assessment of Sustainability of Programme Outcomes.* Bonn: Federation of German Industries.

Kabeer, Naila, Karishma Huda, Sandeep Kaur, and Nicolina Lamhauge. 2012. "Productive Safety Nets for Women in Extreme Poverty: Lessons from Pilot Projects in India and Pakistan." Discussion Paper 28/12, Centre for Development Policy and Research, School of Oriental and African Studies, London.

Kharas, Homi, Constanza Di Nucci, Kristofer Hamel, and Baldwin Tong. 2020. "To Move the Needle on Extreme Poverty, Focus on Rural Areas." *Future Development,* February 21. https://www.brookings.edu/blog/future-development/2020/02/21 /to-move-the-needle-on-ending-extreme-poverty-focus-on-rural-areas/.

Kluve, Joche. 2016. "A Review of the Effectiveness of Active Labour Market Programmes with a Focus on Latin America and the Caribbean." Working Paper 9, ILO, Geneva.

MacLennan, M., ed. 2017. *Debating Graduation Policy in Focus* 39. https://issuu .com/ipc-ig_publications/docs/pif39_debating_graduation.

Macours, Karen, and Renos Vakis. 2014. "Changing Households' Investment Behaviour through Social Interactions with Local Leaders: Evidence from a Randomised Transfer Programme." *Economic Journal* 124 (576): 607–33. doi:10.1111/ecoj.12145.

Mooradian, T., K. Matzler, B. Uzelac, and F. Bauer. 2016. "Perspiration and Inspiration: Grit and Innovativeness as Antecedents of Entrepreneurial Success." *Journal of Economics Psychology* 56: 232–43. doi:10.1016/j.joep.2016.08.001.

Mueller, B. A., M. T. Wolfe, and I. Syed. 2017. "Passion and Grit: An Exploration of the Pathways Leading to Venture Success." *Journal of Business Venture* 32: 260–79. doi:10.1016/j.jbusvent.2017.02.001.

Mullainathan, Sendhil, and Eldar Shafir. 2013. *Scarcity: Why Having So Little Means So Much.* New York: Times Books.

Poulin, Michelle, and Allan Bomuhangi. 2018. *Qualitative Study of Household Livelihood Strategies and Constraints in Zambia.* Washington, DC: World Bank.

Rigaud, K. K., A. de Sherbinin, B. Jones, J. Bergmann, V. Clement, K. Ober, J. Schewe, S. Adamo, B. McCusker, S. Heuser, and A. Midgley. 2018. *Groundswell: Preparing for Internal Climate Migration.* Washington, DC: World Bank. https://openknowledge.worldbank.org/handle/10986/29461.

Schoar, Antoinette. 2010. "The Divide between Subsistence and Transformational Entrepreneurship." In *Innovation Policy and the Economy*, edited by Josh Lerner and Scott Stern, 57–81. Chicago: University of Chicago Press.

UNDESA (United Nations, Department of Economic and Social Affairs). 2018. *Disability and Development Report: Realizing the Sustainable Development Goals by, for and with Persons with Disabilities.* New York: United Nations.

UNDP (United Nations Development Programme). 2015. *Human Development Report 2015: Work for Human Development.* New York: UNDP. https://www.undp.org/content/undp/en/home/librarypage/hdr/2015-human-development-report/.

UNHCR (UN High Commissioner for Refugees). 2018. *Global Trends: Forced Displacement in 2018.* Geneva: UNHCR. https://www.unhcr.org/globaltrends2018.

UNHCR. 2019. "Refugee Livelihoods and Economic Inclusion: 2019–2023 Global Strategy Concept Note." UNHCR, Geneva. https://www.unhcr.org/5bc07ca94.pdf.

USAID (US Agency for International Development). 2017. "Climate Change Risk Profile: West Africa Sahel. Regional Factsheet." Washington, DC: USAID. https://www.climatelinks.org/sites/default/files/asset/document/2017%20April_USAID%20ATLAS_Climate%20Change%20Risk%20Profile%20-%20Sahel.pdf.

Wolfe, M. T., and P. C. Patel. 2016. "Grit and Self-Employment: A Multi-Country Study." *Small Business Economics* 47: 853–74. doi:10.1007/s11187-016-9737-6.

World Bank. 2011. *World Report on Disability: Main Report.* Washington, DC: World Bank. http://documents.worldbank.org/curated/en/665131468331271288/Main-report

World Bank Group. 2020. *World Bank Group Strategy for Fragility, Conflict, and Violence 2020–2025.* Washington, DC: World Bank Group. http://documents.worldbank.org/curated/en/844591582815510521/World-Bank-Group-Strategy-for-Fragility-Conflict-and-Violence-2020-2025.

Promoting Women's Empowerment through Economic Inclusion

The potential to boost the economic empowerment of women takes center stage in many of the programs assessed in this report. Eighty-eight percent of all programs in the survey prioritize female participants, and in 64 percent of these programs, women constitute the majority of participants. Fifteen percent of all programs (and about a fifth of those that reported the number of female beneficiaries) serve only women. Increasing incomes and assets of beneficiaries is a core goal of economic inclusion programs—whether they target women or not—but in addition to pursuing the economic empowerment of women, some programs also seek to empower women in other realms of their lives. These programs use economic inclusion as the starting point, building the skills and confidence of female participants through other interventions such as training and coaching. Seventeen percent of programs in the survey deliberately try to further women's overall empowerment through economic inclusion.

Leaving women out of the productive economy limits economic growth overall and increases inequality. Gender inequality is associated with lower labor productivity and poorer overall economic growth (Kabeer and Natali 2013). Not only does gender equality have an impact on women's individual well-being, it also imparts benefits to future generations and communities (World Bank Group 2015).

Bundled economic inclusion interventions are uniquely placed to address the plurality of constraints poor women face and to empower them beyond the economic domain. Each program component plays a role in promoting improved gender outcomes: productive cash transfers can help women take ownership of a sustainable livelihood that increases assets and the ability to earn income; training builds women's capacity; and coaching helps build social capital through enhanced life skills, self-confidence, and greater awareness of legal rights. The coaching and peer-to-peer exchange that occur during economic inclusion program activities can also help to increase women's agency—elevating their voice, influence, and decision-making power in the community, the household, and their own lives. Increasing women's agency can also be achieved through women's involvement in community institutions and local governance, which can develop their capacity to access and effectively make use of increased economic opportunities, their increased self-esteem, and their increased knowledge about and motivation to exercise their rights (Lazlo 2019).

Key Directions for Gender-Intentional Program Design and Implementation

This section summarizes a range of country experiences to highlight the gender-intentional design and delivery steps in economic inclusion programs. Experience from a range of programs suggests that there is a need to design programs for women that move beyond solely strengthening their economic base to also ensure that program delivery mechanisms are deliberate in addressing the specific constraints of beneficiaries. The observations that follow draw from a portfolio review of World Bank Group operations and the broader literature. Box S2.1 highlights key findings from qualitative and quantitative evaluations.

BOX S2.1   Assimilating the Evidence on Gender and Economic Inclusion Programs

In the review of impact literature in chapter 5, economic inclusion programs were found to hold strong potential for women's empowerment. Programs strengthened women's economic opportunities, increasing their contribution to household income, while asset ownership positively impacted social status in and outside the household. Many programs also contributed to subtle shifts in gender norms by increasing women's mobility. For many women, being able to fulfill parental and community responsibilities helped to increase their self-esteem.

However, impact on women's control over resources and their agency in the household was mixed and highly context specific (see, for example, Banerjee et al. 2015; Bedoya Arguelles et al. 2019; Bandiera et al. 2017; World Bank 2020; Siddiki et al. 2014). Similarly, the impact on women's exposure to intimate-partner violence was also mixed and context specific. Although it is possible that women's participation in economic activities may have exacerbated household tensions when their work was seen as displacing care responsibilities (Holmes and Jones 2013), the limited evidence suggests the opposite, that is, a reduction in violence at least in some contexts (Karimli, Rost, and Ismayilova 2018; Das et al. 2016).

Impacts on women's empowerement were also muted in contexts where social norms restricted women's movement and participation outside the home or the community. In Pakistan, for example, few women participated in economic activities outside their homes and thus needed support from male household members (Kabeer et al. 2012).

Similarly, a combination of a cash grant and training for women in two contexts had different short-term outcomes. In Uganda, a combination of finance and human capital interventions was sufficient to create new enterprises and help women grow their businesses (Blattman, Fiala, and Martinez 2014). In Sri Lanka, the same combination helped new entrants but did not help existing entrepreneurs grow, suggesting binding social constraints for women entrepreneurs (de Mel, McKenzie, and Woodruff 2014).

Household endowments and relationship dynamics also influence a program's impact on women. Women cannot avail themselves of opportunities if they do not have the resources or support from family or community members to balance paid work and unpaid family care work. For instance, in Haiti women with cooperative partners who provided them support as they engaged with the program were better able to take advantage of opportunities the program offered than women with no partners. Also, women with partners who were uncooperative fared poorly in the program (Shoaf and Simanowitz 2019). In West Bengal, participants who had early success in the Trickle Up graduation program, "fast climbers," had more adult males in the family or in their extended network than "slow climbers." The slowest climbers were women with uncooperative husbands, who were a drain on household resources (Kabeer et al. 2012).

Gender-Sensitive Program Design

Targeting women as the primary recipient of economic inclusion programs does not automatically ensure female control over assets. Evidence shows that simply providing access to resources will not lead to meaningful change in a woman's life if she does not have the power to make decisions about the use of resources. The potential for enhanced access will not translate into improved well-being (Bardasi and Garcia 2014). Deliberate targeting is coupled with intentional female-focused design in the Targeting the Ultra Poor program implemented by the Microfinance Investment Support Facility for Afghanistan. The program is open to male-headed households, but targeting criteria place more weight on the selection of female-headed households, that are more vulnerable. However, regardless of whether the primary program beneficiary is female or male, the program makes a substantial effort to ensure that women are the main recipients of the consumption support stipends in order to increase their influence and bargaining power in the household. The women are also actively engaged in the technical training for the productive activity, even if they are not the direct recipients of the program. These strategies have helped begin to increase the voice and status of women in the household despite the fact that the program operates in a very challenging and fragile context (Bedoya Arguelles et al. 2019).

The training and coaching components of economic inclusion programs are effective for increasing the life skills, self-confidence, and agency of women. Among survey respondents, programs that predominantly serve women have a stronger emphasis than those programs that do not on life-skills building (72 percent versus 40 percent) and financial training (82 percent versus 60 percent). The coaching component can also be adjusted to strengthen outcomes for women: programs that primarily serve women, when compared with programs that do not, tend to include more health and nutrition guidance (63 percent versus 27 percent) and discussions around social issues affecting the family, such as child marriage and intrahousehold dynamics (68 percent versus 27 percent).

Gender-sensitive economic inclusion programs can help reduce the gap in access to financial services in developing countries.[1] Among survey respondents, 74 percent of the programs serving a majority of women link them to financial services as compared to 59 percent for programs that do not predominately serve women. Some programs, such as India's Tejaswini Socioeconomic Empowerment of Adolescent Girls and Young Women program and the São Tomé and Principe's Social Protection and Skills Development Project, also draw attention to addressing literacy constraints, especially for older adolescent females.

Livelihoods are not gender neutral, and different livelihoods have specific time and physical labor requirements. Gendered market analysis helps programs develop livelihoods options most suitable for women. In particular, programs need to ensure women have appropriate access to information about prices and exert control over the sale of their goods (de Montesquiou and Sheldon 2018). In places like Coastal Sindh in Pakistan, restrictions on women's mobility in the public domain significantly limit their ability to engage in certain livelihoods and make them dependent on intermediaries both to provide inputs and sell outputs (Hashemi, de Montesquiou, and McKee 2016; and Kabeer et al. 2012). Home-based activities such as raising poultry or producing honey involve low-intensity tasks, and both allow for time for other activities such as household chores and childcare, although they may also reinforce gender norms with women taking on low-productivity activities that can be done at home.

Engaging men while implementing programs for women is essential to ensure their buy-in and facilitate behavior change. Preexisting social, economic, institutional, and environmental conditions are essential factors to consider when supporting women's empowerment, especially favorable gender norms and the quality of spousal relationships (Kabeer et al. 2012). Increasingly, programs are working with men to influence how women are viewed and treated in the household, redistribute care and income-generation responsibilities, reduce the risk of gender-based violence, and challenge accepted gender roles. For example, some programs hold focused discussions with male household members around the role of women and the importance of shared housework and financial decision-making. In Malawi, Concern Worldwide is trying to better understand how programs can improve intrahousehold decision-making with a couples' empowerment training that is being evaluated through a randomized controlled trial implemented by the Trinity College Impact Evaluation Unit. In Zambia, the government has partnered with BRAC to incorporate interventions for engaging men, such as a community gender dialogue, into its economic inclusion program for rural women. The Eastern Recovery Project in the Democratic Republic of Congo also uses sensitization to ensure program adaptations are not met with resistance by male household members and do not create community animosity.

Engaging the community, particularly social networks, is important in the effort to challenge social norms. Many programs utilize existing community groups or create new ones to provide a safe place for women to interact and build social capital. Groups can include village organizations, savings or producer groups, or affinity groups, and each can serve as a platform to deliver key program components, such as training and coaching, making programs more efficient by delivering their interventions to groups and drawing on the strength of mutual support. At JEEViKA in Bihar, India, women's village organizations are used to help programs identify ostracized and excluded households. Some programs engage with community leaders, local governments, and other key actors in the community to raise awareness about women's issues. For example, a Trickle Up project in India promoted gender justice through collective action by mobilizing women's groups, training participants in gender rights, and encouraging them to develop and strengthen culturally relevant gender justice initiatives. Trickle Up assisted them in documenting their own gender justice experiences to share with and motivate others in their communities. Trickle Up also promotes sexual and reproductive rights for girls and young women and rights to girls' education in Guatemala and other countries (Arévalo, Kaffenberger, and de Montesquiou 2018). Cambodia's Livelihood Enhancement and Association of the Poor project prioritizes women in the formation of thrift groups, which allow women to collectively save money while building social capital.

Gender-Sensitive Program Delivery

It is important to make it easier for women to participate in programs by delivering components in a manner that addresses the specific constraints they face. The following touches on particularly salient factors.

Staffing. Economic inclusion interventions require significant capacity building of staff at all levels and the endorsement of leadership, especially when implemented through existing government structures. Making women's empowerment a key objective of a program adds a layer of complexity and training in order to increase staff's capacity to handle gender issues. It is important to train local staff to recognize their own biases and help them understand how gender barriers intersect with other forms of discrimination based on race, ethnicity, sexual orientation, religion, and other aspects of identity. In certain contexts, cultural norms can make it difficult for women to interact with male program staff. In Afghanistan, the Targeting the Ultra Poor program is making a deliberate effort to hire females, although this is challenging in a fragile country with strong patriarchal culture where few women are qualified to take on this type of job. In Mauritania, the Adaptive Safety Net program also found it difficult to hire female staff because travel was challenging, either because the women had small children or because their travel was not culturally sanctioned.

However, hiring women as frontline staff is often critical given the broader coaching role they are expected to play and the engagement with sensitive subjects they often must deal with, such as gender-based violence or family planning. While the importance of having female frontline providers is clear, recruiting them is not without challenges in contexts where female literacy levels are low or their ability to work outside the home might be limited. In order to mitigate the challenges of recruiting female staff members, the Girls' Education and Women's Empowerment and

Livelihoods Project (GEWEL) program in Zambia is setting up a network of women volunteers in communities to deliver life and business skills training and to coach beneficiaries, thus removing the imperative to travel.

Payments and delivery mechanisms. Digitization of transfers, access to digital financial services, and e-coaching may make it easier for women to access services and content from home, easing mobility and time constraints. However, in delivering program components, there is a need to factor in women's limited ownership and access to key assets, including phones and bikes. The GEWEL program in Zambia is adapting the delivery of program components to better serve women. It has developed a unique payment system to deliver the grants, and women can choose the delivery option that suits them best. Fundación Capital in Latin America is ensuring that women have ownership by providing the digital delivery of funds into digital accounts opened in their names. Digital financial services can help foster women's financial inclusion in places where women have access to phones but bank accounts are still often held by men. The confidentiality that digital transfers enables may increase the prospect for women to have control over the resources and mitigate the risk of having funds appropriated by other family members (Chamberlin et al. 2019).

Childcare and flexibility. Childcare can constrain participation in economic inclusion programs for many women. Organizations operating in Afghanistan, India, Pakistan, and Zambia adapt their program delivery to accommodate women by providing sessions near beneficiaries' homes and allowing flexible arrangements to increase participation. For example, the Tejaswini program in India provides training closer to women's houses so that they can attend with their children. In some cases, providing childcare facilities, or compensation for childcare, can also help alleviate constraints (de Montesquiou and Sheldon 2018).

The Challenges

There is growing recognition that the decades of focus on women's economic empowerment have failed to bring about significant structural improvements in women's broader autonomy, voice, and agency. Mainstream approaches to women's economic empowerment improve access to resources but fail to acknowledge that social, political, and market systems are structured in a way that reflects and reinforces the societal inequalities that shaped them (Razavi and Miller 1995; Kabeer 2005; Cornwall 2014).

Without directly confronting the issues of power and social justice—that is, transforming the political, social, and structural dimensions of gender inequality— gender injustice will continue to exacerbate poverty and hinder social development (Kabeer and Natali 2013; UN Women 2013; Cavalcanti and Tavares 2016; World Bank 2019). In Kenya, the BOMA project includes interventions to address men and boys, reduce community-level sociocultural barriers, and address the gender-based division of labor, unequal control over political and economic resources, and domestic and public violence (Arévalo, Kaffenberger, and de Montesquiou 2018). In Bangladesh, BRAC encourages village community organizations that bring women together to exercise their collective voice and action and achieve empowerment in their communities to enable women to organize and mobilize in the public space. Meanwhile, JEEViKA, in Bihar, India, has created a federation of self-help groups.

Economic inclusion programs can have unintended adverse impacts. By making women primary beneficiaries, some programs may reinforce traditional gender roles or increase women's work burden by requiring them to attend project activities and manage microenterprises on top of their usual care responsibilities (Yoong, Rabinovich, and Diepeveen 2012, World Bank 2014, Van den Bold, Quisumbing, and Gillespie 2013). Program design and delivery may exacerbate tensions among household members (Pavanello et al. 2018). In Zambia, for example, interviewed beneficiaries complained about the challenge of balancing training attendance with care and income-generating activities. As a result, the project adjusted the timing of program activities to ensure time-consuming activities, such as life and business skills trainings, did not overlap with intensive agricultural periods, such as planting or harvesting. However, "time poverty" among women is a deeply contextual issue. In Afghanistan, both the primary women beneficiaries and other women in the household were found to have an excess amount of available time. The increased labor for women that came from Afghanistan's Targeting the Ultra Poor program had positive employment outcomes without generating additional stress for the women involved (Bedoya Arguelles et al. 2019).

Although not a common risk, cash transfers can in some cases increase intimate-partner violence due to the women's engagement in economic activities being perceived as a threat to traditional masculinity and gender roles in the household (Prevention Collaborative 2019; Buller et al. 2018). It is as crucial to engage men to mitigate this risk as it is to change cultural norms more broadly. The GEWEL program in Zambia is partnering with BRAC to incorporate proven interventions in this space, including couples training and gender dialogue at the community level. Putting in place gender-sensitive grievance redress mechanisms, such as multiple reporting channels, including anonymous reporting and reporting through trusted focal points. A gender-based violence referral system can also play an important prevention and response role.

Measuring women's economic empowerment is challenging. In Afghanistan, an early evaluation of the Targeting the Ultra Poor program was found to have no impact on gender outcomes when using an index focused on household finances and expenditures, such as that used in the original graduation research per Banerjee et al. (2015). However, after constructing a broader index, the program was found to lead to significant increases in women's empowerment. Women's power over decision-making about their own bodies and over how they use their time was stronger, and there was an increase in their participation in income-generating activities as a result of participating in the program. They had greater political involvement and improved social capital as represented by their having identity cards and reaching out to community leaders (Bedoya Arguelles et al. 2019).[2] This is an important argument for the need to broaden the scope of measurement tools to include different empowerment dimensions in addition to financial decision-making when assessing the gender impacts of economic inclusion programs. A new generation of impact evaluations is in the pipeline that will use a broader set of indicators to examine different dimensions of women's empowerment, including intrahousehold decision-making, self-esteem, psychosocial well-being, and social capital.

Future Directions

Significant efforts to build women's economic empowerment are already under way, and early evidence suggests that when carefully designed with a gender-sensitive lens, economic inclusion programs can improve women's access to income, help them better manage their assets, and enable them to improve their status in the household. Going forward, greater attention is required to track and monitor the effect and impact of program design choices. Getting households to work better together may help increase women's empowerment. There is also strong potential to mobilize local community groups to further the collective strength of female beneficiaries.

Notes

1. There is still a gap of 7 percentage points between men and women when it comes to owning a bank account (Demirgüç-Kunt et al. 2018).
2. In Afghanistan, women's empowerment is driven by an increase in women's decision-making power over their own bodies and time, an increase in their participation in income-generating activities (which follows from the program), and an increase in political involvement and social capital (for example, having an ID, reaching out to community leaders). See Goldstein (2019).

References

Arévalo, I., M. Kaffenberger, and A. de Montesquiou. 2018. *2018 State of the Sector Synthesis Report*. Washington, DC: World Bank.

Bandiera, Oriana, Robin Burgess, Narayan Das, Selim Gulesci, Imran Rasul, and Munshi Sulaiman. 2017. "Labor Markets and Poverty in Village Economies." *Quarterly Journal of Economics* 132 (2): 811–70.

Banerjee, A., E. Duflo, N. Goldberg, D. Karlan, R. Osei, W. Parienté, J. Shapiro, B. Thuysbaert, and C. Udry. 2015. "A Multifaceted Program Causes Lasting Progress for the Very Poor: Evidence from Six Countries." *Science* 14 (348): 1260799.

Bardasi, Elena, and Gisela Garcia. 2014. "Social Safety Nets and Gender: Learning from Impact Evaluations and World Bank Projects." World Bank, Washington, DC.

Bedoya Arguelles, Guadalupe, Aiden Coville, Johannes Haushofer, Mohammad Razaq Isaqzadeh, and Jeremy Shapiro. 2019. "No Household Left Behind: Afghanistan Targeting the Ultra Poor Impact Evaluation." Policy Research Working Paper WPS 8877, World Bank, Washington, DC.

Blattman, Christopher, Nathan Fiala, and Sebastian Martinez. 2014. "Generating Skilled Self-Employment in Developing Countries: Experimental Evidence from Uganda." *Quarterly Journal of Economics* 129: 697–752. doi:10.1093/qje/qjt057.

Buller, Ana Maria, Amber Peterman, Meghna Ranganathan, Alexandra Bleile, Melissa Hidrobo, and Lori Heise. 2018. "A Mixed-Method Review of Cash Transfers and Intimate Partner Violence in Low- and Middle-Income Countries." *World Bank Research Observer* 33 (2): 218–58. doi:10.1093/wbro/lky002.

Cavalcanti, T., and J. Tavares. 2016. "The Output Cost of Gender Discrimination: A Model-Based Macroeconomics Estimate." *Economic Journal* 126 (590): 109–34. https://doi.org/10.1111/ecoj.12303.

Chamberlin Wendy, Liz Kellison, Jeni Klugman, and Jamie Zimmerman. 2019. "Enhancing Women's Economic Empowerment through Digital Cash Transfers: Digitize/Direct/Design: The D3 Criteria." Bill and Melinda Gates Foundation, Seattle, WA. https://www.findevgateway.org/sites/default/files/publications/files/_bmgf_d3_criteria_june_1_2019.pdf.

Cornwall, Andrea. 2014. "Women's Empowerment: What Works?" WIDER Working Paper, United Nations University World Institute for Development Economics Research, Helsinki. doi:10.1002/jid.3210.

Das, Narayan C., Sibbir Ahmad, Anindita Bhattacharjee, Jinnat Ara, and Abdul Bayes. 2016. "Grant vs. Credit Plus Approach to Poverty Reduction: An Evaluation of BRAC's Experience with Ultra Poor." CFPR Working Paper 24, BRAC, Dhaka.

de Mel, S., D. McKenzie, and C. Woodruff. 2014. "Business Training and Female Enterprise Start-Up, Growth, and Dynamics: Experimental Evidence from Sri Lanka." *Journal of Development Economics* 106: 99–210.

de Montesquiou, Aude, and Tony Sheldon, with Syed M. Hashemi. 2018. *From Extreme Poverty to Sustainable Livelihoods: A Technical Guide to the Graduation Approach.* 2nd ed. Washington, DC: World Bank. https://www.microfinancegateway.org /library/extreme-poverty-sustainable-livelihoods-technical-guide-graduation-approach-second-edition.

Demirgüç-Kunt, Asli, Leora Klapper, Dorothe Singer, Saniya Ansar, and Jake Hess. 2018. *The Global Findex Database 2017: Measuring Financial Inclusion and the Fintech Revolution.* Washington, DC: World Bank. doi:10.1596/978-1-4648-1259-0.

Goldstein, Markus. 2019. "Some Good News from Afghanistan." *World Bank Blogs: Development Impact.* June 19. https://blogs.worldbank.org/impactevaluations /some-good-news-afghanistan.

Hashemi, Syed M., Aude de Montesquiou, and Katharine McKee. 2016. "Graduation Pathways: Increasing Income and Resilience for the Extreme Poor." World Bank, Washington, DC.

Holmes, Rebecca, and Nicola Jones. 2013. *Gender and Social Protection in the Developing World: Beyond Mothers and Safety Nets.* London: Zed.

Kabeer, Naila. 2005. "Gender Equality and Women's Empowerment: A Critical Analysis of the Third Millennium Development Goal." *Gender and Development* 13 (1): 13–24. doi:10.1080/13552070512331332273.

Kabeer, Naila, and Luisa Natali. 2013. "Gender Equality and Economic Growth: Is There a Win-Win?" IDS Working Paper 417, Institute of Development Studies, London. doi:10.1111/j.2040-0209.2013.00417.x

Kabeer, Naila, Karishma Huda, Sandeep Kaur, and Nicolina Lamhauge. 2012. "Productive Safety Nets for Women in Extreme Poverty: Lessons from Pilot Projects in India and Pakistan." Discussion Paper 28/12, Centre for Development Policy and Research, School of Oriental and African Studies, London.

Karimli, Leyla, Lucia Rost, and Leyla Ismayilova. 2018. "Integrating Economic Strengthening and Family Coaching to Reduce Work-Related Health Hazards among Children of Poor Households: Burkina Faso." *Journal of Adolescent Health* 62 (1): S6–S14. doi:10.1080/00220388.2019.1677887.

Laszlo, S. 2019. "The Gender Transformative Potential of Graduation Programs." GrOW Research Working Paper Series 25, Institute for the Study of International Development, McGill University, Montreal.

Pavanello, Sara, Pamela Pozarny, Ana Paula de la O Campos, and Nynne Warring. 2018. *Research on Rural Women's Economic Empowerment and Social Protection: The Impacts of Rwanda's Vision 2020 Umurenge Programme (VUP).* Rome: FAO.

Prevention Collaborative. 2019. "Evidence Brief: Cash Transfers and Intimate Partner Violence: Findings from a Review of Quantitative and Qualitative Studies in Low- and Middle-Income Countries." Prevention Collaborative. https:// prevention-collaborative.org/wp-content/uploads/2019/10/EVIDENCE-BRIEF -CASH-TRANSFERS-IPV-low-res-final-4.pdf.

Razavi, Shahra, and Carol Miller. 1995. "Gender Mainstreaming: A Study of Efforts by the UNDP, the World Bank and the ILO to Institutionalize Gender Issues." Occasional Paper Series, Research Institute for Social Development, Geneva.

Shoaf, Emma, and Anton Simanowitz. 2019. *Pathways to Sustained Exit from Extreme Poverty: Evidence from Fonkoze's Extreme Poverty 'Graduation' Programme.* Brighton, UK: Institute of Development Studies.

Siddiki, Omar Faruque, Rebecca Holmes, Ferdous Jahan, Fahim Subhan Chowdhury, and Jessica Hagen-Zanker. 2014. How *Do Social Safety Nets Contribute to Social Inclusion in Bangladesh? Evidence from the Chars Livelihoods Programme and the Vulnerable Group Development Programme.* London: Overseas Development Institute.

UN Women. 2013. *Annual Report 2012–2013*. New York: UN Women. https://www.cbd
.int/financial/mainstream/unwomen-ar2012-13.pdf.

Van den Bold, M., A. R. Quisumbing, and S. Gillespie. 2013. "Women's Empowerment
and Nutrition: An Evidence Review." IFPRI Discussion Paper 1294, International
Food Policy Research Institute, Washington, DC.

World Bank. 2014. *Social Safety Nets and Gender: Learning from Impact Evaluations
and World Bank Projects*. Washington, DC: World Bank.

World Bank. 2019. *The Little Data Book on Gender 2019*. Washington, DC: World Bank.

World Bank. 2020. *Women, Business and the Law 2020*. Washington, DC: World Bank.
doi:10.1596/978-1-4648-1532-4.

World Bank Group. 2015. *World Bank Group Gender Strategy (FY16–23): Gender
Equality, Poverty Reduction, and Inclusive Growth*. Washington, DC: World Bank.

Yoong, Joanne, Lila Rabinovich, and Stephanie Diepeveen. 2012. *The Impact of
Economic Resource Transfers to Women versus Men: A Systematic Review: Technical
Report*. London: EPPI Centre, University of London.

CHAPTER 4

Moving to Scale through Government-Led Programs

KEY MESSAGES

Many government programs are at a nascent stage of scaling up. A sustainable approach to scaling up involves careful design across several programmatic and institutional dimensions. This is a critical prerequisite before the expansion of program coverage.

The Partnership for Economic Inclusion (PEI) Landscape Survey 2020 shows that more than 50 percent of existing government-led programs have the potential to cover between 5 and 10 percent of the extreme poor. In these, economic inclusion programs are devised as a discrete intervention, supporting a wider set of policies. In many instances, these programs are underpinning a push toward comprehensive and universal social protection.

Coordination across ministries is necessary to link different complementary programs. Complementarities and convergences help single-ministry programs achieve economies of scale in implementation and strengthen policy coherence.

FUTURE DIRECTIONS

Documentation of effective operational models and delivery systems in different contexts is required to facilitate effective design and coordination of economic inclusion programming. A wide range of possible configurations of partners, programs, and structures is under way, but there are gaps in documentation and guidance.

Leveraging existing digital infrastructure is critical to strengthen program management and increase efficiency. Digital solutions can help leapfrog some delivery constraints and increase cost-effectiveness, and they will grow in prominence as social distancing restrictions affect training and coaching activities in the wake of the COVID-19 crisis.

Market and value chains links can increase the productivity of livelihood activities and bolster program sustainability. Mesolevel links will help alleviate difficult access to markets, infrastructure, and production inputs, and the potential for increased private sector engagement is high.

Introduction

Global discourse on reaching scale with economic inclusion programs is often limited to expanding the number of people served. Yet there are a number of other dimensions of scaling up that need to be factored in for government-led economic inclusion programs to reach scale. This chapter explores the programmatic and institutional aspects of moving to scale. The discussion builds on the political economy discussions in chapter 2.[1]

Many government-led programs are in their infancy, while others are only in early stages of scaling up. As noted in chapter 1, economic inclusion programs at scale tend to be incorporated into broader policy and programming.

As programs mature, it will be important to document and learn from the different ways governments increase coverage and adapt their design and delivery to do so, based on their contexts, maturity of the social protection and other government systems, and level of decentralization. The process will also be influenced locally by how governments are set up, which ministries hold the institutional mandate for social protection, whether a coordination mechanism exists or needs to be created, and a myriad of other contextual considerations. In the years to come, process documentation and operational research will be essential to build a body of knowledge and guidance on how to bring economic inclusion programs most efficiently to scale.

To achieve economic inclusion "at scale," several programmatic and institutional mechanics needed to embed programs in government systems must be considered together with political economy considerations. Table 4.1 outlines the programmatic, institutional, and policy dimensions of scale explored in this report. It is implicit in this framework that implementing at scale requires a systemic and iterative process of adaptation across several dimensions—in program dimensions such as layering of new

TABLE 4.1   Dimensions of Scale: Programmatic and Institutional

Dimensions of scale	Focus	Description	Expected results
Increased coverage	Programmatic aspects	Expansion of programmatic coverage by including more people and/or communities in a given location or replication in different locations.	Improve, widen, and/or deepen program outcomes
Functional expansion		Expansion by increasing the scope of activity, in which a program starts with a single focus but then layers in or links additional multisectoral interventions	
Policy and strategy	Institutional aspects	Institutionalization through policy, strategy, and programming decisions—reinforced by legal, budgetary, and financing decisions to allow effective performance at scale	Improve efficiency; improve fiscal and policy coherence
Organizational		Expansion of organizational coordination and capacity at different levels (central, local, community level); identification of overall governance mechanisms (including cross-ministerial); and engagement of partnerships (including with groups at community level, nongovernmental organizations [NGOs], and private sector).	
Operational		Operationalization through building or leveraging delivery systems, especially with respect to digital and community platforms	

Source: World Bank, with adaptations from Carter, Joshi, and Remme 2018; Cooley and Linn 2014.

activities and components, in institutional dimensions such as budgeting, financing, and evolution of digital platforms, to name a few.[2]

Moving to scale will require progress on several dimensions, some of which may be considered important prerequisites to test and adapt before expanding the case load of beneficiaries. A program that has included more people through expansion of coverage geographically may have also implemented system-level changes in government policy, perhaps in partnership with various partners to expand capacity.

In practice, scaling up will be supported through a number of customized programmatic arrangements (FAO 2018; Slater et al. 2016; Soares et al. 2017; Tirivayi, Knowles, and Davis 2013; Maldonado et al. 2016). In an ideal world, economic inclusion programs would be customized and coherent in the context of national policy, organized to overlap and converge with other related programs, and pursued with clear and effective targeting. In practice, economic inclusion programs tend to fall under either of two approaches: single or complementary. A single approach is achieved when additional components are added to a program. This is typical in low-capacity settings, newly initiated approaches, or where government coordination may be especially challenging. A complementary approach coordinates across different programs with a common objective. Complementary approaches are more typical where programs advance and mature or where systems are better established for such coordination.

Programmatic Adaptations to Scale

In order to reach scale, economic inclusion programs need to adapt along a range of programmatic dimensions, including the increase of beneficiary coverage and the expansion of program functions. Among government-led programs, coverage remains modest, but more than one-third of government programs have recently undergone functional expansion, most commonly among social safety net (SSN) programs. Many economic inclusion programs have the potential to scale up.

Increasing coverage refers to scaling-up programs to include more people or communities in a given location or replicating the program in different locations. Beyond coverage expansion, programmatic adaptations to scale up often also involve functional scaling up—increasing the scope of activity, where initially a program starts with a single focus but then layers on or links additional multisectoral interventions.

Increased Coverage

At present, 95 government-led programs in the Partnership for Economic Inclusion (PEI) Landscape Survey 2020—those that shared the number of current beneficiaries— serve over 18 million households, or more than 85 million individuals. This represents an overwhelming majority of the total beneficiaries reached by economic inclusion programs globally (93 percent of both households and individuals).[3]

In terms of the different entry points to scaling up, among government programs, 45 percent of programs featured in the report are classified as SSN programs.[4] SSN programs in the PEI Landscape Survey 2020 account for 58 percent of the total individuals reached, while livelihoods and jobs (L&J) programs make up 53 percent of government-led programs and account for 42 percent of total individuals reached.[5]

Given the targeted nature of economic inclusion programs, the analysis considers "coverage equivalents" across different thresholds—the national poverty line, the extreme poverty line, and the Multidimensional Poverty Index—with each metric providing varying perspectives around poverty.[6] For instance, in Bangladesh, coverage rates of government-led programs are 3 percent relative to total population, 12 percent relative to poverty (as measured by the national poverty line), 20 percent relative to extreme poverty, and 7 percent relative to multidimensional poverty. Note that while the overall analysis covers 53 countries, some metrics report fewer, owing to data gaps. Box 4.1 provides an overview of the methodological approaches in estimating coverage of economic inclusion programs, combined with the challenges that may limit this analysis.

The coverage of government-led programs appears modest relative to total population size but slightly higher when comparing the number of beneficiaries to various poverty lines; in any case, in most contexts there is great potential to scale up.[7] Just one individual program, the Tanzania Productive Social Safety Net, serves slightly more than 10 percent of Tanzania's population. The program scale-up was driven by a strong policy initiative to increase outreach and an effort to decentralize program delivery, which led to broad national coverage. The majority of individual programs serve less than 1 percent of their country's total population (see figure 4.1, panel a). When individual programs are aggregated at the country level—and assuming no overlapping beneficiaries among

---

BOX 4.1   **Estimating Coverage of Economic Inclusion Programs**

For this report—based on the Partnership for Economic Inclusion (PEI) Landscape Survey 2020—the "coverage" of a country's economic inclusion programs is considered to be the number of beneficiaries reached by all its programs relative to the total population. The estimates delineate coverage in terms of households (direct beneficiaries) and individuals (direct plus indirect beneficiaries). The individual figure is determined by multiplying direct beneficiaries by average household size. This follows an accepted estimation approach across social protection programs globally (Milazzo and Grosh 2008; Beegle et al. 2018). Estimates do not account for the potential spillover and community effects of an intervention.

Given the tailored nature of economic inclusion programs, the report also considers "coverage equivalents," defined as the number of direct plus indirect beneficiaries reached by a program relative to the total population and estimated poverty thresholds, including the national poverty line, extreme poverty line, and the Multidimensional Poverty Index. These equivalent measures provide important illustrations of the potential coverage of programs that have a strong poverty focus. They also recognize a wider debate on poverty measurement thresholds. However, the approach has shortcomings. The program data provided for this study do not capture beneficiary welfare, so the study could not identify whether reported beneficiaries are poor or not. At best, these figures show the potential scale of programs, if they were perfectly targeted.

Broadly speaking, three challenges limit the analysis: First, there are data gaps, so the information presented should be considered as a lower-bound estimate; just 201 out of 219 programs reported beneficiary data. This points to obvious monitoring gaps in program implementation. Second, in conducting this study, PEI drew on census information to determine average household size. This may underestimate the true nature of coverage, since poorer households are usually larger than average. Also, this level of disaggregated information was not systematically available for all countries. Third, PEI did not account for potential overlaps across programs. To minimize the risk of overlap, PEI cross-checked its own survey data with government administrative data, when possible, and made the decision to report on individuals, whether indirect or direct beneficiaries.

FIGURE 4.1 **Distribution of Program Coverage Rates by Share of Population**

a. Based on four alternative measures (individual government-led programs)

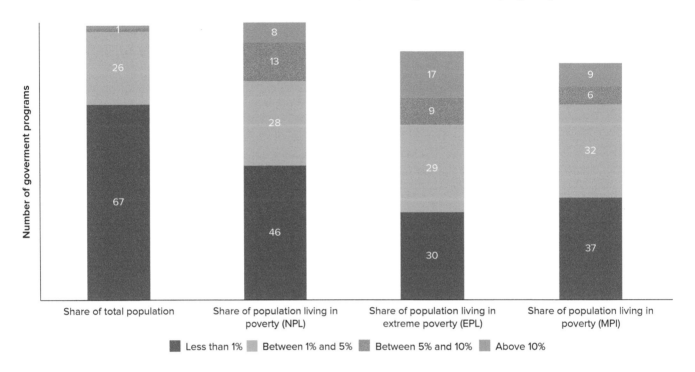

b. Based on four alternative measures (sum of individual government-led programs by country)

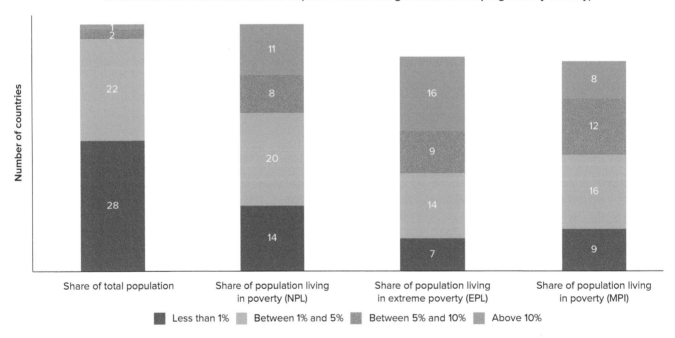

Source: Partnership for Economic Inclusion, World Bank.

Note: NPL = national poverty line; EPL = extreme poverty line; MPI = Multidimensional Poverty Index. The analysis is based on 95 government-led programs (those providing data on the number of beneficiaries), representing 53 countries. Data are presented by program and aggregated at the country level. The poverty headcount is missing for seven countries using the purchasing power parity (PPP) $1.90 per day line or extreme poverty line, and eight countries using the MPI. This figure assumes perfect targeting.

programs—22 out of 53 countries have coverage of between 1 and 5 percent of the total population, as shown in figure 4.1, panel b.

The scale of economic inclusion interventions is modest in part because they began recently and in part because they are most relevant for the poorest subset of the population. South Asia and Sub-Saharan Africa have a large number of people living in poverty, which offers great potential to scale up. Although there is a good base of economic inclusion programs operating in many countries in these regions, the aggregated coverage of programs in the majority of these countries ranges from 1 to 5 percent. Four countries in Sub-Saharan Africa—Ethiopia, Sudan, Tanzania, and Uganda—have programs that build on SSN systems and have managed to achieve coverage greater than 5 percent.

However, expressed as a share of the extreme poor, coverage is slightly higher. The PEI Landscape Survey 2020 shows that 21 countries have the potential to cover between 5 percent and 10 percent of the extreme poor through a combination of existing programs. This presentation of a coverage "equivalent" to extreme poverty provides a more accurate reflection of program objectives and approaches. Economic inclusion programs are devised as discrete interventions, supporting a wider set of policies. In many instances these programs are underpinning a push to comprehensive and universal social protection. As highlighted in box 4.1, although the analysis highlights gaps in coverage, there are strong methodological challenges and assumptions embedded in it.

Many government-led programs surveyed are in the process of expanding coverage, and there is a strong potential to scale up. Fifty-seven percent of these have expanded coverage in the past two years by adding more beneficiaries in a province, region, and/or district or across the country. At present, only 15 percent of government-led programs surveyed operate in a single state or region, while 59 percent serve beneficiaries in multiple states or regions, and a further 26 percent operate nationally. Geographic expansion is largely dependent upon a country's administrative structure and the physical location of target populations. While it is too early to identify trends in economic inclusion programming, there is some evidence that governments are incorporating nongovernment-led programs, which could lead to increased coverage of beneficiaries. For example, in Ethiopia from 2009 to 2011, a small pilot project implemented by the Relief Society of Tigray in the north served as the basis for the design of the government's Household Asset Building Program, which aimed to enhance the productive capacity of the poorest recipients of the public works productive safety net program (PSNP).

Functional Expansion

In the PEI survey, more than a third of the cohort of government-led programs had undergone functional expansion (enhancement of the scope of their activities) in the past two years, often in conjunction with coverage expansion. Scope enhancement was somewhat more common among SSN programs (44 percent) than among L&J programs (26 percent). This is consistent with a growing emphasis on supplementing SSNs with livelihood interventions.

Expanding the scope of a single program is usually a gradual process, with many programs starting with a base intervention and gradually layering interventions. For example, building resilience to climate change became a key rationale for Sahel governments to enhance the scope of their SSNs with elements of adaptive social protection, including economic inclusion (see case study 1). The bundling of multisectoral interventions, a fundamental feature of economic inclusion programming, requires significant administrative capacity. Most SSN programs have added components gradually; in Côte d'Ivoire the Productive Social Safety Net project provided cash transfers to poor households in the first year of operation, introducing additional livelihood interventions only in its third year (World Bank 2015).

While a number of livelihood programs have managed to implement a suite of interventions, others have taken a phased approach to manage complexity at scale. For instance, in India, programs like the Andhra Pradesh Inclusive Growth Project (AGRIGP) and the Bihar Rural Livelihoods Project, or JEEViKA, focused initially on developing self-help groups and other community-based organizations to promote financial inclusion. In later years, these programs progressively added skills training, livelihood support, and links.

Some programs are expanding the scope of their interventions in response to changing needs and contexts. Several programs reported their plans for increased emphasis on resilience, including SSN programs like the upcoming Mali Access to Finance and Income Generating Opportunities Project. Other programs increased their emphasis on market development, including L&J programs like Argentina's Proyecto de inclusión socio-económica en áreas rurales, Bolivia's Rural Alliances Project, and India's AGRIGP for small farmers and producers.

In certain countries, functional expansion takes the form of program convergence, in which components of two or more existing discrete programs serve the same group of beneficiaries. For instance, in Brazil, the Acre Social and Economic Inclusion and Sustainable Development Project provides coordinated interventions to the poor in one state, including cash transfers (Bolsa Família), health, agroforestry production systems, and agricultural extension services (World Bank 2008). Similarly, in India, JEEViKA leverages its community-based structure to link participants to SSN, agriculture, enterprise development, skills training, and financial inclusion programs. In Panama, the pilot Productive Inclusion Program in indigenous territories is part of broader economic inclusion programming and is linked with the cash transfer program Red de Oportunidades. Ideally, this type of complementary program would introduce links and referrals across existing programs. This type of link would ideally help improve existing delivery platforms. In practice, however, varying levels of policy coherence and coordination determine whether this approach is effective in delivering a suite of interventions.

Institutional Adaptations to Scale

Institutional, policy, strategy, organizational, and operational settings influence whether an economic inclusion program scales up or not. Today, through system-level changes, such as in policy or budgeting, small-scale programs are being institutionalized. Institutionalization might happen by including a small-scale pilot or program in government policy and financing, expanding organizational capacity (either in-house or through partnerships), or building delivery systems or utilizing existing systems, depending on the context. An example of institutionalization is the Adaptive Social Protection Program in the Sahel. This program was launched in March 2014 to support the design and implementation of adaptive social protection programs and systems in six Sahel countries (Burkina Faso, Chad, Mali, Mauritania, Niger, and Senegal). The program entails a combination of policies and interventions to help poor and vulnerable households build resilience, reduce the impact of climatic change and other shocks, and foster access to income-earning opportunities. The social protection programs use existing SSNs as a base on which to build complementary activities, with a strong focus on training in basic skills and livelihood diversification, sanitary and health practices, and nutrition awareness.

A number of small-scale pilots or programs, including those led by nongovernmental organizations (NGOs), are also being institutionalized through policy, programming, legal, budgetary, or other system-level changes. For example, the organization Fonkoze has institutionalized the Chemin Lavi Miyò program in Haiti as the primary way to work with poorest beneficiaries. As their incomes and assets grow, participants can access some of the organization's other services, in particular, microfinance. And the Ghana Productive Safety Net Programme (PSNP) program builds on a series of smaller pilots, including one that for almost a decade has been testing ways to increase access to income-generating activities for extremely poor households. This process of institutionalization helps expand the understanding of scaling-up beyond just programmatic aspects and acknowledges that institutional and political settings influence whether a program will scale up or not. Organizational capacity and robust delivery systems are also critical dimensions of effective scale up.

Policy and Strategy Adaptations

Economic inclusion programs often have a strong link to national policy and strategy frameworks. Seventy-six percent of the programs in the survey are integrated with a government program or a government strategy or policy pertaining to growth, poverty reduction, social protection and labor, migration and forced displacement, recovery and resilience, or agriculture and rural development. Ministries that typically lead government economic inclusion programs are ministries of development and planning (17 percent), ministries of social development and protection (26 percent), labor (15 percent), agriculture (12 percent), finance (9 percent), and environment (6 percent).

In the past two years, 33 percent of government-led programs surveyed have adapted institutionalization structures, illustrating the current policy momentum for this agenda. Programs that are scaling up institutionally are often strongly linked to national policy and strategy frameworks. For example, the Satat Jeevikoparjan Yojana (SJY) scale-up in Bihar, India, as highlighted in case study 2, benefits from being integrated into a larger institutionalized economic inclusion effort: JEEViKA at the state level and the National Rural Livelihoods Mission (NRLM) at the national level. SJY is strongly aligned to state- and national-level policy objectives and is considered a key piece of JEEViKA's overall policy goal of "saturation," that is, inclusion of and service provision for the poor. SJY's scale-up benefits from state and national funding, and JEEViKA's well-developed and adaptive delivery systems and infrastructure, all of which have supported an altogether new programmatic approach. NRLM, having been conceptualized at the national level based on the lessons of JEEViKA and similar programs in other states, offers a broad landscape in which to institutionalize the experiences of SJY at a national scale.

Rwanda's Vision 2020 Umurenge Programme (VUP), introduced in 2008, combines public works with financial support in the form of transfers, financial literacy training, and credit. There was strong high-level commitment to the program, which was due to the convergence of interests around the view that persistent poverty and inequality directly created political instability. As a result, the VUP became an integral part of the government's development strategy, with public financing constituting a significant portion of the cost and expanding program coverage to roughly 6 percent of the population (Lavers 2016). Approximately 45 percent of programs led by the ministries of labor and development and planning have adapted institutional structures in the process of scale-up.

Financing is an important part of sustainability, and it links to political economy decisions, discussed in chapter 2. Over half (55 percent) of programs surveyed led by governments are also funded in whole (29 percent of these) or in part (71 percent) by them, with 36 countries having dedicated budget lines for expenditures in this area. Furthermore, the majority of programs in ministries of labor (69 percent of government-led programs), agriculture (58 percent), development and planning (61 percent), and social development and protection (60 percent) have a dedicated budget line for economic inclusion programming. This demonstrates a high level of government ownership and commitment to this agenda. For example, Peru's Haku Wiñay is a government-funded program with an established budgetary line and resources offering greater fiscal continuity. As a result, it has been institutionalizing as it rolled out systematically to different parts of Peru over the years (see case study 4). Survey data disaggregated by region reveal that 92 percent of programs in Latin America and the Caribbean receive government funding, whereas in Sub-Saharan Africa only about 31 percent receive government funding. Of those government-led programs that have institutionalized in the past two years, 63 percent have received government funding. In terms of entry points to scale, 56 percent of SSN and 54 percent of L&J programs have acquired government funding.

At the same time, donor financing has an important role to play, both by filling financing gaps and because of the associated technical expertise that accompanies such financing. The funding that underpins the efforts of those programs surveyed is often provided by a mix of donors, the most prevalent being multilateral agencies, which fund most economic inclusion programs (71 percent of all programs and 79 percent of government-led programs), including the World Bank, multilateral organizations such as the European Union and United Nations agencies, and bilateral agencies like the United Kingdom's Department for International Development, the US Agency for International Development, Ireland's IrishAID, and Germany's Deutsche Gesellschaft für Internationale Zusammenarbeit (GIZ).[8] The World Bank is financing 37 percent of all economic inclusion programs, mostly government-led programs.[9] For example, in Bihar the national and state governments, World Bank, catalytic philanthropic funding for technical assistance, and research support have combined synergistically to support SJY (see case study 2).

Organizational Adaptations

Most programs that have expanded in size and scope have also expanded their organizational capacity. Bundling multisectoral interventions requires that all the government agencies involved have significant administrative capacity and clear institutional mandates. Over the past two years, 41 percent of government programs surveyed have expanded their organizational capacity. This might be by increasing in-house capacity or through partnerships with other institutions, depending on the context. In Peru, the Haku Wiñay program uses expert farmers called *yachachiq*, who advise and help the program participants in the improvements of their farming techniques. The profile of these yachachiq varies from region to region, but they are often young peasants who have previously worked in NGO projects or in other social programs and therefore can provide advice and guidance to their neighbors. Their presence in the communities has alleviated the need to identify or procure a third-party partner organization to deliver the coaching component (see case study 4). Although it is an NGO program, Fonkoze in Haiti provides an interesting example of organizational scaling. Fonkoze determined that safe housing was an essential part of their Chemen Lavi Miyò economic inclusion program because leaky roofs hindered the economic progress of beneficiaries. The organization's entrepreneurial culture led them to offer construction training and deliver basic materials to participants despite those elements not being initially part of the organization's mandate (de Montesquiou and Sheldon 2018).

Economic inclusion packages are bundled together in different ways: some bundles are provided by one program only (single programs) while other bundles are knitted together by linking several programs (complementary programs). Roughly 76 percent of government-led programs in the survey are single programs. In some instances, single programs may also choose to refer program participants to additional services provided by organizations outside the program, such as referring people for health care provision, but the core economic inclusion package is still provided through the program, including through partner organizations. Among government programs, 69 percent of SSN programs and 81 percent of L&J programs are single programs in the survey.

Complementary programs face the challenges of policy coherence in program design and effective coordination during implementation. In most cases, despite stated intentions and agreements, the synergies between programs are typically not well articulated in policy, program design, or implementation. Some countries are working to deepen coordination across programs, as Brazil did with its Brasil Sem Miséria program, in which respective ministries had integrated their registries to achieve better joint-targeting programs, such as the Bolsa Família (conditional cash transfer), Promotion of Rural Productive Activities (Fomento cash grant), the Bolsa Verde (grants in the Amazon forest), and Cisternas (access to water facilitation to rural activities).[10]

The majority of complementary programs in the survey are led by governments (57 percent). These are coordinated interventions built on existing systems and programs, which may be helping to avoid duplication of government interventions and to improve efficiencies. In many cases, despite good intentions and formalized agreements, coordination between programs remains difficult: governments need to focus on strengthening operational capacity and effective coordination in order to do this effectively (GIZ 2017). In Chile, the Ministry of Social Development takes the lead in coordinating the delivery of a range of social services and benefits provided by different government institutions under the Programa Familias for the poorest and most vulnerable. In Indonesia, the Ministry of Social Affairs is also working to integrate its poverty-targeted programs. Selected recipients of Indonesia's conditional cash transfer program (Program Keluarga Harapan) are encouraged to join either the Kelompok Usaha Bersama Program (a business entrepreneurship program through which families receive support to set up sustainable microenterprises) or the new social entrepreneurship program Kewirausahaan Sosial or both. The goal is to create a ladder of support to foster the further development of microbusinesses with higher potential.

Forging partnerships with NGOs and the private sector (including financial services providers) for program delivery is critically important for economic inclusion programs. Box 4.2 discusses some of the key roles NGOs play in program design and implementation. The complexity of bundled interventions makes it difficult for a single agency to deliver them. It is also inefficient for a single agency to do so, except in fragile or conflict- or violence-affected settings, where there are serious service delivery gaps. Among the government-led programs in the survey, 67 percent partner with NGOs and 63 percent with the private sector for implementation, financing, and technical support. Eighty-seven percent of government programs surveyed are supported by donors (such as the World Bank). The most common roles for NGO and private sector partners are providing technical assistance and the delivery of components. Regular performance evaluation of partners such as NGOs and private sector service providers is an essential part of efficient implementation and can be nurtured through performance-based contracting.

Lead organizations often partner with other organizations or actors to implement program components, bring in specialized expertise, and overcome capacity constraints. These partners are mostly NGOs, community members, and governments at different levels. In Brazil, the World Bank–supported Bahia Sustainable Rural Development Project is working to scale up productive alliances, better integrate with the market at both the private and institutional levels, and strengthen the contribution of other public sector institutions and policies. In the Sahel, the governments partnered with Trickle Up both for the design of the program and for the delivery phase, sometimes also including communities through group formations and community agents to deliver the programs.

Government-led programs may rely more on other implementing partners than nongovernment-led programs. This is partly because national governments may

BOX 4.2   Beyond Direct Delivery: NGOs as Catalyzers for Scale

Nongovernmental organizations (NGOs) implement nearly half of all economic inclusion programs worldwide, but serve only 7 percent of beneficiaries. However, coverage data must not minimize the critical role NGOs play in the scaling up of economic inclusion programs.

First, some NGOs directly implement programs at a very large scale. Examples include BRAC's Ultra-Poor Graduation Program, Village Enterprise's Kenya Core Programming, and World Vision's Livelihood Technical Program. This is true especially in fragile and conflict- or violence-affected settings, as is the case with Concern Worldwide's Building Resilient Communities in Somalia, and Humanity and Inclusion's Alliance for Community Resilience program (with a consortium of seven NGOs) in West Africa.

Program design support. Beyond direct implementation, there are several roles that NGOs play. They provide extensive support to the design of government programs with technical assistance. This provision of multiyear technical support and capacity building to governments is accelerating the pace at which governments are adopting economic inclusion programs and is catalyzing a new wave of adaptive learning.

Program delivery support. NGOs also frequently support governments in delivering economic inclusion programs: 67 percent of governments surveyed partner with NGOs for this purpose. Depending on government capacity levels in a country, NGOs may take on different parts of program delivery. For example, in the Sahel Adaptive Social Protection Program, Trickle Up helps the government hire and train frontline staff in some regions, while directly implementing coaching components in lower-capacity regions. In Bihar, the Indian NGO Bandhan Konnagar provides technical support to JEEViKA, the Bihar Rural Livelihoods Project, to help it adapt and roll out the approach of Satat Jeevikoparjan Yojana (SJY). Both examples are highlighted in this publication's case studies.

Documenting and testing innovations. When providing technical assistance or implementing programs, NGOs are often at the forefront of documenting country-level innovations, helping to fill some global knowledge gaps. Some NGOs are testing innovations aimed at right-sizing economic inclusion package components. For example, in Kenya, Village Enterprise has recently completed a randomized controlled trial demonstrating successful results of a low-cost economic inclusion package. The BOMA Project and Concern Worldwide are testing innovations in delivery mechanisms in East Africa. Such lessons are critical to helping governments around the globe adapt programs to their country context and their current and expected future fiscal space.

Building capacity. NGOs often help to build capacity in the government programs they support through design, delivery, and technical assistance. BRAC, Fundación Capital, Trickle Up, and other providers of technical assistance to governments play a key role in delivering training and drafting tools and technical guides to help governments in their economic inclusion programming.

Pioneering new funding mechanisms. Finally, by pioneering innovative funding mechanisms, some NGOs are engaging new funders in the field. For example, in 2017, Village Enterprise mobilized funding for an economic inclusion program through a development impact bond in Uganda. This pioneering effort was followed by significant investment from various donors and philanthropists, who were keen to learn about the effectiveness of outcome-based funding mechanisms to leverage additional funding for scaling up. More work is needed in terms of understanding how government systems can make use of these new funding mechanisms.

not be best suited to beneficiary-level work. In fact, they often rely on regional and local governments, NGOs, or private-sector organizations to undertake the program activities that involve individual beneficiaries, such as program targeting, delivery of program components, and beneficiary monitoring.[11] Figure 4.2 offers a breakdown of the roles played by the lead government agency and partner organizations in government-led programs.

Operational Adaptations

To reduce cost and facilitate links with other social policy, a number of economic inclusion programs leverage existing delivery systems (see chapter 6). Thirty-three percent of all programs surveyed and 43 percent of government-led programs are currently utilizing government social registries, beneficiary registries, and other government databases to identify program participants. Among government-led programs, this is more common in programs operating in the regions of Latin America and the Caribbean and South Asia (62 percent and 40 percent, respectively) than it is in those in Sub-Saharan Africa (27 percent). Using a government registry is also more common in government programs that have an SSN as an entry point (58 percent) than in those with L&J as the entry point (32 percent). In addition, government programs use information systems across the program delivery chain to advance implementation on the ground and support overall program management (figure 4.3, panel a).

Digital technology is utilized in 85 percent of all government-led programs surveyed.[12] Data digitization increases transparency and accountability in service

FIGURE 4.2 **Percentage of Government-Led Programs Where the Lead Government Agency Plays Selected Roles**

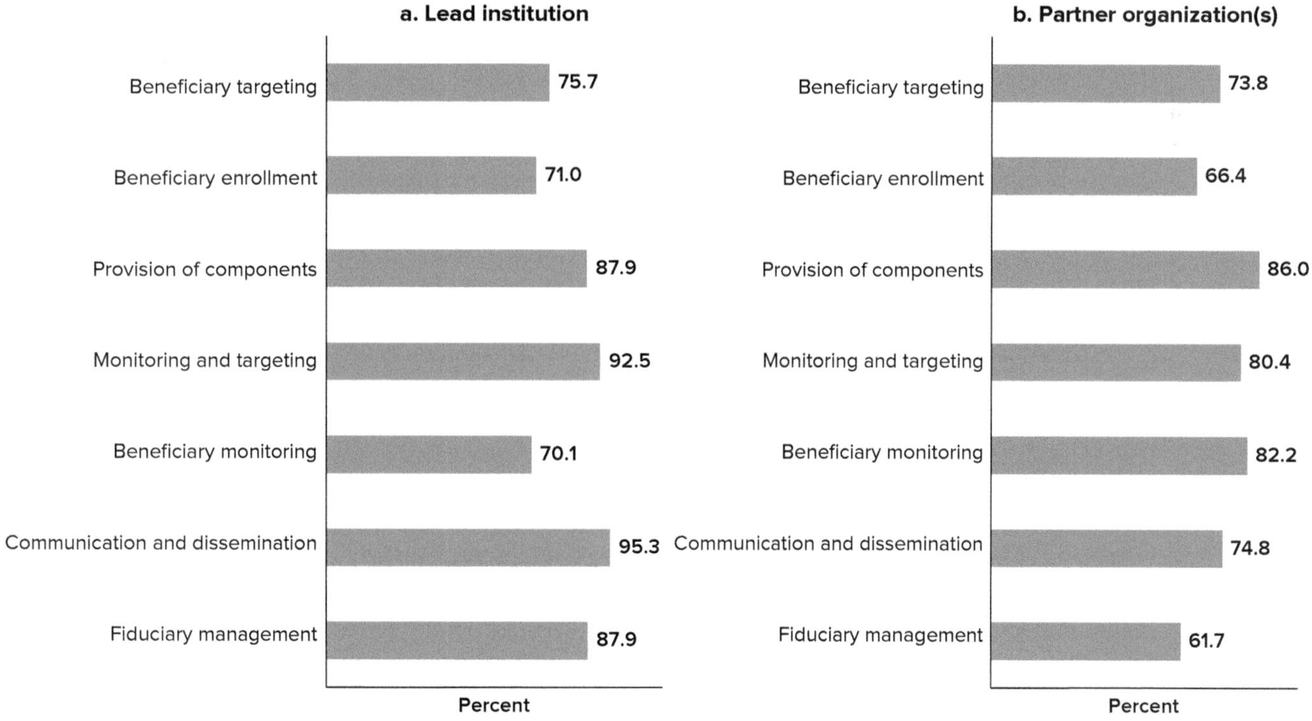

a. Lead institution

Role	Percent
Beneficiary targeting	75.7
Beneficiary enrollment	71.0
Provision of components	87.9
Monitoring and targeting	92.5
Beneficiary monitoring	70.1
Communication and dissemination	95.3
Fiduciary management	87.9

b. Partner organization(s)

Role	Percent
Beneficiary targeting	73.8
Beneficiary enrollment	66.4
Provision of components	86.0
Monitoring and targeting	80.4
Beneficiary monitoring	82.2
Communication and dissemination	74.8
Fiduciary management	61.7

Source: Partnership for Economic Inclusion, World Bank.

Note: Percentage of all government-led programs (N = 107). Both the lead government agency and other partners can play the same role in the same program.

FIGURE 4.3 **Digital Technology: Percentage of Government-Led Programs Using Digital Technology for Program Management and Delivery**

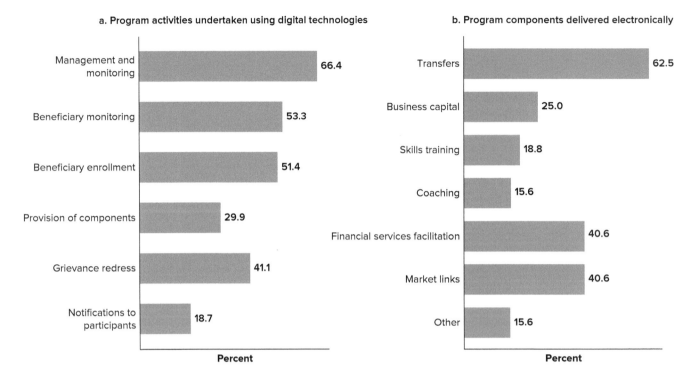

Source: Partnership for Economic Inclusion, World Bank.

Note: Panel a shows percentages of all government-led programs (N = 107). Panel b shows percentages of government-led programs providing components digitally (N = 32). Multiple responses were possible.

delivery and makes data-driven decision-making possible for governments. Several programs expressed the need for robust and responsive market information systems, including the Mozambique Social Protection Project, Nigeria Youth Employment and Social Support Operation, and the Mexico Social Protection System Project. Regionally, the use of digital technology is immensely popular in South Asia and is almost equally as important in Latin America and the Caribbean and Sub-Saharan Africa.

Government complementary programs are more likely than single interventions, among those surveyed, to leverage digital technologies for overall program management and monitoring (77 percent and 63 percent, respectively). Information systems also facilitate information exchange and coordinated delivery across government agencies and nongovernment implementing partners. This is vitally important for economic inclusion programs that combine multiple interventions. However, the use of digital technologies also poses new challenges in terms of building capacity, integrating information systems, and ensuring data protection.

Apart from aiding management and monitoring, digital technology plays a growing role in the direct delivery of services. Thirty percent of government-led programs use digital technology to deliver at least one intervention, such as electronic payments, digital financial services, e-coaching, and e-training (see figure 4.3, panel b). With the exception of skills training, government programs use digital technologies at higher rates than nongovernment programs, especially in delivering transfers or financial support, access to savings, and market information.

The rapid diffusion of new mobile and internet technologies also presents an opportunity to utilize technological innovations to reach beneficiaries. However, digital divides may remain across location, income groups, gender, and age; economic inclusion beneficiaries are less likely to be connected or familiar with digital interfaces. The use of technology needs to be balanced with the need to reach those offline.

Operations: Leveraging Community Structures for Program Delivery

Seventy-three percent of government-led programs included in the survey utilize community structures, including local governance groups (65 percent), formalized producer organizations (53 percent), and informal community savings and credit groups (39 percent). Community structures may be engaged in program delivery, including for training, coaching, and savings facilitation (see figure 4.4). Whether the economic inclusion programs are primarily at the household or individual level, community mobilization components allow programs to build agency and to support program implementation. Engaging the community in a program's implementation can help generate change at the community level. By creating opportunities for social interaction, programs build social capital and influence attitudes and behaviors across social and economic domains. This potentially can generate spillover effects for the broader community, amplifying and sustaining program impact. When the poor have limited social networks to start with, interventions that support the formation of peer groups, profitable social bonds, and cooperative arrangements can yield concrete economic returns (Macours and Vakis 2014; Blattman et al. 2016).

Eighty-six percent of government programs that leverage community structures also support the development of these community platforms, either by developing new structures or strengthening existing ones. Government programs that support the development of producer organizations in their efforts to integrate participants with markets are more likely to leverage community structures than programs that do not (94 percent versus 68 percent). For example, JEEViKA relies on a large cadre of community members trained to support programming efforts. These grassroots women leaders serve as paraprofessionals, resource persons, and functionaries trained in the areas of institutional capacity building, community mobilizing, bookkeeping, and providing links with commercial banks and livelihood support services.[13]

FIGURE 4.4 **Percentage of Program Components Implemented through Community Groups or Structures**

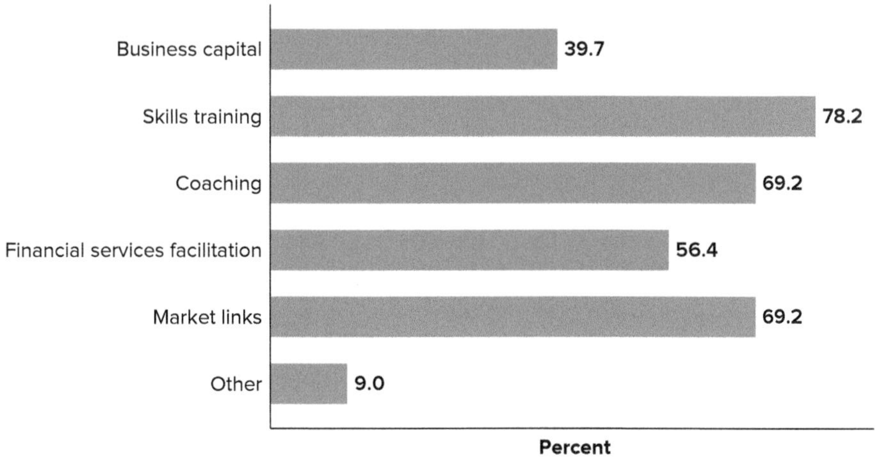

Source: Partnership for Economic Inclusion, World Bank.

Note: Percentage of government programs leveraging community structures (N = 78).

Village organizations enable JEEViKA to extend a host of livelihood supports, including grants to support farmer producer groups mobilized across self-help groups, community-level poultry units, and greenhouses. They also enable initiatives to promote community health; water access, sanitation, and hygiene (WASH) practices; and a host of other services (see case study 2). In Peru, Haku Wiñay is implemented with the support of *executing nuclei*—groups of 80 to 100 rural households. The nuclei have communal legitimacy because they are integrated with and directed by members of the community (see case study 4).

Future Directions

Many government-led economic inclusion programs are at a nascent stage of implementation and must refine their policies and strategies in order to scale up. Scaling up entails not just a simple increase in coverage but a flexible process by which governments develop economic inclusion programs along programmatic and institutional priorities. There are multiple dimensions to consider in order to reach scale; understanding this can dramatically increase the number of people served.

The number of participants served will grow as national economic inclusion programs scale up, but they will eventually plateau, because the programs are designed to serve a subset of the population. These programs are only a part of a wider set of a government policy and underpin a push toward comprehensive and universal social protection. Despite the growth in economic inclusion programming by governments, the scale of these programs is still relatively small compared to need. At present, the PEI survey shows over 50 percent of existing government-led programs have the potential to cover 5 percent to 10 percent of the extreme poor.

Coordination across ministries is necessary to link complementary programs. Complementarities and convergences help single-ministry programs to achieve economies of scale in implementation and strengthen policy coherence. Bundling interventions requires significant administrative capacity, and most programs that have expanded in size and scope have also expanded their organizational capacity. Programmatic adaptations are typically accompanied by some form of institutional adaptation. Depending on context, these include small-scale pilots or programs in government policy and financing, expanding organizational capacity (either in-house or through partnerships), and building delivery systems or leveraging existing systems.

Successful government-led interventions require strong local partnerships. Documentation of good practice in effective government-NGO collaboration can catalyze innovation and learning. Forty-one percent of government programs have expanded their organizational capacity over the past two years, for example, by increasing in-house capacity through partnerships with other institutions. Community structures may be engaged in program delivery, including for training, coaching, and savings facilitation.

Documentation of effective operational models and delivery systems in different contexts is required to facilitate effective design and coordination of economic inclusion programming. With a wide range of possible configurations of partners, programs, and structures under way, documentation and guidance is a gap. Documenting the programmatic and operational lessons from these government programs as they scale up will allow for an increased understanding of how to efficiently reach scale depending on context, administrative structure, capacity, and fiscal resources.

Leveraging existing digital infrastructure is critical to strengthen program management and increase efficiency. Digital solutions can help leapfrog some delivery constraints and increase cost-effectiveness, and they will grow in prominence as social distancing restrictions affect training and coaching activities in the wake of the COVID-19 crisis. Thirty percent of government-led programs provide access to program components through digital platforms, but digital divides still remain across location, income groups, gender, and age.

Market and value chain links can increase productivity of livelihood activities and bolster program sustainability. Mesolevel links will help alleviate difficult access to markets, infrastructure, and production inputs, and the potential for increased private sector engagement is high. Moving forward it will be important to understand how L&J interventions can be further scaled up, reducing the barriers for very poor and vulnerable people to enter job markets. Community-based development approaches and other sectoral interventions (such as agricultural development programs) might also provide opportunities to foster synergies among poverty reduction programs.

Notes

1. For the purposes of this chapter, all descriptions and figures related to economic inclusion programs refer to those programs included in the Partnership for Economic Inclusion (PEI) Landscape Survey 2020, or a subset of those programs, if so indicated.
2. Adapted from Uvin 1995, cited in Hartmann and Linn 2008.
3. Beneficiary data are based on 94 of the 106 government-led programs in 53 countries. Twelve programs did not report beneficiary numbers. The analysis of program coverage excludes data from JEEViKA, which is an outlier program in the overall sample.
4. This report identifies three entry points: social safety nets, livelihoods and jobs, and financial inclusion. These are the foundational interventions on which economic inclusion programs are built.
5. This excludes data from JEEViKA, which is an outlier program in the overall sample.
6. The Multidimensional Poverty Index measures the prevalence of poverty based on indicators that go beyond monetary metrics and span three dimensions: health, education, and standard of living. The Multidimensional Poverty Index is developed by the Oxford Poverty and Human Development Initiative at the University of Oxford.
7. The coverage analysis is based on 95 of the 107 government-led programs in 53 countries. Twelve programs did not report beneficiary numbers.
8. This is based on 217 out of the 219 surveyed programs that provided data on the level and the type of organization financing the economic inclusion program.
9. Much of the World Bank financing is in the form of loans to governments, thus this figure also includes funding that will ultimately be provided to the beneficiaries by the recipient governments. The World Bank is made up of the International Bank for Reconstruction and Development (IBRD) and the International Development Association (IDA). These two institutions provide different types of lending instruments to countries based on income category. IBRD lends to governments of middle-income and creditworthy low-income countries. IDA provides interest-free loans—called credits—and grants to governments of the poorest countries. On occasion, countries may be eligible to receive financing from both lending sources, called blended finance. Of World Bank–financed economic inclusion programs, 57 percent are IDA, 29 percent are IBRD, and 12 percent are blended. The remaining 2 percent of programs are in locations that do not fit into a lending category: West Bank and Gaza, Cyprus, and Sint Maarten (Dutch part).
10. The Brasil Sem Miséria strategy was discontinued following the impeachment of President Dilma Rousseff in 2016.
11. The survey asked programs to indicate which organizations, apart from the lead organization, perform the main roles. There were initially significant errors and inconsistencies in how programs responded to these questions. While the Partnership for Economic Inclusion management team followed up with programs to clarify some of these issues, this section presents broad trends rather than actual percentages, as these may not accurately represent the extent to which different organizations play the various roles captured through the survey.

12. The survey asked programs to indicate the activities undertaken using digital technologies. This figure represents the percentage of programs that use digital technologies for any program activity.

13. As of 2019, community institutions were staffed by more than 120,000 trained community professionals and resource persons in cadres of specialized staff, all from the local area.

References

Beegle, Kathleen G., Aline Coudouel, Monsalve Montiel, and Emma Mercedes. 2018. *Realizing the Full Potential of Social Safety Nets in Africa*. Washington, DC: World Bank.

Blattman, Christopher, Eric P. Green, Julian Jamison, M. Christian Lehmann, and Jeannie Annan. 2016. "The Returns to Microenterprise Support among the Ultrapoor: A Field Experiment in Postwar Uganda." *American Economic Journal: Applied Economics* 8 (2): 35–64.

Carter B., A. Joshi, and M. Remme. 2018. *Scaling Up Inclusive Approaches for Marginalised and Vulnerable People*. K4D Emerging Issues Report. Brighton, UK: Institute of Development Studies.

Cooley, Larry, and Johannes F. Linn. 2014. *Taking Innovations to Scale: Methods, Applications and Lessons*. Washington, DC: Results for Development Institute.

de Montesquiou, Aude, and Tony Sheldon. 2018. *From Extreme Poverty to Sustainable Livelihoods: A Technical Guide to the Graduation Approach*. 2nd ed. Washington, DC: PEI.

FAO (Food and Agriculture Organization of the United Nations). 2018. "FAO and Cash +: How to Maximize the Impacts of Cash Transfers." FAO, Rome.

GIZ (Deutsche Gesellschaft für Internationale Zusammenarbeit). 2017. *Linking Social Protection with Productive Inclusion: Innovative Approaches and Enabling Factors for Inter-Sectoral Coordination*. Bonn: GIZ.

Hartmann, Arntraud, and Johannes Linn. 2008. "Scaling Up: A Framework and Lessons for Development Effectiveness from Literature and Practice." *SSRN Electronic Journal*. doi:10.2139/ssrn.1301625.

Lavers, Tom. 2016. "*Understanding Elite Commitment to Social Protection: Rwanda's Vision 2020 Umurenge Programme*." WIDER Working Paper 093, World Institute for Development Economic Research, Helsinki.

Macours, Karen, and Renos Vakis. 2014. "Changing Households' Investment Behaviour through Social Interactions with Local Leaders: Evidence from a Randomised Transfer Programme." *Economic Journal* 124 (576): 607–33. doi:10.1111/ecoj.12145.

Maldonado, Jorge H., Rocio Moreno-Sánchez, J. A. Gómez, and V. L. Jurado, eds. 2016. *Protection, Production, Promotion: Exploring Synergies between Social Protection and Productive Development in Latin America*. Bogotá: Universidad de los Andes.

Milazzo, Annamaria, and Margaret Grosh. 2008. "Social Safety Nets in World Bank Lending and Analytical Work: FY2002–2007." Social Protection Discussion Paper SP 0810, World Bank, Washington, DC. http://documents.worldbank.org/curated/en/920421468155739339/Social-safety-nets-in-World-Bank-lending-and-analytical-work-FY2002-2007.

Slater, R., S. Wiggins, L. Harman, M. Ulrichs, L. Scott, M. Knowles, P. Pozarny, and G. Calcagnini. 2016. *Strengthening Coherence between Agriculture and Social Protection: Synthesis of Seven Country Case Studies*. Rome: FAO.

Soares, Fabio Veras, Marco Knowles, Silvio Daidone, and Nyasha Tirivayi. 2017. *Combined Effects and Synergies between Agricultural and Social Protection Interventions: What Is the Evidence So Far?* Rome: FAO.

Tirivayi, N., M. Knowles, and B. Davis. 2013. *The Interaction between Social Protection and Agriculture: A Review of Evidence.* Rome: FAO.

Uvin, P. 1995. "Fighting Hunger at the Grassroots: Paths to Scaling Up." *World Development* 23 (6): 927–39.

World Bank. 2008. "Brazil: Acre Social and Economic Inclusion and Sustainable Development Project." World Bank, Washington, DC. http://documents.worldbank .org/curated/en/871561468021550743/Brazil-Acre-Social-and-Economic-Inclusion -and-Sustainable-Development-Project.

World Bank. 2015. "Côte d'Ivoire: Productive Social Safety Net Project." World Bank, Washington, DC. http://documents.worldbank.org/curated/en/902201468000929877 /Cote-d-Ivoire-Productive-Social-Safety-Net-Project.

Linking Economic Inclusion and Markets for the Poorest

While economic inclusion programs typically seek to address the multiple constraints that poor households confront, it is increasingly important for these programs to address constraints beyond the household. These include underlying factors that constrain opportunities for local economic growth, such as proximity to physical markets, regional market depth, access to connective infrastructure, and production. Strengthening links to markets for inputs, labor, goods, and services is important to alleviate spatial-based poverty and to increase income-generating opportunities for the extreme poor and vulnerable. Although this is an area of considerable interest, it is a relatively new frontier for many programs featured in this review.

As many of the world's extreme poor live in isolated, rural localities where access to markets is limited, there is an immediate interest in understanding rural market dynamics and strategies to link households to local, regional, and international markets. A vibrant rural sector requires not only that stakeholders support productive markets but also that they prioritize small rural producers, resilience building, and the enhancement of the economic and productive capacity of the rural poor (FAO 2017). Such efforts entail working with key market players to improve interaction and negotiation with informal workers, producers, and entrepreneurs. Furthermore, to develop a thriving rural sector, it is important to address the challenges and opportunities posed by migration and rural development. Rural households and communities can maximize the benefits of migration by enhancing and diversifying rural employment opportunities, especially for women and youths; helping the poor to better manage risks; and leveraging remittances for investments in the rural sector.

While economic inclusion programs have a strong rural focus, the importance of urban market links is coming into focus. Due to limited labor demand and rising informality in rural areas, there has been an increase in migration to urban centers, presenting the poorest with both opportunities and challenges. By 2045, the number of people living in cities worldwide will increase 1.5 times, to 6 billion. Demand for food will grow by an estimated 70 percent from 2010 to 2050, and 83 percent of that growth is expected to be in urban markets (World Bank 2019). In urban areas, it is especially important to look beyond household-level constraints and link economic inclusion interventions with economic sectors and processes that present economic growth opportunities. This is especially true among urban agricultural markets, where opportunities are emerging to increase off-the-farm employment in agribusiness.

Emerging Practices

Given that training and coaching play critical roles in economic inclusion programs, these initiatives are well positioned to empower the beneficiaries of them to engage in local markets, manage risks, and build assets. Because these programs are designed to support people facing high levels of vulnerability, economic inclusion interventions often aim to strengthen resilience. Such efforts include helping households stabilize consumption and income, develop insurance mechanisms, and protect key assets. For those people with relativity low levels of vulnerability, economic inclusion interventions aim to promote opportunity, either through income expansion or asset growth.

Economic inclusion programs that enhance market access follow a mix of market integration strategies (appendix E). The Partnership for Economic Inclusion (PEI) Landscape Survey 2020 reveals that programs facilitate access to markets by developing producer organizations (51 percent) and provide links to service providers (67 percent) and agricultural extension services (65 percent). In addition, as further evidenced in the 2020 survey, programs facilitate access to improved inputs (65 percent), technology (58 percent), and capital (39 percent). Several key interventions that address the considerable challenges faced in linking extremely poor and vulnerable households to markets are outlined below. Each intervention provides activities that can strengthen both resilience and opportunity.

Linking the extreme poor to cooperatives and producer networks

Poor rural producers very often lack the capacity, or the level of organization needed, to access formal markets in a structured way. Operating as part of a group (for example, producer alliances, self-help groups, farmer groups, and so forth) can help overcome these constraints and enable smallholder farmers to gain access to goods and services previously unavailable. For example, producer alliances and cooperatives are common tools for improving the knowledge and skills of their members in a range of activities as well as improving access to information, helping members access lump sums of cash through savings and/or credit, and linking producers to wider commercial networks. Producers operating in groups have more negotiating power and access to producer-to-producer links that involve longer-term cooperative arrangements among firms that are built on interdependence, trust, and resource pooling to jointly accomplish common goals (USAID, FHI 360, and World Vision 2017). In Argentina, for example, the Socio-Economic Inclusion in Rural Areas Project promotes stronger formal group organization by supporting (1) small family producers to increase their organizational capacity and reach a minimum level of formalization and (2) groups of small family producers with preexisting market links that could be further developed as sustainable formal links through productive alliances. Although community networks are likely weaker in urban contexts, some programs have shown success working in urban centers and with urban communities (for example, in Bangladesh, Ethiopia, Sierra Leone, and Uganda).

Public works development

Public works programs are important avenues for income support and short-term employment and are featured across different economic inclusion programs documented in the survey. Embedded in economic inclusion programs, public works programs have the potential to address different priorities, including temporary employment and the development of community infrastructure. Better community infrastructure (for example, roads and irrigation systems) can increase market output, lower transaction costs, and improve market access, thereby raising the profitability of small producers and enterprises. Furthermore, the additional income from public works programs enables households to accumulate savings, which can ultimately be used for more productive investments. Income transfers that are regular and predictable preform an insurance role, thus altering participants' risk management capacity and willingness to take risks (Gehrke and Hartwig 2015). While the impacts of public works programs are heavily debated and their operation requires a great deal of capacity, they provide an avenue for linking household and community aspects of development. In Uganda, the Third Northern Uganda Social Action Fund aims to provide effective income support through labor-intensive public works (LIPWs) and livelihood investment support to build the resilience of poor and vulnerable rural households. The LIPWs include various labor-intensive subprojects to create community assets, including roads, other paved areas, and market shelters, to increase the accessibility of markets and social services. In the urban context, the Urban Youth Employment Project for Papua New Guinea incorporates an LIPW component that provides youth with temporary employment opportunities focused on simple road maintenance, cleaning, and environmental protection activities, including vegetation control and drain cleaning.

Value chain development

Value chain development involves strengthening the product-to-market systems. Value chains contain multiple stages, from preparation and distribution of primary inputs to primary production, various processing steps, packaging, distribution, marketing, retail, and ultimately disposal of the product. The objective of value chain programming is to increase incentives for the links to improve performance, productivity, and trade and, ultimately, provide poverty alleviation and economic opportunities for poor producers. Value chain and economic inclusion interventions go hand in hand, and their symbiosis can help create sustainability. Demand-side interventions stimulate production, which generates job and earning opportunities for the workforce, while supply-side interventions provide the labor that firms and other actors in the value chain require, Box S3.1 illustrates an example.

BOX S3.1 **Economic Inclusion in the Rice Value Chain: A Pilot Project in Côte d'Ivoire**

Economic opportunities for a large and diverse population in the agricultural sector can be created through on- and off-the-farm input provision, mechanization services, transport, processing, and distribution. The Jobs Group of the World Bank, in partnership with the Côte d'Ivoire Productive Social Safety Net (PSSN) Project, is piloting economic inclusion in value chains through rice value chains.

PSSN provides beneficiaries quarterly cash transfers and offers economic inclusion activities, including formation of savings groups, entrepreneurship training, the provision of small business grants, and coaching. For the pilot, smallholder farmers, small- to medium-sized mills, and a national microfinance institution are collaborating under an agreement: smallholders receive inputs on credit from the financial institution based on having a contract with the mill to deliver a specified amount of rice of a certain quality and at a certain price at harvest. The mill also receives working capital credit from the microfinance institution to buy the rice at harvest and hires a liaison agent to provide basic extension services and maintain regular contact with farmers. The World Bank supports the platform by facilitating exchange between partners in different localities through local and national coordinators. It also provides technical assistance to mills and pays for an agricultural liaison officer in the microfinance institution to reduce transaction costs.

BOX S3.2   **Strengthening Environmental and Natural Resource Links**

Economic inclusion programs that protect and ensure the sustainable management of natural resources not only address pressing environmental concerns but also help strengthen both resilience and opportunity. Often, these programs also build the capacity of multiple stakeholders (including governments, households, communities, and the private sector) to improve planning for more sustainable use of natural resources in different geographic environments.

A number of these programs support investments in infrastructure and technology to spur the development of sectors that have the potential to create environmental as well as economic value, for example, marine fishing and agroforestry. Many programs also support the development of value chains that are protective of the environment and that create alternative income-generating opportunities for resource-dependent communities, for example, value chains of nontimber forest products, such as medicinal plants, bamboo, and honey production. As an example, the Ethiopia Resilient Landscapes and Livelihoods Project (RLLP) aims to improve climate resilience and land productivity and increase access to diversified livelihood activities in selected rural watersheds. It is government-led and relies on local community structures for program delivery. Building on lessons learned through implementation of the World Bank's Sustainable Land Management Project, the RLLP will complement core investments in watershed restoration with a set of associated activities supporting sustainable livelihoods. Activities include funding community-level green infrastructure, introducing climate-smart agriculture (CSA), improving land tenure, and encouraging new income-generating activities through community groups and links to value chains.

Natural resource management

The risk of climate change and other environmental shocks creates barriers to market access for the extreme poor. The integration of climate and disaster risk considerations in the planning and design of economic inclusion programs will help prevent poor and vulnerable households from falling deeper in poverty, reduce their overall exposure to potential risk, and contribute to long-term adaptation to climate change. Sustainable natural resource management interventions can provide much-needed employment opportunities for vulnerable populations as well as maintain and enhance productivity of households' and communities' agricultural, forestry, and fisheries assets. Communities can receive income support through land rehabilitation and forest work schemes. In addition, landscape, coastal, and fisheries programs can be scaled up further to create jobs and support livelihoods and market access. Activities include watershed and landscape management, weather-based index insurance, cash transfers conditioned on the adoption of climate-smart agriculture (CSA), and improved climate-related knowledge provision through extension services (World Bank 2015). See box S3.2 for more on the role of the environment and natural resources in economic inclusion.

Challenges in Linking to Markets

Barriers to market links need to be identified and addressed to successfully integrate beneficiaries. Economic inclusion programs have an advantage as they already address multiple constraints across the individual, household, community, local economy, and institutional levels. Going further, careful analysis of the structures of informality—access to finance, the regulatory regime, cultural context, gender dimensions, and so forth—will be critical.

Across the individual, household, and community levels, the extreme poor face many constraints to participating in markets. Some of these include limited capacity and resources, small-scale production, strong risk aversion, limited mobility, informal rules and norms, limited knowledge of markets, poor management skills, and lack of empowerment. Extremely poor women face added constraints in interacting in markets, including the risk of physical, sexual, and other gender-based violence; inadequate legal protection or enforcement of existing laws; traditional gender roles and expectations; and lack of control over resources (in particular, property) (USAID, FHI 360, and World Vision 2017). In mitigating such constraints, in Peru, Haku Wiñay encourages the development of inclusive business groups consisting of approximately a dozen participants who come together for common productive activities, the commercialization of agricultural products, or both. Groups receive special training and support to launch their activities—usually in textiles and ceramic crafts, baking and gastronomy, rural tourism, dairy products and byproducts, small animal rearing for sale, fish farming, and cattle fattening.

At the local economy level, information asymmetries prevail, leading to high transaction costs. Improving market productivity and earnings requires an in-depth understanding of the constraints and opportunities in a market system. Market assessments provide programs with insight on the market viability of specific interventions as well as the competitive landscape for beneficiaries (CGAP 2012). The Cash Transfer and Economic Inclusion Program in Egypt has launched a rapid market assessment to identify demand- and supply-side constraints as well as available business opportunities. With this information and previous research, the Forsa program has begun to successfully map key sectors and economic activities, value chains, clusters, and partners for collaboration.

The institutional and policy environment is especially important in linking markets to the extreme poor. Multidimensional programs require careful coordination and coherence across ministries, at different levels of government, and among nongovernment partners. The lack of institutional clarity, roles, and responsibilities among ministries and local authorities may challenge the provision of market services, trading, certification, and revenue programs. Furthermore, coordination constraints among market actors (other enterprises, buyers, intermediaries, and sellers) limit access to high-value markets and service providers. Strong, mutually beneficial relationships among market actors facilitate the transfer of information, skills, and services. As an example, Haku Wiñay, either directly or in collaboration with municipalities, encourages small-scale opportunities for trade, such as weekly fairs or festivals targeting certain products, where participants sell their products in a less daunting environment than traditional markets.

Furthermore, government policies and regulations play a key role in shaping the market environment. An inappropriate policy and regulatory framework can lead to the distortion of market efficiency, increasing costs for participants and impeding the development of the market system. Furthermore, market systems respond to developments in the macroeconomy and can be subject to considerable macroeconomic volatility. Changes in exchange rates, real supply, and international monetary reserves can have severe impacts on commodity prices. The added level of insecurity in international and domestic markets can have severe consequences on local markets and small producers. Macroeconomic factors, including climate factors, should be considered for business cycle analysis and public risk management schemes for the stabilization of markets (de Winne and Peersman 2016).

Future Directions

Although market links are well documented in the literature, this is relatively new territory for economic inclusion programming. Economic inclusion programs provide a comprehensive strategy to address the multiple constraints that the extreme poor face in accessing productive markets. Linking economic inclusion programs to markets is complex and multilayered and requires a holistic view in analysis, implementation, and coordination efforts. Moving forward, it will be important to understand which constraints can be addressed in the context of economic inclusion programs and which will require greater coordination across the government policy space.

References

CGAP (Consultative Group to Assist the Poor). 2012. *Graduation Lessons Learned from Bandhan's Targeting the Hard Core Poor Program in Urban Settings.* Washington, DC: CGAP.

de Winne, Jasmien, and Gert Peersman. 2016. *Macroeconomic Effects of Disruptions in Global Food Commodity Markets: Evidence for the United States.* Munich: CESifo.

FAO (Food and Agriculture Organization of the United Nations). 2017. *Social Protection Framework: Promoting Rural Development for All.* Rome: FAO.

Gehrke, Esther, and Renate Hartwig. 2015. *How Can Public Works Programmes Create Sustainable Employment?* Bonn: Deutsches Institut für Entwicklungspolitik.

USAID, FHI 360, and World Vision. 2017 *Integrating Extremely Poor Producers into Markets Field Guide.* 4th ed. Durham, NC: FHI 360.

World Bank. 2015. "Future of Food: Shaping a Climate-Smart Global Food System." World Bank, Washington, DC.

World Bank. 2019. "Expanding Market Opportunities and Inclusive Private Sector Engagement in Agribusiness." World Bank, Washington, DC. https://www.worldbank.org/content/dam/Worldbank/document/Trade/CompSector_Agribusiness.pdf.

CHAPTER 5
An Assessment of Program Impacts

KEY MESSAGES

A review of evaluations of 80 programs in 37 countries shows that a broad range of economic inclusion programs have shown promising and potentially sustained impact on a wide range of outcomes. A bundled set of interventions shows greater impact on income, assets, and savings relative to stand-alone interventions.

The discussion on program impact needs to be rebalanced to reflect the shifting landscape from stand-alone nonprofit-led programs to government-led programs. The evidence from nonprofit-led programs is indicative of persistent impact, supporting the hypothesis that economic inclusion programming can potentially launch the extreme poor into an upward trajectory. Evidence on impact at scale is also cautiously positive. As government-led economic inclusion programs continue to be embedded in broader social policy, community spillover effects will become increasingly important, and beneficiaries will likely benefit from complementary programs or refresher interventions to sustain income growth.

Although there is a strong evidence base, it does not yet go far enough in addressing several ongoing debates in economic inclusion programming. A number of critical knowledge gaps constrain evidence-based program design and delivery.

FUTURE DIRECTIONS

The next wave of evaluations looks set to focus on government programs at scale and will help isolate the mechanisms of impact of economic inclusion programming across entry points and for different groups. This will have important operational implications for identifying cost-effective bundles of interventions and lessons on the effectiveness of different delivery models.

A critical learning agenda is emerging to help address evidence gaps. These include complementing impact evaluations with real-time operational research, program-monitoring assessments, and qualitative fieldwork to identify opportunities to enhance program performance.

There is a need for a more systematic evidence base, using comparable outcomes and indicators to conclusively establish the overall impact of the government-led economic inclusion programs at scale. In the coming years, a meta-analysis of the impact evidence will be an important contribution to the policy debate on the feasibility and sustainability of scaling up economic inclusion programming.

Introduction

Optimism about economic inclusion programming to improve income and resilience of the extreme poor is warranted. There is a large and growing body of research on the impact of these programs, especially those whose entry point is based on advancing livelihoods and jobs (L&J). The initial evidence base was driven primarily by programs led by nongovernmental organizations (NGOs). In particular, the evaluation of pilot projects modeled after BRAC's Targeting the Ultra Poor (TUP) program, conducted by the Ford Foundation and the Consultative Group to Assist the Poor (CGAP) in six countries, made a significant contribution to the evidence base in diverse contexts (Banerjee et al. 2015). Subsequently, the evidence base has broadened to include a number of government-led programs, whose evidence typically had not been considered in discussions of economic inclusion because it is often trapped in sectoral silos. In this review, evidence is synthesized from a range of sectors, covering evaluations of both NGO-led and government-led programs in the past decade. While the diversity in program design and in evaluations makes comparative analysis of impact challenging, this synthesis provides a resource on the state of knowledge on the impact of economic inclusion programming.[1]

However, the evidence presented here does not go far enough in addressing several ongoing debates in economic inclusion programming. This is an inevitable gap as the evidence catches up with country implementation. This chapter highlights critical gaps in understanding the mechanisms and drivers of impact, especially for large-scale programs with social safety nets (SSNs) and financial inclusion (FI) as entry points for different groups. The evaluations of NGO-led programs remain the first wave of knowledge, as they unpack the evidence and test alternative design and delivery modalities. Ideally, this should lead to another wave of learning and evaluation of government-led programs to conclusively establish whether these patterns are replicated at scale.

This chapter focuses on four efforts. First, it assesses the overall short-, medium-, and long-term impacts of economic inclusion programs across a variety of income and resilience indicators and highlights whether these impacts can be sustained at scale. This analysis is based on a review of impact evaluations. Second, the chapter assesses this evidence to examine two key features of economic inclusion programming: the state of our knowledge regarding the bundling of multiple interventions relative to stand-alone interventions and the observed heterogeneity of impacts across population groups. Third, the chapter draws on both impact evaluations and nonevaluative qualitative and operational research to identify key drivers of impact. Fourth, the chapter identifies key directions to filling critical knowledge gaps through the pipeline of upcoming research.

Review of the Impact Literature: Method, Sample, and Caveats

In this synthesis, we review impact evaluations of 80 economic inclusion programs in 37 countries (see figure 5.1). These programs were identified from a number of different sources, including the Partnership for Economic Inclusion (PEI) Landscape Surveys of 2018 and 2020, evaluations listed in online research databases, and in systematic reviews of economic inclusion programs (see appendix B for details). Three programs had only a qualitative evaluation; all others had at least one quantitative evaluation, either experimental (randomized controlled trial) or quasi-experimental.

The evaluated programs in this synthesis cut across diverse institutional arrangements, contexts, and program typologies. The evidence base is largely balanced with respect to the distribution across government-led and nongovernment-led programs, at

FIGURE 5.1 **Distribution of Reviewed Programs**

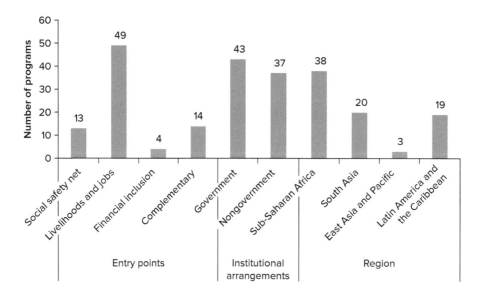

Source: Partnership for Economic Inclusion, World Bank.

Note: Complementary programs in the review typically link social safety nets with livelihood interventions to promote economic inclusion. Data labels refer to number of reviewed programs in each category.

least with respect to overall impact on primary outcomes. The evidence is also fairly representative of the distribution of economic inclusion programming across regions (see chapter 3), with the majority of evaluated programs in Sub-Saharan Africa (48 percent), followed by South Asia (25 percent) and Latin America and the Caribbean (24 percent). However, there is a considerable gap in the scope of available evidence with respect to evaluations of SSN-plus interventions (16 percent) relative to evaluations of L&J interventions (61 percent).[2] This seems surprising given that SSNs are among the most frequently evaluated social policy interventions in the world.[3] This gap exists because this review captures a much narrower set of evaluations of SSN-plus interventions, i.e., those featuring livelihood interventions that are bundled with regular cash transfers or public works programs. However, the complementary programs in the review typically link SSNs with livelihood interventions to promote economic inclusion.[4]

While this diversity is a valuable contribution of the report, it raises several challenges with respect to the comparability of evidence. Impact evaluations reflect the diversity in program design and context, such that outcomes, indicators, and estimates of impact size reported vary widely across studies (see box 5.1). As a result of this diversity, the following allowances have been made:

- Given the limited number of evaluations of SSN-plus programs, the evidence base and findings are presented across all three entry points (figure 5.2 and figure 5.3), rather than disaggregating by entry point. While a total of 107 studies for 80 programs were reviewed for the synthesis, the summary of overall impact findings reflects 97 quantitative impact evaluations for the 71 programs for which complete information on impact estimates from the studies could be obtained.

- There is considerable variation in the precise indicators reported, limiting the possibility of reporting precise ranges of impact sizes. There is also a strong publication bias, with studies reporting positive results on what works, thus presenting an overly positive picture of the evidence. In this synthesis, the focus is on summarizing the direction of impact (when significant to at least the 10 percent level).

BOX 5.1   Gaps in the Evidence and Challenges in Making Comparative Statements

Uneven coverage of different program entry points. The single programs reviewed are predominantly those addressing livelihoods and jobs (L&J), as evidence for social safety net (SSN) programs and financial inclusion (FI) programs is low. The evidence base on complementary programs is mostly available for Latin America and the Caribbean. Although complementary programs are also more common than single programs in East Asia and the Pacific, no evaluations are yet available.

Lack of comparability across evaluations. Studies differ widely with respect to the outcomes and indicators examined and estimates of treatment effects (the size of the impact). The choices are rational, based on the differing program objectives, research priorities, and data availability, but the variation limits our ability to provide an estimated range of effect size. There are also information gaps in some evaluations. While a total of 107 studies (including 4 qualitative evaluations) for 80 programs were reviewed for this synthesis, the summary of findings reflects 97 quantitative impact evaluations for 71 programs for which complete information on impact estimates from the studies could be obtained.

Positive bias. There is a strong publication bias, that is, publicly available studies tend to emphasize results on what works, presenting an overly positive picture of the evidence. We try to mitigate against this risk by including a large number of third-party evaluations and experimental randomized controlled trials (RCTs) (which may be expected to be less susceptible to positive bias relative to retrospective evaluations as the control group is predefined). We would expect publication bias to be stronger for pilot projects and nongovernment-led programs (where financing may depend on results), but most of these evaluations are RCTs. A promising development is that the research pipeline is strong, and many planned evaluations are registered, with researchers posting details of the design, methodology, and hypothesis before starting data collection.

Limited evidence on long-term impact. Program duration varies across programs as does the timing of impact evaluations. The overwhelming majority of programs provide time-bound interventions (of one to three years on average). There are some exceptions: for example, in SSN-plus programs, the SSN is typically open-ended while the "plus" components are time bound. For comparability, we define *short-term* impact as measured immediately after a program concludes, typically one to two years after program start (i.e., when beneficiaries enroll in the program). *Medium term* is defined as impact measured three to four years after program start, and *long term* as more than four years after program start. Evaluations of long-term impact are limited to only three programs: (1) Bangladesh (Targeting the Ultra Poor, different phases); (2) Uganda (Youth Opportunity Program, YOP; Women's Income-Generating Support, WINGS); and (3) India (Targeting the Hard-Core Poor program, West Bengal); as well as an experiment in Ethiopia. This chapter focuses primarily on short- and medium-term impacts, where there is more evidence, and comments on possible directions of long-term impact for this small subset of programs.

Challenges in generalizing and unpacking evidence. Not all studies provide sufficient details on the context in which the program operates. This has implications for the extent to which the evidence from specific (often small-scale) programs and contexts can be generalized to other contexts, other population groups, or at scale (Pritchett and Sandefur 2013). With a few exceptions, most evaluations are not designed to isolate channels of impact. We speculate on the drivers of impact by drawing on nonevaluative qualitative and operational research (see appendix B for a bibliography).

FIGURE 5.2 **Distribution of Studies Reporting on Specific Outcomes, by Lead Agency**

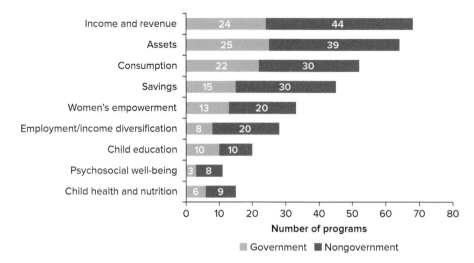

Source: See appendix B for the detailed bibliography.

Note: This summary reflects 97 quantitative impact evaluations for 71 programs for which complete information could be obtained.

FIGURE 5.3 **Summary of Evidence on Overall Impact**

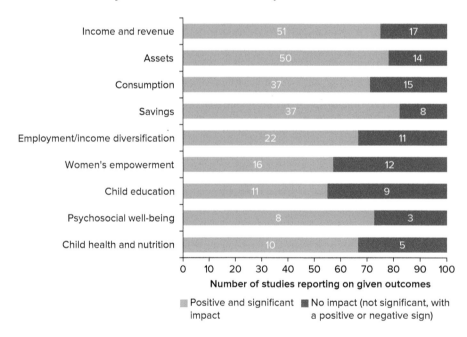

Sources: See appendix B and its bibliography for a summary of the reviewed programs and studies. This summary reflects 97 quantitative impact evaluations for 71 programs for which complete information from the studies could be obtained.

Note: In each outcome, the count of evaluations includes those that reported at least one indicator with a positive impact that was significant at the 10 percent level or higher or that reported no impact (i.e., none of the indicators in the outcome category were significant even at the 10 percent level, regardless of sign). None of the evaluations reported a significant negative impact for all indicators in the outcome category, although many nonsignificant impacts were negative in sign. If an evaluation reported more than one indicator in the broad outcome, the indicator at the highest level of aggregation was used (e.g., total asset index rather than the number of goats or total household consumption rather than household food consumption).

Despite these caveats, the evidence base is strong for the primary outcomes of economic inclusion programming: enhancing income and assets. Other commonly reported outcomes relate to savings and consumption. A large number of studies also report on employment (including on diversification of income sources) and women's empowerment outcomes. Only a few studies report on child outcomes (health, nutrition, or education) or on psychosocial well-being. The evidence base is smaller for government-led programs relative to nongovernment-led programs, particularly on psychosocial indicators of well-being, women's empowerment, and savings.

In coming years, coordinated evaluation agendas hold the promise of establishing a more comparable body of evidence as well a deeper understanding of the channels of impact. This chapter draws on two such recently concluded research agendas (Banerjee et al. 2015; Maldonado et al. 2016). In the near future, a meta-analysis would be feasible, with the inclusion of comparable evidence from multicountry evaluations by, for example, the Food and Agriculture Organization of the United Nations (FAO 2018; Soares et al. 2018), Innovations for Poverty Action and the World Bank (Bossuroy et al. 2019), and the World Food Programme and the World Bank. In addition, over the next two years, a rich research pipeline of program-specific evaluations, including of SSN-plus interventions, will emerge that responds to the critical knowledge gaps identified in this chapter (see appendix B for details).[5]

Evidence of Overall Impact

A broad range of economic inclusion programs have shown promising—and potentially sustained—impact on a wide range of outcomes. Figure 5.3 presents a summary of the direction of impact across reviewed studies.[6] Economic inclusion programs have helped participants invest in productive assets and to save, earn, and consume more than they could have without these programs. These absolute gains are typically quite small in size but often represent large increases for the poorest, given their low baseline values. Most programs increase household resilience to shocks by diversifying livelihoods and sources of income, facilitating savings and access to affordable credit, and building social networks. Many programs empower women by enhancing economic opportunities and social status (see spotlight 1). Evidence of impact on child well-being in participating households is more limited but suggests these programs may increase investments in human capital.

Short-Term Impact

Enhancing incomes and assets

By enabling more effective risk management, most programs (78 percent) enable participants to invest in productive assets. Programs with a business financial support element (such as an asset transfer or lump-sum cash grant) mitigate against the uncertainty of asset loss, while those with an SSN element (such as a regular cash transfer or public works) provide certainty and ease liquidity constraints, allowing poor households to maintain their investments. In programs with an asset transfer or cash grant element, these impacts are generally larger than the value of the initial transfer, suggesting that households have been able to increase, and often diversify, their asset holdings, typically their livestock. This suggests this is not merely a program effect. However, estimates of the size of increase vary widely.[7]

Many programs (82 percent) enable beneficiaries to save and reduce indebtedness, although this does not always translate into increased access to formal sources of finance. Not surprisingly, this impact is more common for programs that encourage the formation of savings groups, suggesting at least some of this may be a program effect. For instance, Tanzania's Productive Social Safety Net (PSSN) increased the share of participating households that were saving by 3.9 percentage points, representing an increase of 29 percent relative to nonparticipating households. This impact was likely due to the formation of savings groups. However, there is some evidence from Kenya's Rural Entrepreneur Access Program (REAP) that shifts in saving behavior occur even before the introduction of such groups and that impacts persist after the program ends (Gobin, Santos, and Toth 2016). There is also the added benefit of reduced indebtedness to high-interest informal lenders. In India, community-driven livelihood programs such as Indira Kranti Pratham and JEEViKA reduced debt-servicing costs and increased access to low-cost credit (Prennushi and Gupta 2014; Deininger and Liu 2013; Hoffmann et al. 2017). In a similar program, India's National Rural Livelihood Mission (NRLM), an additional 2.5 years of membership in self-help groups increased total household savings by 28 percent and reduced the share of informal loans in total debt by 20 percent over baseline values (Kochar et al. 2020).

Economic inclusion programs broaden opportunities for poor households, enabling them to diversify incomes as household members shift from casual wage employment to farm and nonfarm self-employment. Among the programs reporting on employment outcomes, 67 percent reported a significant impact on the time participants spent working or a shift from wage to self-employment. Because most poor people are typically employed as casual wage workers in precarious, seasonal, and sometimes hazardous work, economic inclusion programs provide an opportunity to shift to more productive self-employment in farm or nonfarm activities. For women, this is often a significant occupational transformation.[8] For labor-unconstrained households, this also offers an opportunity to diversify household income, with some members continuing as wage workers while others start subsistence businesses, typically in livestock rearing, fisheries, and petty trade. While SSN programs tend to emphasize income diversification for resilience, L&J programs tend to do so for sustained income growth.

In most cases, the increased investment in productive assets and the shift in employment patterns translates into higher income. Most programs (75 percent of those reporting on this outcome) increased overall household or per capita incomes.[9] The four SSN programs reporting an impact on income found a significant positive impact. For most L&J programs, this increased income effect persisted for one or two years after participants exited the program. In almost all cases, these improvements were driven by increased income from livestock or nonfarm petty trade that persisted for one or two years after program exit. In addition, programs often encourage adoption of good business practices, with these translating into income growth in some cases (such as youth in Uganda and Ethiopia and men in Sri Lanka) but not in others (such as women in Sri Lanka) (Blattman, Dercon, and Franklin 2019; Blattman, Fiala, and Martinez 2014; de Mel, McKenzie, and Woodruff 2012).

Although absolute gains tend to be small, even small increases can be meaningful, given low baseline values. Estimates of effect sizes vary considerably, but most participants in economic inclusion programs tend to experience small absolute gains. In Bangladesh, participants (all women) in phase 1 of TUP increased their total annual earnings by only $23 two years after program completion (and $26 four years after program completion), but this small amount represented a 34 percent increase two years after program completion (and 38 percent four years after) over their preprogram earnings (Bandiera et al. 2013). There are, however, some programs that have had larger impacts. In Afghanistan, participants in the TUP program increased their total monthly household income and revenues from productive activities by approximately $19 relative to nonparticipants (a 23 percent increase) (Bedoya et al. 2019). In Uganda, participants in the Youth Opportunity Program (YOP) increased their monthly cash earnings by approximately $8.50 (41 percent) relative to nonparticipants, while participants in the Women's Income-Generating Support (WINGS) program experienced an increase of approximately $5.19 (66 percent) relative to nonparticipants (Blattman, Fiala, and Martinez 2014; Blattman et al. 2016).

Improving household welfare and building resilience

Economic inclusion programs increase overall welfare in both monetary and nonmonetary dimensions. Many economic inclusion programs (71 percent of those reporting on consumption outcomes) protect poor households against destitution, enabling them to cover their basic needs, maintain consumption levels, and enhance food security. The limited evidence on child outcomes finds largely positive impacts, suggesting that these programs may increase investments in human capital and belying the concern that the income-generating activities promoted by these programs crowd out investments in human capital.[10]

By increasing economic opportunities and asset ownership for women participants, several programs also served to empower women. The quantitative evidence on women's empowerment suggests only marginally positive impacts (with 57 percent of the 28 studies reporting on this outcome finding a positive impact). However, qualitative assessments are overwhelmingly positive, pointing to improvements in mobility, social status, household decision-making, and psychological well-being as critical outcomes for all participants but especially for women. See, for example, Moreno-Sánchez et al. (2018) and Moreno-Sánchez, Martínez, et al. (2018) for Colombia's Produciendo Por Mi Futuro (PxMF).

Most programs make households more resilient to shocks and stresses. They accomplish this by providing regular, predictable transfers, by facilitating asset accumulation, income diversification, access to low-cost credit, and social networks (all of which provide some protection against risk and help households adopt nonerosive coping strategies) or both. A handful of SSN programs also report increased use of insurance products, reducing vulnerability to health shocks.[11] These features help participants prepare, cope with, and recover from shocks.

In particularly shock-prone areas, programs strengthened household resilience ex ante. In Ethiopia, the Pastoralist Areas Resilience Improvement and Market Expansion (PRIME) project supported pastoralist households in coping with drought-induced animal mortality. During a period of multiple droughts, participants experienced a 40 percent lower decline in food security relative to nonparticipants (Smith et al. 2019). In the Sahel, SSN programs helped households cope with the multiple and recurrent shocks (including drought, desertification, floods, conflict, and economic and health shocks) prevalent in the region. In Burkina Faso, for example, in addition to experiencing improvements in well-being, income, assets, and savings, participants in a cash-plus program also reduced their use of negative coping strategies in the first year of the program (FAO 2016). In Bangladesh, two economic inclusion programs increased awareness about disaster preparedness while also helping households cope with seasonal food insecurity during droughts or floods (Siddiki et al. 2014; Hernandez et al. 2016; HTSPE 2011).

Particularly relevant as the world grapples with the COVID-19 crisis, some programs explicitly support livelihood recovery after shocks. In Madagascar, the Fiavota program helped households revive their income-generating activities in severely drought-affected areas, with participants earning approximately $7 more per month compared to nonparticipants (Rakotomana, Randrianatoandro, and Ravelosoa 2018).

Impact over the Medium and Long Terms

Many of these impacts are sustained in the medium term. We define medium-term impact as measured three to four years after enrollment in the program; for one-off or time-bound programs, this is typically one or two years after beneficiaries exit the program. The following are examples:

- *Programs offering time-bound interventions in Bangladesh (TUP), six CGAP–Ford Foundation pilot sites (in India–West Bengal, Ghana, Ethiopia, Pakistan, Peru, and Yemen), and Rwanda (Concern Worldwide Rwanda's Graduation Program).* Short-term gains in asset ownership, income, employment, and well-being remained positive and significant in the medium term. However, effect sizes were generally smaller in magnitude, and the trajectories varied across countries, with gains continuing to increase on some dimensions in some countries and starting to decline in others. See figure 5.10 for effect sizes over time and across countries (Bandiera et al. 2017; Banerjee et al. 2015; Misha et al. 2019; Ahmed et al. 2009; Devereux and Sabates 2016; Emran, Robano, and Smith 2009). In two CGAP–Ford Foundation pilot sites (India–Andhra Pradesh and Honduras), participants experienced no significant gains (or decline) in assets, incomes, or consumption over time (Banerjee et al. 2015; Bauchet, Morduch, and Ravi 2015).

- *Programs offering one-off capital grants and short-duration training (five days) to youth in Uganda and Ethiopia.* Short-term increases in occupation, hours of work, and earnings were sustained in the medium term. Capital stocks, however, started to converge between participants and nonparticipants toward the end of four years (Blattman, Dercon, and Franklin 2019; Blattman, Fiala, and Martinez 2018).

- *Programs providing an open-ended component (typically a cash transfer) in addition to time-bound interventions.* In Ethiopia, among households receiving the Household Asset-Based Program, those receiving a longer duration of the Productive Safety Net Program (PSNP) (five years as opposed to just one year) were able to significantly increase their crop yields and boost their agricultural productivity (Hoddinott et al. 2012).

Over the longer term—for up to seven years—some of these impacts continued to be sustained for the two programs for which this evidence is available.[12] The Targeting the Hard-Core Poor (THCP) program in West Bengal had positive and accelerating long-term impact with respect to economic opportunities and material well-being of beneficiaries even seven years after being enrolled in the program (nearly six years after program completion). For instance, the asset index (including production and household assets) was 0.89 standard deviations larger in the short term, 1.00 standard deviation larger in the medium term, and 0.99 standard deviations larger in the long term, relative to the baseline. Sustained improvements are also evident for total household income and consumption, while psychosocial impacts that had dissipated in the medium term improved in the long term (Banerjee et al. 2016). In Bangladesh, TUP also had sustained positive impact on income, savings, and food security for up to seven years. Long-term impact on asset ownership, however, was mixed: some studies found a sustained and even accelerating increase in productive assets (including land holdings) (Bandiera et al. 2017; Raza, Das, and Misha 2012; Asadullah and Ara 2016), but others found that vulnerability to shocks had resulted in asset losses for some households (Krishna, Poghosyan, and Das 2012).

However, longer-term impacts start to dissipate or reduce in size nine to ten years after program enrollment. In Bangladesh, some long-term impacts on assets, savings, employment, and food security persist even nine years after program enrollment, but effect sizes are very small (Asadullah and Ara 2016) or persisted only for existing entrepreneurs but not for others (Misha et al. 2019).[13] A recent 10-year evaluation of the THCP program in West Bengal shows positive impacts on assets, income, consumption, and health persist even ten years later. For instance, beneficiaries still had higher asset ownership compared to nonbeneficiaries but the size was smaller after ten years relative to after seven years (0.35 standard deviations higher relative to 0.8 standard deviations). The impact on income and revenues, on the other hand, persisted at the same level (0.3 standard deviations higher than nonparticipants) even after ten years (Banerjee et al. 2020). In Ethiopia and Uganda, only some changes persisted, as most long-term impacts of L&J programs dissipated (Blattman, Dercon, and Franklin 2019; Blattman, Fiala, and Martinez 2018). For instance, nine years later, YOP participants in Uganda remained slightly more likely than nonparticipants to be in skilled trades, rather than in petty business, and to have household assets and livestock (Blattman, Fiala, and Martinez 2018). This declining long-term impact was partly due to catch-up by the nonparticipants, whose incomes, earnings, and consumption grew slightly faster than those of participants (in Bangladesh and Uganda), and partly due to coverage expansion of SSNs (in Bangladesh).

These findings are indicative of persistent impact on a range of outcomes, suggesting that these are not just short-term program effects of time-bound asset transfers, cash grants, or savings group mobilization. The fact that impacts persist at least in the medium term suggests that economic inclusion programming can, at minimum, launch the extreme poor into an upward trajectory. In addition, a handful of program evaluations find accelerating long-term impact of up to seven years and persisting for up to ten years. These findings are indicative of the potential of these programs to unlock poverty traps. Further research is warranted on a broader set of programs to conclusively establish whether this is the case.[14]

In the meantime, expectations need to be appropriately calibrated: impact of a one-off or time-bound intervention will be more likely to persist in the long term if the original participants have the option of receiving discrete "refresher" interventions over time, such as training and coaching to grow enterprises, labor market intermediation, support for market links, and so forth. Alternatively, the duration of support may need to be extended, especially in harsh ecosystems and settings of fragility, conflict, and violence (FCV). In other words, economic inclusion programming is far more likely to lead to transformative solutions to poverty and to sustained long-term income growth for the poorest if embedded in a continuum of support, at the micro and meso levels.

Impact at Scale

While a number of government-led programs have shown positive impact on incomes, assets, savings, and consumption, the effects are heterogeneous.[15] The breadth and depth of the evidence base on government-led programs is more limited relative to that of nongovernment-led programs (see figure 5.2). The majority report positive impacts on assets (67 percent of programs reporting on this outcome), savings (100 percent), and employment outcomes (including diversification) (75 percent). More than half the studies of government-led programs also find positive impact on income and consumption. We review these examples to highlight three main concerns in scaling up programs:

1. Sustaining impact as a program scales up coverage (and scope)

2. Achieving impact when economic inclusion programming scales up through complementary programs that link to existing SSNs and L&J

3. Realizing indirect spillover effects on the wider local economy

Some government-led programs have managed to sustain positive impact even as they expand functional scope and coverage to a large number of beneficiaries. In India, the NRLM (and its state-level precursors)[16] built grassroots platforms of women's self-help groups linking women to finance, livelihood opportunities, and other social programs. The state-level program in Andhra Pradesh increased access to finance, asset holdings, social networks, and well-being in the short and medium terms (Prennushi and Gupta 2014; Deininger and Liu 2009, 2013). In Bihar, poor households benefited from access to lower-cost credit and increased their ownership of assets over two years (Hoffmann et al. 2017). Several of these impacts were sustained in seven additional states under NRLM, with an increase in household income (a 19 percent increase over preprogram income), number of income sources, savings, and links to government programs. However, impact on assets, overall consumption, or women's empowerment were more limited or not yet apparent in these states. For instance, although intra-household decision-making was not affected, the program helped women, especially those with some education, gain greater confidence in engaging with the community (Kochar et al. 2020).

Some complementary SSN and L&J programs have helped households increase household productivity and income, diversify income, and accumulate assets, including:

- Large-scale livelihood programs in Peru (Haku Wiñay) and Colombia (PxMF) that link with their countries' conditional cash transfer programs (Juntos and Más Familias en Acción, respectively)[17] offer a comprehensive bundle of interventions. These have helped participants increase their asset holdings, improve productivity, and shift from agricultural wage employment to self-employment, thereby raising income, consumption, and personal well-being (Escobal and Ponce 2016, Moreno-Sánchez, Maldonado, et al. 2018).

- Large-scale SSN programs that link their beneficiaries with existing livelihood programs have also experienced similarly positive results for some outcomes. In Ethiopia, households benefiting from PSNP and the Household Asset Building Program increased assets (livestock holdings and farm equipment), productivity, and food security (Berhane et al. 2014; Hoddinott et al. 2012; Sabates-Wheeler and Devereux 2012). Other complementary unconditional cash transfer and livelihood programs also increased asset accumulation and well-being in Lesotho and Malawi (FAO and UNICEF 2018; Pace et al. 2017).

- Some overlapping SSN and agriculture development programs have also increased productivity, income diversification, and financial inclusion in Brazil, El Salvador, and Peru.[18] In El Salvador, the complementarity of a conditional cash transfer and agricultural development program increased income diversification for small- and medium-scale farmers and access to credit for subsistence farmers (de Sanfeliú, Ángel, and Shi 2016).

However, many such complementary programs fall short of their potential to achieve positive synergies. For some overlapping and complementary programs in Brazil, Colombia, Kenya, Mexico, and Peru, despite the positive impact of the individual programs, there was no additive or multiplicative impact of the combination (Costa, Helfand, and Souza 2018; Yúnez-Naude et al. 2016; Moya 2016; Jensen, Barrett, and Mude 2017; Aldana, Vásquez, and Yancari 2016).[19] This may be because the complementary programs are not particularly well designed or effectively coordinated to provide a bundled set of interventions or because the bundle does not collectively address the multiple constraints faced by participants.

Finally, we do not know enough about the indirect impact that large-scale economic inclusion programs might have on the broader local economy. Scaled-up programs may generate spillover effects in two ways: through network effects, such as demonstration effects or the sharing of information with nonparticipants, or through general equilibrium effects (economic multipliers). The handful of studies that report spillover effects on nonparticipants in a community find evidence of behavioral change and increased personal and social empowerment (Raza, Van de Poel, and van Ourti 2018; Misha et al. 2019; Deininger and Liu 2009). However, there remain concerns about sustaining implementation quality and hence impact on these outcomes (Hoffmann et al. 2018). Less is known about economic multipliers that may influence local economywide impact on material outcomes at scale. Program design and contextual factors matter: we would expect greater price effects for programs with high transfers, with large numbers of participants per locality, and in isolated communities with reliance on local rather than regional or national markets (see box 5.2).

BOX 5.2 **Achieving Economic Inclusion in FCV Settings**

Several economic inclusion programs operating in fragility, conflict, and violence (FCV) settings have had positive impacts on the income and resilience of the extreme poor. For instance, Afghanistan's Targeting the Ultra Poor (TUP) program had a greater impact relative to similar programs in stable contexts (Bedoya et al. 2019). Similarly, Concern Worldwide Burundi's Terintambwe, the Trickle Up graduation program in Burkina Faso, and Fonkoze's Chemen Lavi Miyò (CLM) in Haiti had positive impacts on incomes, assets, savings, and child outcomes (Devereux et al. 2015; Karimli, Bose, and Kagotho 2019; Roelen and Saha 2019). In Côte d'Ivoire, a microenterprise program Projet d'Insertion Socio-Economique (PRISE), increased the likelihood of entry into self-employment as well as savings and investments, although it had no impact on earnings (Premand and Marguerie 2020). In contrast, a public works program (Projet d'Urgence de Création d'Emploi Jeunes et de Développement des Compétences, PEJEDEC) increased earnings from self-employment by approximately $12 (a 32 percent increase compared to nonparticipants) but had no impact on participation in wage- or self-employment (Bertrand et al. 2017). Another public works–plus program (Urban Youth Employment Program, UYEP) in Papua New Guinea was able to translate temporary wage employment into formal sector employment by directly influencing employer preferences (Hoy and Naidoo 2019).

However, program disruption due to conflict can undermine impact. In South Sudan's Youth Business Start-Up Grant Program, youths who received training and a cash grant substantially increased savings and consumption by about a 1.0 standard deviation and in psychological well-being by 0.8 standard deviations. Impacts were similar for men and women. Those who expected to receive the combination but received only training, due to program disruption following the outbreak of conflict, experienced no impact on savings and a small decline in consumption. For women, program disruption also led to a severe reduction in trust by 0.9 standard deviations (Müller, Pape, and Ralston 2019). In many cases, provision of economic opportunities is a means to improve social cohesion, especially for at-risk youth in FCV settings. Impact has been mixed on this front.

(Box continues next page)

BOX 5.2   **Achieving Economic Inclusion in FCV Settings** *(continued)*

In Côte d'Ivoire, the PRISE program was able to increase group participation and solidarity in the locality, even though there was little impact on broader indicators of social cohesion such as exposure to violence (Premand and Marguerie 2020). Similarly, the UYEP program in Papua New Guinea had a substantial positive impact on participants' interactions with their peer group and social behavior, but more limited effects on the socioeconomic causes of crime (Ivaschenko et al. 2016).

Factors That Mediate Impact

With a few exceptions, most evaluations are not designed to isolate mechanisms of impact. This is a critical knowledge gap with respect to two core elements of economic inclusion programming:

- Bundling of interventions

- Focusing on the extreme poor and vulnerable

The emerging evidence reveals the importance of coordinating multiple interventions vis-à-vis stand-alone interventions. However, most programs have heterogeneous impacts, with the poorest and most vulnerable experiencing the fewest gains. For programs that target both men and women, there is some evidence of differential impacts. Much of this evidence comes from NGO-led programs and from experimental studies (some of which build on government programs). More recently, there have been some evaluations of government-led programs that explore these questions, and a pipeline of forthcoming research is anticipated that could start to answer these questions more definitively, including for government-led programs.

Bundled Interventions Have a Larger Impact Than Stand-Alone Interventions

A core feature of economic inclusion programming is combining different interventions to address multiple constraints; such interactions are likely to drive overall program impact. While stand-alone interventions can also impact incomes, assets, and resilience, a single intervention—a regular cash transfer, an asset transfer or a cash grant, business training, agricultural extension services, or access to finance—would not necessarily help those facing multiple constraints, or would do so to a lesser extent.[20]

A comprehensive suite of interventions has larger and more sustained impact on income, assets, and savings relative to stand-alone interventions. In pilot programs in Ghana (Graduating the Ultra Poor, GUP), South Sudan (TUP), and Uganda (Village Enterprise microenterprise program), the classic graduation package had significant positive impact on income, assets, consumption and food security, and women's empowerment. In all three countries, stand-alone interventions had much more limited impact.

- In Ghana's GUP, a stand-alone savings intervention had a short-term impact on assets, income, consumption, and savings. However, only the recipients of the full set of interventions (with or without a savings component) were able to grow businesses, invest in assets and savings, and sustain income gains in the medium term (figure 5.4). Similar findings emerged for a stand-alone asset transfer relative to the classic graduation bundle (even without a savings component) (Banerjee et al. 2018).

- In South Sudan's TUP, a stand-alone cash grant increased consumption levels but had no impact on asset wealth relative to the comprehensive program (Chowdhury et al. 2017).

- In Uganda's Village Enterprise program, a stand-alone cash grant improved asset ownership but had no other impact, although a combination of the grant with light-touch behavioral interventions possibly facilitated a shift from wage to self-employment and reduced child labor (Sedlmayr, Shah, and Sulaiman 2019).

These findings suggest that the poorest population groups derive higher economic value from a lump-sum cash grant or an asset transfer when also provided with complementary training, coaching, and regular transfers.[21] In Peru, there was considerable heterogeneity in the bundle of interventions accessed by different households under Haku Wiñay; this had implications for the magnitude of impact.[22] Grouping households into terciles based on the intensity of interventions, the tercile that received the lowest-intensity bundle increased income by 35 percent, as compared with a 51 percent increase for the tercile that received the highest-intensity bundle. Impact on resilience to shocks (and on empowerment) was significant only for the tercile receiving the highest program intensity (Escobal and Ponce 2016).

In livelihood programs, bundling lump-sum cash grants with training and group formation can increase household incomes and welfare relative to either intervention in isolation. The cash grant eases capital constraints, training addresses human

FIGURE 5.4 **Comprehensive Package Showing Larger and More Sustained Impact Than Stand-Alone Interventions (Ghana, GUP)**

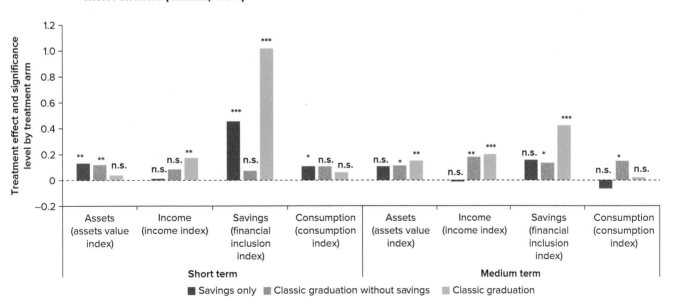

Source: Banerjee et al. 2018.

Note: All outcomes plotted on the vertical axis are economic indices (of assets, income, savings, and consumption). Program duration was two years; short-term impact is estimated at the end of the program (two years after the start) and medium-term impact at three years after the start of the program. GUP = Graduating the Ultra Poor.

* significance at 10 percent, ** 5 percent, *** 1 percent. n.s. = not significant.

capital constraints, and group formation helps the poorest households form social networks. In Uganda's WINGS, youths who were provided with a cash grant of $150, basic training *and* were mobilized into savings groups increased their incomes by a 0.15 standard deviation (significant at 10 percent) relative to those who received only the grant and basic training (figure 5.5). In addition, supervision increased their chances of business survival (Blattman et al. 2016). Similarly, in Sri Lanka, an experimental study found that a combination of cash grant and training was successful in getting women to start a subsistence business. Business training alone also increased business ownership but to a lesser extent, and the combination was needed to boost profits and capital stock (de Mel, McKenzie, and Woodruff 2014).

A combination of asset transfers and training has a similarly larger positive impact on household income and consumption relative to stand-alone interventions. In Rwanda's Girinka ("one cow per poor family") program, this effect persisted: households that received both the livestock asset transfer and training had higher milk production, livestock productivity, earnings, and asset accumulation in the long term.[23] In particular, complementary training provided at the same time as the asset transfer led to self-perpetuating gains over time; subsequent training, possibly of lower quality, did not have the same impact (Argent, Augsburg, and Rasul 2014). These findings are striking in contexts where households have weak links to markets and might be expected to have lower returns to such investments. In Burundi's Terintambwe program, beneficiaries highlighted the importance of training and coaching that provided them the knowledge and confidence required to maximize their returns from the asset transfer and income support (Roelen and Devereux 2019).

Similarly, while cash transfers ease consumption constraints and enable risk taking, bundling livelihood interventions can amplify impact by further easing production constraints. These effects seem to vary depending on the nature of the additional intervention. In drought-affected areas, the government of Nicaragua added layers to a conditional cash transfer (Atención a Crisis) in the form of either a lump-sum cash grant (with some coaching) or vocational training. The combination of the cash grant with the regular transfer increased average income and consumption and increased household resilience to the negative impact of droughts, partly due to their role in

FIGURE 5.5 **Bundling Cash Grants, Training, and Group Formation (Uganda, WINGS)**

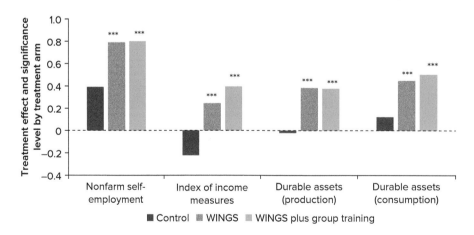

Source: Blattman et al. 2016.

Note: Nonfarm self-employment is the percentage of total beneficiaries in the control/treatment arm; all the other indicators are z-scores. Core program includes a cash grant and basic training and supervision. WINGS = Women's Income-Generating Support program.

* significance at 10 percent, ** 5 percent, *** 1 percent. n.s. = not significant.

facilitating income diversification.[24] Households eligible to receive the cash grant were 13 percentage points more likely to be self-employed in nonagricultural activities, relative to just 4 percent of those receiving either the cash transfer alone or the cash transfer combined with training (figure 5.6). Those eligible to receive the cash grant also had substantially higher profits from nonagricultural self-employment, approximately a 15 to 20 percent annual return on the initial cash grant ($200) even two years after the program ended (Macours, Premand, and Vakis 2012). Similarly, in Burkina Faso and Niger, a cash-plus program had greater positive impact on income, asset accumulation, and food security than a stand-alone asset transfer (FAO 2016).

In public works programs, the impact of bundling livelihood interventions appears to be more muted and context specific. In Côte d'Ivoire's Projet d'Urgence de Création d'Emploi Jeunes et de Développement des Compétences (PEJEDEC), a public works–plus program, participation in public works alone had a significant positive impact on savings and on well-being, but all program variants had similarly insignificant impacts on income and assets (figure 5.7). However, self-employment earnings of youths who received the basic entrepreneurship training in addition to participating in the public works program were higher than those engaged only in the public works (Bertrand et al. 2017). In Papua New Guinea, youth who participated in the public works–plus variant of the Urban Youth Employment Program (UYEP) were substantially more likely to be in formal employment in the short term, relative to those who participated only in the public works variant. The positive employment impact of the public works–plus was achieved through screening candidates on ability and by combining job-matching assistance and on-the-job training with wage subsidies to employers. Fewer than 15 percent of employers reported willingness to keep the same number of placements without a subsidy (Hoy and Naidoo 2019).

Figure 5.6 **Layering Regular Cash Transfers with Livelihood Interventions (Nicaragua, Atención a Crisis)**

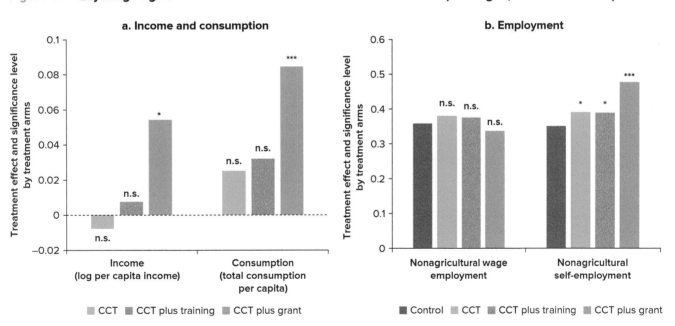

Source: Macours, Premand, and Vakis 2012.

Note: Panel a indicators plotted on the vertical axis are monetary values in local currency units. Panel b indicators are participation in economic activity. Pilot duration was one year; medium-term impact is estimated three years after the start of the program (two years after pilot completion). CCT = conditional cash transfer.

* significance at 10 percent, ** 5 percent, *** 1 percent. n.s. = not significant.

FIGURE 5.7 **Bundling Public Works Programs with Other Livelihood Interventions (Côte d'Ivoire, PEJEDEC)**

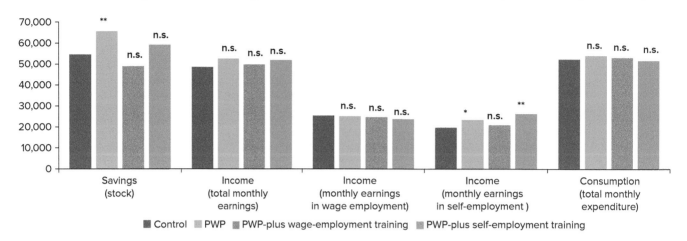

■ Control ■ PWP ■ PWP-plus wage-employment training ■ PWP-plus self-employment training

Source: Bertrand et al. 2017.

Note: PWP = public works program. All outcomes plotted on the vertical axis are monetary values in the shared Central African currency (CFAF). Short-term impact is estimated 12–15 months after program completion (with program duration approximately 7 months). PEJEDEC = Projet d'Urgence de Création d'Emploi Jeunes et de Développement des Compétences.

* significance at 10 percent, ** 5 percent, and *** 1 percent. n.s. = not significant.

Some complementary programs also display these positive synergies, with the cumulative impact greater than that of the individual programs. For instance, in Brazil the overlapping implementation of Bolsa Família (a conditional cash transfer) and Pronaf (a subsidized agricultural credit) had a greater aggregate impact on land productivity and income than the individual programs (Garcia, Helfand, and Souza 2016). In Malawi, the joint impact of an unconditional cash transfer and farm input subsidy was about 22 percent larger than that of the sum of the impacts of the stand-alone programs on the value of production (Daidone et al. 2017). As previously noted, however, many complementary programs do not have any additive or multiplicative impact of the combined programs.

It is possible that in some contexts further bundling may be necessary to address the multiple constraints faced by the target populations. In Peru (prior to Haku Wiñay), complementary programs—a conditional cash transfer (Juntos) and technical training (Sierra Sur)—influenced the adoption of new technologies and increased assets. However, these changes did not translate into higher income in the absence of financial or other support (Aldana, Vásquez, and Yancari 2016). Similarly, in Côte d'Ivoire, the Projet d'Insertion Socio-Economique program (PRISE) found very little difference across different variants (combining training with semicredit, cash grant, or establishment of village savings and credit association). Possibly, additional interventions, such as a regular cash transfer, may have been necessary in the fragile, postconflict setting (Premand and Marguerie 2020).

In summary, the emerging evidence suggests that a bundled set of interventions has greater impact than its constituent stand-alone interventions. However, knowledge of this key aspect of economic inclusion programming is still limited. Further research is needed to conclusively establish this finding, particularly if this holds at scale, for different population groups, and across a range of contexts. It is also important to better understand the marginal impact (and costs, see chapter 6) of each intervention, relative to the overall impact of the program, in order to identify cost-effective bundles for different population groups and contexts.[25]

Heterogeneity of Impact: Not Everyone Benefits to the Same Extent

Program impact often varies across participants, with greater impact on incomes and assets for the least poor among the target population. For instance, in the medium term, the impact of the classic graduation pilots on the asset index among people at the 90th percentile was more than 14 times greater than among those at the 10th percentile (Banerjee et al. 2015). In Afghanistan, a similar program (TUP) also found significantly higher impact on livestock holdings for the top relative to the bottom quintile (Bedoya et al. 2019). In Bangladesh's TUP, these differences persist over time, with medium-term effects on savings and assets being greater at the 95th relative to the 5th percentile (Bandiera et al. 2017). This seems to hold in SSN-plus programs too. In Côte d'Ivoire, the PEJEDEC program also had substantially higher impact on income and savings for youths at the top end of the distribution relative to those at the bottom, although these differences were muted after the program closed (Bertrand et al. 2017).

With respect to other dimensions of social exclusion, the picture may be more nuanced, especially in community-based programs. In Andhra Pradesh, Scheduled Tribes experienced greater increases in savings, livestock assets, consumption, and education outcomes compared to other participants in the state-level (pre-NRLM) program (Prennushi and Gupta 2014). Similarly, in Bihar's JEEViKA, landless households (predominantly Scheduled Caste) benefited more than landowning households with respect to reductions in cost of credit (Hoffmann et al. 2017). These patterns held in seven other states under NRLM, with greater gains to Scheduled Caste and Tribe households (Kochar et al. 2020). (For more on Scheduled Casts and Tribes, see case study 2.)

However, absolute gains are largely positive across the distribution. In some programs, the poor experienced larger impacts on food security, psychological well-being, and human capital investments. The classic graduation pilots, for example, increased food security only toward the lower end of the distribution, at the 25th percentile (Banerjee et al. 2015). Similar programs in Afghanistan (TUP) and Colombia (PxMF) yielded greater and more sustained improvements in subjective well-being and aspirations for the poorest and for those who started the program with lower life satisfaction compared to other participants (Moreno-Sánchez, Maldonado, et al. 2018; Bedoya et al. 2019).

Participants also differ with respect to their trajectories during the program and after program exit (in the case of time-bound programs). Many participants—referred to as "improvers" or "fast climbers"—experience positive changes during the program and manage to sustain these changes afterward. These sustained changes include increasing income; diversifying income; increasing resilience to shocks; investing in their children's health, nutrition, and education; and planning for the future with some degree of confidence. Another group of participants—referred to as "late improvers" or "slow climbers"—might only gradually start to show improvements. Yet others—referred to as "decliners"—who may or may not have experienced positive changes during the program are unable to sustain whatever changes they experienced and end up on a downward trajectory. Among this latter group, some ("crash outs") may even fall back to preprogram levels (see figure 5.8). See Sabates-Wheeler, Sabates, and Devereux (2018) for trajectories of Concern Worldwide Rwanda participants, Shoaf and Simanowitz (2019) for Chemen Lavi Miyò in Haiti, and Sengupta (2012) for the classic graduation pilot in Ethiopia. These trajectories can vary across participants, depending on a number of factors mediating impact, as examined in the following material.

FIGURE 5.8 **Participant Trajectories in Time-Bound Economic Inclusion Programs**

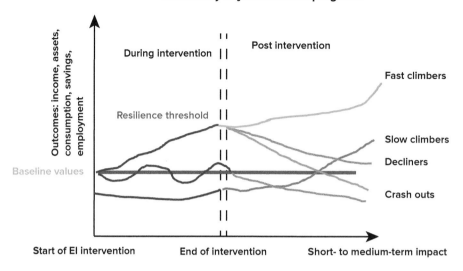

Beneficiary trajectories in EI programs

Source: Adapted from Sabates-Wheeler, Sabates, and Devereux 2018, figure 2.

Note: In this figure, EI (economic inclusion) intervention can refer to the entire program, such as the classic graduation programs, or to a livelihood component in a social safety net–plus program.

Drivers of Impact

A number of factors enable—or constrain—economic inclusion in different contexts and for different population groups. Getting the design right is important for all social policy, but it is critically so for economic inclusion programming that seeks to address multiple constraints for the poor. Program design features vary enormously, with respect to the bundling and sequencing of different interventions, as well as the adequacy, intensity, and duration of support.[26] This can drive both the size and the heterogeneity of impact. On the one hand, if a poverty trap exists, impact will vary depending on the distance of participants from the threshold and whether the program is designed to provide just the right amount of support. On the other hand, variations in participant characteristics can also affect participants' choices (such as between short-term consumption and long-term investments), their returns from livelihoods, and thus their trajectories after exposure to the program.

Thus, impacts vary across different types of programs, for similar programs in different contexts, and for the same program with different population groups. The main factors that drive impact include the ecosystem in which program participants operate—that is, institutional factors that determine program design and delivery as well as markets and community-level factors—and the characteristics of participating households and individuals (figure 5.9).

Context: Institutions

Institutional capacity, of both local administrative structures and the reach of private sector and nongovernment partners, can influence impact. Staff capacity is critical in economic inclusion programs, with a mix of technical, managerial, communication, and interpersonal skills required. The bundling of interventions and use of digital solutions require partnerships between the government and the private sector, NGOs, and

FIGURE 5.9 **Factors That Mediate Program Impact**

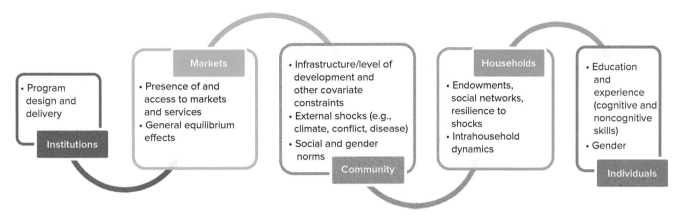

Source: Adapted from Sabates-Wheeler and Devereux 2013; Shoaf and Simanowitz 2019; and Huda 2009.

civil society. Uneven implementation across geographic locations can lead to variable impact across groups (Berhane et al. 2014), or can dilute impact, especially as programs scale up (Hoffmann et al. 2018).[27]

In particular, as reviewed in chapter 2, complementary programs require policy coherence and effective interagency coordination to unlock positive synergies across constituent programs. In most contexts, positive synergies from coordinated interventions are more likely to emerge where there are significant market failures, such as those faced by small farmers and rural microentrepreneurs. In these cases, cash transfers provide liquidity and certainty, while the complementary livelihood interventions and financial services address production constraints, including technical knowledge and access to inputs, credit, and markets (Tirivayi, Knowles, and Davis 2013; Soares et al. 2017). However, these synergies will not necessarily materialize when programs are merely overlapping in geographic coverage, without any attempt at joint policy articulation or operational coordination (Slater et al. 2016). Programs designed for different target groups (in terms of poverty status, land or asset ownership, education, and ability, for example) would not achieve much complementarity in coverage or have much aggregate impact on economic inclusion.[28]

Context: Markets and communities

The broader ecosystem in which program participants operate shapes local livelihoods and mediates impact from economic inclusion programs that seek to influence these livelihoods. These contextual factors include communitywide characteristics, such as location (for example, concerning remoteness and connectivity), level of development (such as availability and quality of infrastructure and services), local economy (including economic growth, agroclimatic conditions, labor demand, and purchasing power), access to input and output markets (including integration of local markets with regional or national markets), and exposure to shocks (especially climate, conflict, and disease).

As a result, similar programs can yield very different outcomes in different locations. The evaluation of the CGAP–Ford classic graduation pilot projects implemented in a very wide range of contexts revealed significant impacts in all but one case, but the size varied across the pilots (see figure 5.10) (Banerjee et al. 2015; J-PAL and IPA Policy Bulletin 2015).

FIGURE 5.10 **Impact of Similar Programs Can Vary Substantially in Different Contexts: Evidence from the CGAP–Ford Foundation Classic Graduation Pilot Projects**

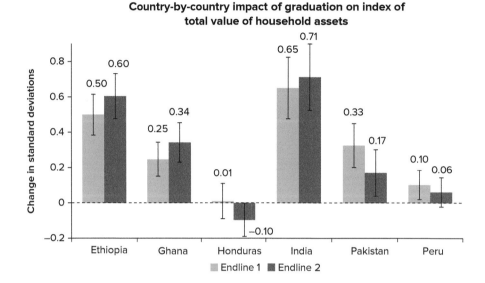

Country-by-country impact of graduation on index of total value of household assets

Source: J-PAL and IPA Policy Bulletin 2015.

Note: These percentage changes are over small baseline values. Endline 1: two years after program start; endline 2: three years after program start.

* significance at 10 percent, ** 5 percent, and *** 1 percent. n.s. = not significant.

Similarly, in India, the same model had significant impact on incomes and assets in one India state but not in another, largely due to differences in the local economy (Bauchet, Morduch, and Ravi 2015). In Peru's Haku Wiñay, for example, heterogeneity of outcomes is associated with the level of economic dynamism of the local area (Asensio, Fernández, and Burneo 2016).[29] In harsh ecosystems and FCV contexts, achieving impact is feasible but can be particularly challenging (box 5.2). In particular, shocks can disrupt program delivery such that households receiving partial inputs or inputs of a poorer quality than planned tend to fare poorly, in both material and psychosocial terms (Müller, Pape, and Ralston 2019).

Economic inclusion programming at scale needs to address these covariate constraints, particularly with respect to facilitating market access (see spotlight 3). Large-scale programs can generate spillover effects—positive and negative—especially in contexts where there are significant market failures (see box 5.3). For instance, programs promoting self-employment may lead to constrained market supply or market saturation if local input or output markets are weakly integrated with regional or national markets. Program participants in Paraguay and Colombia experienced market saturation in poorly integrated local markets (CADEP 2017; Sheldon 2016). However, this was not the case for program participants in Bangladesh, which had better regional market integration (Banerjee et al. 2015; Bandiera et al. 2017).

In addition, community norms can promote or restrict the extent to which participants benefit from the opportunities offered by economic inclusion programs. For instance, some communities have a strong practice of sharing in mutual support networks. While this is an important informal SSN, such sharing of in-kind and cash transfers from economic inclusion programs can dilute the expected impact (Sabates-Wheeler, Lind, and Hoddinott 2013). In the Sahel, successful people face community pressure toward generosity to show solidarity with other community members (Bossuroy, Koussoubé, and Premand 2019). Many programs involve communities heavily in the selection of beneficiaries; while this is

BOX 5.3   **Spillover Impact on Communities and the Local Economy**

Livelihood programs that promote self-employment and microenterprises can potentially generate positive or negative spillover effects. In particular, integration with regional markets is important, as there are limits to how many similar enterprises a single community can support. In Paraguay's Sembrando Oportunidades Familia por Familia and Colombia's PxMF, participants reported low profitability due to lower than anticipated sales at low prices, as the small local market was flooded and resources were limited in the community. These low profit margins were reinforced by poor connectivity with markets for remote communities and weak input markets, which led to reliance on a few vendors providing poor-quality chickens and feed in some areas (CADEP 2017; Sheldon 2016). However, this may not be the case for all programs and in all contexts. In Bangladesh's Targeting the Ultra Poor (TUP) program, the program-induced shift from casual wage employment to self-employment for participants increased local casual wages but did not have negative spillover effects on village livestock prices. This was possibly because there were dynamic regional livestock markets in the program areas. Also, general equilibrium effects may be small if scale-up takes the form of geographic expansion of a narrowly targeted program. Although the poor benefit, there might only be a modest impact on the village economy's overall asset stock, output markets, and labor markets (Banerjee et al. 2015; Bandiera et al. 2017).

For stand-alone social safety net (SSN) programs, there is considerable evidence of positive local economy impacts. In seven Sub-Saharan countries, a public works program and cash transfers generated substantial income multipliers (Taylor, Thome, and Filipski 2016; Filipski et al. 2017). In Ethiopia, for example, the PSNP had substantial impact on supply, demand, wages, and prices in both PSNP and non-PSNP areas. There was considerable variation across regions, depending on program design as well as contextual factors, such as the structure of the local economy, types of household activities, and degree of integration with outside markets.

Complementing SSNs with livelihood interventions can also have substantial spillover effects on the local economy, especially when each mitigates possible negative impacts of a stand-alone intervention. For example, much of the rationale for the expansion of cash and livelihood interventions in Malawi has been to compensate for the removal of ineffective and expensive farm input subsidies (Kagin et al. 2019; Filipski et al. 2017).

critical in building support and utilizing local knowledge, it can also result in the crowding out of other support, especially when programs are rationed. For instance, in Rwanda, participants in the Concern Worldwide graduation program were removed from the beneficiary lists of the government program, Vision 2020 Umurenge Programme, to make room for others not receiving any support (Devereux and Sabates 2016). These local norms are harder to shift through program design.

Context: Households and individuals

At the household level, initial endowments determine the magnitude of an impact. Most of the programs reviewed here found that households with prior asset ownership, more labor availability in the household or extended family, and better social relations were in a better position to take advantage of the opportunities offered by economic inclusion programs. The effect of prior asset ownership is particularly important if there are complementarities between asset types, such as land and livestock (Sabates-Wheeler, Sabates, and Devereux 2018). The age, sex, and skills of the labor pool available to households is important in defining its trajectory. Across the board, labor-constrained households, such as single-headed households (especially with a female head) and those with a large number of dependents, tend to fare worse.

Social networks help households manage risk and access formal and informal SSNs.[30] Participants in many programs reported increased participation in community meetings and social events as well as improvements in trust and in the degree of integration with their communities. For previously marginalized households, these social networks improved living conditions in both tangible ways, such as access to information and opportunities as well as cooperation in the form of labor sharing, cooperative cash cropping, and informal finance (Blattman et al. 2016), and intangible ways, such as by shaping attitudes and aspirations for the future (Macours and Vakis 2014). Some programs increased access to other government social programs and services (Escobal and Ponce 2016; Kochar et al. 2020). At the same time, there were also negative impacts in terms of resentment and abuse, loss of informal means of support, and sometimes even theft by nonparticipating households, particularly in contexts with limited natural resources (Siddiki et al. 2014) or rigid social hierarchies (Kabeer et al. 2012).

Shocks can halt or even reverse progress toward economic inclusion, but this effect is tempered by household resilience. In many programs, households that were unable to improve or maintain their socioeconomic situation (decliners or crash outs) were adversely affected by a series of shocks that overwhelmed their ability to cope. While shocks upended many upward trajectories, some households (improvers) had the resilience to overcome these setbacks and rebuild their livelihoods. This greater resilience was due to better risk management (in terms of greater diversification) and reliance on nonerosive coping strategies. However, the ability to diversify incomes itself depends on attitudes to risk and skills, some level of capital to invest in alternative activities, and household labor availability, while nonerosive coping mechanisms require some resources and access to credit and social networks.[31] For instance, in Haiti's Kore Lavi program, participants who had joined village savings and loans associations were more likely to adopt resilient coping strategies (CARE 2019). These are important levers for economic inclusion programs to influence.

Individual characteristics, such as education and experience, are also important in differentiating participant trajectories. Participants with some prior experience, especially business experience, are able to make more informed decisions about livelihood options offered by economic inclusion programs and to increase their returns. This is particularly important for programs promoting self-employment. For instance, in Bangladesh's TUP, while most participants were able to move to self-employment in the short to medium term, only existing entrepreneurs managed to sustain their business (relative to nonparticipants) in the long term (Misha et al. 2019). In many cases, particularly complementary programs, participants are typically selected based on an assessment of capability, employability, and business acumen of potential participants (see chapter 3). Even then, differences in education can impact income gains (Aldana, Vásquez, and Yancari 2016) and employment outcomes (Acosta and Avalos 2018). Some programs found younger participants benefited more than older participants, and, in some cases, positive income and labor supply impact was experienced only by younger and more educated participants (Almeida and Galasso 2010).

Program trajectories are often gendered, with intrahousehold dynamics and gender norms constraining progress toward economic inclusion. For women, social norms, labor availability, and relationship dynamics in the household are important determinants of participant trajectories and overall program impact. In Rwanda, male-headed households were better placed to take up new opportunities, leading to greater improvements in assets and food security relative to female-headed households. For instance, examining asset trajectories, only 36 percent of households grouped as improvers were female-headed, compared to 29 percent of decliners and 56 percent of crash outs (Sabates-Wheeler, Sabates, and Devereux 2018). The reverse was true in Bangladesh, where the program targeted women. In this case, female-headed households substantially increased their incomes in the short term, relative to male-headed households, and were able to match them over time (Misha et al. 2019).

At the same time, personal agency and noncognitive abilities, such as drive, initiative, risk taking, and an entrepreneurial spirit, can also put some individuals and their households on a path of sustained income generation. This is particularly relevant for programs promoting self-employment. Many participants are self-employed by necessity; only some participants are self-employed by choice and have the necessarily entrepreneurial experience and traits to succeed (see chapter 3). In the Sahel subregion, for example, many focus group participants associated behavioral skills such as being hard working, determined, and courageous with success in farm or nonfarm activities (Bossuroy, Koussoubé, and Premand 2019). In West Bengal, indigenous women were among the fast climbers, despite being the most marginalized group and despite dealing with resentment and barriers to advancement in their communities. This was largely because they viewed the program as their only chance to improve their situation, while the self-help group approach taken by the program helped forge strong horizontal social bonds (Kabeer et al. 2012). In complementary programs, differences in the take-up of various constituent components in the program can also influence overall impact (Escobal and Ponce 2016).

Future Directions

This synthesis makes a strong case for the potential of a broad range of economic inclusion programs to impact a wide range of outcomes across diverse contexts. While the first round of evidence came from NGO-led programs, a new wave of evidence will soon emerge from government-led operations, which are increasingly moving to scale. There is a need to ensure that this emerging evidence base balances long-term evidence generation with monitoring and learning that ultimately strengthens program performance in real time. In this context, key priorities going forward are as follows:[32]

First, a more systematic evidence base, using comparable outcomes and indicators, would conclusively establish the overall impact of economic inclusion programming across all three entry points, at scale, and over time. In this context, greater effort is needed to expand the evidence base to evaluate the following programs:

- SSN-plus and FI programs
- Government-led programs[33]
- Programs operating in FCV settings

In addition to the upcoming coordinated research agendas (see appendix B), the next wave of evaluations could draw on the framework presented in chapter 1 to identify common research questions and report on a common set of outcomes and indicators. Depending on study comparability, a meta-analysis could combine evidence from multiple evaluations to provide estimates of effect sizes, disaggregated by program entry points, institutional arrangements, program size, and context. The evidence base on the long-term sustainability of impacts also needs to be broadened beyond the current small set of programs. In particular, there is little information on the long-term impact of government-led programsprograms and on the nature of "refresher" interventions and other support that may be required for sustained long-term income growth for the poorest. Finally, addressing existing knowledge gaps will require complementing impact evaluations with real-time operational research (such as constraints analysis and other diagnostic studies, performance monitoring, process evaluations, etc.) to identify opportunities to enhance program design and performance. Beyond knowing what works in terms of cost-effectiveness and scalability, program implementers need greater understanding on how to operationalize programs and make them work.

Second, a critical learning agenda is investigating differences in program impact across population groups and understanding the factors driving differences in beneficiary trajectories across fast climbers, slow climbers, and crash outs. About 39 percent of programs that reported undertaking an impact evaluation in the PEI Landscape Survey 2020 plan to evaluate customized bundles for different groups. This will require supplementing impact evaluations with operational research to allow cost-effective program customization to suit different characteristics and constraints (see box 6.2 in the next chapter for some emerging evidence on these strategies). A key priority is reconciling the differences between quantitative and qualitative research with respect to impact on women and children. This is critical to design economic inclusion programs that amplify positive impacts (such as personal empowerment and human capital and intergenerational outcomes), avoid unintended negative impacts (such as gender-based violence and child labor), and potentially course-correct and customize support depending on beneficiary trajectories.[34]

Third, the next wave of evaluations needs to help unpack the bundling of interventions. Although the emerging evidence suggests that bundling interventions is critical for impact, this comes with higher cost and complexity (see chapter 6). Further research is necessary to identify the marginal contribution of constituent interventions to overall impact, the role of timing and sequencing in maximizing the impact of a bundled set of interventions, and corresponding implications for cost-effectiveness. This knowledge would benefit operational teams in identifying a bundle that is well sequenced, appropriate to the context, and retains the positive impact of the program at a lower cost. This is particularly important for the scalability of high-cost interventions, such as coaching and training, whose marginal contribution to overall cost-effectiveness we do not yet know.[35]

Fourth, program evaluations need to be part of broader program monitoring, evaluation, and learning agendas. Supplementing impact evaluations with process evaluations and operational research would enable a deeper understanding of the mechanisms of impact, particularly the role of implementation and overall program performance, both for programs with proven impact and those with no discernible impact. In particular, impact and process evaluations of alternative program delivery models can help identify workable solutions for a variety of program innovations and refinements for a range of contexts, including, for instance, technology-based solutions in hard-to-reach contexts. This has taken on greater urgency in light of the COVID-19 containment measures.

Notes

1. This synthesis must be offered with one note of caution: the results presented here are unavoidably subject to publication bias, as publications usually present only positive findings. It should also be noted that this is *not* a meta-analysis, and consequently we cannot present estimates of average impact across programs.

2. SSN-plus refers to *social safety nets–plus*, where the "plus" is additional inputs, service components, or links to external services, that complement the cash transfer. There is also a significant gap with respect to FI interventions, which largely mirrors the fact that this is often a secondary, rather than primary, entry point (see chapter 2).

3. As highlighted in chapter 2, stand-alone SSN interventions—like cash transfers—have shown an array of productive impacts, although sometimes with small size effects and often when these were not an explicit program objective. SSNs have led to investments in agricultural assets, inputs and livestock, business and enterprise, and savings, besides improving well-being (in terms of consumption, food security, and human capital) (Bastagli et al. 2016; Ralston, Andrews, and Hsiao 2017; Davis et al. 2016; O'Keefe, Dutta, and Palacios 2020).

4. These feature well-known SSNs, such as Ethiopia's productive safety nets program (linked to the Household Asset Building Program) and Brazil's Bolsa Família (linked to the agricultural credit program, Pronaf).

5. Of the total number of programs surveyed for this report, 80 percent have not yet been evaluated, as most are relatively recent.

6. Program duration: For ease of comparability across studies, we define *short-term* impact as measured immediately after a program concludes or in one to two years after program start (that is, when beneficiaries enroll in the program); *medium term* as three to four years after program start; and *long term* as four or more years after program start.

7. Examples include the following: the CGAP–Ford Foundation pilots in Ethiopia, Honduras, Ghana, India, Pakistan, and Peru increased total asset value by 0.26 standard deviations relative to the baseline (Banerjee et al. 2015); Paraguay's Sembrando Oportunidades Familia por Familia increased total asset value by 0.31 standard deviations relative to that of nonparticipants (and 0.42 standard deviations compared to the baseline of participants) (Maldonado et al. 2019); and Afghanistan's TUP program increased livestock assets and household assets by 1.06 and 0.36 standard deviations, respectively, relative to nonparticipants (Bedoya et al. 2019).

8. In Afghanistan, where women's labor participation is very low, the TUP program increased women's labor participation (including market work, self-employment, or job searching) by 22 percentage points (above a 35 percent average among nonparticipants) (Bedoya et al. 2019). In Tanzania's PSSN, for example, women were 7.6 percentage points more likely to work on nonfarm activities relative to nonparticipating women. Men, however, were 6.5 percentage points more likely to work on farm activities relative to other men (Rosas et al. 2019).

9. For example, Kenya's REAP increased the per capita income of participating groups by 34 percent (0.246 standard deviations) compared to nonparticipating groups (Gobin, Santos, and Toth 2016). In the six CGAP–Ford Foundation pilots, participating households increased their total income by 0.383 standard deviations (Banerjee et al. 2015).

10. Only 15 studies report on child health outcomes and 20 studies on education outcomes. In Bangladesh, TUP improved nutrition, reducing the likelihood of being underweight for children under 5 years of age by 10 percentage points (Raza, Van de Poel, and van Ourti 2018). Although older children increased hours spent on own-family livestock rearing and cultivation, this did not crowd out schooling (Bandiera et al. 2017). Haiti's Chemen Lavi Miyò program resulted in no reduction in care for children and reduced the occurrence of children being sent to work as domestic help (Roelen and Saha 2019), while Burkina Faso's Trickle Up program reduced children's exposure to hazardous work (Karimli, Bose, and Kagotho 2019). See Roelen, Sherer, and Himmelstine (2020) for a review of impact on children.

11. A qualitative evaluation of Rwanda's Vision 2020 Umurenge Programme found increased usage of insurance products due to links made through the program (Gahamanyi and Kettlewell 2015). Similarly, Tanzania's PSSN increased take-up of health insurance, with 33 percent of participating households enrolled in a health insurance plan compared to just 11 percent of nonparticipating households (Rosas et al. 2019).

12. These results should be at best treated as indicative of the possible directions of programs, as long-term evidence up to seven years is limited to two programs (and an experiment) and up to nine to ten years to three programs only (see box 5.1).

13. Existing entrepreneurs managed to sustain their business (relative to nonparticipants) even nine years after program exit. However, households that had engaged primarily in begging or

in domestic or casual wage work were able to sustain their newly created businesses only in the medium term. After nine years, the majority of these households had fallen back to their original employment (Misha et al. 2019). See box 3.3 in chapter 3 on differential profiles of reluctant and transformational entrepreneurs.

14. The long-term impact of stand-alone interventions, including SSNs, is also not yet conclusively established. See, for example, Millán et al. (2019).

15. This is a key concern in scaling up social policy. For stand-alone interventions (including SSNs, microcredit, financial literacy, and women's empowerment programs), there is some evidence of heterogeneity in effect sizes across programs, with smaller effect sizes in government-led programs relative to experiments or NGO-led programs (Vivalt 2019). The evidence on economic inclusion programs at scale is more limited and, given the diversity in programs, we cannot compare effect sizes.

16. In Andhra Pradesh, Indira Kranti Pratham (IKP); in Bihar, JEEViKA (see case study 2).

17. About 80 percent of Haku Wiñay families and 60 percent of PxMF families received consumption support through the existing conditional cash transfer programs (Juntos and Más Familias en Acción, respectively) (Sheldon 2016).

18. In Brazil, Bolsa Família and Pronaf (Garcia, Helfand, and Souza 2016); in El Salvador, Comunidades Solidarias Rurales and Fondo de Inversión Social para el Desarrollo (de Sanfeliú, Ángel, and Shi 2016); in Peru, Juntos and agricultural credit (Loayza 2015).

19. In Brazil, Bolsa Família and the International Fund for Agricultural Development rural development program (Costa, Helfand, and Souza 2018); in Colombia, Familias en Acción and Oportunidades Rurales (Moya 2016); in Mexico, Prospera and Procampo (Yúnez-Naude et al. 2016); in Chile, Ingreso Ético Familiar (IEF) and enterprise support programs (El Fondo de Solidaridad e Inversión Social, FOSIS) (Fernández et al. 2016); in Kenya, Hunger Safety Net Program and index-based livestock insurance (Jensen, Barrett, and Mude 2017). The programs examined in these studies predate more comprehensive economic inclusion programming in some of the countries (notably, Brazil, Chile, Colombia, and Mexico).

20. See footnote 3 for evidence on stand-alone SSNs. The evidence on active labor market programs (including business grants and training) is mixed. For instance, training programs are likely to have a positive effect on post-program employment rates but not necessarily on earnings, at least in developing countries (Kluve 2016; Betcherman, Olivas, and Dar 2004; Ibarraran and Shady 2009; Card, Kluve, and Weber 2015). It is possible that effects may be more positive for women, especially if constraints on accessibility and child care are addressed (Buvinic and Furst-Nichols 2014), but many would not pass a cost-benefit test (Blattman and Ralston 2015; McKenzie 2017). The small evidence base for farmer field schools suggests impact on knowledge and practices, as well as agricultural production and farmers' incomes, at least in small pilot projects (Waddington et al. 2014). Financial services such as savings, insurance, and, to a lesser extent, payments have substantial positive impact on building household resilience and empowering poor women; the evidence on other services, such as credit, is more mixed and contextual (El-Zoghbi, Holle, and Soursourian 2019).

21. There may also be important noneconomic benefits. For instance, in Burkina Faso's Trickle Up livelihood program, supplementing the classic graduation package with family coaching on child protection issues improved children's mental health functioning, fostered a supportive parenting environment, and reduced exposure to family violence (Karimli, Rost, and Ismayilova 2018; Ismayilova et al. 2018).

22. About 20 percent of Haku Wiñay participants did not qualify for the conditional cash transfer (Juntos) and so did not receive regular cash transfers for consumption support. There were also differences in interventions offered and take-up.

23. Households that received training with the asset transfer were more likely to produce milk (approximately 1.5 liters of milk more per day relative to less than 1 liter per day); this translated into a $0.82 increase in household income from milk, equivalent to about 66 percent of an untrained household's daily income.

24. All variants had a positive impact on child outcomes (Macours, Schady, and Vakis 2012).

25. Emerging evidence from BRAC's CFPR-TUP (Das et al. 2016) and Côte d'Ivoire's PRISE (Premand and Marguerie 2020) provide some insights with respect to program variants with a cash grant versus a credit or semicredit (chapter 6).

26. See chapter 3 for a review of the global landscape of economic inclusion programs and chapter 6 for a detailed discussion on adequacy and component costs for a subset of programs.

27. This chapter does not investigate program performance to understand the extent to which deviations from the intended program design may drive impact.

28. For instance, Chile sought to complement its social protection program (IEF) with entrepreneurship through a public service (FOSIS) but had no impact. It is possible that the IEF beneficiaries (poor elderly and people living in the streets) did not have the right profile, with limited means or skills to participate in the business proposal contests required to access the FOSIS programs (Fernández et al. 2016). Similarly, the lack of aggregate impact of the Oportunidades and Procampo programs in Mexico between 2002 and 2007 may have been due to differences in their target populations; Procampo beneficiaries were not necessarily poor and hence not covered by Oportunidades (Yúnez-Naude et al. 2016).

29. Household and individual characteristics also play a role in explaining heterogeneity. See case study 4.

30. These include horizontal networks, which can provide financial support and share business expertise, and vertical networks, which facilitate opportunities and access to credit and government programs.

31. See Smith et al. (2019) for an analysis of resilience capacity among pastoralist beneficiaries of the PRIME program in drought-prone areas of Ethiopia.

32. Some of these will be addressed through the upcoming research pipeline (appendix B).

33. While the emerging evidence on the short- and medium-term impact of government-led programs is promising, many programs continue to rely largely on nonevaluative performance assessments. Among programs that reported undertaking an impact evaluation in the PEI Landscape Survey 2020, about 26 percent are planning to evaluate impact at scale.

34. For instance, Innovations for Policy Action (IPA) and Village Enterprise are planning to evaluate the impact of a livelihood program in Ghana on intimate-partner violence and women's empowerment. About 5 percent of the programs reporting a planned impact evaluation in the PEI Landscape Survey 2020 plan to evaluate intergenerational impact.

35. A subset of programs that reported undertaking an impact evaluation in the PEI Landscape Survey 2020 plan to evaluate the impact of various bundles (40 percent), sequencing (10 percent), impact on noncognitive skills (4 percent), and the marginal impact of some interventions (such as market links, 15 percent). For instance, IPA, Heifer International, and the Ford Foundation are planning to evaluate the impact of alternative bundles (including cognitive behavioral therapy) in Ghana. Upcoming multicountry research on SSN-plus bundling in the Sahel also seeks to answer these questions (Bossuroy et al. 2019).

References

Acosta, Pablo, and Jorge Avalos. 2018. "The Philippines Sustainable Livelihood Program: Providing and Expanding Access to Employment and Livelihood Opportunities." World Bank Social Protection Policy Note 13, Washington, DC.

Ahmed, A. U., Mehnaz Rabbani, Munshi Sulaiman, and Narayan C. Das. 2009. "The Impact of Asset Transfer on Livelihoods of the Ultra Poor in Bangladesh." Research Monograph Series 39, Research and Evaluation Division, BRAC, Dhaka.

Aldana, U., T. Vásquez, and J. Yancari. 2016. "Sierra Sur and Juntos: An Analysis Based on the Joint Implementation of Both Programs in Chumbivilcas, Cusco, Perú." In *Protection, Production, Promotion: Exploring Synergies between Social Protection and Productive Development in Latin America*, edited by J. H. Maldonado, R. Moreno-Sánchez, J. A. Gómez, and V. L. Jurado. Bogotá: Universidad de los Andes.

Almeida, Rita K., and Emanuela Galasso. 2010. "Jump-Starting Self-Employment? Evidence for Welfare Participants in Argentina." *World Development* 38 (5): 742–55. https://doi.org/10.1016/j.worlddev.2009.11.018.

Argent, Jonathan, Britta Augsburg, and Imran Rasul. 2014. "Livestock Asset Transfers with and without Training: Evidence from Rwanda." *Journal of Economic Behavior and Organization* 108: 19–39.

Asadullah, M. Niaz, and Jinnat Ara. 2016. "Evaluating the Long-Run Impact of an Innovative Anti-Poverty Program: Evidence Using Household Panel Data." IZA Discussion Paper 9749, Institute of Labor Economics, Bonn.

Asensio, Raúl, Juan Fernández, and María Luisa Burneo. 2016. "Validación herramienta de género FAO para servicios de asesoramiento rural en Perú: Estudio de caso Haku Wiñay." Manuscript, Instituto de Estudios Peruanos, Lima.

Bandiera, Oriana, Robin Burgess, Narayan Das, Selim Gulesci, Imran Rasul, and Munshi Sulaiman. 2017. "Labor Markets and Poverty in Village Economies." *Quarterly Journal of Economics* 132 (2): 811–70.

Bandiera, Oriana, Robin Burgess, S. Gulesci, I. Rasul, and Munshi Sulaiman. 2013. "Can Entrepreneurship Programs Transform the Economic Lives of the Poor?" IZA Discussion Paper 7386, Institute of Labor Economics, Bonn.

Banerjee, Abhijit, Esther Duflo, Raghabendra Chattopadhyay, and Jeremy Shapiro. 2016. "The Long-Term Impacts of a 'Graduation' Program: Evidence from West Bengal." J-PAL Working Paper, Cambridge, MA. https://www.povertyactionlab.org/evaluation/graduating-ultra-poor-india.

Banerjee, Abhijit, Esther Duflo, Nathaneal Goldberg, Dean Karlan, Robert Osei, William Parienté, Jeremy Shapiro, Bram Thuysbaert, and Christopher Udry. 2015. "A Multifaceted Program Causes Lasting Progress for the Very Poor: Evidence from Six Countries." *Science* 348 (6236):1260799.

Banerjee, Abhijit, Dean Karlan, Robert Darko Osei, Hannah Trachtman, and Christopher Udry. 2018. "Unpacking a Multi-faceted Program to Build Sustainable Income for the Very Poor." NBER Working Paper 247271, National Bureau of Economic Research, Cambridge, MA.

Banerjee, Abhijit V., Esther Duflo, and Garima Sharma. 2020. "Long-Term Effects of the Targeting the Ultra Poor Program." NBER Working Paper w28074, National Bureau of Economic Research, Cambridge, MA.

Bastagli, Francesca, Jessica Hagen-Zanker, Luke Harman, Valentina Barca, Georgina Sturge, Tanja Schmidt, and Luca Pellerano. 2016. *Cash Transfers: What Does the Evidence Say? A Rigorous Review of Programme Impact and of the Role of Design and Implementation Features*. London: Overseas Development Institute.

Bauchet, Jonathan, Jonathan Morduch, and Shamika Ravi. 2015. "Failure vs. Displacement: Why an Innovative Anti-Poverty Program Showed No Net Impact in South India." *Journal of Development Economics* 116: 1–16.

Bedoya, Guadalupe, Aidan Coville, Johannes Haushofer, Mohammad Isaqzadeh, and Jeremy Shapiro. 2019. "No Household Left Behind: Afghanistan Targeting the Ultra Poor Impact Evaluation." Policy Research Working Paper 8877, World Bank, Washington, DC.

Berhane, Guush, Daniel O. Gilligan, John Hoddinott, Neha Kumar, and Alemayehu Seyoum Taffesse. 2014. "Can Social Protection Work in Africa? The Impact of Ethiopia's Productive Safety Net Programme." *Economic Development and Cultural Change* 63 (1): 1–26. doi:10.1086/677753.

Bertrand, M., Bruno Crépon, Alicia Marguerie, and Patrick Premand. 2017. "Contemporaneous and Post-Program Impacts of a Public Works Program: Evidence from Côte d'Ivoire." Working Paper, World Bank and J-PAL, Washington, DC. https://www.povertyactionlab.org/evaluation/youth-employment-and-skills-development-cote-divoire.

Betcherman, G., K. Olivas, and A. Dar. 2004. "Impacts of Active Labor Market Programs: New Evidence from Evaluations with Particular Attention to Developing and Transition Countries." World Bank Social Protection Discussion Paper 0402, Washington, DC.

Blattman, Christopher, Stefan Dercon, and Simon Franklin. 2019. "Impacts of Industrial and Entrepreneurial Jobs on Youth: Five-Year Experimental Evidence on Factory Job Offers and Cash Grants in Ethiopia." Working Paper 2019-65, University of Chicago.

Blattman, Christopher, Nathan Fiala, and Sebastian Martinez. 2014. "Generating Skilled Self-Employment in Developing Countries: Experimental Evidence from Uganda." *Quarterly Journal of Economics* 129: 697–752. doi:10.1093/qje/qjt057.

Blattman, Christopher, Nathan Fiala, and Sebastian Martinez. 2018. "The Long-Term Impacts of Grants on Poverty: Nine-Year Evidence from Uganda's Youth Opportunities Program." NBER Working Paper 24999, National Bureau of Econoic Research, Cambridge, MA.

Blattman, Christopher, Eric P. Green, Julian Jamison, M. Christian Lehmann, and Jeannie Annan. 2016. "The Returns to Microenterprise Support among the Ultrapoor: A Field Experiment in Postwar Uganda." *American Economic Journal: Applied Economics* 8 (2): 35–64.

Blattman, C., and L. Ralston. 2015. "Generating Employment in Poor and Fragile States: Evidence from Labor Market and Entrepreneurship Programs." Unpublished paper. http://dx.doi.org/10.2139/ssrn.2622220.

Bossuroy, Thomas, Estelle Koussoubé, and Patrick Premand. 2019. *Constraints to Productive Employment Faced by Safety Nets Beneficiaries in the Sahel Results of a Multi-country Qualitative Assessment.* Washington, DC: World Bank.

Bossuroy, Thomas, Julia Vaillant, William Parienté, Christopher Udry, Harounan Kazianga, Dean Karlan, Markus Goldstein, and Patrick Premand. 2019. "Promoting Productive Inclusion and Resilience among the Poor: Multi-country RCT of the Sahel Adaptive Social Protection." *AEA RCT Registry, August 29.* https://doi.org/10.1257/rct.2544-4.0.

Buvinic, M., and R. Furst-Nichols. 2014. "Promoting Women's Economic Empowerment: What Works?" *World Bank Research Observer* 31: 59–101.

CADEP (Centro de Análisis y Difusión de la Economía Paraguaya). 2017. *Evaluacion de proceso del programa Sembrando Oportunidades Familia por Familia.* Report prepared for La Plataforma de Evaluación y Aprendizaje del Programa Graduación en América Latina. Asunción, Paraguay: Centro de CADEP.

Card, D., J. Kluve, and A. Weber. 2015. "What Works? A Meta Analysis of Recent Active Labor Market Program Evaluations." IZA Discussion Paper 9236, Institute of Labor Economics Bonn.

CARE. 2019. *Kore Lavi Safety Net Beneficiary Resilience Assessment: Listening, Reflecting and Learning on Resilience and Food Security.* Washington, DC: USAID.

Chowdhury, Reajul, Elliott Collins, Ethan Ligon, and Munshi Sulaiman. 2017. "Valuing Assets Provided to Low-Income Households in South Sudan." Discussion Paper, BRAC University, Dhaka, Bangladesh.

Costa, Lorena Vieira, Steven M. Helfand, and André Portela Souza. 2018. *No Impact of Rural Development Policies? No Synergies with Conditional Cash Transfers? An Investigation of the IFAD-Supported Gavião Project in Brazil.* Rome: International Fund for Agricultural Development.

Daidone, S., B. Davis, M. Knowles, R. Pickmans, N. Pace, and S. Handa. 2017. *The Social Cash Transfer Programme and the Farm Input Subsidy Programme in Malawi: Complementary Instruments for Supporting Agricultural Transformation and Increasing Consumption and Productive Activities?* Rome: FAO.

Das, Narayan C., Sibbir Ahmad, Anindita Bhattacharjee, Jinnat Ara, and Abdul Bayes. 2016. "Grant vs. Credit-Plus Approach to Poverty Reduction: An Evaluation of BRAC's Experience with Ultra Poor." CFPR Working Paper 24, BRAC, Dhaka.

Davis, Benjamin, Sudhanshu Handa, Nicola Hypher, Natalia Winder Rossi, Paul Winters, and Jennifer Yablonski. 2016. *From Evidence to Action: The Story of Cash Transfers and Impact Evaluation in Sub-Saharan Africa.* Oxford: Oxford University Press.

de Mel, Suresh, David McKenzie, and Christopher Woodruff. 2012. "One-Time Transfers of Cash or Capital Have Long-Lasting Effects on Microenterprises in Sri Lanka." *Science* 335: 96266. doi:10.1126/science.1212973.

de Mel, Suresh, David McKenzie, and Christopher Woodruff. 2014. "Business Training and female Enterprise Start-Up, Growth, and Dynamics: Experimental Evidence from Sri Lanka." *Journal of Development Economics* 106 (C): 199–210.

de Sanfeliú, Margarita Beneke, Amy Ángel, and Mauricio Arturo Shi. 2016. "Conditional Cash Transfer Programs and Rural Development in El Salvador." In *Protection, Production, Promotion: Exploring Synergies between Social Protection and Productive Development in Latin America*, edited by J. H. Maldonado, R. Moreno-Sánchez, J. A. Gómez, and V. L. Jurado. Bogotá: Universidad de los Andes.

Deininger, Klaus, and Yanyan Liu. 2009. "Economic and Social Impacts of Self-Help Groups in India." Policy Research Working Paper 4884, World Bank, Washington, DC.

Deininger, Klaus, and Yanyan Liu. 2013. "Economic and Social Impacts of an Innovative Self-Help Group Model in India." *World Development* 43: 149–63. doi:10.1016/j.worlddev.2012.09.019.

Devereux, Stephen, Keetie Roelen, Ricardo Sabates, Dimitri Stoelinga, and Arnaud Dyevre. 2015. *Final Evaluation Report: Concern's Graduation Model Program in Burundi.* Brighton, UK: Institute of Development Studies.

Devereux, Stephen, and Ricardo Sabates. 2016. *Final Evaluation Report: Enhancing the Productive Capacity of Extremely Poor People in Rwanda.* Dublin: Concern Worldwide and IDS.

El-Zoghbi, Mayada, Nina Holle, and Matthew Soursourian. 2019. "Emerging Evidence on Financial Inclusion: Moving from Black and White to Color." CGAP Focus Note, Consultative Group to Address Poverty, Washington, DC.

Emran, M. S., V. Robano, and S. C. Smith. 2009. "Assessing the Frontiers of Ultra-poverty Reduction: Evidence from Challenging the Frontiers of Poverty Reduction/Targeting the Ultra-poor, an Innovative Program in Bangladesh." *Economic Development and Cultural Change* 62: 339–80.

Escobal, Javier, and Carmen Ponce, eds. 2016. *Combinando protección social con generación de oportunidades económicas: Una evaluación de los avances del programa Haku Wiñay.* Lima: Grupo de Análisis para el Desarrollo.

FAO (Food and Agriculture Organization of the United Nations). 2016. *Les transferts productifs (CASH+) au Niger et au Burkina Faso: Une approche innovante pour renforcer les moyens d'existence vulnérables au Sahel.* Rome: FAO.

FAO. 2018. *FAO and Cash+: How to Maximize the Impacts of Cash Transfers.* Rome: FAO.

FAO and UNICEF. 2018. *Impact Evaluation of Lesotho's Child Grants Programme (CGP) and Sustainable Poverty Reduction through Income, Nutrition and Access to Government Services (SPRINGS) Project.* Rome and Geneva: FAO and UNICEF.

Fernández, Maria Ignacia, Maria Fernanda Leiva, Jorge Ortega, and Macarena Weason. 2016. "Synergistic Effects between Ingreso Ético Familiar and the Enterprise Support Programs in Chile, 2012–2014." In *Protection, Production, Promotion: Exploring Synergies between Social Protection and Productive Development in Latin America*, edited by J. H. Maldonado, R. Moreno-Sánchez, J. A. Gómez and V. L. Jurado. Bogotá: Universidad de los Andes.

Filipski, Mateusz, J. Edward Taylor, Getachew Ahmed Abegaz, Tadele Ferede, Alemayehu Seyoum Taffesse, and Xinshen Diao. 2017. *General Equilibrium*

Impact Assessment of the Productive Safety Net Program in Ethiopia. New Delhi: International Initiative for Impact Evaluation (3ie).

Gahamanyi, Vincent, and Andrew Kettlewell. 2015. "Evaluating Graduation: Insights from the Vision 2020 Umurenge Programme in Rwanda." *IDS Bulletin* 46 (2).

Garcia, F., S. M. Helfand, and A. P. Souza. 2016. "Conditional Cash Transfers and Rural Development Policies in Brazil: Exploring Potential Synergies between Bolsa Família and Pronaf." In *Protection, Production, Promotion: Exploring Synergies between Social Protection and Productive Development in Latin America*, edited by J. H. Maldonado, R. Moreno-Sánchez, J. A. Gómez and V. L. Jurado. Bogotá: Universidad de los Andes.

Gobin, Vilas J., Paulo Santos, and Russell Toth. 2016. "Poverty Graduation with Cash Transfers: A Randomized Evaluation." Monash University Economics Working Papers 23-16, Melbourne.

Hernandez, Ricardo, Akhter U. Ahmed, Arifeen Akter, Nusrat Zaitun Hossain, Samira Choudhury, and Mehrab Malek. 2016. *An Evaluation of the Program on Enhancing Resilience to Natural Disasters and the Effects of Climate Change in Bangladesh*. Dhaka: International Food Policy Research Institute.

Hoddinott, John, Guush Berhane, Daniel O. Gilligan, Neha Kumar, and Alemayehu Seyoum Taffesse. 2012. "The Impact of Ethiopia's Productive Safety Net Programme and Related Transfers on Agricultural Productivity." *Journal of African Economies* 21 (5): 761–86. doi:10.1093/jae/ejs023.

Hoffmann, Vivian, Vijayendra Rao, Upamanyu Datta, Paromita Sanyal, Vaishnavi Surendra, and Shruti Majumdar. 2018. "Poverty and Empowerment Impacts of the Bihar Rural Livelihoods Project in India." International Initiative for Impact Evaluation (3ie), New Delhi.

Hoffmann, Vivian, Vijayendra Rao, Vaishnavi Surendra, and Upamanyu Datta. 2017. "Relief from Usury: Impact of a Community-Based Microcredit Program in Rural India." Policy Research Working Paper 8021, World Bank, Washington, DC.

Hoy, Christopher, and Darian Naidoo. 2019. "The Marginal Benefit of an Active Labor Market Program Relative to a Public Works Program: Evidence from Papua New Guinea." *IZA Journal of Development and Migration* 10. doi:10.2478/izajodm-2019-0003.

HTSPE. 2011. *Bangladesh: Independent Impact Assessment of the Chars Livelihoods Programme: Phase 1 Final Report*. Hemel Hempstead, UK: HTSPE.

Huda, Karishma. 2009. "Mid-term (12 Month) Trickle Up India TUP Process Evaluation: CGAP–Ford Foundation Graduation Pilot." BRAC Development Institute, Dhaka.

Ibarraran, P., and D. R. Shady. 2009. "Evaluating the Impact of Job Training Programmes in Latin America: Evidence from IDB Funded Operations." *Journal of Development Effectiveness* 1 (2): 195–216.

Ismayilova, Leyla, and Leyla Karimli. 2018. "Harsh Parenting and Violence against Children: A Trial with Ultrapoor Families in Francophone West Africa." *Journal of Clinical Child and Adolescent Psychology* 49: 1–18. doi:10.1080/15374416.2018.1485103.

Ismayilova, Leyla, Leyla Karimli, Jo Sanson, Eleni Gaveras, Rachel Nanema, Alexice Tô-Camier, and Josh Chaffin. 2018. "Improving Mental Health among Ultra-Poor Children: Two-Year Outcomes of a Cluster-Randomized Trial in Burkina Faso." *Social Science and Medicine* 208: 180–89. doi:10.1016/j.socscimed.2018.04.022.

Ivaschenko, Oleksiy, Darian Naidoo, David Newhouse, and Sonya Sultan. 2017. "Can Public Works Programs Reduce Youth Crime? Evidence from Papua New Guinea's Urban Youth Employment Project." *IZA Journal of Development and Migration* 7 (1): 9. doi:1086/s40176-017-0101-7.

J-PAL and IPA Policy Bulletin. 2015. "Building Stable Livelihoods for the Ultra-Poor." Abdul Latif Jameel Poverty Action Lab and Innovations for Poverty Action, Cambridge, MA.

Jensen, Nathaniel D., Christopher B. Barrett, and Andrew G. Mude. 2017. "Cash Transfers and Index Insurance: A Comparative Impact Analysis from Northern Kenya." *Journal of Development Economics* 129: 14–28. doi:https://doi.org/10.1016/j.jdeveco.2017.08.002.

Kabeer, Naila, Karishma Huda, Sandeep Kaur, and Nicolina Lamhauge. 2012. "Productive Safety Nets for Women in Extreme Poverty: Lessons from Pilot Projects in India and Pakistan." Discussion Paper 28/12, Centre for Development Policy and Research, School of Oriental and African Studies, London.

Kagin, Justin, J. Edward Taylor, Luca Pellerano, Silvio Daidone, Florian Juergens, Noemi Pace, and Marco Knowles. 2019. *Local Economy Impacts and Cost-Benefit Analysis of Social Protection and Agricultural Interventions in Malawi*. Rome: Food and Agriculture Organization of the United Nations.

Karimli, Leyla, Bijetri Bose, and Njeri Kagotho. 2019. "Integrated Graduation Program and Its Effect on Women and Household Economic Well-being: Findings from a Randomised Controlled Trial in Burkina Faso." *Journal of Development Studies* 56 (7): 1–18. doi:10.1080/00220388.2019.1677887.

Karimli, Leyla, Lucia Rost, and Leyla Ismayilova. 2018. "Integrating Economic Strengthening and Family Coaching to Reduce Work-Related Health Hazards among Children of Poor Households: Burkina Faso." *Journal of Adolescent Health* 62 (1): S6–S14. doi:10.1080/00220388.2019.1677887.

Kluve, J. 2016. *A Review of the Effectiveness of Active Labour Market Programmes with a Focus on Latin America and the Caribbean*. Geneva: International Labour Office Research Department.

Kochar, Anjini, Bidisha Barooah, Chandan Jain, Geeta Singh, Nagabhushana Closepet, Raghunathan Narayanan, Ritwik Sarkar, and Rohan Shah. 2020. *Impact Evaluation of the National Rural Livelihoods Project*. Impact Evaluation Report 128. New Delhi: International Initiative for Impact Evaluation (3ie).

Krishna, Anirudh, Meri Poghosyan, and Narayan Das. 2012. "How Much Can Asset Transfers Help the Poorest? Evaluating the Results of BRAC's Ultra-poor Programme (2002–2008)." *Journal of Development Studies* 48: 254–67. doi:10.1080/00220388.2011.621942.

Loayza, Cesar Del Pozo. 2015. "Impact Assessment of Conditional Cash Transfers and Agricultural Credit on the Accumulation of Productive Assets by Rural Households in Peru." *Policy in Focus: Social Protection, Entrepreneurship and Labour Market Activation* 12 (2).

Macours, Karen, Patrick Premand, and Renos Vakis. 2012. "Transfers, Diversification and Household Risk Strategies: Experimental Evidence with Lessons for Climate Change Adaptation." Policy Research Working Paper 6053, World Bank, Washington, DC.

Macours, Karen, Norman Schady, and Renos Vakis. 2012. "Cash Transfers, Behavioral Changes, and Cognitive Development in Early Childhood: Evidence from a Randomized Experiment." *American Economic Journal: Applied Economics* 4 (2): 247–73.

Macours, Karen, and Renos Vakis. 2014. "Changing Households' Investment Behaviour through Social Interactions with Local Leaders: Evidence from a Randomised Transfer Programme." *Economic Journal* 124 (576): 607–33. doi:10.1111/ecoj.12145.

Maldonado, Jorge H., Viviana Leon-Jurado, John Gomez, Daniel Rodriguez, and Laura I. Villa. 2019. "The Graduation Approach for the Reduction of Extreme Poverty: Impact Evaluation of Sembrando Oportunidades Familia Por Familia in Paraguay." Documento CEDE no. 2019-19. http://dx.doi.org/10.2139/ssrn.3411131.

Maldonado, Jorge H., Rocio Moreno-Sánchez, J. A. Gómez, and V. L. Jurado, eds. 2016. *Protection, Production, Promotion: Exploring Synergies between Social Protection and Productive Development in Latin America*. Bogotá: Universidad de los Andes.

McKenzie, D. 2017. "How Effective Are Active Labor Market Programs in Developing Countries? A Critical Review of Recent Evidence." Policy Research Working Paper 8011, World Bank, Washington, DC.

Millán, Teresa Molina, Tania Barham, Karen Macours, John A. Maluccio, and Marco Stampini. 2019. "Long-Term Impacts of Conditional Cash Transfers: Review of the Evidence." *World Bank Research Observer* 34 (1): 119–59. doi:10.1093/WBGro /lky005.

Misha, Farzana, Wameq Raza, J. Ara, and E. Poel. 2019. "How Far Does a Big Push Really Push? Long-Term Effects of an Asset Transfer Program on Employment Trajectories." *Economic Development and Cultural Change* 68 (1): 41–62. doi:10.1086/700556.

Moreno-Sánchez, Rocío, Jorge H. Maldonado, Vanesa Martínez, and Arturo Rodríguez. 2018. "Qualitative Evaluation of the Poverty-Alleviation Program Produciendo por mi Futuro in Colombia." Working Paper 24, Centro de Estudios Sobre Desarrollo Economico (CEDE) Bogotá.

Moreno-Sánchez, Rocío, Vanesa Martínez, Jorge H. Maldonado, and Arturo Rodríguez. 2018. "Changes in Subjective Well-Being, Aspirations and Expectations in Participants of Poverty Alleviation Programs: A Qualitative Analysis of Produciendo Por Mi Futuro in Colombia." Working Paper 3, Centro de Estudios Sobre Desarrollo Economico (CEDE), Bogotá.

Moya, A. 2016. "Rural Poverty Alleviation Programs in Colombia: An Assessment of the Synergies between Oportunidades Rurales and Familias en Acción." In *Protection, Production, Promotion: Exploring Synergies between Social Protection and Productive Development in Latin America*, edited by J. H. Maldonado, R. Moreno-Sánchez, J. A. Gómez and V. L. Jurado. Bogotá: Universidad de los Andes.

Müller, Angelika, Utz Pape, and Laura Ralston. 2019. "Broken Promises: Evaluating an Incomplete Cash Transfer Program." Policy Research Working Paper 9016. World Bank, Washington, DC.

O'Keefe, Philip, Puja Vasudeva Dutta, and Robert Palacios. 2020. *Diverse Paths: The Dynamic Evolution of Social Protection in Asia and the Pacific*. Washington, DC: World Bank.

Pace, N., S. Daidone, B. Davis, S. Handa, M. Knowles, and R. Pickmans. 2017. "One Plus One Can Be Greater Than Two: Evaluating Synergies of Development Programmes in Malawi." *Journal of Development Studies* 54 (11): 2023–60. doi:10.1080/00220388.2017.1380794.

Premand, Patrick, and Alicia Marguerie. 2020. *Résultats de l'Evaluation d'Impact du Projet d'Insertion Socio-Economique pour les populations vulnérables de l'Ouest de Côte d'Ivoire (PRISE)*. Washington, DC: World Bank.

Prennushi, Giovanna, and A. Gupta. 2014. "Women's Empowerment and Socio-Economic Outcomes Impacts of the Andhra Pradesh Rural Poverty Reduction Program." Policy Research Working Paper 6841, World Bank, Washington, DC.

Pritchett, Lant, and Justin Sandefur. 2013. "Context Matters for Size: Why External Validity Claims and Development Practice Don't Mix." Center for Global Development Working Paper 336, Washington, DC.

Rakotomanana, Faly, Zo Tahiana Randrianatoandro, and Julia Rachel Ravelosoa. 2018. *Mid-term Evaluation Results: The Fiavota Program—Main Report*. Geneva and Washington, DC: UNICEF and World Bank.

Ralston, Laura R., Colin Andrews, and Allan Jer-Yu Hsiao. 2017. "The Impacts of Safety Nets in Africa : What Are We Learning?" Policy Research Working Paper WPS 8255, World Bank, Washington, DC.

Raza, W. A., N. C. Das, and F. A. Misha. 2012. "Can Ultra-Poverty Be Sustainably Improved? Evidence from BRAC in Bangladesh." *Journal of Development Effectiveness* 4 (2): 257–76.

Raza, Wameq A., Ellen Van de Poel, and Tom van Ourti. 2018. "Impact and Spillover Effects of an Asset Transfer Programme on Malnutrition: Evidence from a Randomised Control Trial in Bangladesh." *Journal of Health Economics* 62: 105–20.

Roelen, K., and S. Devereux. 2019. "Money and the Message: The Role of Training and Coaching in Graduation Programming." *Journal of Development Studies* 55 (6): 1121–39.

Roelen, Keetie, and Amrita Saha. 2019. *Fonkoze's CLM Ultra Poverty Programme: Understanding and Improving Child Development and Child Well-being—Endline Report*. Brighton, UK: Institute of Development Studies, University of Sussex.

Roelen, K., M. Sherer, and C. L. Himmelstine. 2020. "The Role of Graduation Programming in Promoting Early Childhood Development: An Overview of the Evidence." *Journal of the British Academy* 8 (s2): 133–61.

Rosas, Nina, Samantha Zaldivar, Maria Julia Granata, Gaew Lertsuridej, Nicholas Wilson, Albina Chuwa, Rainer Kiama, Mayasa Mahfoudh Mwinyi, and Asia Hassan Mussa. 2019. *Evaluating Tanzania's Productive Social Safety Net: Findings from the Midline Survey*. Washington, DC: World Bank.

Sabates-Wheeler, Rachel, and Stephen Devereux. 2012. "Cash Transfers and High Food Prices: Explaining Outcomes on Ethiopia's Productive Safety Net Programme." *Food Policy* 35 (4): 274–85.

Sabates-Wheeler, Rachel, and Stephen Devereux. 2013. "Transforming Livelihoods for Resilient Futures: How to Facilitate Graduation in Social Protection Programmes." *Development and Change* 35 (4): 274–85.

Sabates-Wheeler, Rachel, Jeremy Lind, and John Hoddinott. 2013. "Implementing Social Protection in Agro-pastoralist and Pastoralist Areas: How Local Distribution Structures Moderate PSNP Outcomes in Ethiopia." *World Development* 50: 1–12. https://doi.org/10.1016/j.worlddev.2013.04.005.

Sabates-Wheeler, R., R. Sabates, and S. Devereux. 2018. "Enabling Graduation for Whom? Identifying and Explaining Heterogeneity in Livelihood Trajectories Post-Cash Transfer Exposure." *Journal of International Development* 30: 1071–95.

Sedlmayr, Richard, Anuj Shah, and Munshi Sulaiman. 2019. "Cash-Plus: Poverty Impacts of Alternative Transfer-Based Approaches." *Journal of Development Economics* 102418. https://doi.org/10.1016/j.jdeveco.2019.102418.

Sengupta, Anasuya. 2012. *Pathways out of the Productive Safety Net Programme: Lessons from a Graduation Pilot in Ethiopia*. Dhaka: BRAC Development Institute.

Sheldon, Tony, ed. 2016. *Preserving the Essence, Adapting for Reach: Early Lessons from Large-Scale Implementations of the Graduation Approach*. New York: Ford Foundation.

Shoaf, Emma, and Anton Simanowitz. 2019. *Pathways to Sustained Exit from Extreme Poverty: Evidence from Fonkoze's Extreme Poverty 'Graduation' Programme*. Brighton, UK: Institute of Development Studies.

Siddiki, Omar Faruque, Rebecca Holmes, Ferdous Jahan, Fahim Subhan Chowdhury, and Jessica Hagen-Zanker. 2014. *How Do Social Safety Nets Contribute to Social Inclusion in Bangladesh? Evidence from the Chars Livelihoods Programme and the Vulnerable Group Development Programme*. London: Overseas Development Institute.

Slater, R., S. Wiggins, L. Harman, M. Ulrichs, L. Scott, M. Knowles, P. Pozarny, and G. Calcagnini. 2016. *Strengthening Coherence between Agriculture and Social Protection: Synthesis of Seven Country Case Studies*. Rome: FAO.

Smith, Lisa, Tim Frankenberger, K. Fox, S. Nelson, and T. Griffin. 2019. *Ethiopia Pastoralist Areas Resilience Improvement and Market Expansion (PRIME) Project Impact Evaluation: Endline Survey Report*. Prepared for the US Agency for International Development. Washington, DC: USAID.

Soares, Fabio Veras, Marco Knowles, Silvio Daidone, and Nyasha Tirivayi. 2017. *Combined Effects and Synergies between Agricultural and Social Protection Interventions: What Is the Evidence So Far?* Rome: FAO.

Taylor, J. E., K. Thome, and M. Filipski. 2016. "Local Economy-wide Impact Evaluation of Social Cash Transfer Programmes." In *The Promise of Social Protection: Social and Productive Impacts of Cash Transfer Programmes in Sub-Saharan Africa*, edited by B. Davis, S. Handa, N. Hypher, N. Winder Rossi, P. Winters, and J. Yablonski. Oxford: Oxford University Press.

Tirivayi, N., M. Knowles, and B. Davis. 2013. *The Interaction between Social Protection and Agriculture: A Review of Evidence.* Rome: FAO.

Vivalt, Eva. 2019. "How Much Can We Generalize from Impact Evaluations?" Unpublished paper. Australian National University.

Waddington, Hugh, Birte Snilstveit, Jorge Hombrados, Martina Vojtkova, Daniel Phillips, Philip Davies, and Howard White. 2014. *Farmer Field Schools for Improving Farming Practices and Farmer Outcomes: A Systematic Review.* Campbell Systematic Reviews 6. Oslo: Campbell Collaboration.

Yúnez-Naude, Antonio, George Dyer-Leal, Fabiola Rivera-Ramírez, and Omar Stabridis-Arana. 2016. "The Fight against Poverty Program and Rural Development Policies in Mexico: Impact Assessments and Alternative Policies." In *Protection, Production, Promotion: Exploring Synergies between Social Protection and Productive Development in Latin America*, edited by J. H. Maldonado, R. Moreno-Sánchez, J. A. Gómez, and V. L. Jurado. Bogotá: Universidad de los Andes.

CHAPTER 6
Assessing the Cost of Economic Inclusion Programs

This chapter provides one of the first standardized multicountry cost disaggregations of government- and nongovernment-led economic inclusion programs globally. The analysis has real-time value for policy dialogue and is based on a newly developed Partnership for Economic Inclusion (PEI) Quick Costing Tool 2020 applied across 34 programs globally.

This costing analysis is a critical step toward understanding cost optimization and cost-effectiveness in economic inclusion programs. Costing discussions have been fraught with methodological challenges and minimal available information.

The cost of economic inclusion programs tends to be driven by a single intervention, such as cash grants, asset or input transfers, or social safety net (SSN) transfers. Human resource and staff costs are more prominent cost drivers in complex projects, whose costs are driven by multiple components, rather than those driven by one component.

Program "sticker prices" can be misleading and mask considerable heterogeneity. The price range of the economic inclusion programs sampled varies substantially depending on design and target groups. Sticker prices need to be understood based on their adequacy and impact.

FUTURE DIRECTIONS

There is a strong operational demand to better understand cost effectiveness and program sustainability. The PEI Quick Costing Tool 2020 provides a simple starting point to frame these debates. The tool will evolve as further evidence and know-how emerges.

Researchers assessing the impact of economic inclusion programs should systematically collect and report on cost data in addition to impact sizes. The systematic understanding of costs will allow governments to make sense of program cost-benefit ratios and guide their policy choices.

Reliable costing data offer considerable scope to further understand cost optimization. Optimizing costs includes, but is not limited to, variations in size and cost recovery of cash grants; variations in intensity of modality, frequency, and content of training; and in coaching.

Introduction

Policy discourse on economic inclusion programs has typically focused on the pursuit of a "sticker price" to identify investment worthiness or cost-effectiveness. A reframing of the expectations regarding both a sticker price approach and the utility of cost data is overdue.

Various impact evaluation studies (Bedoya et al. 2019; Ara et al. 2017; Bauchet, Morduch, and Ravi 2015; Banerjee et al. 2015; Bandiera et al. 2013) have tried to determine the cost of economic inclusion programs (see appendix B for a full list of impact evaluation studies), and some have also assessed the cost-effectiveness of them by estimating their internal rate of return. A review of these studies reveals a large variation in cost per beneficiary, between $41 and $2,253 (in 2011 purchasing power parity, PPP).[1] One estimate that considers the size of an asset transfer required to escape poverty (a poverty-trap-based estimation) finds the appropriate size is $504 (in 2007 PPP) (Balboni et al. 2020). Given the variations in costs, it is important to reset expectations of a sticker price by undertaking a detailed and standardized costing survey that goes beyond a cost-effectiveness assessment.

Program cost analysis is a critical tool to inform not just cost-effectiveness but also program design decisions. Assessing program costs can enable policy makers and program designers to identify limitations and opportunities to inform program activity and policies. To begin with, total program costs are defined as including the following:

- The direct cost of each benefit provided to the beneficiaries of a program

- The indirect cost of providing those benefits, such as administrative or implementation costs and beneficiary identification costs

- The direct cost associated with the beneficiaries' participation in program activities, such as their travel costs or the cost of enrolling in a mobile wallet service to receive cash transfers in electronic form

- The opportunity cost of beneficiaries' participation in program activities, including the monetized value of time that they forego from other productive activities in order to attend program activities

Disaggregating total program costs can enable programs to assess the affordability and scale of a project with available resources or understand the relative cost share of each component.

Disaggregated costing analysis entails the disaggregation of the total cost of a program into the categories noted as well as any further disaggregation. The latter could include the indirect cost of providing benefits, the costs of implementation at the national versus province or district level, and the direct cost of each program component benefit. This analysis can be done on a yearly basis or, for rapidly evolving programs and policy contexts, in shorter timeframes. As discussed in chapter 1, economic inclusion programs tend to be quite varied even as they all focus on providing a multipronged intervention to the poor. The process of correctly designing an appropriate economic inclusion program can be quite complex and cumbersome, and information on cost structures can provide important guidance to designing such a program and broader policy making, as in the case of other poverty alleviation transfer programs (Caldés, Coady, and Maluccio 2006).

Cost-effectiveness analysis is particularly important for economic inclusion interventions, given that it involves multiple components. Cost-effectiveness analysis is the estimation of the return from the program cost from an investment point of view, and, depending on the quality of impact data available, it could be disaggregated. This type of analysis is particularly important for economic inclusion programs as they rely on layering multiple interventions. While this multiplicity brings greater impact (chapter 5), it also brings greater administrative complexity (chapters 3 and 4) and potentially higher costs. Undertaking a cost-effectiveness analysis can, therefore, be quite informative in terms of whether the impact generated by a bundled intervention is worth the investment. But there are various methodological limitations, as discussed in the following sections, that can render cost-effectiveness analysis less convincing and useful. Moreover, such analysis cannot be undertaken regularly, given the data requirements. Cost-effectiveness analysis will typically be undertaken with an impact evaluation, which can take three to five years to implement.

Costing data on economic inclusion programs is minimally available and largely incomplete when disaggregated. Only 20 out of 76 impact studies noted in chapter 5 report on total cost, and only 15 of them provide some form of disaggregation. At the same time, programs implemented by nongovernmental organizations (NGOs) are disproportionately represented, compared to the universe of programs presented in chapter 3, with 19 of these 20 studies reporting on NGO programs. Of those that provide disaggregated data, grant, asset transfer, and consumption support tend to be the most commonly reported intervention, constituting between 15 percent and 67 percent (with an average of 38 percent) of total cost.

Cost-effectiveness studies have some methodological challenges that make cross-context analyses challenging for the following reasons:

- Many social programs tend to have multiple objectives, some of which are not quantifiable and hence remain unaccounted for in cost-effectiveness studies.

- Measurement methodologies can vary across studies and contexts, resulting in the benefits of an intervention being constructed differently than in others and hence being incomparable. For example, to quantify benefits, Bandiera et al. (2017) use household consumption, whereas Blattman et al. (2016) use total household nondurable consumption, while Banerjee et al. (2015) use nondurable consumption, assets, and total consumption, varying by year of estimation.

- Contexts and target groups are not always comparable.

- The quality of impact and cost data may vary across programs.

- Inaccurate assumptions about the long-term sustainability of impacts may easily be made. For instance, Kidd and Athias (2019) discuss how both Banerjee et al. (2015) and Bandiera et al. (2013) assume that the gains from the program they studied would last every year until the death of a beneficiary, despite there being mixed evidence of long-term sustainability of impacts. As a result, comparisons across programs can be quite imperfect and may not capture the full value of a program.

The PEI Quick Costing Tool 2020 was developed to demystify the cost of economic inclusion programs. As detailed in the following text, the focus of this survey is on understanding the more operational aspects of economic inclusion programming rather than just the cost-benefit analysis. The survey is also expected to serve as a template, with revisions and the benefit of hindsight, for similar future exercises. The objective of this exercise is to develop an early understanding of the range of costs of economic inclusion programs and the cost drivers, including the complexity of the programs and the modality of delivery, the costs of delivering these interventions, and the underlying intervention costs and dosage. Note that this costing exercise is limited to the direct cost of each benefit provided to the beneficiaries and the indirect cost of providing those benefits, defined in this introduction's third paragraph, and therefore does not include beneficiary costs of participation due to the time requirements of collecting these data points. As desirable as it may be to do so, this report does not include a cost-benefit analysis—due to the lack of simultaneous availability of impact data for the programs that reported on cost—but it does reflect on some existing literature.

The PEI Quick Costing Tool 2020

For the PEI Quick Costing Tool 2020, PEI gathered and analyzed self-reported cost data from 34 programs globally, ensuring that the programs represented a mix of income, geographic, and sociopolitical contexts as well as implementation modalities. These programs are from 25 countries, primarily from Sub-Saharan Africa and South Asia together with a few each from the other regions. While 24 of these programs are government-led, 10 are NGO-led.[2] In terms of program typologies, 12 are social safety net (SSN) and 22 are livelihoods and jobs (L&J) programs. About 8 of these programs are implemented in contexts of fragility, conflict, and violence (FCV), as defined by the World Bank. A summary of the programs for which cost information was received is included in table 6.1 by operational lead, region, and context, and compared to the sample of programs in the Partnership for Economic Inclusion Landscape Survey 2020 in chapter 3. Appendix C has additional information.

TABLE 6.1   Percentage Representation of Programs: PEI Quick Costing Tool 2020 and PEI Landscape Survey 2020

	PEI Quick Costing Tool 2020	PEI Landscape Survey 2020
Lead implementing agency		
Government	70.6%	48.9%
Nongovernmental organization	29.4%	51.1%
Region		
East Asia and Pacific	5.9%	5.9%
Europe and Central Asia	2.9%	2.4%
Latin America and the Caribbean	5.9%	18.7%
Middle East and North Africa	5.9%	7.3%
South Asia	20.6%	14.6%
Sub-Saharan Africa	58.8%	51.1%
Entry point		
Livelihoods and jobs	64.7%	63%
Social safety nets	35.3%	35.2%
Financial inclusion	0.0%	1.8%
Fragility, conflict, and violence (FCV)		
No	76.5%	74.4%
Yes	23.5%	25.6%
Income group		
Low income	52.9%	37.5%
Lower middle income	38.3%	42.9%
Upper middle income	8.8%	16.4%
High income	0.0%	3.2%
Total programs	**34**	**219**

Source: World Bank.

The cost data reported by program teams are for the full integrated package of layered interventions. This naturally brings up the issue of attribution to the economic inclusion program, as there could be costs linked to other underlying programs that may be included or, depending on the bookkeeping practices in-country, excluded from the reported costs. To the extent possible, the costs have been disaggregated through further consultations with the task team and a review of program documents, as detailed below. Note that there are specific cost categories that are less amenable than others to this disaggregation approach. These include staff costs (for administrative and intervention delivery), monitoring and evaluation costs, and targeting costs. Box 6.1 provides further details on some issues with the costing survey.

BOX 6.1   **Complications and Limitations of the PEI Quick Costing Tool 2020**

While some of the following issues are inherent to the costing of economic inclusion programs, others are common to any costing exercise for any set of programs, particularly when undertaken in a short timeframe.

Comparability across economic inclusion programs. Economic inclusion programs vary quite substantially depending on target beneficiaries, the set of constraints they try to tackle, the choice of constituent instruments, and how they intend to incorporate the latter into a consolidated economic inclusion package. For example, social protection programs that provide consumption support, grants, and skills training targeted explicitly at the extreme poor are quite distinct from agriculture programs that incentivize the formation of productive alliances and provide matching grants to poor farmers.

Variations in cost-accounting standards and in levels of data disaggregation. The costing survey sought to gather detailed information on each intervention broken down by its various elements, such as direct benefit cost, cost of monitoring, and cost of targeting. The cost-accounting and monitoring systems varied by project, as did the level of disaggregation of available data.

Complications with assigning costs to administrative expenses. Except for interventions that directly transfer a certain amount of benefit to the target group (for example, cash grants and transfers), many interventions of economic inclusion programs have constituent cost items that look like administrative expenses but are actually part of the direct implementation costs. For example, staff costs and travel per diem costs represent a major set of cost items in implementing skills training and savings groups. These are also the key components of administrative costs, which makes it difficult to isolate administrative costs from implementation costs. Ideally, administrative cost would be defined as any portion of staff and travel per diem costs that is not used for direct program implementation, but the current analysis does not undertake this estimation exercise. Hence, costs reported as staff cost by programs is reported in this analysis as "delivery and staff cost" to be true to what this cost category includes. Box 6.2 cites details of a separate costing exercise undertaken by the Sahel Adaptive Social Protection Program, which distinguishes between administrative costs and direct program implementation costs.

Exclusion of some government costs directly linked to project. Many government-led economic inclusion projects are jointly implemented by government staff and project implementation units comprised of consultants recruited for this purpose. The costing

(Box continues next page)

BOX 6.1   Complications and Limitations of the PEI Quick Costing Tool 2020 *(continued)*

data received from such projects typically exclude the government staff costs, among them the staff costs of government employees at headquarters and at other, decentralized levels. This exclusion is due to complications with obtaining such data from ministries as well as estimating staff time and cost allocations to a project because government staff tend to be engaged on multiple projects and tasks as part of their duties.

Exclusion of opportunity costs and hidden costs of participation. The cost estimations do not include the opportunity cost of beneficiaries' participation in the program, nor do they include the costs incurred to attend training sessions or travel to payment points to receive cash grants. These exclusions apply to both monetary and time costs.

Cost-effectiveness analysis limited by lack of simultaneous access to impact assessment results. Of the 35 projects that reported costing information, impact evaluation results are available for only 1 project at the time of this writing, namely, the National Rural Livelihoods Program in India (Kochar et al. 2020).

FIGURE 6.1   Sample Program Percentage Cost Structure

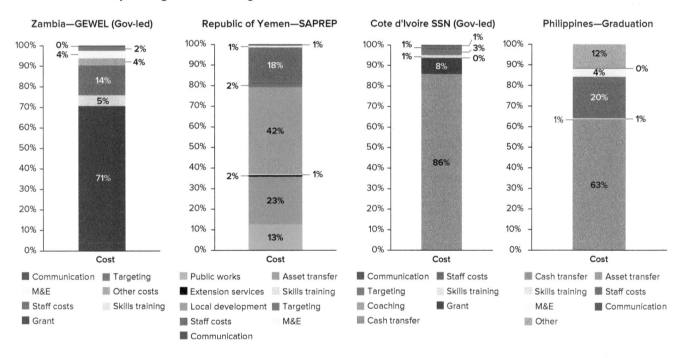

Note: GEWEL = Girls' Education and Women's Empowerment and Livelihoods Project; SAPREP = Smallholder Agricultural Production Restoration and Enhancement Project; SSN = social safety net; M&E = monitoring and evaluation.

* NGO-led program. Refer to appendix C for details.

The analysis of costing data, supplemented by details from program documents, is largely descriptive in nature and uses various robustness checks for quality assurance. Figure 6.1 is a sample template of programs' costing data. A multipronged approach was used for quality assurance. First, to supplement and rationalize findings from the cost survey data analysis, the PEI team uses project appraisal documents, operations manuals, and information available on program websites. Second, a sensitivity analysis was done on the PPP conversions to check if specific years may be biasing the cost trends across countries. Third, the team undertook multiple detailed discussions with each country team or organization to confirm data and analysis: (1) right after the raw data was received from each program, (2) after the initial cross-program draft analysis was undertaken, and (3) after this chapter was written. Fourth, findings are included from another independently undertaken costing exercise by the Sahel Adaptive Social Protection Program (SASPP), which was conducted over a longer period of time and uses a more sophisticated costing tool. It is described in box 6.2 as a comparison and to add nuance to some of the findings (for example, on staff costs) from the PEI Quick Costing Tool 2020. Fifth, extensive consultations were undertaken with technical experts at the World Bank and the Partnership for Economic Inclusion network to ground-truth the findings.

BOX 6.2   **Economic Inclusion Program Costs in the Sahel Adaptive Social Protection Program (SASPP)**

A thorough costing exercise was undertaken across the four countries that implemented the productive measures developed as part of the Sahel Adaptive Social Protection Program (SASPP) (Burkina Faso, Mauritania, Niger, and Senegal). The Sahel ASP Program developed a rigorous costing template to clearly break down costs for each specific intervention and costs related to program administration. For each component, the key cost items, such as transport, equipment, materials, housing, and restoration, are listed and informed by project teams and social safety net (SSN) agencies. Management and supervision costs were factored in, including the time costs for all staff involved in the country program (from the government, nongovernmental organization (NGO) partners, or the World Bank). This allows for a very precise estimation of the cost of each intervention and for separately reporting administrative or nonintervention-specific costs.

The total cost of the productive measures amounts to about $250–260 (2011 $235–246 at purchasing power parity, PPP) per beneficiary in Niger and Burkina Faso, $430 (2011 $407 PPP) in urban Senegal, and $570 (2011 $446 PPP) in Mauritania. The cash grant was the largest cost driver, accounting for between 40 percent (Mauritania) and 70 percent (Burkina Faso) of the total cost of implementation. It was calibrated based on international experience to about 70 percent of the annual household consumption of beneficiaries. The cost of the grants largely reflects the cost of living in the different contexts. The training components, including life skills and microentrepreneurship trainings, were delivered for $50–100 per beneficiary depending on the country.

Beyond the cost of living, the main differences across countries reflect the scale of operations but also the level of integration of the program with national SSN systems. Scale mattered: per capita nonintervention costs were higher in Mauritania, which established the program for about 2,000 household beneficiaries, than in Burkina Faso, which delivered it to almost 18,000 households. The existence of established delivery systems also enabled the program to minimize costs related to the identification of beneficiaries, the constitution of groups, and the delivery of repeated frontline services, such as savings facilitation and coaching. In Niger and Senegal, where community volunteers were trained and supervised by local program staff, the savings and coaching components cost under $20 per beneficiary. In Mauritania, where qualified NGO workers provided those services with a much higher ratio of beneficiaries to providers, the same activities cost $180. Similarly, administrative costs, which include monitoring and evaluation and targeting costs, were lower in contexts that made use of existing systems. See figure B6.2.1 for details by program.

(Box continues next page)

BOX 6.2 **Economic Inclusion Program Costs in the Sahel Adaptive Social Protection Program (SASPP)** *(continued)*

FIGURE B6.2.1 **Per Capita Program Costs by Components**

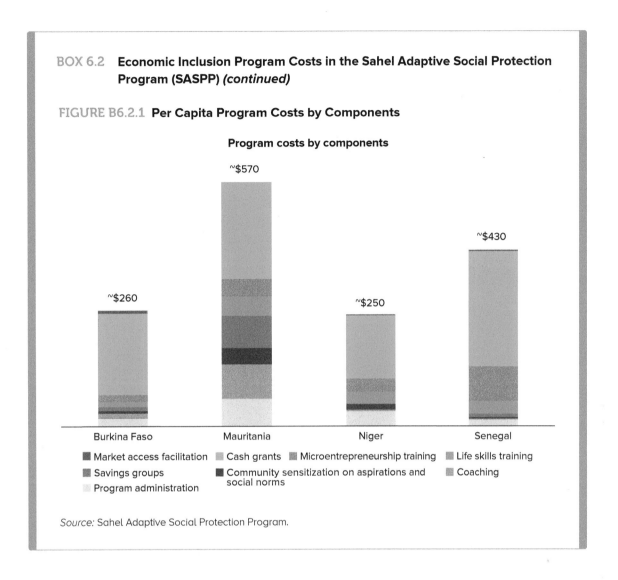

Program costs by components

■ Market access facilitation   ■ Cash grants   ■ Microentrepreneurship training   ■ Life skills training
■ Savings groups   ■ Community sensitization on aspirations and social norms   ■ Coaching
▨ Program administration

Source: Sahel Adaptive Social Protection Program.

Overall Cost of Economic Inclusion Programs

The overall price tag for economic inclusion programs varies substantially, and the "sticker price" approach to costing economic inclusion programs can be faulty. The total cost of economic inclusion programs is between $41 and $2,253 (in 2011 PPP) per beneficiary over the duration (3.6 years on average) of each program.[3] This variance continues when the programs are further broken down by entry points (see figure 6.2): SSN programs range from $77 to $2,253 (2011 PPP) and, L&J programs range from $41 to $2,076 (2011 PPP). The variation is higher for SSN programs. The Afghanistan Targeting the Ultra Poor (TUP) program is not included in the analysis in this chapter, as it is deemed to be an outlier due to its substantially higher cost per beneficiary despite being tagged as an L&J program. Along similar lines, the cost per beneficiary for NGO-implemented programs in the survey, all classified as L&J, ranges from $41 to $778 (2011 PPP). Note that these variations in program costs reflect their different objectives and design elements, including the intervention dosage or adequacy, sequencing, duration of interventions, programmatic contexts, and target beneficiary groups. For example, NGO program costs for L&J programs are in a lower range than L&J government programs. This comparison, however, can be quite misleading as the target group may be different. For example, Argentina's Socio-economic Inclusion in Rural Areas Project (Proyecto de Inclusión Socio-Económica en Áreas Rurales, PISEAR) provides matching grants of larger sizes to its producer groups, that consist of less poor but

FIGURE 6.2 **Overall Price Tags for Economic Inclusion Programs, Surveyed Countries ($ PPP)**

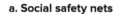

a. Social safety nets

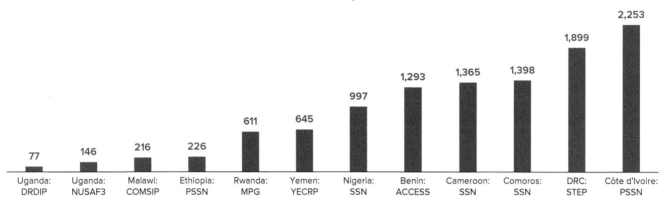

b. Livelihoods and jobs

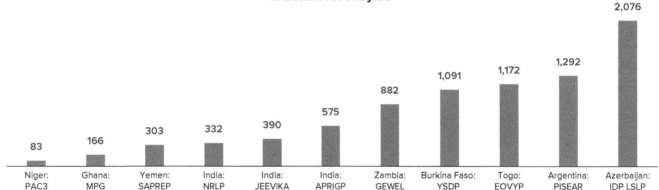

c. Nongovernmental organization (NGO)* livelihoods and jobs

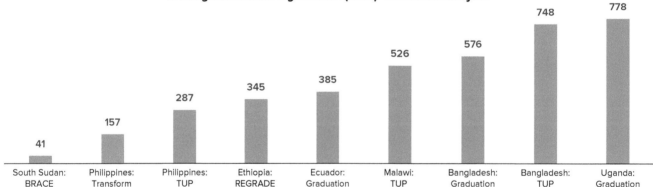

Source: PEI Quick Costing Tool 2020, World Bank.

Note: See appendix C for all program names and details.

* NGO-led programs only. All other programs are government led. Refer to appendix C for details.

vulnerable family producers, whereas many of the NGO programs target the ultrapoor individually. Moreover, it must also be recognized that there are likely other NGO programs that have a higher range of cost than that reported here, driven either by the context in which they operate (especially in FCV settings) or their design.

While the cost and impact relationship is unclear, it is worth considering if there is a minimum dosage threshold below which programs should be deemed to not have the type of impact necessary to meet their objectives. For example, perhaps, programs costing less than $400 (2011 PPP) per beneficiary have a lower range of impact than programs costing more than this threshold. While this is likely, it is important to note that lower unit costs are a factor not only of program design but also of program evolution. Some of these programs, such as the Third Northern Uganda Social Action Fund (NUSAF3) in Uganda and the Support Rural Income Generation of the Poorest in the Upper East Region Project (SRIGP) in Ghana, have relatively new programs under implementation within larger SSN programs. These programs will likely mature and develop into more sophisticated and costly economic inclusion programs as the economic inclusion sector in these countries develop.

Bundling of Interventions and Complexity

Even though economic inclusion programs are multisectoral, in many cases their cost is driven by a single component. This is likely a result of the evolution of such programs or due to a mechanism used to reduce complexity in program management. Many economic inclusion programs allocate between 50 and 86 percent of their overall cost to one component. These components tend to be either cash or in-kind transfers or wages through public works programs in the case of SSN programs. For L&J and financial inclusion (FI) programs, these components tend to be lump-sum cash grants or transfers of inputs or assets. Figure 6.3 illustrates this pattern with more than a dozen program examples.

This dominance of a single component could be due to several reasons. First, programs may build on existing interventions and then introduce smaller-scale add-ons to improve the productive impact of the program as a whole, as in the case of the functional expansion of an SSN program. Second, program designers may view a multiplicity of interventions as potentially increasing complexity and hope that by prioritizing an intervention that is less resource-intensive, the program management complexities and costs can be minimized. Third, perhaps these components correspond to the identified binding constraints to economic inclusion in these contexts.

FIGURE 6.3 **Largest Cost Component as a Percentage of Total Cost, Selected Programs**

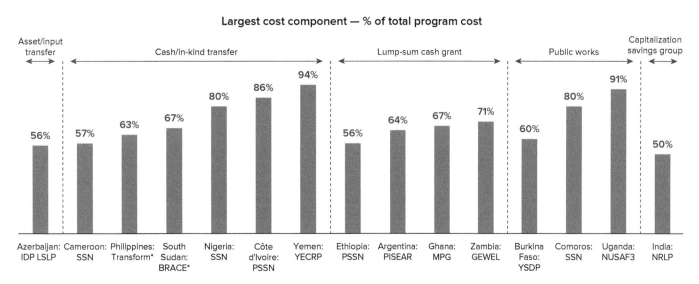

Source: PEI Quick Costing Tool 2020, World Bank.

Note: See appendix C for all program names and details.

* NGO-led programs. All other programs are government led.

The costs of SSN programs are slightly more frequently driven by a single component than the costs of L&J programs. On average, 60 percent of the total cost of SSN programs consists of a single component, compared with 44 percent of the cost of L&J programs. The cost differences are likely driven by the different evolutionary paths of the two sets of programs, with SSN programs being driven by the legacy and objectives of their foundational SSN programs. L&J programs, on the other hand, tend to have less of this legacy and hence can be more squarely focused on resolving the multiplicity of constraints to the beneficiaries' economic inclusion.

Government-led programs' costs are more often driven by a single component than those of NGO-led programs. On average, across all government-led programs, the cost share of the biggest component is 53 percent, whereas it is 37 percent across all NGO-led programs. Even for rigorously evaluated NGO-led programs, the average cost share of the biggest reported component is 33 percent of total program cost (Bandiera et al. 2013, 2017; Bedoya et al. 2019; Blattman et al. 2016; Blattman, Dercon, and Franklin 2019; Sedlmayr, Shah, and Sulaiman. 2019; Banerjee et al. 2015; Bauchet, Morduch, and Ravi 2015; Ismayilova et al. 2018; Gobin, Santos, and Toth 2016). At the same time, while 13 out of 24 government-led programs have a component that constitutes half or more of the total program cost, that is the case for only 2 out of 10 NGO-led programs. NGO-led programs tend to be stand-alone programs and hence have no programmatic legacies to build on, unlike government-led programs. At the same time, they tend to be smaller in scale, in terms of beneficiaries and geographic coverage, and they can therefore more easily afford (in both monetary and nonmonetary resources) to design and implement more complex interventions.

As expected, economic inclusion programs in more complex FCV contexts tend to be less complex than those not in FCV contexts, that is, their cost structures are driven by a single component. A majority of economic inclusion programs in these contexts (five out of eight programs) have a single component that drives more than 50 percent of overall costs. The average cost share of the biggest component in FCV contexts is 53 percent, as compared with 47 percent in other contexts. FCV contexts (not programs) tend to be more complex than other settings, because some of the basic infrastructure and capacity needed to design and implement programs may be missing. Nevertheless, these programs continue to have a substantial number of components as they try to address the severity of deprivations across multiple constraints to economic inclusion.

Delivery and staff costs tend to be lower for programs that fiscally prioritize one component vis-à-vis those that prioritize multiple components. Key cost items in delivering economic inclusion programs are those that are human resource intensive, such as savings groups and training. As highlighted in box 6.1, this cost tends to be accounted as staff costs. Most of the surveyed programs reported their total staff cost as comprised of the following:

- The cost of implementing certain components, such as savings groups and training

- The human resource cost of administering other components, such as grants, inputs, and cash transfers

These will be referred to as *delivery* and *staff* costs. Delivery and staff costs range between 1 percent and 45 percent of the total cost of economic inclusion programs. On average, they account for 13 percent of overall cost for programs where one component drives the majority of total costs (that is, less complex programs), but 26 percent of overall program cost for programs that fiscally prioritize multiple components. Both government-led and NGO-led programs incur higher delivery and staff costs, as a share of total program cost, for programs that fiscally prioritize multiple components—9 percent versus 16 percent for government-led programs and 26 percent versus 32 percent for NGO-led programs. See figure 6.4 for program-specific data.

FIGURE 6.4 **Delivery and Staff Costs as a Percentage of Total Costs, Largest Cost Component versus Multiple Cost Component Programs, All Surveyed Programs, and Government-Led Programs**

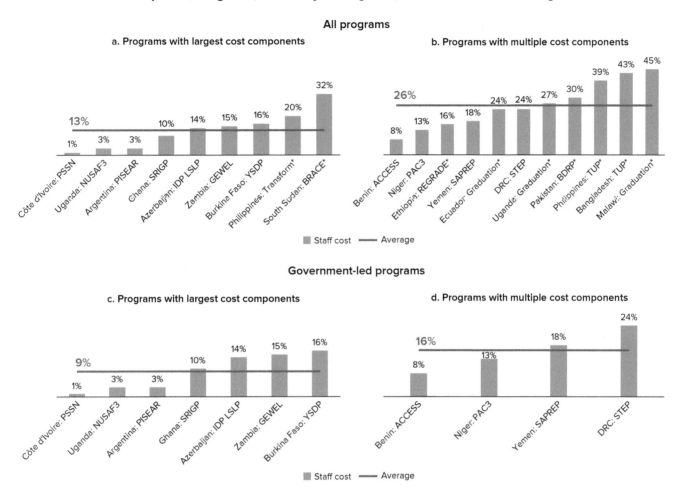

Source: PEI Quick Costing Tool 2020, World Bank.

Note: See appendix C for all program names and details.

* NGO-led programs. All other programs are government led.

Delivery and staff cost incurred by SSN programs is lower than that incurred by L&J programs. It is, on average, 10 percent of the total costs for SSN programs compared to 18 percent of the total cost for L&J programs. While this trend is based on a small subset of SSN programs, it likely reflects the existing SSN implementation infrastructure upon which the programming builds. In L&J programs themselves, these costs tend to be higher for programs that are more complex, that is, those that fiscally prioritize multiple program components.

Component Dosage and Adequacy

The following analysis is based on programs that provided disaggregated data on underlying components. The sample of programs, therefore, varies across different interventions. Components reported by three or fewer programs are not included. Adequacy is calculated as cost ($ 2011 PPP) of a component (for example, grant size) divided by average annual per capita consumption ($ 2011 PPP) of the bottom 20 percent of households in the relevant country.

Lumpy cash grants (lump-sum transfers for productive investments) are provided more often and at higher value to beneficiaries in L&J programs than in SSN programs. This differing method may reflect differences in the underlying objectives or primary entry points between the two types of programs. L&J programs are squarely focused on improving productive outcomes, whereas SSN initiatives primarily aim to improve consumption and, for a subset of beneficiaries, their productive outcomes as well. Fewer SSN programs provide any cash grants to their beneficiaries compared to L&J programs. At the same time, the average grant size for SSN programs is $222 (2011 PPP), whereas for L&J programs it is $416 (2011 PPP), excluding Burkina Faso. By design, Burkina Faso provides a substantially higher grant to youths selected through business plan competitions to create small business and microenterprises, rather than for self-employment. See table 6.2 for the range of grants and their adequacy.

TABLE 6.2 **Lumpy Cash Grants, by Program Type for Selected Programs: Grant Size and Adequacy**

Typology	Program name	Country	Grant size per beneficiary (2011 US$, PPP)	Adequacy: Share of average consumption per capita per annum (bottom 20%)
Livelihoods and jobs	Socioeconomic Inclusion in Rural Areas Project (PISEAR)	Argentina	923	35%
	Support Rural Income Generation of the Poorest in the Upper East Region Project (SRIGP)	Ghana	95	78%
	Girls' Education and Women's Empowerment and Livelihoods Project (GEWEL)	Zambia	622	339%
	Enabling Sustainable Graduation out of Poverty for the Extreme Poor in Southern Malawi,* Concern Worldwide	Malawi	401	134%
	Resilience Programming with the Graduation Model and Evidence Building for Structural Dialogues (REGRADE),* Concern Worldwide	Ethiopia	486	99%
	Graduating to Resilience,* AVSI	Uganda	146	41%
	Employment Opportunities for Vulnerable Youth Project (EOVYP)	Togo	239	N.A.
Social safety nets	Productive Social Safety Net (PSSN)	Côte d'Ivoire	284	70%
	Productive Safety Net Program (PSNP)	Ethiopia	487	99%

Source: PEI Quick Costing Tool 2020, World Bank.

* NGO-led programs. All other programs are government led. Refer to appendix C for details. PPP = purchasing power parity.

L&J programs tend to provide cash grants in two installments as compared to one installment by SSN programs. Installment payments are likely to reduce the income effect on household consumption of receiving a large sum of money all at once, and they may reduce chances of theft or fraud that may result from receiving a large sum of money at once.

Some L&J programs provide larger grants as cofinancing to less poor but vulnerable producers as part of the customization of benefits to different groups. Note that these are not included in table 6.2. Azerbaijan's Internally Displaced Persons Living Standards and Livelihood Project provides grants worth $1,469 (2011 PPP) per beneficiary to income-generating groups comprised on average of 11 people from the community of internally displaced people (IDPs) with viable business plans.[4] This grant allows them to register and operate as local liability companies and open bank accounts. The beneficiaries contribute their own savings, worth 5 percent of the overall grant size, to these accounts, and each self-help group that reaches a required savings threshold is then supported with a financial grant of not more than $15,000 to start a new microenterprise. These business plans are typically higher-value-addition activities, such as milk processing, incubation for egg production, and trade in agricultural machinery.

Similarly, Argentina's PISEAR project, implemented by the Ministry of Agriculture, provides matching grants to its beneficiaries, who are less poor than those who receive lumpy cash grants, to enable them to form productive alliances between producer groups and buyers. These grants average $3,144 (2011 PPP) per beneficiary household, and producer groups are expected to cofinance a minimum of 30 percent of the total cost of each productive alliance subproject. This is in addition to the lumpy cash grants listed in table 6.2 that are provided to other poorer beneficiaries.

While asset and input transfers also seem more likely to be provided to beneficiaries of L&J programs than SSN beneficiaries, the actual value of transfers between the two is similar. Most programs provide asset or input transfers worth between $3.30 and $420 (2011 PPP) per beneficiary. The value of these transfers varies substantially, likely driven by the value of the actual asset transferred, but also by the contexts in which these transfers are made. For example, while some programs provide small seed kits worth $3.30, others provide livestock worth $250 to $420, and still others provide planting materials and seed and breed development services worth $127 (all values in 2011 PPP). There are also programs that provide a substantially higher value of transfers, such as Azerbaijan's Internally Displaced Persons Living Standards and Livelihood Project, which provides for income-generating activities. Sulaiman (2018) finds similar variability in in-kind transfer values across contexts. See Table 6.2 for this range.

Regular cash transfers (consumption support) are provided by 40 percent of programs, with SSN programs being more generous by virtue of providing them for longer periods of time. About 40 percent of the programs surveyed provide consumption support through cash or in-kind transfers to their beneficiaries, with SSN programs providing larger total benefits through longer regular transfers. The average value of consumption support provided per capita per month by L&J programs is $8.80 (2011 PPP), while the average amount provided by SSN programs is $5.70 (2011 PPP). While these figures are comparable, it is noteworthy that SSN programs provide consumption support for a longer period (28 months on average) than L&J programs do (14 months on average). Among L&J programs, regular transfers are typically time bound, because they are supposed to compensate for the opportunity costs of time consumed until the point when an income stream from the livelihood activity starts up. By contrast, the regular transfers issued in

TABLE 6.3   Asset Transfers, by Program Type for Selected Programs: Transfer Size and Adequacy

Typology	Program	Country	Asset provided	Grant size per beneficiary (2011 US$, PPP)	Adequacy: Share of average consumption per capita per annum (bottom 20%)
Livelihoods and jobs	Internally Displaced Persons Living Standards and Livelihoods Project (IDP LSLP)	Azerbaijan	Toolkits, small machinery, hairdressing, mechanics, and so forth	1,469	61%
	Targeting the Ultra Poor (TUP),* BRAC	Bangladesh	Productive grant and livestock	212	37%
	Graduation Model Approach,* HIAS	Ecuador	Productive grant and livestock	421	48%
	Targeting the Ultra Poor (TUP),* BRAC	Philippines	Productive grant and livestock	248	33%
	Andhra Pradesh Rural Inclusive Growth Project (APRIGP)	India	Planting material, seed and breed development kits	128	24%
	Smallholder Agricultural Production Restoration and Enhancement Project (SAPREP)	Yemen	Livelihood kits and farm restoration start-up packages	73	NA
	Transform Program,* International Care Ministries	Philippines	Small seed kits	3	NA
Social safety nets	Eastern Recovery Project (STEP)	DRC	Establishing storage and agroprocessing facilities as well as small hydroelectric plants to power irrigation and processing equipment	261	168%
	Minimum Package for Graduation (MPG)	Rwanda	Productive grant and livestock	269	100%

Source: PEI Quick Costing Tool 2020, World Bank.

Note: DRC = Democratic Republic of Congo.

* NGO-led programs. All other programs are government led. Refer to appendix C for details. PPP = purchasing power parity.

SSN programs are meant to provide for the basic consumption needs of beneficiaries and for much longer. See table 6.4 for program-level details.

Similarly, programs that give beneficiaries access to public works jobs provide wages in about the same range across the two program types, although with a greater total benefit size through SSN programs. The average value of daily wages provided by L&J programs and SSN programs is $5.60 and $4.30 (both in 2011 PPP), respectively (pegged to minimum wages in the country). The annual value of these wages, which typically are earned for just the months of program participation, is equivalent

TABLE 6.4 **Cash Transfers, by Program Type for Selected Programs: Transfer Size and Adequacy**

Typology	Program	Country	Transfer per capita per month (2011 US$, PPP)	Adequacy: Share of average consumption per household per annum (bottom 20%)
Livelihoods and jobs	Graduation Model Approach,* HIAS	Ecuador	13.1	15%
	Transform Program,* International Care Ministries	Philippines	14.0	6%
	Enabling Sustainable Graduation out of Poverty for the Extreme Poor in Southern Malawi,* Concern Worldwide	Malawi	13.9	46%
	Targeting the Ultra Poor (TUP),* BRAC	Philippines	5.1	6%
	Resilience Programming with the Graduation Model and Evidence Building for Structural Dialogues (REGRADE),* Concern Worldwide	Ethiopia	3.7	7%
	Graduating to Resilience (Graduation),* AVSI	Uganda	3.2	8%
Social safety nets	Social Safety Nets Project (SSN)	Cameroon	12.2	24%
	Productive Social Safety Net (PSSN)	Côte d'Ivoire	8.8	24%
	National Social Safety Nets Project (SSN)	Nigeria	2.5	5%
	Yemen Emergency Crisis Response Project (YECRP)	Yemen	0.6	NA
	Support to Communes and Communities for the Expansion of Social Services (ACCESS)	Benin	4.2	NA

Source: PEI Quick Costing Tool 2020, World Bank.

* NGO-led programs. All other programs are government led. Refer to appendix C for details.

PPP = purchasing power parity.

to 9 percent and 14 percent of the average consumption per capita per annum of the poorest 20 percent of the respective country's population. Yet SSN programs provide a greater number of days of work, with more than 100 days compared to about 50 days for L&J programs. The rationale for this is the same as that provided for cash and in-kind transfers. See table 6.5 for program-level information.

Skills training, including vocational training, is another common intervention provided to beneficiaries of economic inclusion programs, particularly in L&J programs. These programs provide training to beneficiaries as a one-off intervention.[5] The duration of trainings ranges from 1 to 30 days, with the average cost per beneficiary rising with duration. Half of these trainings are provided at the individual or household level, while the other half are provided to beneficiary groups and at the community level. The content of such training may include human capital awareness-raising, life skills training, microentrepreneurship, and grassroots management (for example, community procurement and participatory evaluation of poverty and needs).

The cost per beneficiary of the formation of savings groups varies substantially across programs, likely stemming from differences in their duration. The major limitation in analyzing the implementation cost of the savings group component is that it is based on only four programs: the JEEViKA project (not including the Satat Jeevikoparjan Yojana (SJY) included in case study 2) in Bihar, India; the National Rural

TABLE 6.5   **Public Works Wages, by Program Type for Selected Programs: Transfer Size and Adequacy**

Typology	Program	Country	Wages per day (2011 US$, PPP)	Public works: Share of average consumption per household per annum (bottom 20%)
Social safety nets	Social Safety Nets Project (SSN)	Cameroon	3.9	10%
	Eastern Recovery Project (STEP)	DRC	2.6	20%
	Minimum Package for Graduation (MPG)	Rwanda	3.3	16%
	Third Northern Uganda Social Action Fund (NUSAF3)	Uganda	3.1	8%
	Support to Communes and Communities for the Expansion of Social Services (ACCESS)	Benin	4.1	NA
	Social Safety Nets Project (SSN)	Comoros	4.5	NA
Livelihoods and jobs	Youth Employment and Skills Development Project (YSDP)	Burkina Faso	6.5	14%
	Programme d'Actions Communautaires (PAC3)	Niger	2.8	4%
	Smallholder Agricultural Production Restoration and Enhancement Project (SAPREP)	Yemen	8.9	NA
	Employment Opportunities for Vulnerable Youth Project (EOVYP)	Togo	4.0	NA

Source: PEI Quick Costing Tool 2020, World Bank.

Note: DRC = Democratic Republic of Congo. PPP = purchasing power parity.

Livelihood Project (NRLP), under the National Rural Livelihood Mission (NRLM) in India; and L&J programs implemented by Concern Worldwide in Malawi and Ethiopia. While both programs in India cost about $331 per beneficiary over the total duration of each program, the Concern Worldwide programs cost only $18 per beneficiary in Ethiopia and $1.30 per beneficiary in Malawi (all amounts in 2011 PPP).

Even after taking program duration into account, the difference in cost per beneficiary per month is quite varied, likely because of their underlying objectives. The programs in the NRLM focus sharply on improving financial access by providing capitalization support, resulting in improved productive outcomes, whereas the Concern programs focus on improving productive outcomes through a simultaneous focus on multiple constraints, with the lack of financial access being one. This is also evident in the cost structure: savings groups constitute 50 percent of JEEViKA's overall cost, whereas the largest components of Concern Malawi and Concern Ethiopia constitute only 32 percent and 16 percent, respectively, of the overall cost.

Implementation Costs

Targeting

Economic inclusion programs often use a mix of targeting methods, and costs vary substantially across programs. Overall, the targeting cost varies from as low as 0.3 percent, in Niger's agriculture program, Programme d'Actions Communautaires, to 5.5 percent in Cameroon's National Social Safety Net Project. L&J programs tend to use a mix of geographical, categorical, and community-based targeting methods, while SSN programs rely heavily on proxy means tests and community-based targeting. The choice of targeting method likely depends on three factors:

1. The target population group under consideration

2. Any policy frameworks that dictate goals for targeting efficiency

3. The foundational program on which the economic inclusion program builds

Targeting costs are largely driven by household-based assessments, either household surveys for categorical or poverty targeting (including registries) or intensively managed community-based targeting. But higher costs are associated with some targeting methods more than others—for example, they are higher with the inclusion of proxy means tests. This trend is in line with Grosh (1994, 45), who finds that "the median total administrative costs as a share of total program costs were 9 percent for individual assessment, 7 percent for geographic targeting, and 6 percent for self-targeting."

The targeting cost of SSN programs tends to be higher than that of L&J programs. Notwithstanding the small sample size, the targeting cost of SSN programs is, on average, 4.5 percent, whereas it is 1.8 percent for L&J programs. The difference is largely driven by the targeting needs of the broader SSN program, which must develop a targeting process sufficient to build a robust SSN system. In fact, it is likely that the majority of the reported targeting cost is attributable to the broader SSN component of the program because of the difficulty of accounting for the marginal cost of selecting SSN beneficiaries for the additional economic inclusion component. The cost of economic inclusion programs is lower when they use existing systems. Benin's ACCESS program and Niger's PAC3 program build on existing SSN systems and on previous phases of the project and thereby have seemingly lower targeting costs. This relationship with the use of existing systems is confirmed even when the more detailed costing exercise undertaken by the Sahel Adaptive Social Protection Program is utilized. See box 6.2 for this and other insights.

Monitoring and Evaluation

Monitoring and evaluation (M&E) costs are roughly similar for all L&J programs, whether they are led by government or NGOs, ranging between 0.1 percent and 5 percent of total costs. Information on M&E costs for SSN programs is unavailable, as the programs did not report those costs separately. Among L&J programs, the average cost seems to be lower for government-led programs. This may be due to the less structured way M&E is likely undertaken in government programs, which might also be why, primarily, government-led SSN programs do not report M&E separately. At the same time, it might also reflect the stronger accountability systems that are normally in place for NGO-led programs.

Assessing Cost Effectiveness and Exploring Cost Optimization Strategies

The relationship between the magnitude of impact and cost is largely unclear. An interesting finding from Sulaiman (2018) is that higher program cost does not necessarily translate to higher impacts (measured by increase in consumption), and, similarly, lower program cost does not imply lower impacts. As explained earlier, this may be because the measured impacts are an underestimation of true impacts. For example, there may be primary outcomes (such as income or assets ownership), but there may also be local spillovers that are of interest but that are not incorporated in or represented by consumption increases. Nevertheless, the fact that greater expenditure does not necessarily result in greater impact also highlights the scope for improving effectiveness at any level of cost.

The rate of return on economic inclusion programs is quite varied and sensitive to impact dissipation rates. According to Bandiera et al. (2017), the rate of return for BRAC's TUP program is 16 percent per year, whereas Afghanistan's TUP program and Uganda's Women's Income-Generating Support (WINGS) program show an average return to investment of 26 percent (Bedoya et al. 2019) and 24 percent (Blattman et al. 2016), respectively. Blattman, Dercon, and Franklin (2019) evaluate a start-up grant-and-training program and an industrial job placement program in Ethiopia and find minimal returns—not enough to cover the cost of the programs.

While differing elements of intervention design could lead to these different outcomes, it is interesting to note that a similar variance is observed even for the same intervention when it is implemented in different contexts. Banerjee et al. (2015) evaluate a six-country pilot of the CGAP–Ford Foundation graduation program and find rates of return (per year) between 7 percent in Ghana and 23 percent in India, with an average of 12 percent (not including negative benefits in Honduras). Their analysis of cost-effectiveness is among the most robust among all impact studies of economic inclusion programs and the analysis reports on annual impact dissipation rate. They find that at annual rates of dissipation of the impact size, 1.8 percent in Ghana, 2.6 percent in Peru, 5 percent in Pakistan, 10 percent in Ethiopia, and 31 percent in India, the benefits and cost of the programs are equalized. In other words, largely moderate dissipation of impacts can nullify the investment case for such programs.

For governments to scale up economic inclusion programming, an important consideration is how to sustain impact at lower cost. For large-scale programs, especially when led by government, there are trade-offs with respect to adequacy and customization versus cost and complexity. At the same time, not all groups face the same constraints or need the same level of support; customizing the program for different groups may be more cost-effective than implementing a standardized package. Box 6.3 summarizes some recent innovations to optimize on costs, without diluting impact, that could inform the design of large-scale government-led programs.

BOX 6.3 **Innovative Mechanisms to Optimize on Costs**

Variations in size and cost recovery of the cash grant. In Bangladesh, BRAC modified the Challenging the Frontiers of Poverty Reduction: Targeting the Ultra Poor (CFPR-TUP) program, varying the nature of the asset transfer (grant versus loan) and the provision of a cash transfer for consumption support for different segments in the ultrapoor population. Both variants increased assets, income, self-employment, consumption, and diet diversity, and although the least intensive variant had lower impact, it also cost much less (Das et al. 2016). In West Bengal, however, a similar pilot (varying grant versus credit by segments of the ultrapoor population) was discontinued due to practical challenges with loan repayment after program exit (Sheldon 2016). In Sri Lanka, the large-scale program Samurdhi transitioned in 2014 from grants to a mix of grant and credit for all participants, with variations depending on vulnerability and repayment capacity (Tilakaratna and Sooriyamudali 2016).

Variations in intensity of modality, frequency, and content of training and coaching. In Burundi, the Terintambwe Program divided its beneficiaries into two experimental groups—a "high treatment" group and a "low treatment" group, with some participants receiving more intensive support from case managers than others, who received fewer visits. An evaluation found that program impact did not significantly vary between high- and low-intensity participants (Devereux et al. 2015). In Uganda, the Women's Income-Generating Support (WINGS) program varied the frequency and, thereby, the content of its most expensive program component (which cost two to three times the grant amount), supervision or coaching. The first two visits focused on holding beneficiaries accountable to their business plans, and later visits provided advice. Results of an evaluation show that two visits were as good as five visits in improving the business survival rate, even as supervision by itself did not improve income and food security.

Shifting from individual to group-based interventions. Shifting from individual to group focus can reduce administrative costs and the monitoring burden. The Uganda Village Enterprise program managed to reduce its costs by a third compared to the six-country study of the CGAP–Ford Foundation pilots by Banerjee et al. (2015) using group-based training and keeping the intervention to a shorter duration (Sedlmayr, Shah, and Sulaiman 2019). Despite the low cost, it achieved impact in terms of increases in self-employment activities, improved assets, higher subjective well-being, and higher consumption. In Kenya, The BOMA Project's group-based Rural Entrepreneur Access Program (REAP) had similar positive impacts.

Entrepreneurial group formation. Group formation can also amplify outcomes and serve as a tool for sustainability, by promoting social networks and group-based production and marketing. In Uganda, the Youth Opportunities Program (YOP) supported group-based microenterprises rather than individual businesses. Operating in groups allowed participants to negotiate discounts from trainers (Blattman, Fiala, and Martinez 2014). Another program in Uganda, WINGS, which supported individual microentrepreneurs, enabled half of them to form self-help groups. While group formation did not necessarily increase the size, survival, or profitability of the businesses of the individual participants, it doubled their earnings relative to those of participants who were not in the groups, mainly by increasing cooperation in the form of labor sharing, cooperative cash cropping, and informal finance. It also mitigated resentment and abuse that participants faced from nonparticipating households in the neighborhood

(Box continues next page)

BOX 6.3   **Innovative Mechanisms to Optimize on Costs** *(continued)*

(Blattman et al. 2016). Such group formation, typically for savings but also for joint market-related activities, is a core feature of many livelihood programs, including India's National Rural Livelihood Mission and JEEViKA, as discussed in case study 2.

Deepening financial inclusion through digital finance and mobile money. By making digital payments of grants, some economic inclusion programs can connect some of the poorest households to the financial system. The payment service providers benefit as well, as they can access a large pool of unbanked households, thereby increasing their customer base. Through innovative products such as microloans, payment service providers can continue to engage some of these households, either individually or even as groups. In making microloans, digital transaction history could also provide some markers of the quality of lending. At the same time, delivery systems need to be careful about not excluding those who are unable to access digital platforms. In Kenya, REAP used a digital finance platform to promote the use of various financial instruments for savings, loans, and payments. However, low literacy and numeracy levels, lack of familiarity with mobile technology, and preferences for savings in cash and livestock limited participants' usage of digital financial products (Tiwari, Schaub, and Sultana 2019).

More research is needed to answer these questions fully. Fortunately, there is a rich pipeline of program-specific research (see appendix B for the thematic research planned by the programs in the Partnership for Economic Inclusion (PEI) Landscape Survey 2020) as well as multicountry research agendas on SSN programming (World Bank 2019) and complementary programming involving SSN together with agricultural and other livelihood programs (Maldonado et al. 2016; FAO 2018).

Future Directions

This chapter deliberately moves away from pursuing a "sticker price" costing approach and to that of "costing to design and context." This is driven by the realities of the economic inclusion programming landscape reflected in chapter 3 and is well founded in the observed variation in cost per beneficiary from existing impact evaluation literature as well as the PEI Quick Costing Tool 2020.

The chapter also pivots toward the broader and more timely use of costing data for programming and policy making. Costing data, particularly disaggregated data, can be highly informative to the process of designing programs (including assessing affordability and potential scale, and the extent to which beneficiaries' multiple constraints are addressed) and to the monitoring of expenditures for the purpose of identifying bottlenecks to implementation.

Going forward, it is critical that economic inclusion program implementers, both government and nongovernment, and policy makers innovatively use and make available costing data. The analysis in this chapter is based on a small subset of economic inclusion programs, but as reflected in chapter 3, there are at least 219 programs currently being implemented globally. Increasing the number of programs reporting cost information would allow for better and more robust analysis, particularly by program types, regions, target groups, and so forth. Besides any follow-up data collection exercises by researchers or practitioners, a data dashboard has been developed by the Partnership for Economic Inclusion and is one avenue through which cost data can be reported and analyzed (https://www.peiglobal.org/pei-data-portal).

At the same time, it is important that researchers assessing the impact of economic inclusion programs systematically collect and report on cost data in addition to impact sizes. Besides programmatic data, impact literature is another source of costing data and is significant when it comes to estimating cost-effectiveness. Here again, the costing template developed as part of this chapter's rapid survey could be a starting point for further revision and use. Often impact literature does not report disaggregated cost data but, as shown earlier, this can be quite operationally relevant—after all, impact assessments are often undertaken to make a case for further investments and scale up of programs.

It would also be useful to further refine and develop the PEI Quick Costing Tool 2020 to improve its relevance to endogenous and exogenous programmatic evolution. There are a couple of reasons. First, as highlighted earlier, the costing tool has various limitations given the rapid nature of the costing survey. These include the incorporation of beneficiary costs in terms of both direct and opportunity costs of participation as well as parsing staff costs into their benefit delivery and administrative components. Second, economic inclusion programs will likely evolve further over the next many years to reflect the improved knowledge and learning on such programming, particularly in response to exogenous shocks, such as COVID-19. The PEI Quick Costing Tool 2020 would need to evolve to respond to these changing programmatic needs as well as to mitigate many of the limitations identified.

Notes

1. It is important to note that the 2011 US$, PPP is used for cost comparison, because it is the least common denominator across all projects surveyed.
2. In this chapter, "NGO-led" is used, as only governments and nongovernmental organizations (NGOs) submitted costing data.
3. Note that here we do not divide the total cost by duration of each program. Although dividing by duration would help standardize the comparison across programs, it is misleading, as duration of economic inclusion packages is an important aspect of the program's design. Those that are designed such that their beneficiaries receive a set of interventions over a longer duration of time (perhaps because they are slow climbers or highly vulnerable) will likely cost more than those that are of shorter duration. In discussing adequacy of benefits, however, we standardize by duration.
4. The Youth Support Program, which has different grant sizes and components.
5. The only exception is the Microfinance Investment Support Facility for Afghanistan, which provides its training at two separate times and consists of training in rearing and keeping assets, encouragement of personal and group savings, and basic financial literacy.

References

Ara, J., N. Das, M. Kamruzzaman, and T. Quayyum. 2017. "Walking on Two Legs: Credit Plus Grant Approach to Poverty Reduction." CFPR Working Paper no. 25, BRAC Research and Evaluation Division, Dhaka.

Balboni, Clare, Oriana Bandiera, Robin Burgess, Maitreesh Ghatak, and Anton Heil. 2020. "Why Do People Stay Poor?" STICERD Economic Organisation and Public

Policy Discussion Papers Series 067, Suntory and Toyota International Centres for Economics and Related Disciplines, London School of Economics.

Bandiera, Oriana, Robin Burgess, Narayan Das, Selim Gulesci, Imran Rasul, and Munshi Sulaiman. 2013. "Can Basic Entrepreneurship Transform the Economic Lives of the Poor?" IZA Discussion Paper 7386, Institute of Labor Economics, Bonn.

Bandiera, Oriana, Robin Burgess, Narayan Das, Selim Gulesci, Imran Rasul, and Munshi Sulaiman. 2017. "Labor Markets and Poverty in Village Economies." *Quarterly Journal of Economics* 132 (2): 811–70.

Banerjee, Abhijit, Esther Duflo, Nathaneal Goldberg, Dean Karlan, Robert Osei, William Parienté, Jeremy Shapiro, Bram Thuysbaert, and Christopher Udry. 2015. "A Multifaceted Program Causes Lasting Progress for the Very Poor: Evidence from Six Countries." *Science* 348 (6236): 1260799.

Bauchet, Jonathan, Jonathan Morduch, and Shamika Ravi. 2015. "Failure vs. Displacement: Why an Innovative Anti-Poverty Program Showed No Net Impact in South India." *Journal of Development Economics* 116: 1–16.

Bedoya, Guadalupe, Aidan Coville, Johannes Haushofer, Mohammad Isaqzadeh, and Jeremy Shapiro. 2019. "No Household Left Behind: Afghanistan Targeting the Ultra-Poor Impact Evaluation." Policy Research Working Paper 8877, World Bank, Washington, DC.

Blattman, Christopher, Stefan Dercon, and Simon Franklin. 2019. "Impacts of Industrial and Entrepreneurial Jobs on Youth: Five-Year Experimental Evidence on Factory Job Offers and Cash Grants in Ethiopia." Working Paper no. 2019–65, University of Chicago.

Blattman, Christopher, Nathan Fiala, and Sebastian Martinez. 2014. "Generating Skilled Self-Employment in Developing Countries: Experimental Evidence from Uganda." *Quarterly Journal of Economics* 129: 697–752. doi:10.1093/qje/qjt057.

Blattman, Christopher, Eric P. Green, Julian Jamison, M. Christian Lehmann, and Jeannie Annan. 2016. "The Returns to Microenterprise Support among the Ultrapoor: A Field Experiment in Postwar Uganda." *American Economic Journal: Applied Economics* 8 (2): 35–64.

Caldés, Natalia, David Coady, and John A. Maluccio. 2006. "The Cost of Poverty Alleviation Transfer Programs: A Comparative Analysis of Three Programs in Latin America." *World Development* 34 (5): 818–37.

Das, Narayan C., Sibbir Ahmad, Anindita Bhattacharjee, Jinnat Ara, and Abdul Bayes. 2016. "Grant versus Credit Plus Approach to Poverty Reduction: An Evaluation of BRAC's Experience with Ultra Poor." CFPR Working Paper 24, BRAC, Dhaka.

Devereux, Stephen, Keetie Roelen, Ricardo Sabates, Dimitri Stoelinga, and Arnaud Dyevre. 2015. *Final Evaluation Report: Concern's Graduation Model Program in Burundi.* Dublin: Concern Worldwide.

FAO (Food and Agriculture Organization of the United Nations). 2018. *FAO and Cash +: How to Maximize the Impacts of Cash Transfers.* Rome: FAO.

Gobin, Vilas J., Paulo Santos, and Russell Toth. 2016. "Poverty Graduation with Cash Transfers: A Randomized Evaluation." Economics Working Paper 23–16, Monash University, Melbourne.

Grosh, Margaret. 1994. *Administering Targeted Social Programs in Latin America: From Platitude to Practice.* Washington, DC: World Bank.

Ismayilova, Leyla, Leyla Karimli, Jo Sanson, Eleni Gaveras, Rachel Nanema, Alexice Tô-Camier, and Josh Chaffin. 2018. "Improving Mental Health among Ultra-Poor Children: Two-Year Outcomes of a Cluster-Randomized Trial in Burkina Faso." *Social Science and Medicine* 208: 180–89. doi:10.1016/j.socscimed.2018.04.022.

Kidd, Stephen, and Diloá Athias. 2019. "The Effectiveness of the Graduation Approach: What Does the Evidence Tell Us?" *Pathways' Perspectives on Social Policy in International Development* 27.

Kochar, Anjini, Bidisha Barooah, Chandan Jain, Geeta Singh, Nagabhushana Closepet, Raghunathan Narayanan, Ritwik Sarkar, and Rohan Shah. 2020. "Impact Evaluation of the National Rural Livelihoods Project." Impact Evaluation Report 128. International Initiative for Impact Evaluation (3ie), New Delhi.

Maldonado, Jorge H., Rocio Moreno-Sánchez, J. A. Gómez, and V. L. Jurado, eds. 2016. *Protection, Production, Promotion: Exploring Synergies between Social Protection and Productive Development in Latin America*. Bogotá: Universidad de los Andes.

Sedlmayr, Richard, Anuj Shah, and Munshi Sulaiman. 2019. "Cash-Plus: Poverty Impacts of Alternative Transfer-Based Approaches." *Journal of Development Economics* 144 (May). doi:10.1016/j.jdeveco.2019.102418.

Sheldon, Tony, ed. 2016. *Preserving the Essence, Adapting for Reach: Early Lessons from Large-Scale Implementations of the Graduation Approach*. New York: Ford Foundation.

Sulaiman, Munshi. 2018. "Livelihood, Cash Transfer, and Graduation Approaches: How Do They Compare in Terms of Cost, Impact, and Targeting?" In *Boosting Growth to End Hunger by 2025: The Role of Social Protection*, edited by Fleur Stephanie Wouterse and Alemayehu Seyoum Taffesse, 102–20. Washington, DC: International Food Policy Research Institute. doi:10.2499/9780896295988_08.

Tilakaratna, Ganga, and Chinthani Sooriyamudali. 2016. *Samurdhi/Divineguma Programme*. Institute of Policy Studies of Sri Lanka. Colombo.

Tiwari, Jaya, Emily Schaub, and Naziha Sultana. 2019. "Barriers to 'Last Mile' Financial Inclusion: Cases from Northern Kenya." *Development in Practice* 29 (8): 988–1000. doi:10.1080/09614524.2019.1654432.

World Bank. 2019. *Resilience through Economic Inclusion: Sahel ASP Thematic Activity–Sahel Adaptive Social Protection (SASPP)*. Concept Note, Regional Analytical Program. Washington, DC: World Bank.

PART B
Case Studies

Productive Inclusion Measures and Adaptive Social Protection in the Sahel

Introduction

Against the backdrop of recurring climate shocks and deep poverty, governments in Africa's Sahel region have introduced economic inclusion programs for national beneficiaries of social safety nets (SSNs). Over the last decade, the governments of Burkina Faso, Chad, Mali, Mauritania, Niger, and Senegal have established national SSN programs that provide regular and predictable cash transfers to poor and vulnerable households, focusing strongly on women as the primary recipients of the transfers. The programs help to address chronic poverty and acute food insecurity.

Many households also face constraints to improving their incomes, productivity, and resilience. To address these constraints, countries expanded their SSN systems and complemented cash transfer programs with productive measures. These efforts have been implemented by national government institutions, with support from the World Bank and its development partners through the Sahel Adaptive Social Protection Program (SASPP)—see box CS1.1 and World Bank (2017).

This case study describes the implementation of a coherent set of productive inclusion measures through national SSN programs in four Sahel countries: Burkina Faso, Mauritania, Niger, and Senegal.[1] It also provides insights into the challenges and opportunities of delivering productive inclusion programs at scale through government systems. Preliminary operational insights are already emerging, including the importance of government leadership and institutional coordination; the value of broader investments in the SSN system; and the need for flexibility in delivery arrangements, depending on the country context.

BOX CS1.1   The Sahel Adaptive Social Protection Program Funding

The Sahel Adaptive Social Protection Program (SASPP) is supported by a multidonor trust fund (MDTF) managed by the World Bank. The United Kingdom's Department for International Development (DFID) provided an initial contribution to the MDTF of £46 million ($63 million) over five years (2014–19). Since then, new donors have joined the MDTF. Agence Française de Développement (AFD) contributed approximately $7 million in 2018, and a philanthropic foundation provided $1.35 million to support the multicountry impact evaluation of productive inclusion measures and a further $1.35 million to support program implementation in Burkina Faso. Germany's Federal Ministry for Economic Cooperation and Development (BMZ) recently committed €50 million, which will enable SASPP to continue until at least 2025.

This case study was written by Edward Archibald (independent consultant), Thomas Bossuroy (World Bank Group, WBG), and Patrick Premand (WBG).

The robust evidence base being built will inform a potential scale-up of productive measures in the region and beyond. The productive measures are being tested through a multicountry impact evaluation led by a team of researchers from the World Bank and several universities in partnership with Innovations for Poverty Action (IPA), a research and policy organization. The evaluation will be complemented by operational learning and process evaluations. Its findings will be disseminated in 2020–21, benefiting future discussions of an expansion within the region.

The operational lessons offered in this case study are intended to support other governments that may consider delivering productive measures for poor and vulnerable households through the platform of a national SSN program.

Context

The Sahel is home to some of the poorest countries in the world. Although poverty rates have fallen in recent decades, the levels of poverty across the region remain high.[2] Measured by the international poverty line of $1.90 a day, the poverty headcount ratios in the Sahel (latest year) are 49.7 percent in Niger, 49.3 percent in Mali, 43.7 percent in Burkina Faso, 38.4 percent in Chad, and 38.0 in Senegal. Although the ratio is low in Mauritania at 6.0 percent, this rate increases to 33.0 percent when measured by the national poverty line. When the international poverty line of $3.20 a day is applied—a proxy for vulnerability to poverty—these rates increase markedly to about 66 percent for all countries except Mauritania (World Bank 2018b). The Sahel region is also increasingly exposed to conflict and insecurity, contributing since 2011 to an increase in the number of refugees, internally displaced persons, asylum seekers, and stateless persons (World Bank 2018b, 2019a, 2019b).

In the Sahel, the incidence of poverty is higher in rural areas, where inhabitants largely depend on agriculture. Urban poverty rates are more than 30 percentage points lower than rural rates, with the exception of Senegal. Large proportions of people move in and out of poverty as well. For example, between 2006 and 2011, 45 percent of poor households in Senegal escaped poverty, but during the same period 40 percent of nonpoor households fell into it, leaving the poverty rate almost unchanged (World Bank 2018b).

The risks posed by climate change loom large in the Sahel. Large covariate shocks such as drought regularly affect the region, and the number of persons affected by drought has been increasing in recent decades. This trend is expected to continue because of climate change (World Bank 2018b). Although climate models on future rainfall patterns in the Sahel show considerable divergence in predictions (Park, Bader, and Matei 2015), it is generally accepted that rainfall has been more erratic in the region (Bolwig et al. 2011), which is expected to induce additional flooding, drought, pests, and temperature shocks (World Bank 2018b).

Climatic shocks have a strong tendency to disproportionately affect the poorest and most vulnerable, underscoring the need to diversify livelihoods and strengthen resilience. Agriculture is the dominant sector for employment in the Sahel, and more than 80 percent of all employment is vulnerable—such as self-employed workers or those helping in household enterprises. Many households also have limited savings, assets, and access to the finance that could help them manage the impacts of climatic shocks. For example, households in Senegal affected by a natural disaster between 2011 and 2016 were 9 percentage points more likely than other households to fall into extreme poverty (Dang, Lanjouw, and Swinkels 2014). Many households are ill-equipped to face seasonal lean periods and shocks, experiencing both acute and chronic periods of food insecurity (World Bank 2018b). Poor households often rely on coping mechanisms that will eventually have negative consequences on their human capital or earnings, such as taking out high-interest loans, reducing consumption, withdrawing children from school, or selling household and productive assets (sometimes at highly reduced prices).

Populations are growing across the region, and yet the human development indicators remain poor. Most Sahel countries expect a doubling of their current population before 2050. Niger recorded the highest annual population growth rate, 4 percent, in the region over the 2010–15 period, and its population is expected to increase threefold by 2050. All countries in the region rank low on the World Bank's Human Capital Index, with future generations estimated to fulfill only between 30 percent (Chad) and 42 percent (Senegal) of their economic potential when they reach adulthood. The index is particularly influenced by the low levels of educational attainment. Although economic inclusion programs have the potential to support households facing poverty and multiple interrelated challenges, the programs also need to be tailored to the characteristics and constraints faced by this population.

Gender empowerment is an urgent priority in the Sahel, with women having low levels of education and employment. Access to basic education remains a challenge in the region, particularly for girls, which has implications for future income (see box CS1.2). Between 2011 and 2014, net school attendance for girls was approximately 50 percent in Chad, Mali, and Niger (OECD 2020). Persistent barriers to girls' education include early marriage and early motherhood and a division of household labor by gender. Girls suffer from low literacy rates such as just 15 percent in Niger and 34 percent in Mali (OECD 2020), which affect their ability to engage in productive employment. Women's labor participation rates are lower than men's, with a gap of 49 percentage points in Niger.

The rise and the potential of safety nets

In recent years, governments across the region have made significant investments in creating national social protection systems and programs that provide regular cash transfers to poor and vulnerable households. Social protection interventions in the Sahel have generally focused on providing direct emergency responses to drought, food prices, or other seasonal shocks. Over the past decade, however, governments have begun to set up more permanent national social protection systems, including implementing regular cash transfers to poor and vulnerable households. SSN programs now cover more than 4.5 million beneficiaries in Burkina Faso, Chad, Mali, Mauritania, Niger, and Senegal, and most of the cash transfer recipients are women. These programs generally identify and enroll beneficiaries through a combination of geographic and household targeting, using either community-based targeting or proxy means testing. The transfers aim to provide consumption support and reduce food insecurity, as well as facilitate investments in children's human capital and in livelihoods.

BOX CS1.2 **Girls in Burkina Faso: Less Likely to Attend School, with Implications for Future Income**

Almost half of primary school–age children in Burkina Faso are not enrolled in school, and girls are one of the groups at the highest risk of nonattendance. The gender gap in attendance is already notable at the primary school level, with a difference of 4 percentage points between boys and girls (World Bank 2019c). Girls not finishing primary school are more likely to earn income from agriculture, a sector with low average productivity. Completion of primary school reduces the chances of staying in agriculture by 23 percentage points (World Bank 2019c).

They are provided for two to three years in Burkina Faso, Chad, and Niger and up to five years in Mauritania and Senegal (World Bank 2019a).

The maturity of SSN systems varies across the Sahel region. Government-led SSN systems in Chad and Mauritania are somewhat nascent and have focused on establishing the foundations of a system, accompanied by a phased expansion of cash transfers to beneficiaries. By contrast, countries such as Niger and Senegal are substantially more advanced, having well established delivery platforms and national programs with coverage of almost 3.5 million individuals between them.

With their growing coverage and efforts to set up delivery systems to reach and serve the poor, SSN systems provide a platform for delivering productive inclusion measures efficiently at scale.

Identifying constraints to productivity and resilience: The diagnostic phase

Productive inclusion measures are intended to tackle the key binding constraints faced by the poor. Identifying those constraints accurately is a necessary first step toward designing effective economic inclusion programs. Prior to designing productive measures for the Sahel Adaptive Social Protection Program, the World Bank and partner governments undertook a range of qualitative and quantitative assessments to identify and prioritize the main constraints faced by SSN beneficiaries in their income-generating activities. A quantitative constraint analysis was undertaken by IPA, and qualitative research was carried out by international and local researchers. The qualitative studies highlighted some of the main constraints faced by poor households in the Sahel:

- Access to capital
- Technical and business skills
- Access to markets (for inputs and outputs)
- Social norms, particularly affecting women and the socially disadvantaged
- Psychosocial and aspirational constraints
- Capacity to manage risk (Bossuroy, Kossoubé, and Premand 2017)

The quantitative and qualitative diagnoses were complemented by a literature review of local and international experiences. Consultations were also organized in each country with nongovernmental organizations (NGOs), civil society organizations, and government partners.

The diagnostic studies and consultations suggested that these multiple constraints be addressed through a set of interventions that does the following:

- Reduces the poorest households' exposure to risk and vulnerability
- Facilitates diversification of their income-generating activities
- Improves their capacity to plan their finances and manage risk in the short to medium term
- Develops their skills
- Enables them to acquire and accumulate productive assets
- Builds an enabling environment in which women are supported and empowered to take new initiatives

Designing the content of productive measures

A joint design process was set up across the six Sahel countries with SSN programs— Burkina Faso, Chad, Mali, Mauritania, Niger, and Senegal. That process led to consensus on a package of productive measures. A regional workshop was convened by the World Bank in 2016 with participation by the governments of the six countries, NGOs, development partners, and researchers. The objective was to take stock of the diagnostic studies and decide on packages of productive measures that could be implemented and tested across participating countries, with technical support from a regional activity led by the World Bank and its technical partners. The results of the diagnoses and consultations on local experiences were combined with evidence about the most promising interventions gleaned from the international literature.

BOX CS1.3 Overview of Productive Inclusion Measures in the Sahel

Component 1: Group formation and coaching
Coaches facilitate program activities (such as mobilization of beneficiaries for meetings and coordination with service providers) for groups of 15–25 individual beneficiaries. They also provide individual and group coaching. They meet with beneficiary groups on a regular basis and organize follow-up visits with individuals every few months. Sessions are intended to identify and resolve the constraints facing beneficiaries.

Component 2: Community sensitization on aspirations and social norms
This measure seeks to address the aspirational or psychosocial constraints facing many individuals, particularly women, in undertaking new initiatives and income-generating activities. A short video is shown to all community members, telling the story of poor, food-insecure individuals who overcome many barriers and successfully engage in productive investments. After the video, a group discussion is facilitated on themes such as aspirations, social dynamics, and women's empowerment.[a]

Component 3: Facilitation of savings groups for beneficiaries
Using the village savings and loan association model, coaches help beneficiaries form community savings groups and provide ongoing technical support to help manage the groups.

Component 4: Life skills training
To further help address the psychosocial barriers faced by beneficiaries, a week-long, group-based training session covers topics such as self-esteem, personal initiative, aspirations, social norms, and spousal, gender, and generational roles.

Component 5: Microentrepreneurship training
This week-long, group-based training covers basic business skills. It focuses on cross-cutting microentrepreneurship skills, including basic accounting and management principles, market research, planning and scheduling, saving, and investing. The training also covers the risks and opportunities of income-generating activities that beneficiaries are interested in initiating or expanding.

Component 6: One-time lump sum cash grant
After savings groups are formed and have received training, beneficiaries work with coaches to develop a business plan that outlines how they will invest funds in agricultural or nonagricultural activities. Beneficiaries are then given an unconditional lump sum cash grant of $140–$275 (the amount varies across countries, according to income level and available budget).

Component 7: Facilitation of access to inputs and markets
Coaches help to locate suppliers for inputs for beneficiaries' investments (such as seeds for agricultural initiatives) and facilitate group purchases to help reduce unit costs. Although this is a separate component, in practice it is integrated with coaching.

a. The following sample videos are available: Niger, short version, https://vimeo.com/239508182/b14fd77540; Senegal, long version, https://vimeo.com/264707787.

BOX CS1.4   **Characteristics of the Village Savings and Loan Association Model**

As part of the productive package, the measure on village saving and loan associations (VSLAs) seeks to address constraints to financial inclusion. Financial institutions have a limited reach in the Sahel. In Niger, for example, less than 4 percent of adults have a bank account and less than 2 percent borrow from a financial institution, including 1 percent of women (World Bank 2018a, 3). Mutual savings associations (*tontines*) are widespread across the region, but they generally do not replace the need for informal networks and family ties to access credit. The VSLA instrument is a more structured saving instrument that includes a credit facility. The model has a range of key characteristics.

Affinity and ownership. Members know each other and come from similar economic backgrounds with common interests. All rules applicable to the VSLA are decided by the group for each cycle: cost of the share, interest rate, penalty fees, solidarity contribution, and loan maturity. Rules can be voted on, but consensus is the norm.

Accountability. All financial transactions (savings and loans) are conducted during a full meeting of the VSLA to ensure transparency and accountability.

Purchase of shares. Savings are generated when members purchase shares in the VSLA. The value of one share, agreed on by the group, can vary over time, depending on the members' saving capacity. Members have the option to purchase between one and five shares per VSLA meeting.

Loans. Each member is allowed to take a monthly loan, and repayment is spread over three months with an interest rate agreed on by the group—generally 5–10 percent. Members are not allowed to accumulate loans. The fund for loans is the total of the shares currently owned by members, the interest generated by previously repaid loans, and payments for penalties.

Solidarity. Members contribute not only to their savings, but also to a separate fund to support members in need, which is distributed based on a group consensus.

Autonomy. Members control the group's resources and rules—not external actors or nongovernmental organizations, which may be engaged to provide support.

Sources: Facilitation Guide, Associations Villageoises d'Épargne et de Crédit, 2017; Mallé (2020).

The productive measures were defined to address coherently the identified constraints. For selected cash transfer beneficiaries, the regular cash transfers would be complemented by a package of time-bound productive measures consisting of seven components: (1) individual and group coaching; (2) community sensitization on aspirations and social norms; (3) village savings and loan associations (VSLAs); (4) life skills training; (5) microentrepreneurship training; (6) a lump sum cash grant; and (7) facilitation of access to inputs and markets. These components are described in more detail in box CS1.3, and the VSLA measure is described in more detail in box CS1.4.

Four countries—Burkina Faso, Mauritania, Niger, and Senegal—elected to implement the productive package that came out of the design process. Chad and Mali implemented productive measures inspired by the diagnostic and consultation phases but with some variations in content.

The productive measures were offered to the beneficiaries of national SSN programs, the overwhelming majority of whom are women. The diagnostics phase influenced the decision by all countries to give priority to female participants because empowerment of women was identified as a critical pathway to greater economic resilience. In some countries, the beneficiary of the productive package was the recipient of cash transfers regardless of the age of the beneficiary, while in other countries steps were taken to ensure that younger women in the household also benefited from productive measures. For example, in Niger the individual recipient of the productive measures was the cash transfer recipient. In Burkina Faso, every adult woman in selected households received regular cash transfers. Every adult woman also benefited from the productive measures, but the lump sum cash grant was given to the youngest adult. In Senegal, the government took steps to give priority to the participation of young women in the household, even when a young woman was not the primary cash transfer beneficiary. In Mauritania, the individual recipient of the productive measures was the cash transfer recipient or a young woman in the household.

The measures are implemented in rural areas in all countries except Senegal, which opted to implement the program in urban and peri-urban areas. The factors affecting Senegal's decision included rising urbanization rates and a predominantly young population that faces limited opportunities for participation in the formal labor market. High job insecurity and labor informality, especially among the poor, youth, and women, are a major policy challenge for the Senegalese government. The government identified the urban and peri-urban areas of Dakar, along with two regional capitals (Kaolack and Thies), with suburbs selected according to the criteria of poverty, urbanization, and unemployment among young people and women.

More than 50,000 households across the four participating countries have received the package of productive measures, as shown in table CS1.1. The average duration of a productive inclusion measure in each country is 12–18 months. As of early 2020, implementation had been completed in Mauritania, Niger, and Senegal, and it was nearing completion in Burkina Faso.

Modalities for delivering productive measures

The productive measures are delivered through national SSN programs, which are operated by government institutions. The government agency in each country responsible for overseeing SSNs is also responsible for the accompanying productive measures, which includes planning, budgeting, monitoring, coordinating, and procuring external

TABLE CS1.1 Coverage of Productive Inclusion Measures across Four Sahelian Countries

	Number of households benefiting from productive inclusion measures
Burkina Faso	17,900
Mauritania	2,000
Niger	16,700
Senegal	14,800
Total	**51,400**

Sources: World Bank 2019b; project documents.

Note: The beneficiary participating in productive activities is a member of the social safety net household but is not necessarily the individual who receives the regular cash transfer.

service providers (such as trainers or payment providers for the lump sum transfer).[3] The SSN agencies have both central-level staff and decentralized staff throughout the country. To accommodate the scale of additional activities, each SSN agency has appointed staff to act as a national focal point for the productive measures and has identified field staff to supervise implementation.

Although the content of the productive measures package is similar across countries, delivery modalities vary across countries. Each national SSN agency tailored its approach to implementation to accommodate its institutional context, delivery systems, scale of operation, and local realities.

In Niger, a combination of SSN agency staff, service providers, and community coaches implemented the productive measures package. As shown in figure CS1.1, beneficiaries elect a member of their community as a coach, and coaches are then trained by field operators from the SSN agency. Once fully trained, the elected coaches facilitate the savings groups and advise beneficiaries on their investments. Field operators supervise overall implementation on behalf of the SSN agency, with one field operator allocated to oversee multiple villages (nine on average). The SSN agency contracts firms to train beneficiaries on life skills and microentrepreneurship. The lump sum cash transfer is effectively a vertical scale-up of the transfer provided by the SSN program—that is, it is provided through a payment agency, using the same delivery mechanism as for the national SSN program.

A second delivery modality involves contracts and partnerships between SSN agencies, training firms, and NGOs (see figure CS1.2). In two provinces of Burkina Faso and Senegal, NGOs provided community volunteer coaches with training and ongoing supervision and support. SSN agency teams supervised implementation by training the NGOs and monitoring their work based on clearly established implementation manuals and field protocols.

Finally, in two provinces of Burkina Faso and in Mauritania NGOs delivered the full package, except for the cash grants, which were paid through the national SSN system. In Mauritania, the NGOs involved are regular government partners in charge of delivering human capital measures in the SSN program, and they extended their role to include

FIGURE CS1.1 **Delivery of Productive Measures by a Combination of SSN Agency Staff, Trainers, and Community Volunteers: Niger**

Source: World Bank.

Note: NGO = nongovernmental organization; SSN = social safety net.

FIGURE CS1.2 **Contracting or Coordinating with NGOs to Deliver the Productive Measures: Burkina Faso, Mauritania, and Senegal**

Source: World Bank.
Note: NGO = nongovernmental organization.

productive measures. In Burkina Faso, NGOs were selected to implement only the productive measures and worked with independent funding mobilized by Trickle Up, a nonprofit international development organization, in partnership with the SSN agency.

The capacity of national SSN agencies to deliver the productive measures was enhanced through technical assistance from external partners. The Sahel Adaptive Social Protection Program facilitated technical assistance at the regional level to support content development for implementation manuals and curricula, as well as training of trainers in each country. This assistance included partnerships with Trickle Up for village savings and loan associations and coaching and with the Centre de Suivi et d'Assistance et de Management (CESAM) for training (see box CS1.5). Similarly, the script and production of video-based community sensitization were carried out in partnership with local communications experts, videographers, and a social psychologist.

These collaborations were established at the regional level for various reasons. First, there were economies of scope because of the similarity of the package implemented in different countries stemming from the cross-cutting nature of the underlying constraints to income-generating activities. Second, collaboration led to cost savings in developing a common set of high-quality materials. And, third, national SSN agencies that had not yet implemented integrated packages of productive measures had capacity constraints in these areas. In addition to regional support, each national SSN agency adapted the core set of operational tools to suit the local needs and context. The technical assistance provided at the regional level complemented the regular supervision and support provided by the World Bank's country teams.

Cost of productive measures

A thorough costing exercise was undertaken consistently across the four participating countries. The Sahel Adaptive Social Protection Program developed a rigorous costing

---

BOX CS1.5 **Providing Technical Assistance for Implementation through Government Systems by Partnering with External Institutions**

Partnership with Trickle Up

Trickle Up is an international nongovernmental organization with extensive experience worldwide in productive inclusion. Trickle Up supported the design of implementation manuals and the training of trainers for two components of the package: coaching and savings groups. This work built on earlier smaller-scale experimentation by Trickle Up in the Sahel. The design of the operational manuals for the Sahel Adaptive Social Protection Program recognized two key factors: (1) the context of extremely poor women in the Sahel and the external and internal constraints they face; and (2) delivery of the package through national social protection programs instead of outside government systems. In addition to developing the operational manuals for national social safety net (SSN) agencies, Trickle Up provided program implementers across five countries with training of trainers on coaching and village saving and loan associations. Training sessions a few months apart were complemented by field visits to provide implementing agencies and field staff with feedback.

Trickle Up also mobilized funding to implement the productive package in two provinces in Burkina Faso, working in close collaboration with the national SSN agency and the World Bank.

Partnership with Centre de Suivi et d'Assistance et de Management

The Partnership with Centre de Suivi et d'Assistance et de Management (CESAM), a training firm based in Benin, supports the development and rollout of training programs across Africa for the International Labour Organization (ILO). CESAM supported the design and adaptation of materials for the behavioral skills and microentrepreneurship training. Based on this content, CESAM then trained trainers in partnership with master trainers in each country. CESAM also developed the training materials for facilitation of access to inputs and markets. These materials were used to train and support coaches to serve as intermediaries and social entrepreneurs to link the beneficiaries with input suppliers for both agricultural and nonagricultural livelihoods.

---

template to clearly break out costs for each specific intervention and costs related to program administration. For each component, the key cost items such as transport, equipment, materials, housing, and restoration were listed and reviewed by the program teams and SSN agencies. Management and supervision costs were factored in, including the time costs of all staff involved in the country program (from government, NGO partners, or the World Bank). This approach allowed precise estimation of the cost of each intervention and separate reporting of specific administrative or nonintervention costs.

Supporting implementation at scale through monitoring and evaluation and regional learning

Although there are differences across the six countries, national SSN agencies tackle many of the same issues in the design and implementation of productive measures. Thus innovations in one country can be pertinent to all. A regional learning agenda was outlined to gather lessons from the implementation of the productive measures and learn about their effectiveness collaboratively. This coordinated learning effort included a multicountry impact evaluation, monitoring and evaluation (M&E) data, and process evaluations.

Multicountry impact evaluation

A multicountry impact evaluation is assessing the impact and cost-effectiveness of the productive measures in Burkina Faso, Mauritania, Niger, and Senegal. The evaluation is addressing a range of priority policy questions such as: What is the impact of a comprehensive package of productive accompanying measures on cash transfer beneficiaries? How can the package be optimized and made more cost-effective? How can one ensure that the package is inclusive and has an impact on the extreme poor? The evaluation is led by a team of researchers at the World Bank in partnership with researchers in several universities and IPA.

The impact evaluation is designed as a randomized controlled trial in which 16,700 beneficiaries from SSN programs in Burkina Faso, Mauritania, Niger, and Senegal were randomized into four groups. All groups receive regular cash transfers through the national SSN program, with variation in the allocation of the accompanying measures as follows:

- *Control group.* This group receives only regular cash transfers with no productive package.

- *Treatment group 1 (Full Package).* This group receives regular cash transfers and the full package of accompanying measures described in table CS1.2.

- *Treatment group 2 (Capital Package).* This group receives regular cash transfers and a capital-centric package, which includes coaching, village savings groups, entrepreneurship training, and a lump sum cash grant. Participating households in this group do not receive sensitization on aspirations and social norms or life skills training. (By testing the program with and without these psychosocial interventions, the evaluation will be able to determine whether addressing participants' aspirations and social norms improves the program's overall effectiveness.)

- *Treatment group 3 (Social Package).* This group receives regular cash transfers and a package of productive measures with a stronger focus on addressing psychosocial constraints, including coaching, village savings groups, community sensitization on aspirations and social norms, life skills training, and entrepreneurship training.

TABLE CS1.2 **Productive Packages Compared through Impact Evaluation**

Control group	Full Package	Capital Package	Social Package
Cash transfers	Cash transfers	Cash transfers	Cash transfers
X	Coaching	Coaching	Coaching
X	Savings groups	Savings groups	Savings groups
X	Community sensitization on aspirations and social norms	X	Community sensitization on aspirations and social norms
X	Microentrepreneurship training	Microentrepreneurship training	Microentrepreneurship training
X	Life skills training	X	Life skills training
X	Lump sum cash grant	Lump sum cash grant	X

Source: World Bank.

Participating households in this group do not receive the lump sum cash grant. (Because the lump sum cash grant is one of the most expensive components of the package, researchers and policy makers are interested in identifying the cost-effectiveness of the transfer itself.)

The impact evaluation will analyze a broad range of outcomes related to economic welfare (consumption, food security, resilience), participation and earnings in income-generating activities (nonagricultural activities, livestock, agriculture, wage work, diversification), as well as psychosocial well-being. Nearly 95 percent of beneficiaries are women, and the impact evaluation will pay special attention to gender empowerment, including by measuring women's engagement in income-generating activities, control over resources, participation in decision-making, agency, relationships with partners, and, more generally, gender attitudes.

M&E data and process evaluation

The capacity of government institutions to implement at scale has been supported by strong monitoring and evaluation. An M&E module was developed specifically for the productive measures, tracking delivery of the package consistently across countries. The M&E module was linked to SSN program management information systems as much as possible. The data were collected through a decentralized approach, with each country developing its own protocols. Technical support was provided by a regional team to build synergies and ensure a coordinated approach.

To complement M&E data, process evaluations have been commissioned in Burkina Faso, Mauritania, Niger, and Senegal, looking in depth at the complex issue of implementing coaching at scale within a government program. Complementary efforts are also under way to summarize operational learning on how to design and implement productive inclusion packages through large-scale, government-led programs. Consultations with various stakeholders (such as governments, World Bank staff, and service providers) will influence the consolidation of implementation lessons.

Perspectives for scaling up

In 2020–21, results from the first phase of the impact evaluation, process evaluations, and operational learning will be disseminated. Over the medium term, the evidence base will inform the design and implementation of the programs evaluated, and it may affect the design and implementation of other programs across the region.

The emerging evidence base has already had an influence on recent initiatives in the Sahel. In Niger, for example, the operational learning has shaped the productive inclusion components of a youth employment project and an operation to support refugees and host communities.[4] The second phase of Niger's Adaptive Safety Net Project also includes a component on productive inclusion, with implementation modalities adjusted according to the results of the impact evaluation. Similarly, the SSN program in Senegal has planned a large scale-up of the productive measures in response to needs arising from the COVID-19 crisis. Meanwhile, the governments of Mauritania and Senegal are discussing the implementation of productive measures as an exit strategy for cash transfer beneficiaries. A new SSN program in Mauritania has incorporated a productive inclusion component for households exiting the national conditional cash transfer program.[5] Youth employment programs in Burkina Faso and Mauritania will include productive measures based on lessons learned from the first phase of implementation.

Lessons

Detailed findings from the impact evaluations and operational learning will be disseminated to governments and other stakeholders in 2020–21. Pending publication of these findings, this section outlines some emerging operational lessons at the institutional and programmatic levels on working at scale.

Institutional and delivery modality lessons

The diagnostic phase was critical to grounding the program design in evidence, but also to creating a consensus around program objectives and facilitating government leadership. The evidence collected through qualitative and quantitative surveys created unique opportunities to look more closely at the daunting challenge of increasing the productivity of poor households and women in particular, to discuss the concrete constraints they face when engaging in economic activities, and to create consensus across various agencies around the objectives of the productive measures.

Government-led national SSN programs offer a platform for implementing productive inclusion measures at scale. National social protection systems were established in the region to support the basic needs of poor and vulnerable households. Although cash transfer programs have had widely documented impacts, they also provide a platform to tackle constraints to economic activities through a combination of cash transfers and direct efforts to promote productive employment. A defining feature of the Sahelian approach to productive inclusion is that national governments successfully led overall implementation. National programs have defined and maintained a coordinated approach, reducing fragmentation of interventions and opening a pathway to scale. This approach has also allowed the delivery of productive measures at relatively low cost. In a context in which there is a need to improve opportunities for the economic empowerment of women, the productive measures provide new opportunities, particularly for younger women.

A multifaceted program requires pragmatic delivery arrangements and solid government coordination. Adaptations at scale require the articulation of delivery arrangements by SSN agencies and the creation of partnerships or sustained contractual relationships with local organizations. Depending on the extent and nature of the existing field activities and on the skills available locally, governments may choose various combinations of actors to deliver the set of productive measures. It is, however, critical that the package of activities be kept coherent, with consistent messages picked up across the measures and coaching as a common thread.

Significant capacity is required at all levels of government (at both the central and local levels) to oversee implementation and ensure close synergies with the relevant programs and agencies.

Investment in delivery systems for national SSN programs lays the foundation for the delivery and expansion of productive inclusion measures. The establishment of national systems facilitates the layering of additional measures that advance economic inclusion objectives and build resilience to shocks. For example, social registries include a substantive cohort of poor and vulnerable households, and they can be used to identify households that may benefit from productive measures; SSN agencies within government can be supported to expand their coordination roles; and delivery mechanisms for SSNs provide an avenue for implementing complementary measures and providing lump sum cash grants to beneficiaries.

Meanwhile, investing in high-quality monitoring data helps to improve the capacity of government agencies to track program implementation. The implementation of complex interventions on a large scale by government systems must be accompanied by comprehensive efforts to build strong M&E systems and integrate data collection protocols in routine operations carried out by partner governments through their own program management information systems.

Programmatic and operational lessons

Despite short time frames and seasonal challenges, the village savings and loan association model has worked well, even in the most remote and deprived communities of the region. Combining VSLAs with cash transfers can boost financial inclusion by directly allowing the poor to participate. The flexibility of the VSLA approach, in which groups establish their own rules, allows it to function in challenging times, such as the lean seasons when many members are facing consumption pressures and are unable to save as much. The timeline of activities needs to factor in the fact that VSLA groups need a few months to get up to speed—that is, reach the point that members have a full understanding of the approach and groups have sufficient resources to start the loan component.

The *VSLA model* is well placed to rapidly increase coverage through horizontal expansion. In Niger, the VSLA approach was easily embedded into the existing beneficiary groups. As part of the SSN project in Niger, beneficiaries were organized in groups, and these groups often organized rotating savings groups (ROSCAs, or *tontines*). As part of the productive measures of the SASPP, groups of beneficiaries were transformed into VSLAs, which facilitated mobilization and allowed VSLAs to quickly get up and running. In other countries, groups had to be formed first, which took a little more time.

Some savings groups are showing encouraging signs of sustainability, with the prospect of links with formal financial institutions. Although support from the national SSN program has concluded in Niger and Senegal, many savings groups continue to operate. There may be scope for additional links between VSLAs and formal financial institutions, such as opening a bank account for a VSLA and encouraging members to open individual bank accounts.

As for the *community coaches*, it is not yet clear whether they can successfully implement multiple layers of interventions. Community-level coaches have already shown a degree of success, with preliminary findings suggesting some strong buy-in

---

BOX CS1.6   **Niger, Where Beneficiaries Continue to Work with Coaches after Project Conclusion**

Anecdotal evidence from Niger suggests some coaches have delivered encouraging results, although substantial variation in the performance of coaches has been noted. Many coaches in Niger have low levels of education and so have at times struggled to use formal coaching materials, even those with signs and pictures. Nonetheless, coaches have gained the trust of beneficiaries. Payments for coaches by the project ended in early 2019, yet groups of beneficiaries in certain communes decided to continue using their own funds to remunerate coaches for their work. These beneficiaries contribute a small amount each week—between $15 and $20 over the nine-month period of the VSLA cycle. Coaches therefore remain active and continue providing close support to beneficiaries. It appears that beneficiaries perceive that one of the advantages offered by coaches is access to markets.

from communities, such as in Niger (see box CS1.6). But the efficiency of coaching large numbers of beneficiaries is not yet established, suggesting potential capacity constraints to expanding coverage through a horizontal scale-up. The profiles of coaches vary widely, and still more must be learned about the optimal profile and what types of technical support or incentives are most effective.

Women are empowered by participation in productive inclusion programs. Evidence from process evaluations strongly suggests that, among other beneficial impacts, women experience increased agency. Membership in VSLAs creates a safe space, which fosters group dynamics and peer learning. Similarly, the psychosocial components help to strengthen community support.

The *community sensitization* on social norms through the use of videos was found to be very suitable for low-skilled individuals and for addressing gender norms. Participation in the video session was high, and process evaluations showed that beneficiaries recalled key aspects of a storyline over a year after a video was projected. Meanwhile, the larger community rallied around the objective of having women lead economic initiatives and contribute to household income, creating a lasting enabling environment for beneficiaries. This platform for delivering messages and triggering social dynamics could be promising for other interventions targeting this population.

Urban and peri-urban environments present various implementation challenges. The Senegal experience reveals that selecting areas for the program can be complex and sensitive where there are few socioeconomic differences between neighborhoods. Furthermore, beneficiaries frequently change residence in urban areas, presenting complications for program implementers. And economic opportunities may reduce the prospects for full attendance at training. There also may be limited locations for appropriate training sites in the neighborhoods where beneficiaries live, and coaches may not live in proximity to all beneficiaries. Training tools also need to be adapted to urban contexts, although the higher level of education among urban beneficiaries facilitates participants' comprehension of the training and related information.

The impact evaluation will address key policy questions identified by stakeholders during the design phase. Until now, relatively little has been known about the impact of different combinations of interventions, or about their effectiveness when implemented at scale in government-led national SSN programs. The systematic efforts to both provide robust findings on the cost-effectiveness of various components and gain a deeper understanding of the constraints and opportunities related to implementation will inform future discussions of a broader rollout.

Notes

1. The Sahel Adaptive Social Protection Program (SASPP) was launched in 2014 to support the design and implementation of adaptive social protection programs and systems in six Sahel countries: Burkina Faso, Chad, Mali, Mauritania, Niger, and Senegal. Of these Sahel countries, this case study covers productive inclusion measures in four: Burkina Faso, Mauritania, Niger, and Senegal. Geographic definitions of the Sahel region vary. Commonly, the Sahel stretches from Senegal on the Atlantic coast, through parts of Mauritania, Mali, Burkina Faso, Niger, Nigeria, Chad, and Sudan to Eritrea on the Red Sea coast.

2. The following terms, as defined, appear in these case studies. *Poor*—those persons whose consumption is below the national poverty line, as defined by the government. Or those who, because of their personal or community characteristics, face barriers in accessing opportunities to earn sustainable livelihoods and have elevated risks of being or staying in poverty or being socially marginalized. *Extreme poor*—those persons whose consumption is less than $1.90 a day (2011 US$ at purchasing power parity, PPP). Also defined as the bottom 50 percent of the poor population in a country or those unable to meet basic needs. *Ultrapoor*—those persons whose consumption is less than $0.95 a day (2011 US$, PPP). Also

defined as those experiencing the severest forms of deprivation such as being persistently hungry or lacking sources of income. *Other vulnerable*—other groups that do not meet any of these criteria such as those just above the poverty line and marginalized groups irrespective of their poverty level.

3. In Burkina Faso, a consultative framework has been established with all program partners. The SSN agency chairs quarterly meetings, which serve as a forum for discussion of achievements, challenges, lessons, and forward planning.

4. See these World Bank–funded operations: Youth Employment and Productive Inclusion Project (P163157) and Niger Refugees and Host Communities Support Project (P164563).

5. See this World Bank–funded operation: Mauritania Social Safety Net System Project II (P171125).

References

Bolwig, S., K. Rasmussen, C. Hesse, T. Hilhorst, and M. Kauffmann Hansen. 2011. "New Perspectives on Natural Resource Management in the Sahel." SEREIN–Occasional Paper No. 21, Sahel-Sudan Environmental Research Initiative.

Bossuroy, T., E. Koussoubé, and P. Premand. 2017. "Constraints to Productive Employment Faced by Safety Nets Beneficiaries in the Sahel: Results of a Multi-country Qualitative Assessment." World Bank, Washington, DC.

Dang, Hai-Anh, Peter F. Lanjouw, and Rob Swinkels. 2014. "Who Remained in Poverty, Who Moved Up, and Who Fell Down? An Investigation of Poverty Dynamics in Senegal in the Late 2000s." Policy Research Working Paper 7141, World Bank, Washington, DC.

Mallé, Y. 2020. *Transforming Village Associations into VSLAs in Niger.* Trickle Up, New York. https://trickleup.org/transforming-village-associations-vslas-niger/.

OECD (Organisation for Economic Co-operation and Development). 2020. *Gender Equality in West Africa.* http://www.oecd.org/swac/topics/gender.htm.

Park, J., J. Bader, and D. Matei. 2015. "Northern-Hemispheric Differential Warming Is the Key to Understanding the Discrepancies in the Projected Sahel Rainfall." *Nature Communications* 6 (5985). https://doi.org/10.1038/ncomms6985.

World Bank. 2017. *Sahel Adaptive Social Protection Program, Annual Report 2017.* Washington, DC: World Bank.

World Bank. 2018a. *Country Partnership Framework for the Republic of Niger, 2018–2022.* Report No. 123736-NE. Washington, DC: World Bank.

World Bank. 2018b. *Sahel Adaptive Social Protection Program, Annual Report 2018.* Washington, DC: World Bank.

World Bank. 2019a. *Promoting Productive Inclusion and Resilience in National Safety Nets: A Four-Country Evaluation in the Sahel—Baseline Report: Mauritania, Niger, Senegal, Burkina Faso.* Washington, DC: World Bank.

World Bank. 2019b. *Sahel Adaptive Social Protection Program, Annual Report 2019.* Washington, DC: World Bank.

World Bank. 2019c. *The Way Forward for Social Safety Nets in Burkina Faso.* Washington, DC: World Bank.

The State of Bihar's Approach to Economic Inclusion: JEEViKA and the SJY Program

Introduction

In the eastern Indian state of Bihar, bordering Nepal, the Bihar Rural Livelihoods Promotion Society (BRLPS), locally known as JEEViKA, is the state's implementing agency of the National Rural Livelihoods Mission (NRLM). JEEViKA has a statewide mandate to mobilize rural women into a variety of community institutions, including (1) affinity-based self-help groups; (2) village organizations (VOs) that are composed of several of these self-help groups; (3) commodity-specific producer groups; and (4) higher federations. These community institutions offer several advantages, as they enable JEEViKA and others to offer capacity building to women collectively and allow women to better access finance, public services, and direct links to markets.

Launched as a state-level partnership and World Bank–funded program, JEEViKA has evolved into a multidimensional effort. It implements the NRLM and the World Bank–funded Bihar Transformative Development Project (BTDP), and it is a platform for targeted delivery of government policies and entitlement programs. Over 13 years of operation, JEEViKA has leveraged its network of self-help groups to achieve the greater financial and economic inclusion of more than 10 million poor rural women.

And yet despite strong economic inclusion programming and interventions shown to increase incomes and assets, JEEViKA's leadership realized that the poorest of the state's population faced challenges in engaging with its programs. JEEViKA's core intervention relies on the self-selection of households into self-help groups and their participation in higher-order economic activities, but these activities were difficult to sustain for the poorest and most vulnerable households.

In an attempt to address this challenge, JEEViKA embarked on a "graduation" pilot, and shortly thereafter an ambitious scale-up, Satat Jeevikoparjan Yojana (SJY). This case study primarily describes SJY, which is intended to serve the poorest people who had been left out of JEEViKA's broader programming. SJY is based on a contextualized graduation approach that aims to integrate 100,000 of the poorest and most vulnerable of the state's households into the VO infrastructure. Specifically, SJY seeks to boost the human capital of the poorest and most excluded households through support of consumption and livelihoods, savings, and training. This multidimensional support is designed to develop the capacities of these households to take better advantage of JEEViKA's core programming and economic inclusion efforts, including access to onward financing for enterprises, market links, food security interventions, and health and sanitation services, among others.

Within JEEViKA's broader economic inclusion programming, SJY is a graduation approach with key adaptations and potentially salient lessons for other programs. It explores new pathways for scale-up by leveraging JEEViKA's community institutions

This case study was authored by Sadna Samaranayake (World Bank Group, WBG), with contributions from Paramveer Singh (JEEViKA), Ajit Ranjan (JEEViKA), Kshovan Guha (JPAL), and Gautam Patel (JPAL).

and financial inclusion infrastructure to implement the program and relies on members of the community to serve as front-line implementers. As a livelihoods-plus approach built on a platform of financial inclusion, JEEViKA tackles economic inclusion from a different entry point than that of social safety nets (SSNs) or cash-plus approaches.

Context

Over the last three decades, India has made significant gains in economic growth and poverty reduction. Alongside its growth, between 1994 and 2012 India halved the share of its population in extreme poverty, bringing it down from 45 percent to 22 percent. The pace of poverty reduction accelerated threefold from 2005 to 2012 relative to the previous decade. Based on a poverty line defined as at or below $1.90 per person per day (2011 US$ at purchasing power parity, PPP), India has lifted more than 160 million people out of poverty in recent years, surpassed only by China (World Bank 2018c). However, India's growth rate has decelerated, and as of 2015 poverty remained an intractable issue, with roughly 176 million people nationwide living below the poverty line. At the time of this writing, India is experiencing a nationwide lockdown in response to COVID-19, which will undoubtedly blunt economic growth and exacerbate poverty conditions.

The social exclusion of specific groups—Scheduled Castes, Scheduled Tribes, other tribes, and minorities[1]—plays a major role in both the prevalence and the persistence of poverty (World Bank 2016c). Twenty-eight percent of India's population belong to Scheduled Castes or Scheduled Tribes, and 43 percent of that total remains poor. Historically determined social hierarchies and norms, including "untouchability" and segregation of livelihoods, land, and asset ownership, ensure that these groups continue to lag behind the general population in income, ownership of productive assets, human capital, and access to resources and services. There is also great regional diversity in the distribution of poverty. Seven of the poorest states, including the state of Bihar, are home to 62 percent of India's poor (World Bank 2018b).

Meanwhile, Bihar is one of India's fastest-growing low-income states, but large parts of the state remain very poor. India's third most populous state, Bihar is home to over 100 million people, 36 million of whom are poor. The state has long suffered from inadequate infrastructure and weak governance. Moreover, progress across social groups in Bihar has been uneven, with stark differences among groups in educational attainment and types of jobs held. The poverty rate for Scheduled Castes in the state is the highest in the country (World Bank 2016b). Bihar also has one of the highest rates of malnutrition in the country, and although its infant mortality is declining, it is still high. Consumption inequality has remained largely unchanged (World Bank 2016a).

Bihar is witnessing several shifting circumstances affecting its working population. Its agricultural productivity is one of the lowest in India, and the productivity of small-holder farmers is even lower than the average across all states (Behera et al. 2013). Against a backdrop of low agricultural production, rural dwellers are beginning to move off the farms and into other kinds of work, although the workforce remains largely farm-based in the areas of dairy, poultry, and enterprises tied to agriculture. There has been an increase in the number of jobs since 2005, but very few workers have salaried jobs, and job creation has lagged behind the expansion of the working-age population. In addition, state-level legislation in 2016 banning the production and consumption of liquor has had a significant impact on poor households reliant on income from the production and sale of country liquor.

Establishing JEEViKA: Setup, scale-up, and use of community structures

Against this backdrop of persistent poverty and inequality, the Bihar Rural Livelihoods Project (BRLP) was launched in 2006 in six districts and 42 blocks of Bihar with the support of a $63 million credit (World Bank 2007). In 2012 the program received additional financing of $100 million to saturate and deepen the program in the six districts (World Bank 2017). The success of BRLP led to the designation of JEEViKA as the state rural livelihoods mission to implement NRLM, the national-level livelihoods program, built on the lessons learned from JEEViKA and similar investments in the states of Andhra Pradesh, Kerala, and Tamil Nadu. In 2014 BRLP was scaled up to include all 534 blocks and 38 districts of Bihar. In 2016 the Bihar Transformative Development Project, a $290 million World Bank project, was initiated to support this scale-up and deepen the next-generation livelihoods approach across Bihar.

Scale-up and community structures

With its scale and outreach in Bihar, JEEViKA is the largest state mission implementing community-based livelihoods programming in India. The program has thus far mobilized more than 10 million rural women into more than 923,000 self-help groups, which are further federated into nearly 60,000 village organizations and 1,045 cluster-level federations. These community institutions have emerged as effective platforms for economic inclusion, linking the poorest to the formal banking system, and for enabling a range of services, including insurance, regular financial literacy, credit counseling, and orientation in sound financial practices, as well as new modes of financial transactions such as digital and mobile banking (World Bank 2018a). This large institutional platform has enabled households from the poorest areas of rural Bihar to collectively access banking services from more than 3,672 rural bank branches. Under the program, community institutions have leveraged credit worth roughly $1.5 billion from banks, while generating nearly $130 million in community savings.

Core operations

As shown in figure CS2.1, JEEViKA's core operations consist of mobilizing, supporting, and extending program services to and through three levels of group structures: self-help groups, village organizations, and cluster-level federations.

Within the village, 12–15 rural women come together to form *self-help groups*. JEEViKA facilitates these groups, which meet regularly, undertake financial savings, and lend internally from the group's common funds. JEEViKA then provides small catalytic funding—a Community Investment Fund—to stimulate financial activity and build the credit history of members. Locally identified resource persons—community mobilizers—facilitate the self-help group meetings and maintain ledgers. With proven credit history and a small corpus generated from savings and interest, the self-help groups are able to leverage larger amounts of credit from banks.

At the village level, 10–15 self-help groups are federated into *village organizations*. These organizations act as an important interface between the local bank branch and the member groups and facilitate ongoing credit links to local banks. Village organizations also facilitate specialized financial products, such as the Food Security Fund, a specialized credit window for collective procurement of food grains in lean seasons, and the Health Risk Fund, a specialized funding window for low-interest loans for health-related costs. Village organizations are also vital platforms for convergence with

FIGURE CS2.1 **JEEViKA Core Services Channeled through Various Levels of Groups and Organizations in the Community**

Source: World Bank.

key government programs and entitlements, and they provide a platform for communities to engage effectively with other public institutions such as schools and *panchayats* (community-level government).

Village organizations are further federated into cluster-level federations (CLFs), each composed of 30–50 village organizations. These federations act as large-scale financial intermediation platforms for addressing a wide variety of the community's financial needs. CLFs monitor the overall financial health of member institutions and act as vital touch points for banks to reach out to the community.

JEEViKA as a platform

Apart from a role in higher-level financial intermediation and representation of their constituent self-help groups, village organizations and CLFs serve as powerful organizational platforms. These structures enable JEEViKA to extend a host of livelihood supports, including grants to support farmer producer groups mobilized across self-help groups, community-level poultry units, and farm infrastructure, as well as initiatives to promote community health, water, sanitation, and hygiene (WASH) practices, and a host of other services. In Bihar, the strength of these institutions is evidenced by the fact that the village organizations and CLFs are the go-to platforms for other public services and nongovernmental organizations (NGOs) seeking to efficiently target the poorest and improve program delivery.

JEEViKA has also initiated interventions on a pilot basis or through convergence with other government programs to enable scaled-up access to public entitlements for the poor. These include access to social security pensions, wage employment, and insurance coverage—facilitating, for example, the enrollment of more than 2.2 million members in the government insurance scheme for women, thereby insuring members against death and disability.[2]

Program implementation through cadres of community implementers

JEEViKA's ability to effectively extend programming across a large and disconnected state depends on its human resource structure, which comprises core JEEViKA staff as well as large cadres of community members who are trained to support programming efforts. Over its years of operations, JEEViKA has strengthened its human resource, monitoring and evaluation, and learning systems at the level of community institutions and at the level of various project management units—block, district, and state

(World Bank 2018a). The human resources system focuses on strong accountability mechanisms and pays special attention to building up local technical specialist support.

As of 2019, community institutions were staffed by more than 120,000 trained community professionals and resource persons (roughly 80 percent of whom were women), composing cadres of specialized staff, all from local communities. These grassroots women leaders serve as paraprofessionals, resource persons, and functionaries trained in institutional capacity building, community mobilizing, bookkeeping, and facilitating links with commercial banks and livelihood support services.

Addressing the persistent exclusion of the poorest

As JEEViKA was expanding its coverage in Bihar, it recognized early on that the very poorest households faced difficulties engaging with its programs and its foundational structure, the self-help group. In part, the self-selective nature of self-help groups, by which women would elect into and organize groups themselves, was discouraging the poorest households, creating "self-exclusion." JEEViKA recognized that the ultrapoor often felt uncomfortable forming groups, sometimes because of an inability to save regularly. The self-help group model relied on saving, group lending, regular meetings, and financial discipline. These were demanding requirements for ultrapoor women, who were often without enough resources for basic consumption, let alone saving and lending. Community stigma and ostracization of poorer and vulnerable women and families contributed to their exclusion as well.

As the project evolved, JEEViKA recognized that certain flexibilities in the self-help group model would be required to encourage the participation of the poorest and that community institutions could play a powerful role. To catalyze the engagement of community institutions in including the poorest, JEEViKA instituted several practices, including introducing *social inclusion* as one of the seven quality indicators in village organizations' performance assessments. This helped village organizations evolve specific strategies, such as working closely with community resource persons as well as social action committees to identify and contact excluded households and encourage them to join. Later, through the efforts of the village organizations, the communities themselves made considerable efforts to identify and include the poorest households and migrant groups (World Bank 2018a).

Extending economic inclusion through contextual graduation

Despite progress made by JEEViKA in the economic inclusion of Bihar's poor, a share of poor households either remained excluded or dropped out of self-help groups. JEEViKA realized that effectively addressing the needs of these poorest households would require more nuanced and more targeted approaches. Without inclusion in the self-help group structure, the omitted households would continue to have no ability to reap the broader benefits of community institutions, access to credit, and the links to other government and nongovernmental programming that leveraged village organizations as a platform for service delivery. JEEViKA understood that assistance in asset building and targeted efforts at boosting household capacities were required, as were household-level interventions for livelihood enhancement. The poorest households also likely required coping strategies for unexpected shocks and a programmatic approach that recognized and accounted for the health and economic setbacks that regularly push the ultrapoor back into the deeper traps of poverty and debt (World Bank 2018a).

In August 2018, the State Cabinet of Bihar approved a budgetary outlay of approximately $120 million for a new program, Satat Jeevikoparjan Yojana (SJY), under JEEViKA's remit. SJY was intended to be a targeted strategy to extend JEEViKA's economic inclusion efforts to 100,000 of its poorest constituents. The program was also seen as an avenue to countering the loss of livelihoods from the recent outlawing of liquor consumption and production in the state.

An earlier pilot graduation program, Targeting the Hard-Core Poor (THCP), had borne many lessons and insights for JEEViKA, including how to augment the graduation approach to work within its core program offerings and infrastructure. Several randomized controlled trials (RCTs) revealed that the graduation approach had positive results on the income, asset, and consumption levels of the poorest, among other indicators (Banerjee et al. 2015). Considered key to its success is the catalytic and combinatory effect of its sequenced inputs, which are thought to result in a "big push" to the household, enabling a rise in income and consumption levels, assets, savings, and human capital dimensions. In scale-up, as in pilot mode, JEEViKA retained core graduation components and the engagement of research and technical partners (see table CS2.1). The Abdul Latif Jameel Poverty Action Lab (J-PAL), a research and policy organization that had conducted several RCTs on graduation approaches, is currently conducting research on the operations of SJY and is planning an impact assessment. Bandhan Konnagar, a West Bengal–based NGO, is providing technical guidance based on its experience as one of the early adapters of graduation programming in India.

SJY is one of the largest known government scale-ups of graduation programming; see box CS2.1 for details of components of the SJY scale-up and, where relevant, shifts from the THCP pilot.

TABLE CS2.1 **SJY at a Glance: Key Scale-Up Components (and Variations from the Pilot)**

Project basics	Components
Participants. Scale-up to 100,000 households across Bihar	***Targeting.*** Scale-up of social mapping + village organization input + verification
Pilot: 2,000 households at two pilot sites ***Project duration.*** July 2018–July 2023 (100,000 households to be identified by July 2021) ***Project leadership.*** JEEViKA, Bihar Rural Livelihoods Promotion Society (government) ***Other support.*** Technical assistance by Bandhan Konnagar and research support by J-PAL ***Cost of scale-up.*** Rs 77,000 (approximately $1,040) per family ***Current status.*** A 100,000 household scale-up of the approach (SJY) is under way, featuring graduation approach inputs and sequencing, with key departures in targeting and program delivery, including through the use of community inputs and cadres. ***Initial findings.*** Process evaluations show roughly 10 percent exclusion errors in targeting but no significant inclusion errors. Program is contending with balancing a fast-paced rollout with quality control and timing of interventions.	**Pilot: Social mapping + Poverty Wealth Ranking + verification at household** ***Consumption support.*** Scale-up of Livelihood Gap Assistance Fund of Rs 1,000 per month for seven months ***Assets.*** Productive assets provided to households in multiple tranches from a list of choices, including livestock, grocery shop, tea and snacks shop, and sewing machines. Scale-up asset value average Rs 60,000 with initial tranche/asset valued at Rs 20,000. **Pilot asset value: Rs 20,000 with initial tranche/asset valued at Rs 5,000** ***Enterprise training.*** Three-day asset-specific training plus refreshers ***Household coaching.*** Eighteen months of weekly sessions at the group and household level conducted by trained community-based master resource persons ***Access to savings.*** Help to open a bank account and motivation to save

Source: World Bank.
Note: SJY = Satat Jeevikoparjan Yojana.

Funding and costs

National, state, World Bank, and philanthropic funding have combined synergistically to support SJY. The cost per household of the SJY intervention is roughly Rs 77,000 ($1,040) per household. Roughly Rs 67,000 ($900)[3] covers direct inputs to the household, including the Livelihoods Gap Assistance Fund and asset transfers (Livelihood Investment Fund). The remaining $140 per household covers human resources (community cadres and staff) and their capacity building.

State-level funding of $120 million supports all transfers and assets to participating households. Funding provided by the national government and the World Bank supports JEEViKA's human resources, systems, and operations at large, including those devoted to the SJY scale-up. In addition to government funding and support, SJY benefits from external philanthropic funding support, which is utilized for technical assistance to the JEEViKA team for operational research and to enhance the monitoring tools used in the SJY scale-up.

Moving to scale leveraging established infrastructure and policy objectives

SJY is a functional expansion of JEEViKA's economic inclusion programming, which has already reached more than 10 million rural women and represents coverage of more than 46.6 million individuals in Bihar. With a goal of reaching 100,000 households

---

BOX CS2.1   SJY at a Glance: Key Scale-Up Components (and Variations from the Pilot)

SJY coverage and targeting

To date, Satat Jeevikoparjan Yojana (SJY) has targeted more than 70,000 ultrapoor households in Bihar in all 38 districts, across 233 of 534 blocks. Rapid targeting of participants has been enabled by leveraging community structures and modifying the original pilot targeting approach. The targeting and selection of beneficiaries in the pilot had closely followed the Bandhan Konnagar and BRAC graduation models[a] and included social mapping, community wealth ranking, and house-to-house verification of program entry criteria. However, this targeting method was considered too time-consuming for a scale-up and was changed significantly for SJY. SJY retained a simpler transect walk and social mapping exercise and simplified the wealth ranking process. In its place, the input of the village organizations was solicited to identify and rank the poorest people. Block-level project implementation units carried out a final check on the endorsed list of SJY participants.

SJY implementation arrangements

Notably, SJY is JEEViKA's first attempt to mainstream a program that works with households as the unit of intervention instead of group structures. To implement SJY at the household level, JEEViKA leans on its organized village organizations, which lend input and support to key functions such as targeting, endorsement of selected households, initial asset procurement, and routing of funds to the households. Active implementation of the program is largely in the hands of community cadres—community resource

(Box continues next page)

BOX CS2.1 **SJY at a Glance: Key Scale-Up Components (and Variations from the Pilot)** *(continued)*

persons—established by JEEViKA to handle functions such as targeting for SJY through intensive community-level drives. Meanwhile, a new type of cadre, consisting of "master resource persons," is dedicated to the SJY program, handling the coaching and household-level work of SJY. JEEViKA staff, together with a Bandhan Konnagar resource person at the block level, provide households with training on specific livelihoods and offer overall supervisory support for the program (see figure BCS2.1).

FIGURE BCS2.1 **Role of Community Cadres in JEEViKA and SJY Core Operations**

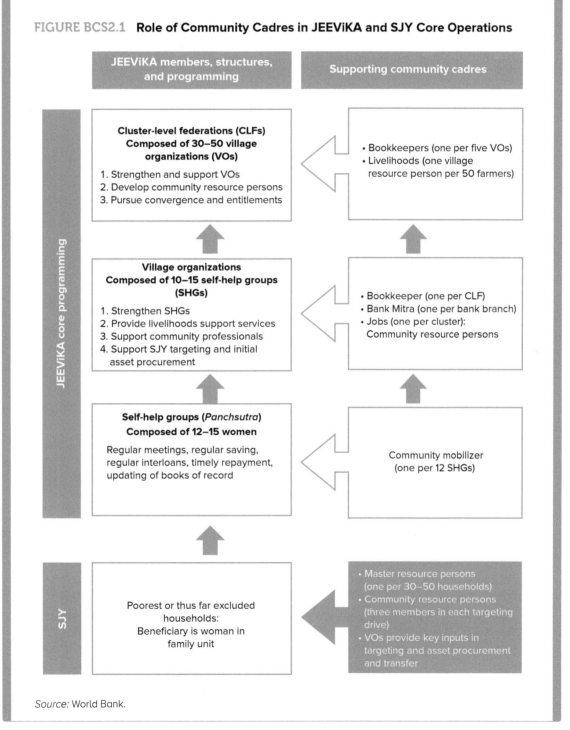

Source: World Bank.

(Box continues next page)

BOX CS2.1 **SJY at a Glance: Key Scale-Up Components (and Variations from the Pilot)** *(continued)*

Productive assets

SJY participants choose a productive asset from a list of choices determined by local context and needs, and then they receive asset-specific skills training and weekly household coaching. After completing the training, they take possession of the assets, typically in two or three tranches. Asset packages may include various types of livestock, sewing machines, farm inputs, inventory for a small shop, or other contextually relevant productive assets. Early trends from households indicate that small-scale trading enterprises and livestock are the preferred options for first tranche assets.

The first tranche value of the Livelihood Investment Fund is pegged at a maximum of Rs 20,000 ($280). Households may choose a diverse activity in the second or third tranche, and the total value of assets is estimated to be Rs 60,000 ($840). Participants also receive a temporary subsistence allowance called the Livelihood Gap Assistance Fund of Rs 1,000 ($14) per month paid over seven months. This allowance is intended to encourage higher consumption and to offset the opportunity costs of learning how to put the new enterprise asset into use before it begins to generate income.

Coaching

Participating households receive weekly coaching. During coaching, master resource persons provide a range of support that may include guidance on care and maintenance of assets, proper care of livestock, guidance on building microenterprises, or help in gaining essential skills such as learning how to sign one's name, basic numeracy, and bookkeeping skills. The weekly coaching sessions also include a social education component, with discussions on topics ranging from nutrition to early marriage and family planning.

a. BRAC is an international nongovernmental organization with headquarters in Bangladesh.

(and coverage of roughly 500,000 individuals), SJY is itself an ambitious scale-up of a contextual and rigorous graduation approach, extending JEEViKA's reach and core services, which are centered around access to financing, market links, and access to public entitlement programs in the direction of livelihoods enhancement for the extreme poor. As of early 2020, more than 70,000 households had been successfully targeted and endorsed to receive the SJY intervention.

JEEViKA's wide coverage and scale can be attributed in part to its institutional structure and staffing. JEEViKA was launched in 2006 as an autonomous agency with an independent executive committee and chief executive officer and a professional staff (see box CS2.2). In later years, the same structure was adopted by several other state rural livelihoods missions and other government agencies. This structure as well as strong training and accountability measures have largely insulated JEEViKA from some of the governance issues that historically have faced the state's agencies, including elite capture and leakage of funds. A long-standing partnership with the World Bank has enabled the program to establish strong financial management systems as well as robust mechanisms for redressing grievances.

BOX CS2.2   **SJY: Key Roles and Funders**

Roles

- *Implementer:* JEEViKA (government)
- *Technical assistance partner:* Bandhan Konnagar
- *Knowledge and learning partner:* J-PAL

Funders

- *Core JEEViKA human resources, systems, and operations:* Jointly funded by the national government of India and World Bank
- *SJY scale-up operational funding:* Funded by state of Bihar
- *Technical assistance and operational research funding:* Philanthropic funding from Co-Impact and IKEA Foundation

---

Note: SJY = Satat Jeevikoparjan Yojana; J-PAL= Abdul Latif Jameel Poverty Action Lab.

The SJY scale-up benefits from being integrated into a larger institutionalized economic inclusion effort: JEEViKA at the state level and NRLM at the national level. SJY is strongly aligned with state and national level policy objectives and is considered a key piece of JEEViKA's overall policy goal of "saturation"—that is, inclusion of and service provision for the poor. SJY's scale-up benefits from state and national funding and JEEViKA's well-developed and adaptive delivery systems and infrastructure, all of which have supported an altogether new programmatic approach that has effectively found its footing in Bihar. NRLM, conceptualized at the national level based on the lessons of JEEViKA and similar programs in other states, offers a broad landscape to institutionalize the experiences of SJY on a national scale.

SJY leverages JEEViKA-catalyzed community structures, such as village organizations and community cadres, effectively institutionalizing community capacity for its program delivery. In the move from pilot to scale-up, one decision rooted the SJY scale-up firmly in the fabric of JEEViKA's core programming: the move to make use of community structures in selecting SJY households and in other key implementation steps. For JEEViKA, a successful shift in programming from a 2,000-household pilot to a 100,000-household scale-up implied that the approach would have to be seamlessly integrated into JEEViKA's core community structures, leveraging their strengths and operational capacity. Village organizations and their constituent self-help groups came to the forefront as a source of inputs into the SJY beneficiary selection process. In addition, community structures are now involved at key implementation junctures, including the channeling of money through village organizations to SJY households and the use of village organization procurement committees to source and distribute assets to households.

Key partnerships supported by catalytic funding

The institutional capacity of JEEViKA to design and implement the SJY scale-up was enhanced through partnerships with several external organizations, which enabled key technical guidance and operational learning support. The expertise and guidance provided by Bandhan Konnagar in a technical assistance capacity and J-PAL South Asia as a knowledge and learning partner allowed a learning-by-doing and iterative approach for JEEViKA.

Bandhan Konnagar provides JEEViKA with dedicated staff who advise community resource persons, master resource persons, and JEEViKA staff on key implementation steps. It has also provided training materials for staff and cadres, program implementation guidelines and tools, and monitoring forms and formats during both the Targeting the Hard-Core Poor pilot and the SJY scale-up.

J-PAL has assumed an operational research role to help ensure effective real-time learning of operational lessons. It regularly reviews operational challenges, and in doing so it observes the implementation of key steps, including targeting, household micro-planning, and asset transfers to date. It then offers feedback to JEEViKA on the efficacy of each step, potential areas for improvement, and, where possible, avenues to facilitate efficiency at scale. In addition to its current role supporting operational learning, J-PAL hopes to conduct a randomized controlled trial of the SJY program in the future.

Catalytic philanthropic funding has been central to equipping JEEViKA with a project management unit, technical assistance, and operational research support for SJY. Although many state, national, and multilateral budgets finance implementation and direct inputs to households, funding for other vital elements of large-scale government programming is not always as readily available. These vital elements include technical assistance, development of the required infrastructure and systems, and research on process and outcomes. Catalytic investments by philanthropic donors and private sector actors can bridge these critical gaps. Grants from Co-Impact[4] and the IKEA Foundation[5] allowed expansion of Bandhan's and J-PAL's involvement beyond the Targeting the Hard-Core Poor pilot, enabling the provision of additional technical inputs to assist in a wider scale-up effort and help ensure effective learning of operational lessons and documentation. In addition, philanthropic funding has supported JEEViKA's investments in monitoring technologies for SJY, including the development of mobile applications to allow implementing staff and community cadres to capture program data and milestones on their phones. All ultrapoor households under SJY are now registered on a mobile application, and programmatic inputs and key outcomes are digitally tracked on the platform.

Lessons

Programmatic lessons

For JEEViKA, both the Targeting the Hard-Core Poor pilot and the SJY scale-up have confirmed the notion that to effectively reach the poorest and most vulnerable people, a more intensive approach is required. Although economic inclusion at scale can be achieved through its core livelihoods and financial inclusion activities, JEEViKA has committed to a higher-touch, and in some ways higher-intensity, graduation approach, working directly with households as opposed to groups to effectively engage the poorest and most persistently excluded.

As SJY and its preceding pilot were being implemented, it quickly became clear that adapting the originally envisioned graduation approach was necessary to effectively institutionalize it within the larger JEEViKA programmatic model. When embarking on the Targeting the Hard-Core Poor pilot, JEEViKA leaders were keen to follow the tried and tested graduation approach as closely as possible to benchmark its operations and ensure impacts. But by the time they decided to scale up SJY, they understood that adaptations were required to allow successful integration of the approach into its core program infrastructure and community cadres.

Unlike in many other global adaptations of graduation approaches, in SJY most of the programmatic changes and lessons learned are related to the *way in which the original graduation components are delivered,* as opposed to changes to the components themselves. JEEViKA has embraced the intensity of graduation approach components, electing not to pare down the model, in contrast to several international government agencies, which have sought to use a "graduation-lite" approach. The most substantive changes have aimed at allowing the program to effectively leverage existing community structures. Graduation program components themselves have not been eliminated or reduced. In fact, in the scale-up the value of asset transfers has tripled on average. And although several global graduation programs are moving to home visits every two weeks, JEEViKA has maintained weekly coaching and coaching at the household level over the 24-month course of the program.

An ambitious mandate to scale up, coupled with the relative novelty of working directly with households, poses ongoing challenges. SJY's priority is to scale up as quickly as possible in order to keep pace with the available funding resources. A clear mandate to scale up puts pressure on identifying, training, and retaining high-quality master resource persons, who are responsible for the bulk of household-level programming inputs. As targeting efforts are under way, community resource persons are being trained in large numbers to conduct targeting activities, and village organizations are being tapped to help identify households through targeting drives.

The results of operational research so far have revealed exclusion errors, but no noticeable inclusion errors. Errors of exclusion, in which deserving households are left out, are reasonable in the early days of a program, are fixable with later rounds of programming, and are less problematic than inclusion errors, which can indicate leakage and elite capture of programs. The early days of SJY have also seen other anomalies, including over-targeting of households with disabilities (proportional to the population). This anomaly is likely because community resource persons and village organizations, in their new roles of household identification, more readily recognize people with disabilities as meeting program entry criteria without nuanced regard of who may have limited means to engage in economic activities.

The fast-paced scale-up has had impacts on households as well. SJY households with completed asset transfers are increasingly competing with other subsistence-level enterprises in the community, as well as with themselves. JEEViKA is in the early stages of tracking whether and where clusters of enterprises could be formed to facilitate aggregated interventions, such as retail marts and cooperatives, to facilitate more streamlined market access and better pricing for farmers and small traders.

As JEEViKA learns in real time about the effectiveness of its programming, it is considering additional methods to mitigate against loss of quality and impacts, while preserving the fast pace of the SJY scale-up. To stem capacity constraints, JEEViKA has moved to quickly recruit and deploy a pool of young professionals to support the program scale-up, and it has instituted training drives to prepare cadres of community resource persons to undertake targeting and to prepare master resource persons for household-level programming. With the support of philanthropic funding, JEEViKA is also constituting a professional project management unit to shore up professional staff in oversight and managerial positions for the scale-up. Because the program is sequential, JEEViKA is batching and phasing activities, attempting to create competencies at scale and, potentially, specialization within activities. The best-performing staff and master resource persons are quickly converted to trainers to extend their expertise, and JEEViKA has appointed dedicated human resources to the program at the district level to ensure ongoing technical oversight. JEEViKA is also considering avenues to standardize and digitize content both for training master resource persons and for training and coaching program participants. It will likely move toward video-based training and modules to be delivered via hand-held projectors.

Institutional lessons

Although it is still at an early stage of implementation, SJY is one of the largest known government scale-ups of graduation programming within a larger economic inclusion effort. Accordingly, SJY and its host program, JEEViKA, have the potential to offer nationally and globally relevant lessons for economic inclusion of the extreme poor. India's National Rural Livelihoods Mission, with its nationwide infrastructure and resources, has nationalized economic inclusion efforts that organize the poor in self-help groups and connect them to formal financial services, public entitlements, and livelihood-enhancing support (World Bank 2011b). If SJY proves successful, the program could demonstrate that such efforts are an effective way to extend economic inclusion, financial inclusion, and the public entitlement offerings of state and national governments to the country's unreached extreme poor. In India, NRLM's national infrastructure can extend SJY lessons across the country. Indeed, NRLM's state agencies have a history of borrowing implementation practices and lessons learned from leading states (World Bank 2011a).

Although many governments look to graduation approaches as a way to move households through and out of government interventions, JEEViKA seeks the opposite result. It regards the approach as a way to boost the capacities of households, enabling them to move on to JEEViKA's core programming. That programming is driven by a statewide "saturation" mandate, the success of which is predicated on self-selection and the election of services by all eligible households. Rather than seeking to move (graduate) SJY households *out* of the program, JEEViKA focuses on the degree to which SJY households can be mainstreamed *into* self-sustaining self-help groups and village organizations.

The SJY experience within JEEViKA provides a possible blueprint for scaling up economic inclusion through the entry point of livelihoods programming, while utilizing financial inclusion building blocks. SJY differs from the better-known "cash plus" approach of government agencies, which leverages social safety net infrastructure and cash transfers to extend economic inclusion programming. It is primarily a livelihoods intervention delivered through financial inclusion infrastructure. Although the intervention itself provides inputs to participating households centered on boosting productive assets and skills, its delivery relies on the support of self-help groups and village organizations. SJY may therefore provide insights into how various global financial inclusion approaches and platforms could be tapped to reach increasingly poorer households. Globally, these approaches and platforms could include government-catalyzed self-help group programs, large-scale village savings and loan programs, and other financial inclusion and community structures.

JEEViKA's SJY program offers insights into how community structures can enhance economic inclusion efforts and, potentially, seed greater impacts at the community level. JEEViKA's self-help groups and higher structures are not merely financial inclusion structures. The prevailing philosophy behind them is one of community mobilization and building the countervailing power of the poor. The approach leverages upstream community structures. It remains to be seen whether economic and social inclusion outcomes can be enhanced by this community participation and leverage.

The use of community cadres to deliver graduation programming could contribute to the discourse around how to ease the persistent capacity constraints of economic inclusion efforts. Distinct from more typical channels of NGO or government service delivery, JEEViKA's training and involvement of large numbers of community members in various cadres could serve as a model for delivering the often high-intensity and high-touch programming of economic inclusion interventions. In addition to enabling program delivery, JEEViKA's model of training large numbers of community workers is intended to empower the community in a real sense as agents of change. It also ensures the transfer of programmatic practice and knowledge to the community.

Implementation of SJY may offer significant lessons on moving to scale-up. If SJY is able to successfully scale up to its target of 100,000 households in three years, it will be in part because of significant previous market-making investments by JEEViKA. These include developing community cadres and infrastructure and investing in value chain development and a rich tapestry of other support services and programs to which JEEViKA attempts to link participants. A scaled-up SJY could shed light on key elements of graduation and economic inclusion programming that have the power to drive, or conversely inhibit, further scale-up. The costs of the program are high, and the sustainability of the approach over a longer term will depend on its ability to evolve strategically into a convergence approach—one in which the resources and benefits of other public programs can be leveraged in support of the poorest people. Because of the phased approach of the program, there is an opportunity for and interest in exploring a convergence approach for a subset of households.

The outcomes of SJY will also offer lessons on adequate dosages of graduation and economic inclusion inputs among poor households, on meeting the capacity needed to deliver comprehensive economic inclusion approaches, and on ways to internalize new programmatic processes into existing operations. In summary, the outcomes will reveal the feasibility of achieving the elusive goal of reaching the last mile of poverty and help determine whether more states and programs may follow a similar path.

Notes

1. Scheduled Castes (SCs) and Scheduled Tribes (STs) are groups recognized in the Indian constitution as having been historically marginalized. The schedules, or lists, provide the basis for affirmative action, enabling the government to establish quotas to give representation for historically and currently disadvantaged groups in Indian society in education, employment, and politics.
2. Figures are as of 2019 based on conversations with JEEViKA staff.
3. Rs 67,000 is the average cost per beneficiary. However, the actual assistance per beneficiary can range from Rs 27,000 to Rs 97,000, depending on when the household graduates, according to program indicators.
4. Co-Impact, engaged in global collaboration for systems change, brings together philanthropists, foundations, and other funders to support efforts to change systems in low- and middle-income countries in education, health, and economic opportunity, with an emphasis on gender and inclusion.
5. The IKEA Foundation, the philanthropic arm of IKEA (the Swedish home furnishings company), works with strong strategic partners in applying innovative approaches to achieve large-scale results. The IKEA Foundation is committed to helping families living in poverty afford a better everyday life while protecting the planet.

References

Banerjee, Abhijit, Esther Duflo, Nathanael Goldberg, Dean Karlan, Robert Osei, William Parienté, Jeremy Shapiro, Bram Thuysbaert, and Christopher Udry. 2015. "A Multifaceted Program Causes Lasting Progress for the Very Poor: Evidence from Six Countries." *Science* 348 (6236): 1260799.

Behera, Debaraj, Arvind Kumar Chaudhary, Vinay Kumar Vutukuru, Abhishek Gupta, Sitaramachandra Machiraju, and Parmesh Shah. 2013. *Enhancing*

Agricultural Livelihoods through Community Institutions in Bihar, India. South Asia Rural Livelihoods Series 3, Note no. 1. Washington, DC: World Bank. http://documents.worldbank.org/curated/en/467261468258525242 /Enhancing-agricultural-livelihoods-through-community-institutions-in-Bihar-India.

World Bank. 2007. *India—Bihar Rural Livelihood Project—"JEEViKA."* Washington, DC: World Bank. http://documents.worldbank.org/curated/en/675101468269084791 /India-Bihar-Rural-Livelihood-Project-JEEViKA.

World Bank. 2011a. *India—National Rural Livelihoods Project.* Washington, DC: World Bank. http://documents.worldbank.org/curated/en/600761468051290938 /India-National-Rural-Livelihoods-Project.

World Bank. 2011b. *The National Rural Livelihoods Project.* Washington, DC: World Bank. https://www.worldbank.org/en/news/feature/2011/07/05/the -national-rural-livelihoods-project.

World Bank. 2016a. *Bihar Poverty, Growth & Inequality.* Washington, DC: World Bank, May. http://documents.worldbank.org/curated/en/781181467989480762 /pdf/105842-BRI-P157572-PUBLIC-Bihar-Proverty.pdf.

World Bank. 2016b. *Bihar–Social inclusion.* Washington, DC: World Bank, May. http:// documents.worldbank.org/curated/en/376521468185928955/Bihar-Social-inclusion.

World Bank. 2016c. *India–Bihar Transformative Development Project.* Washington, DC: World Bank. http://documents.worldbank.org/curated/en/595731467305650771 /India-Bihar-Transformative-Development-Project.

World Bank. 2017. *India—Bihar Rural Livelihoods Project.* Washington, DC: World Bank. http://documents.worldbank.org/curated/en/606701493659325326/India -Bihar-Rural-Livelihoods-Project.

World Bank. 2018a. *A Decade of Rural Transformation: Lessons Learnt from the Bihar Rural Livelihoods Project—JEEViKA.* Washington, DC: World Bank. http://documents.worldbank.org/curated/en/298391515516507115/A-decade -of-rural-transformation-lessons-learnt-from-the-Bihar-Rural-Livelihoods-Project -JEEViKA.

World Bank. 2018b. "India States Briefs." Washington, DC, February 1. https://www .worldbank.org/en/news/feature/2016/05/26/india-states-briefs.

World Bank. 2018c. *India—Systematic Country Diagnostic: Realizing the Promise of Prosperity.* Washington, DC: World Bank. http://documents .worldbank.org/curated/en/629571528745663168/India-Systematic-country -diagnostic-realizing-the-promise-of-prosperity.

Adapting BRAC's Graduation Program to the Changing Poverty Context in Bangladesh

Introduction

BRAC, an international nongovernmental organization (NGO) headquartered in Bangladesh, was already engaged in large-scale development programming when it began to develop its flagship graduation program. Prompted to rethink its approach in the early 2000s when evaluations revealed that its existing programs to promote food security and livelihoods were not serving the needs of the poorest, BRAC developed a new program that was scaled up nationwide within a few years. Building on the experience and infrastructure of its other programs, BRAC saw its program reach over 2 million households by 2020, with some 100,000 female heads of households accepted into the program each year. Randomized controlled trials of BRAC's program revealed sizable economic impacts that have been sustained seven years after participants entered the program (Bandiera et al. 2017).

This case study explores BRAC's experience evolving the graduation approach over the last 20 years, paying special attention to the lessons for governments and NGOs alike that have emerged from the most recent periods of implementation. Specifically, this case study looks at how, since the program started in 2002, BRAC has sought to ensure high program quality and maximize sustainable impacts, at scale, in a changing poverty context. By employing a historical perspective from nearly two decades of program implementation, the study reflects the reality that graduation and economic inclusion programs require staying power enabled by long-term investment and innovation supported by research.

The case study brings into focus aspects of program delivery, emphasizing the principles and processes that have enabled the program's strong impacts and the rigorous learning practices undertaken by BRAC to correct course when the program has shown signs of ineffectiveness. BRAC has attributed the success of the program largely to an ethos of learning and critical self-evaluation that is deeply embedded in the way BRAC has developed and continually improved the program. After nearly 15 years of implementation, however, it became clear that the program's components needed more significant reimagining. BRAC relied heavily on research and evaluation teams to provide the analytical basis for changes to what were previously considered the core elements of its graduation model. This case study looks into how, despite compelling external evidence that BRAC's program was having an impact, the organization transformed the program, introducing new elements not previously associated with graduation programming. It will situate this series of decisions and activities within the broader context of the evolution of the program and the shifting poverty context of Bangladesh since the early 2000s.

This case study was written by Isabel Whisson, with contributions from Rozina Haque, Julie Kedroske, and Munshi Sulaiman (from BRAC), and Imran Matin, Narayan Das, and Syed Hashemi (from BRAC University).

Context

The macroeconomic context in Bangladesh has changed considerably since the early 2000s. The country has experienced steady growth in its gross domestic product (GDP) despite external shocks. Over the last 15 years, the growth rate has remained consistently over 5 percent.[1] There has also been an impressive steady reduction in poverty. In 2000, 49 percent of the population was poor. That rate then declined to 31.5 percent in 2010 and 21.8 percent in 2018. Extreme poverty declined from 34.3 percent in 2000 to 17.6 percent in 2010 and further to 10.5 percent in 2019.[2] Likewise, over the 20-year period per capita incomes increased and food insecurity decreased, and access to financial services expanded significantly, especially in rural areas.

Achievements in the social sectors over the last two decades have also been impressive. Household size has decreased, infant and neonatal mortality rates have fallen, and primary school attendance has become almost universal. These changes have been driven by robust growth in the agriculture sector, increased international remittances, and a thriving export-oriented ready-made garment manufacturing industry (Hill and Genoni 2019). Meanwhile, since the 2000s government programming has increased significantly in quality and efficacy against a backdrop in which NGOs have played a critical role in filling the void in social services since independence in 1972.

See box CS3.1 for details on the policy drivers and poverty context that influenced the early designs of the BRAC graduation approach.

Over the decades, BRAC evolved from a small relief operation into one of the world's largest development organizations, with programs in 11 countries in Asia and

---

BOX CS3.1 Political and Policy Drivers of BRAC's Graduation Programming

Bangladesh came into being in the early 1970s as one of the poorest countries in the world. Emerging from its war of independence with a strong redistributive ethos supported by a highly active and reality-grounded public discourse on poverty and vulnerability, the government galvanized a succession of social and policy initiatives to address poverty. Nongovernmental organization innovations complemented the delivery of social protection services.

A key finding of extensive academic research on poverty dynamics during the 1980s, backed up by BRAC's experience in rural areas, was the heterogeneity of the population in poverty. Researchers and practitioners identified a subgroup of the poor, referred to variously as the hard-core poor, the ultrapoor, or the extreme poor, who earned less and had fewer assets, faced far more limited livelihood opportunities, experienced higher food insecurity and greater vulnerability to periodic economic shocks, and endured more intense social marginalization. Detailed estimates indicated that 27 percent of the rural population was in this category, and they were not being reached by most government and NGO development programs, including microfinance. It was against this backdrop that BRAC implemented in 1987, with the government of Bangladesh and the World Food Programme, its Income Generation for Vulnerable Group Development (IGVGD) program. Subsequently, BRAC's graduation program built on learning from IGVGD. The core idea was to target the poorest—that is, those who are routinely excluded from development programs—and provide an intervention that combined social safety net (SSN) support to ensure basic food security with a livelihood strategy for earning incomes that would eventually negate the need for continued consumption support.

Note: BRAC is an international nongovernmental organization with headquarters in Bangladesh.

Sub-Saharan Africa. In the field of economic inclusion, BRAC is widely associated with the graduation approach—a programming methodology that promotes strong livelihood, social empowerment, and financial inclusion outcomes for the poorest populations. The flagship graduation program, which BRAC launched in 2002 in Bangladesh as a pilot with 5,000 households, now enrolls up to 100,000 households a year. This rapid scale-up was enabled by a large network of branch offices established by BRAC's microfinance program, which already operated nationwide. As of 2020, the program in Bangladesh had reached more than 2 million households—nearly 9 million people. Rigorous evaluations conducted by BRAC's independent research arm and the London School of Economics have revealed significant impacts across a range of development indicators, including income, asset value, consumption, and savings (Bandiera et al. 2017).

Yet after more than a decade of implementation, the drivers of poverty and political economy had begun to shift in Bangladesh, prompting a redesign of BRAC's program. Consistent economic growth and the government's investment in public services have contributed to significantly changing the context of extreme poverty in Bangladesh. According to BRAC, the annual household income of the poorest participants entering the program rose from $80 in 2002 to $188 in 2016. Food insecurity was all but resolved in Bangladesh, as reflected in the higher spending on nonfood expenditures, even by the poorest. The daily per capita food expenditure of households entering the program increased from $0.30 in 2002 to $0.48 in 2016. Indicators of education and hygiene also improved. By 2016, 13 percent of household heads were literate, compared with just 4 percent in 2002, and 43 percent had a sanitary latrine, compared with 7 percent in 2002. It was also increasingly common for the poorest households to have access to some services provided by government, NGOs, or microfinance institutions. In addition to the changed nature of poverty, the geographic spread of poverty in Bangladesh shifted as well. Whereas the program had originally been implemented in 42 districts of Bangladesh (roughly two-thirds of the country), by 2016 the remaining pockets of extreme poverty were concentrated in fewer areas.

Beyond macroeconomic changes in Bangladesh that rendered aspects of the current program less relevant, analysis of data from the randomized controlled trial revealed the significant heterogeneity of impacts. Although the data showed significant positive impacts on average, they obscured the fact that many participants thrived considerably, while many were only nominally better off and did not demonstrate a strong trajectory in livelihood growth (Bandiera et al. 2012). This pattern was clear-cut among older women who often had limited ability to engage in income-generating activities.

BRAC graduation approach, an iterative response

Although BRAC is known for the graduation approach, the effectiveness of the program has been sustained over a long period of time through continual adaptation. Developed in the early 2000s, the program was born out of learning from BRAC's previous long period of program implementation. It was established to address the finding by evaluators at BRAC that its existing programs did not do enough to build the long-term capacity of the poorest households it was reaching across Bangladesh to enter into sustainable livelihoods. A continued assessment of the program's responsiveness to a changing poverty context, enabled by learning processes that were embedded into all aspects of program development, iteration, rollout, scale-up, and implementation, were key to ensuring the program's continued relevance.

From 2002 to 2016, BRAC implemented several iterations of the graduation program. It rigorously targeted the poorest households in communities across the 42 districts of Bangladesh known to have the deepest pockets of extreme poverty. Female heads of households were entered into a program that included (1) a weekly stipend to cover essential needs for the first few months; (2) enterprise training; (3) productive asset transfers (valued at approximately $100); (4) weekly household coaching and monitoring visits; (5) access to savings; (6) biweekly visits from a community health worker; (7) life skills development training; and (8) monthly meetings of the village poverty reduction committee. This program lasted 24 months at a cost of $450–$550 per household. Meanwhile, BRAC realized that another population was slightly better-off than the poorest but was nonetheless too vulnerable for microfinance alone. For this second group, BRAC adjusted the graduation program to include the same components just described, with the stipulation that assets would be transferred as part of a soft loan that participants would have to repay over the course of the program period.

In a more recent round of changes starting in 2017, BRAC again confronted the need to significantly reform its long-standing graduation program. This process was guided by two questions: Which program elements are essential for the extreme poor in the current context? What elements or components of the program could BRAC optimize to be more efficient?

Four design and implementation considerations loomed large in these discussions:

1. *Heterogeneity of impacts.* Women over a certain age invested less time and money in their enterprises and saw smaller economic gains.

2. *Sustainability of impact.* Livelihood packages needed to remain large enough for the poorest households to earn a decent income in an evolving market.

3. *Shifts in financial capacity.* Any continued financial support must account for changing consumption patterns and levels of food security.

4. *Operational and cost efficiencies.* The program design and operations should explore opportunities to simplify or reduce inputs wherever it would not compromise impacts.

Although BRAC was open to revising all the components of the program, it remained faithful to two principles: (1) a focus on reaching the poorest, and (2) delivery of a package of interventions that would empower the poorest households both socially and economically to attain sustainable livelihoods. These principles ensured that staff, who included some with decades of field experience, focused on the outcomes needed in modern-day Bangladesh and not simply on the activities they had been accustomed to implementing. Adaptive program design in support of outcomes was also enabled by a flexible funding agreement in place from 2011 to 2020 with the United Kingdom's Department for International Development (DFID) and Australia's Department for Foreign Affairs and Trade (DFAT).

BRAC segmented participant selection based on age group as well as wealth category. The core program would focus on women under the age of 50. Among this group, participants were split into two groups—the poorest and those slightly better-off—with interventions tailored to each. Women over the age of 50 would receive a less resource-intensive package of support and would be connected to other government services.

The cost per household of implementing the program came down from $550 to approximately $350 for most participants. Although BRAC increased the value of the asset transfers, it also identified cost efficiencies in program components, management, and operations that enabled it to reduce the overall operating costs.

The program rolled out the changes in 2017 in a phased approach, initially to roughly half of its annual capacity—45,000 households—giving staff the space to work out kinks in implementation and enabling cross-learning among field staff. Once the program was scaled back up to 100,000 households in 2018, BRAC targeted the 36 districts in which poverty was most concentrated. The program further accounted for contextual differences in environment between regions. Box CS3.2 provides an overview of the newly designed program.

BOX CS3.2   **Overview of the BRAC Ultra Poor Graduation Program (2017 Onward)**

Targeting
Targeting was based on three approaches: (1) poverty mapping; (2) participatory rural appraisal; and (3) household verification via survey.

Program components for women under age 50
Productive asset transfer. Options include livestock such as cows, goats, and chickens, or a combination of agriculture, fisheries, and small trade. Assets are transferred as an interest-free partial loan valued at $200. Participants in both the poorest and better-off wealth categories repay 30–50 percent and 80 percent of the asset value, respectively, over 24 months.

Livelihood training. Ten days of enterprise development training, of which seven days are tailored to the specific enterprise a participant selected.

Financial services. Savings matched at 1:1, up to $1.20 per month, and credit shield life insurance.

Life skills training. Biweekly group-based training on a range of topics related to child welfare, health, safety, and women's issues.

Household coaching. Biweekly individual household visits to monitor progress of participants, including their enterprises, understanding of life skills topics, and financial management, and to offer guidance and support.

Community mobilization and integration. Bimonthly village social solidarity committees (VSSCs) to promote social integration and raise voices of the extreme poor within the community.

Links to health care. Reserve fund is set aside in the event of medical emergencies, which BRAC would cover. For general ailments, local managers are present at the local government clinic for four hours one day a week to ensure that participants and their families can access health care as needed.

Intervention period. 24 months.

Program cost per household. $350.

Program adaptations for women over age 50
Productive asset transfer. Options include livestock, agriculture, and small trade. Assets are transferred on a grant basis and are valued at $60–$95. Participant does not receive credit shield insurance facility.

Links to government social safety nets. BRAC shares a list of participants with local government officials, so participants can enroll in a range of SSNs for which they may be eligible, including allowances for the elderly, widows, and persons with disabilities and other special programs. Because of government quotas, only a small proportion of participants are successfully admitted.

Intervention period. 12 months.

Program cost per household. $200.

Note: BRAC is an international nongovernmental organization with headquarters in Bangladesh.

BRAC's 2017 programmatic shifts

Revision of participant selection and segmentation

BRAC decided to resegment its target populations to address heterogeneities between the working-age population and the elderly to maximize impact and cost-effectiveness. BRAC observed that participants over age 50 were less likely to reinvest in and grow their assets beyond a certain point, nor did those participants usually have physically able members of the household to support their work. By contrast, participants under age 50 were much more likely to diversify and grow their assets. For example, according to data from households that entered the program in 2007, 19 percent of households without working-age members would enroll in microfinance, compared with 28 percent of households with working-age members. By 2014 these numbers had dropped to 13 percent and 23 percent, respectively.

Among the same cohort, four years after entering the program women over age 50 had increased their annual household income by $82, whereas in households with women under age 50 income increased by $200. The program needed to draw better distinctions between who would benefit from which protective and productive mechanisms. BRAC concluded that among those identified as being in the poorest category, there would always be people with limited productive capacity who must receive some support and be linked to social safety nets (SSNs) to ensure a minimum dignified existence that could be sustained.

Although the most cost-effective solution would have been to exclude the elderly from the program and target households that had productive labor, BRAC took a different approach. To ensure that all households continued to receive support, BRAC adapted its packages of support to target groups based on age and on the slightly varying wealth categories among the working-age extreme poor. Women in households with no family members between the ages of 16 and 50 would receive a similar package of support for 12 months instead of 24 months, receive a productive asset of lower value relative to households with more productive capacity, and receive household visits once a month. For older women, the program would facilitate access to government SSNs, depending on women's eligibility and availability.

BRAC revised its definition of the poorest and which households were eligible for graduation. Previously, it had distinguished between the poorest households and those that had slightly more wealth and productive capacity in the household. Households in the latter category had been required to pay for their assets with soft loans, but received all other graduation program inputs. With the evolution of the poverty landscape in Bangladesh, this group had become fairly indistinguishable from BRAC's mainstream microfinance program clients. BRAC therefore decided the group would not be targeted by the graduation program moving forward. Instead, most of the graduation program would focus on the poorer households with women under age 50. BRAC data indicated that these households invest the most in assets, in diversifying their incomes, and in children's welfare, leading to the greatest benefits over longer periods of time. BRAC recognized that levels of vulnerability would still vary among this group, and therefore within this group it distinguished between those who were the poorest and those who were slightly better-off, adjusting program terms for each. See box CS3.3 for BRAC's selection criteria and segmentation of program participants, revised in 2017.

Changes to program components

Removed consumption stipend. The program removed the weekly stipend of $2.80. When first conceived, the stipend was designed to ensure that households could meet

BOX CS3.3   **Selection Criteria, Ultra-Poor Graduation Program, 2017**

Over age 50
- No family member between the ages of 16 and 50.
- Per capita monthly income not to exceed $20.
- No member of the household is a regular beneficiary of a nongovernmental organization or has a loan with a microfinance or financial institution.

Under age 50: Poorest
- Per capita monthly income not to exceed $20.
- No member of the household is a regular beneficiary of an NGO or has a loan with a microfinance or financial institution.
- Female household members must work (as domestic labor, agricultural labor, and so forth).
- At least two of the following:
  - Household has productive asset value of $6 or less.
  - Household owns 10 decimals[a] of land or less.
  - One or more household members face chronic disease or mental and physical disability.

Under age 50: Better-off
- Per capita monthly income not to exceed $20.
- No member of the household is a regular beneficiary of an NGO or has a loan with a microfinance or financial institution.
- At least two of the following:
  - Household is dependent on irregular income.
  - Household has productive asset value of $12 or less.
  - Household owns 30 decimals[a] of land or less.
  - One or more household members face chronic disease or mental and physical disability.

a. A decimal is one-hundredth of an acre.

their necessary caloric intake and guard against selling off assets to pay for food. By 2016, even the poorest households were able to meet their basic food needs, and the value of the consumption stipend was deemed to bring a negligible financial benefit.

Increased value and choice of productive assets. Conversely, BRAC recognized that the approximate $100 value assigned to the productive assets provided before 2016 was no longer on pace with most markets and had limited income growth potential. The program doubled the value of the productive asset for women under 50, giving households an even bigger push to becoming self-sufficient. This decision was informed by the study by Bandiera et al. (2017), which suggests that BRAC's graduation program in earlier years had broken the poverty trap for the poorest by providing a sufficiently large injection of resources to enable the extreme poor to access productive opportunities otherwise inaccessible to them. Market assessments indicated that a significant increase in asset value would enable households to compete in local markets, bringing sufficient financial returns to participants to make up for the added cost. The program also expanded the number of livelihood options available to participants, taking advantage of new opportunities within local markets and ways to avoid increasing competition between households.

Changed payment for productive assets to partial loans with flexible terms and protections. The profile of participants under age 50 entering the program had changed; they were not as vulnerable or resource-constrained as participants in earlier years. They were more likely than earlier participants to own some land, earn some income, or have been exposed to microfinance (widely available across rural Bangladesh by then). They also demonstrated higher aspirations—wanting to feel a sense of ownership as opposed to dependence on aid. These considerations informed the decision to require all participants under age 50 to repay some of the asset value. Specifically, the poorest would have to repay 30–50 percent of the asset value, and better-off participants would repay 100 percent of the asset value, interest-free, by the end of the 24-month program. Repayment was later reduced to 80 percent for the latter group. The collection of installments would be administered by BRAC's microfinance program. Participants would have a grace period of one month. In addition, all participants would receive two vouchers that entitled them to a 15-day installment deferment. The vouchers gave participants flexibility in the event they faced a period of higher expenses or diminished cash flow. The graduation program leveraged other new products and services being widely offered by BRAC's microfinance program, such as credit shield life insurance for all participants, whereby the repayment balance is forgiven in the event an earner in the household passes away. In such cases, BRAC returns the principal the household had already paid back, plus an additional financial benefit of $118 to support funeral costs.

Increased financial management support. The decision to introduce partial asset value repayment to all participants underscored and increased the importance of coaching support for participants. During household visits, program officers would provide one-on-one guidance on tracking income and expenditures, calculating how much to set aside for savings and installments and planning for income growth or diversification. In addition, BRAC microfinance staff, who administered the biweekly meetings on installment and savings collections, provided routine guidance on the terms and expectations of repayment and savings collection.

Introduced a match savings mechanism. A critical outcome of the program was to build financial resilience by encouraging regular savings behavior and ensuring a sizable savings balance in the event of financial shocks. As program staff conducted learning visits of similar programs implemented in Bangladesh, BRAC learned of a "savings match" component in the government program Ektee Bari, Ektee Khamar (One Farm, One House). As a result, BRAC introduced a match savings mechanism to further give participants an incentive to save regularly. For every 1 Bangladesh taka ($0.01) saved, BRAC would match it two to one, up to a maximum of Tk 100 ($1.20). BRAC later revised the match to one to one to promote greater financial independence.

Alternated individual household visits with group visits. BRAC moved from weekly individual home visits to alternating between biweekly home visits and biweekly group visits. This change enabled BRAC to bring the staff-to-participant ratio down, while maintaining touch points with staff at four times per month.

Revised life skills training curriculum. BRAC added a focus on noncommunicable diseases to the curriculum because such diseases had become a leading cause of higher morbidity and mortality in Bangladesh.

Adjusted terms of village social solidarity committees. Village committee schedules were changed to every two months instead of once a month, with the option to call an emergency meeting sooner if needed. This change helped to reduce the workload of branch managers, who previously were administering 12–13 committees at a time.

Furthermore, sometimes issues raised in the committee meetings could not be resolved within a month.

Linked participants to health and water, sanitation, and hygiene (WASH) services. Instead of continuing to provide participants directly with sanitary latrines, the program linked participants to BRAC's water and sanitation program, thereby reducing costs. The widespread availability of government health services across Bangladesh also meant the program could link participants in need to the health care providers operating locally instead of to BRAC's health program. Program staff would also leverage the village social solidarity committees (VSSCs) to help mobilize financial support if needed. Both changes promoted sustainability of access to health care and support by enabling participants to rely on these mechanisms after the program ended and without BRAC's support.

Factored in localized area contextualization. BRAC factored regional contextual differences among its target locations into slight program adjustments. For example, a third of program sites are located in regions affected by climate change. In those regions, adaptations include alternative livelihood options, awareness-raising on disaster preparedness, and support to make homes and shelters more resilient.

Scale and adaptation through leveraging investments in infrastructure, staff, and learning

BRAC has reached more than 100 million people in Bangladesh through a systematic effort to scale up and leverage its investments in infrastructure, staff, insights, and learning from earlier and existing programs. BRAC is recognized for both its horizontal and functional scale and for implementing expansive programs in microfinance, education, health, human rights and legal empowerment, and disaster preparedness, which address the multidimensional aspects of poverty. Over the years, the organization has expanded to over 2,000 branch offices covering all 64 districts of the country.

BRAC's initial scale nationwide is attributed to community mobilization efforts related to the health care work it undertook in the 1980s as it trained households on how to mix oral rehydration solution. These community mobilization efforts were leveraged to offer microfinance for poor women in rural communities, thereby creating a demand for a network of branches and staff infrastructure that would later be used to offer additional development services, including livelihoods training, human rights awareness-raising and local advocacy, WASH, and other health programs. Outside of Bangladesh, BRAC has largely continued a similar trajectory of using microfinance to develop a presence, layering other development programs alongside it. For example, in Uganda, where BRAC has its largest presence outside of Bangladesh, it serves 208,000 microfinance clients and offers additional development programs in 100 of its 160 branches.

In the graduation and other programs, continuous feedback loops ensured that field insights informed management decisions. The richest insights on program effectiveness from field staff are systematically fed up to management. Regional managers, who spend three weeks a month in the field and one week a month in the head office in Dhaka, collect observations from program officers from across branch locations and identify patterns to be considered or addressed by management in charge of operations. This mechanism for learning was critical to understanding how participants were responding to the program changes. For example, in 2017 anecdotes from program officers, who work directly with households, suggested that a third of eligible households whom the program had classified as being in the "better-off" category of households and therefore were expected to repay the full value of the asset were self-excluding from the program. The program's monitoring and evaluation department verified that the self-exclusion rate of eligible households was roughly 30 percent.

Researchers identified the main reason for this finding: this group felt that the expectation that they would repay the full amount while others paid less than half was unfair, and so they did not want to participate. Thus before scaling back up to 100,000 households in 2018, management brought the repayment expectation down to 80 percent of the asset value, which, among other factors, led to a reduction in self-exclusion rates. To test the design before a full-scale implementation, BRAC cut its normal graduation program intake by over half, enabling staff to learn by doing, with half directly implementing and sharing knowledge and implementation suggestions with others before BRAC expanded.

The scaled-up nature of BRAC's program implies that large-scale organizational shifts are often required to successfully operationalize programmatic shifts. For example, in spite of a strong staff implementation capacity, recent graduation program changes required a shift in the mindset and skills of field staff, many of whom had been implementing the program for more than a decade. To ensure a continued organizational capacity for the program at scale, all field implementation staff received an in-depth orientation around the changes and the rationale behind them, helping to build buy-in. In particular, the program's new emphasis on building participants' capacity to pay installments meant all staff had to be skilled in supporting careful financial planning, monitoring spending, and assessing business plans. To increase efficiency and reduce costs, BRAC streamlined its field management structures, increasing the number of regions and districts under each regional manager. Recognizing the organizational lift required to achieve these programmatic changes at scale, BRAC led an inclusive change management process. From the beginning, the redesign process was enriched by cross-program learning from field officers, management, and research staff involved in consultations, market assessments, design workshops, and program design prototyping. The phased rollout was launched in 2017. All staff were subsequently engaged in assessing the effectiveness of the new design.

BRAC's efforts in graduation have also pivoted toward a new dimension of scale—supporting governments in implementing their own programs through policy advocacy and technical assistance. BRAC recognized that the global magnitude of extreme poverty demanded government-scale programs and that NGOs could do much to support the launch of such programs. Since 2014, BRAC has explored a new modality for scaling the graduation approach by supporting the adoption, implementation, and scale-up of graduation programs by governments through advocacy and in-depth technical assistance. To date, it has worked with the governments of Afghanistan, Guinea, Kenya, Lesotho, Pakistan, the Philippines, Rwanda, and Tamil Nadu (India).

Lessons

The revised program is undergoing a quasi-experimental evaluation to assess the impacts of the redesigned program, and end-line surveys were being conducted at the time of this writing. However, because the characteristics of target groups vary between pre- and post-2017 cohorts, the impacts of the two program designs will not be directly comparable. This section outlines the pertinent lessons for graduation and economic inclusion programs at the programmatic level on how to enable effective adaptation and scale.

Effective adaptation

BRAC's iterative approach to the evolution of its program has been supported by long-term investment with flexible terms. BRAC's program benefited from the stability of a long-standing funding instrument with DFID and DFAT. This arrangement gave BRAC the flexibility to adapt and adjust the program because it was held accountable for outcomes and not for specific program design expectations.

Graduation should be viewed as an adaptive methodology aimed at facilitating key outcomes for the poorest, not as a rigid program model. The understanding that graduation is a set of principles rather than a set of fixed components gave BRAC the creative freedom to make the adjustments demanded by the context, regardless of what had been proved to work previously. Its focus on the needs of the poorest and intended outcomes enabled BRAC to ensure fidelity to the original program's ability to generate sustainable outcomes for the poorest while providing plenty of room for adaptation to the new context. BRAC has continued to apply this approach to other vulnerabilities and pockets of extreme poverty in Bangladesh, such as adaptations for persons with disabilities, refugee host communities, and urban communities, as well as for other NGOs and governments outside of Bangladesh.

Because the contexts of poverty invariably change, graduation programming can add value to a tapestry of antipoverty interventions by maintaining a focus on helping the poorest achieve a basic standard of living through a multidisciplinary approach—one that activates households' latent economic potential. As contexts develop, it can become even harder for the poorest population to keep pace. Graduation programs have a role to play in ensuring the poor's access to opportunities to address their most salient issues. For example, although a variety of SSNs and health services had become available to the poorest, many needed help to access them.

BRAC has sought to be intentional in seeking out the poorest, and it recognizes the changing contexts of poverty mean that the indicators used to identify the extreme poor must be continually reevaluated, in addition to the interventions most appropriate to building social and economic empowerment and financial inclusion outcomes for this population. The poorest are often the most marginalized, and typically they require proactive targeting and identification so they are not left behind. Programs must also be intentional about addressing heterogeneity among the poorest in order to maximize cost-effectiveness and program outcomes. For BRAC, this meant understanding distinctions between women considered to be of "working age" versus women who were older with a limited capacity to engage in income-generating activities. Understanding these distinctions can help inform how certain interventions may be more or less impactful and cost-effective. For example, although older women still needed some level of livelihood support from BRAC, they were less likely to invest in livelihoods, would gradually become less productive, and thus would benefit more from receiving additional support via government SSNs. BRAC therefore intentionally shifted toward allotting a greater portion of programming resources to building the livelihoods of women under age 50.

Continuous learning and evaluation have proved integral to achieving impact at scale. Such a process goes beyond inviting external researchers to conduct evaluations at the end of an implementation period. The use of a range of research, monitoring and evaluation in development, scale-up, adaptation, and implementation measures ensures that insights, questions, or issues about the program's effectiveness can be addressed quickly and efficiently. BRAC credits its ability to achieve a highly impactful program at scale to the deeply embedded role that research and learning had in the development and continued adaptation of the program. Large-scale programs in return create robust opportunities for learning by offering large data sets from which BRAC can more easily identify patterns and understand heterogeneous effects more clearly.

BRAC's field implementation staff have been critical stakeholders in change management. BRAC's evolution of the graduation program has relied heavily on enabling and empowering staff operating at the grassroots to inform decision-making at the highest levels. Feedback loops from the front lines are vital to ensuring that learning and observation are incorporated into senior-level decision-making on program design, adaptation, and operations.

The coaching component of graduation can be a critical element in moving the program in new directions. Coaching is a vital mechanism for monitoring how participants are responding to particular program elements. For example, when BRAC introduced all of its participants to partial loan repayments, the value of individual coaching was reinforced as a mechanism for mitigating risk and easing participants into the new demands on their abilities.

Some participants can contribute to the costs of the program. Where this option is explored, programs must conduct rigorous market assessments to indicate whether livelihoods will generate sufficient returns for participants to pay regular installments and earn a profit. Meanwhile, managers must consider participants' financial capacity to repay loans, and, if repayments are expected of participants, the program must dedicate resources to building financial literacy and skills, building in protections, and carefully monitoring and supporting participants.

Scale

Programs should seek cost efficiencies by leveraging existing structures and services. In fact, all graduation and economic inclusion programs should review the constellation of available services and structures for possible leverage and should design interventions to fill these gaps. Such an effort would promote functional scale by layering on what is available, as well as horizontal scale by identifying cost efficiencies. These efficiencies do not need to be internal to the implementing organization. Although BRAC was able to leverage its own microfinance branch network to scale up the graduation program across Bangladesh, it also took advantage of the ability to link participants to available government SSNs and health care services. Geographic coverage should be driven by where there is the greatest need. Although BRAC maintained the same intake of households, it reduced the geographic scale of the program to focus on areas with the greatest concentrations of extreme poverty. This principle should be maintained, especially where resources limit the ability to scale up nationwide.

For BRAC, an intentional shift toward supporting governments to scale up their own graduation programs implies new learning and innovation and exploring new arrangements for implementation and contexts suitable for graduation. Through its work with governments in different contexts, BRAC has explored a variety of implementing arrangements, from direct government implementation to government–NGO partnerships, seeking to understand which operational approaches apply best in which settings or circumstances. Specifically, BRAC has been exploring how the graduation approach can be adapted to refugee settlements and host communities, urban resettled populations, fragile contexts, violence- and conflict-affected communities, and people with disabilities. BRAC is also seeking to address questions of cost-effectiveness by exploring opportunities to layer onto existing government schemes, such as cash transfers, public works programs, and other livelihood schemes.

BRAC's work implicitly leverages funds that governments and multilateral donors already dedicate to social protection programming. Instead of seeking additional funds to set up new programs, BRAC has found that graduation provides a framework through which existing government programs and measures can be converged, and therefore resources can be leveraged. This convergence also reveals opportunities for interministerial collaboration and cost-sharing among, for example, ministries of agriculture, trade, and industry and small business or labor, where existing programs can be adapted and leveraged to serve the most vulnerable as part of a holistic approach to alleviating extreme poverty on a national level.

Notes

1. Data in this section are from the World Bank's World Development Indicators (database), https://data.worldbank.org/country/bangladesh.
2. Bangladesh Bureau of Statistics, http://bbs.portal.gov.bd/sites/default/files/files/bbs.portal .gov.bd/page/5695ab85_1403_483a_afb4_26dfd767df18/2019-12-17-16-30-614e10bcb101bc1df5 938723cc141c5d.pdf.

References

Bandiera, Oriana, Robin Burgess, Das Narayan, Selim Gulesci, Imran Rasul, Raniya Shams, and Munshi Sulaiman. 2012. "Asset Transfer Programme for the Ultra Poor: A Randomized Control Trial Evaluation." CFPR Working Paper No. 22, BRAC Research and Evaluation Division, Dhaka.

Bandiera, Oriana, Robin Burgess, Das Narayan, Selim Gulesci, Imran Rasul, and Munshi Sulaiman. 2017. *Labor Markets and Poverty in Village Economies*. Oxford, U.K.: Oxford University Press.

Hill, Ruth, and Maria Eugenia Genoni. 2019. *Bangladesh Poverty Assessment: Facing Old and New Frontiers in Poverty Reduction*. Washington, DC: World Bank. http:// documents.worldbank.org/curated/en/793121572582830383/Bangladesh-Poverty -Assessment-Facing-Old-and-New-Frontiers-in-Poverty-Reduction.

Haku Wiñay: An Economic Inclusion Program in Peru

Introduction

Against a backdrop of intense social, political, and economic transformation in its rural areas over the last decades, Peru introduced Haku Wiñay, an economic inclusion program aimed at creating economic gains among the most disadvantaged rural households. The intervention, implemented by the Ministry of Development and Social Inclusion (MIDIS), draws on both new and traditional methodologies, relying on participatory decision-making by organized households, community-level trainers, and community structures.

At its core, Haku Wiñay is characterized by (1) flexibility to adapt the intervention to the productive, social, and cultural dynamics of each rural territory; (2) empowerment of the participating households that play a key role in implementing the local design of the intervention; and (3) recapture of the lessons learned from previous interventions in order to scale them up.

To implement Haku Wiñay, MIDIS relies on the Social Development Cooperation Fund (Foncodes). An agency of the Peruvian government created in 1991, Foncodes was part of a generation of demand-driven rural development programs promoted by several cooperation agencies at the time. Since then, Foncodes has become an important and innovative rural development actor (Asensio 2019) that has been attached to various ministries and, since 2011, has been part of MIDIS. Foncodes is in charge of implementing Haku Wiñay, applying its personnel, methodologies, and experience to the benefit of the program.

Haku Wiñay is primarily a livelihoods intervention that overlaps significantly with Peru's predominant cash transfer program, Juntos. Introduced in 2006, Juntos provides mothers in poor households with a bimonthly payment in exchange for fulfilling a series of conditions relative to their underage children's education, nutrition, and health. Although Juntos is thought to be an important approach to social protection, questions remained about how to sustain economic inclusion of households when their children aged out of eligibility for the program.

Haku Wiñay employs this theory of change: improving the economic inclusion of the rural poor is possible by strengthening a virtuous circle among productive improvements, home improvements, income generation, and market access through capacity development, asset enhancement, and promotion of economic opportunities. The intervention has aimed to simultaneously increase households' income and improve their food security, resulting in expanded economic inclusion of the rural population and greater resilience once the cycle of conditional transfers of the Juntos program ends for a family when its children age out of eligibility. Initially, Haku Wiñay and Juntos were envisioned as complementary—that is, the programs would generate a path for families receiving the conditional transfer to continue to receive support once their children had become ineligible for Juntos. In practice, efforts to limit Haku Wiñay to Juntos participants proved to be infeasible, and now Haku Wiñay operates even in areas where Juntos does not.

This study was authored by Raúl Asensio, Instituto de Estudios Peruanos.

This case study provides insights into how economic inclusion programs can leverage proven and accepted community structures and integrate them in a national program strategy with a view toward replication and scale-up. Participatory decision-making and the engagement of community project management systems and community trainers (*yachachiqs*) have helped Haku Wiñay scale up its work. Replication in certain contexts has required significant adaptations, as well as giving implementers the freedom to apply locally relevant microstrategies that take into account the various contexts of rural poverty found in Peru.

Context

Inequality has characterized Peru's growth story. Poverty in Peru dropped from 58.7 percent in 2004 to 20.5 percent in 2018. This decrease was among the most prominent in Latin America, but it also coincided with an increasing disparity between rural territories—that is, between those that had successfully connected to economic growth dynamics and those that had remained (and remain) at the margins. Widening gaps have also been evident between those households that have successfully engaged in growth dynamics by diversifying their incomes and those that have been challenged to do so.

Recent growth in Peru has also coincided with intense social, political, and economic transformations. The country is urbanizing rapidly, moving away from being a primarily rural economy. As a result, effective territorial management and integration between the capital, Lima, and the large and intermediate cities have become challenging. Lima remains highly populated compared with the rest of the country and contains the largest concentration of the country's wealth and human capital. Even so, the country has seen significant improvements in recent decades. Expanded public services, new road construction, stronger local governments, diversification of economic activities, and the rise to power of mayors with rural farming and peasant backgrounds have all helped to address the challenges. However, these developments have coincided with a surge in conflicts linked to the management of natural resources and the use of public funds, as well as with poverty rates that remain significantly higher in rural areas than in urban areas.

Although challenges remain, in the last few years significant changes have affected the economic and social dynamics in rural areas. Positive trends are evident in educational achievement and the empowerment of women, both through schooling and through improved access to control over agricultural holdings, and advances in infrastructure and rural connectivity are being made as well. Overall, a dependence on farming activities is declining because these activities are being replaced by paid work and employment in the services sector.

The Ministry of Development and Social Inclusion emerged during the first months of President Ollanta Humala's administration as part of an effort to reorganize the country's social protection and inclusion policies, grouping them under the leadership of a single ministry. MIDIS is founded on the *human development* approach, and so it is committed to activating and multiplying the potential of low-income families. It has aspired to become the axis of social policy for the Peruvian state through a comprehensive life cycle approach that addresses the different stages of life of the most disadvantaged populations and a multidimensional approach to well-being. MIDIS's short-term strategies included providing direct assistance programs to enable households to access basic resources.

In both the medium and long term, MIDIS has sought to provide conditions for families so that they themselves can undertake the social and economic strengthening that would allow a break in intergenerational poverty. In doing so, MIDIS has assumed two responsibilities, which in other countries may correspond to two ministries: (1) it coordinates and ensures the implementation of social policy among sectors and levels of government; and (2) it implements the most important social safety net interventions, including the conditional cash transfer program (Juntos) and the school feeding program (Qali Warma).

Haku Wiñay coverage, targeting, implementation, and cost

Haku Wiñay owes its creation to the confluence of three factors. First, a window of political opportunity opened during the first years of the Humala administration, making it possible to design a new style of social program with an emphasis on productive inclusion. Second, a community of academics, experts, and practitioners emerged who focused on development policy, extracted lessons, and proposed new economic inclusion initiatives. And, third, there had been a long-standing tradition of economic development and inclusion interventions in Andean rural areas—one that had generated knowledge that accumulated in public institutions, among nongovernmental organizations (NGOs), and among rural households that interacted with social programs and development interventions.

Social inclusion interventions in Peru developed considerably during the 1990s, when a series of demand-driven programs, supported by international aid and technical assistance, were introduced. Programs such as Foncodes and the National Program for the Management of Water Basins and Land Conservation (Pronamachs) were early efforts that bore lessons for Haku Wiñay, as were the experiences of several Peruvian NGOs and international cooperation programs, including the Puno-Cusco Corridor Program developed by the International Fund for Agricultural Development (IFAD). These programs helped to overcome the economic challenges faced by rural Peruvians during the 1990s and contributed to a decline in rural poverty in the first decade of the 21st century.

By 2010, however, a growing consensus among academics and policy makers was that these interventions were insufficient to tackle persistent rural poverty. A new strategy was needed—one that would draw on prior lessons and leverage the strength of the growing Peruvian economy. Haku Wiñay was envisioned as an approach that would leverage the experience and lessons of the past to create an innovative program tailored to the new economic context of Peru's rural areas.

Haku Wiñay was launched in 2014, building on the lessons of a pilot program, Mi Chacra Productiva, launched two years earlier. Haku Wiñay's objective was to provide rural households with the tools they needed to take advantage of new opportunities arising from the dynamics of economic growth through the improvement and diversification of agricultural production and rural market access. Haku Wiñay was conceived as a time-bound intervention consisting of four components over a three-year period. Each household remains in the program for a maximum of three years, divided into three stages:

- Stage 1, *implementation*, covering components 1 and 2 of the program

- Stage 2, *appropriation*, covering component 3

- Stage 3, *consolidation*, covering component 4

These components and the accompanying productive assets and technologies are outlined in more detail in box CS4.1.

BOX CS4.1 **Haku Wiñay's Components and Accompanying Productive Assets and Technologies**

Component 1: Strengthening and consolidating rural family production systems
Each home receives two to four visits each month from a local operator, known as the productive *yachachiq*, who provides individualized technical assistance, training, and productive assets. The primary goal is to help households implement productive assets and technologies and to train households in their use. The productive assets and technologies offered vary according to the local area and market dynamics. They can include small irrigation systems at the household level, open field vegetable gardens and rustic greenhouses, cultivation of associated pastures, smaller animal breeding management (guinea pigs, hens, sheep), improvement of Andean crops (grains and tubers), management of cocoa and coffee cultivation in mountain areas, and other productive investments with local impacts (such as barns for alpacas, beekeeping, mini-parcels for producing rice, and *cochas* for aquaculture and fish processing).

Component 2: Improvements for healthy homes
Technical assistance from the productive yachachiqs also focuses on home improvements such as installing better stoves and appropriate safe water and solid waste disposal systems. The productive assets and technologies offered include improved kitchens, safe water, solid waste management, and other improvements in the home's organization and health (such as separation of spaces). This component also includes assistance and guidance on healthy practices, which are coordinated with local health establishments.

Component 3: Promotion of inclusive rural businesses
Groups of households work together to prepare a business profile to be publicly supported by CLAR (Local Committee for the Allocation of Resources) through a business plan competition. The executing nuclei (groups of 80–100 rural households created ad hoc for implementation of the project) provide winning groups with specialized technical assistance (assets and services) according to the type of business. These services are offered by technicians and professionals, including the financial yachachiqs (see component 4).

Component 4: Capacity building, providing training in financial literacy, and promoting savings
All households participating in Haku Wiñay receive training in simple financial operations. This training is carried out by specialists, financial yachachiqs (not the productive yachachiqs). Often the training is carried out jointly with the Juntos program. Component 3 business groups can also receive more complex training in the financing of inclusive businesses.

Current coverage

As of April 2020, over 246,000 households had received support from Haku Wiñay, including the some 115,000 homes where the Haku Wiñay cycle of intervention has concluded. These numbers represent a significant scale-up in coverage in the Peruvian context. According to the current targeting criteria, it is estimated that Haku Wiñay has reached approximately 47 percent of homes that could potentially fulfill the requirements to participate in the intervention.

To scale up, Haku Wiñay has followed an incremental approach to deploying efforts in new territories. Progressively, new departments have been incorporated, and coverage has been extended to other regions throughout the country. From the southern highlands to the northern highlands and the jungle, Haku Wiñay is present today in all of the country's regions, except for the department of Tumbes, where the target population is not significant in number. In 2013 Haku Wiñay expanded to the departments of the Peruvian jungle. In this region, the program is called Noa Jayatai ("We are going to grow" in the Shipibo language). The operating scheme is similar and includes the same four components, although with some adaptations to respond to the social and economic contexts of the jungle regions. Similarly, productive technologies and home improvements are also adapted to the local cultural context.

Targeting

Beneficiaries are able to self-select into the program in predetermined program implementation areas. These areas are selected based on a high incidence of rural poverty and with a view toward minimizing potential discord. The central criterion for selecting areas of intervention has become the predominance within each community of homes with subsistence economies. To define this in operational terms, Haku Wiñay looks at farmland utilization as an indicator. *Subsistence economy* is defined as a household with a property of less than 1.3 hectares (the median size of national plots, according to the agricultural census of 2012). In addition to this central criterion, as of 2020 Haku Wiñay beneficiaries are characterized by the use of 75 percent or more of available household labor for agricultural activities; the use of 75 percent or more of property for agricultural purposes; and simultaneously, limited sales and market value of agricultural production.

Although Haku Wiñay households overlap significantly with Juntos recipients, engagement in Juntos is no longer an explicit inclusion criterion for Haku Wiñay. Other guidelines for the selection of implementation areas include location in districts with over 40 percent of households living in poverty; in priority districts for the reduction of chronic child malnutrition; in areas with at least 40 households; and in areas in which 60 percent or more of households exhibit at least one unmet basic need.

Implementation

Implementation of Haku Wiñay relies on oversight by government agencies and the participation and support of households and communities. As noted, the program is overseen by Foncodes, an agency within MIDIS that is staffed primarily by both agricultural science professionals and social science professionals. Increasingly, Foncodes and MIDIS are leveraging the rise of a new generation of professionals who have farming and peasant backgrounds and who have benefited from university training. They can therefore leverage both training and a deep knowledge of local culture and practice.

Haku Wiñay is implemented with the support of its so-called *executing nuclei*. The concept of executing nuclei as an avenue for program delivery was inherited by Haku Wiñay from previous Foncodes interventions. Executing nuclei are groups of 80–100 rural households created ad hoc for implementation of the project. Each nucleus has a board of directors whose members have been selected by the beneficiaries or users of the intervention. The executing nuclei are in charge of the funds received to finance Haku Wiñay activities and pay the *yachachiqs*. The nuclei have communal legitimacy because they are integrated and directed by members of the community, and they are not involved in determining who participates in the program—the program is open to all households in the selected areas. They also create bureaucratic efficiency because of their ability to receive and manage funds from the public budget, authorized by a special rule established when Foncodes was founded. Executing nuclei are supervised and supported by local Haku Wiñay offices, which also approve their formation.

For the front-line delivery of technical assistance and training to households, Haku Wiñay relies on the farmer-to-farmer training model, based on the figure of the yachachiq (or trainer). Meaning "the one who knows" in the Quechua language, the yachachiq is a local expert hired to train his or her neighbors or households in nearby communities. Yachachiqs, selected through a public contest held by the Foncodes regional office, are largely responsible for the delivery of Haku Wiñay components 1 and 2, with the support of the professionals who work in Foncodes's regional offices. One of the advantages of engaging yachachiqs, in addition to their knowledge of the local language, is that they are embedded in the communities' sociocultural dynamics and therefore have privileged insight into their area and into the characteristics and needs of rural families. The use of yachachiqs has worked well in regions where there is already a critical mass of peasants with experience of working with social programs and NGOs. By contrast, it has been more challenging in areas where the concept of yachachiqs is more nascent.

When deciding how the program will be implemented in their communities, Haku Wiñay households have ample margin for autonomy. The first two intervention components (technology transfer for improving the farm and the home) are designed in such a way that each community can adapt them to their own particular social and economic dynamics.

Productive assets and technologies transferred to households

Haku Wiñay offers users a menu of potential productive assets and technologies to be transferred, as well as a menu of home improvements. Each community must select from both the technology and home improvement menus which improvements it will implement, up to a limit of $1,700 per household. This selection is made collectively at the executing nucleus level through a community diagnostic workshop held prior to the intervention itself. The technologies included in the menu have been validated as operational and sustainable in contexts of low resources (for additional detail on the various productive assets and technologies, see box CS4.1). To implement these technologies, participants count on guidance from Haku Wiñay and, in some cases, from other state institutions that deliver certain supplies or assist in training or logistics issues. As participants in the intervention, households are required to help with the installation of these technologies (as unpaid labor) and commit to their sustainability.

Promoting market access through inclusive rural business groups and competitions

To further improve the population's income, Haku Wiñay encourages the development of inclusive businesses and facilitates market links. Inclusive business group participants are chosen through competitions carried out at the end of the second year of the intervention. Inclusive business groups consist of three to five Haku Wiñay recipients seeking to carry out common productive activities, or the commercialization of agricultural products, or both. The winning groups receive special training and support to launch their activities during the third year of the intervention. The most common inclusive businesses are textiles and ceramic crafts, bakery and gastronomy, rural tourism, dairy products and by-products, small animal rearing for sale, fish farming, and cattle fattening.

To further develop their businesses, the winning groups rely on Foncodes's support for resources, advice, and efforts to establish active market links. Support of these rural inclusive business groups stimulates small business opportunities, which may mean pursuing transactions with provincial capitals and previously inaccessible markets. In addition, Haku Wiñay, either directly or in collaboration with municipalities, encourages small-scale opportunities for trade, such as weekly fairs or festivals targeting a certain product. In such venues, participants can sell their products in an environment less daunting than that found in traditional markets.

Funding and costs

The activities of Haku Wiñay are funded by the government as a budgetary line item, replenished on an annual basis. The Haku Wiñay intervention costs roughly $1,700 per household across three years of the intervention. Figures CS4.1 and CS4.2 show the intervention's evolution and the budgetary investment. Between 2012 and 2018, Haku Wiñay received 1,031 million nuevos soles from the Peruvian government (approximately $310 million).

Impacts and results

Haku Wiñay has been the subject of several studies and evaluations that speak to the program's operations, results, and impact. The most important quantitative evaluation was carried out by Escobal and Ponce (2016), although it was conducted at an early stage of the development of Haku Wiñay and in a limited number of regions. This evaluation found an average increase of 7.8 percent in the incomes of the households in the

FIGURE CS4.1 Number of Households Participating in Haku Wiñay, July 2014–April 2020

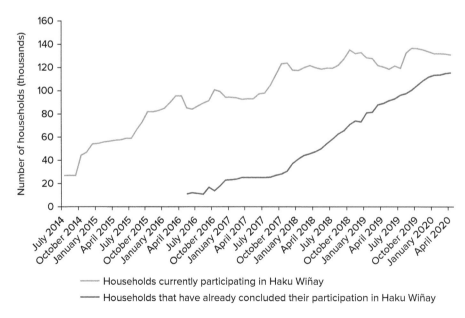

Households currently participating in Haku Wiñay
Households that have already concluded their participation in Haku Wiñay

Source: Info MIDIS, http://sdv.midis.gob.pe/Infomidis/#/.

FIGURE CS4.2 **Number of New Participant Households in Haku Wiñay per Year and Annual Budget, 2012–18**

Source: Info MIDIS, http://sdv.midis.gob.pe/Infomidis/#/.

program compared with the households in the control group (Escobal and Ponce 2016). These increases, which mainly affected households that participated in component 3 (inclusive businesses), were accompanied by a change in income generation strategies: the percentage of income from independent work or work based on self-employment increased, while the percentage of income from dependent work, including agricultural labor for others, decreased, indicating that households were now more autonomous. From a subjective point of view, 67 percent of households perceived their own income to be higher than before the intervention. In food security, the evaluation found statistically significant changes in the production of vegetables and greens, as well as in the number of chickens, guinea pigs, and eggs produced. Subsequent qualitative studies have shown results along the same lines—that is, a significant but limited impact on income and a greater impact on food security (Díez Hurtado and Correa Aste 2016). A pending new quantitative evaluation is intended to study the evolution of the program in recent years in a greater number of regions, including jungle departments.

Almost all studies of Haku Wiñay point to a heterogeneity of results and outcomes. Differences are associated both with each household's participation in the program and with the characteristics of the territories where the intervention is being carried out. At the territorial level, studies such as that by Asensio, Fernández, and Burneo (2016) have found that the level economic dynamism of each territory correlates with the success experienced by families. In rural areas with relatively dynamic markets, the Haku Wiñay interventions enable families to access productive assets to take better advantage of these dynamics. In areas with less dynamism, the results are more limited. At the participant level, studies show that individual dispositions and household characteristics, including the relative economic condition of the household and levels of interest in engaging in the program play a role in levels of success (Escobal and Ponce 2016). Further studies are expected to examine factors such as how the program could be influenced by psychological variables, including perceptions of what can be achieved on the farm and perceived control over life events (Aldana et al. 2018). See box CS4.2 for a discussion on the gender-related dimensions of Haku Wiñay programming.

BOX CS4.2   **Gender Dimensions of Haku Wiñay**

The design of Haku Wiñay does not include an explicit gender-based approach. Nevertheless, the program may, as implemented, facilitate more progressive perceptions of women's roles that go beyond those assigned by traditional gender systems, and facilitate the inclusion of women in community decision-making opportunities, such as in the executing nuclei. In these meetings, women may acquire skills and abilities that they later may put to use in other areas of community life, although this was not an explicit goal of Haku Wiñay.

Women's participation is noteworthy in the productive business component, but it is hard to quantify with precision. Their increased participation may stem from the fact that these businesses often focus on new areas of family productive activity. Generally, in Andean areas the prevailing division of labor sees men tending to work in consolidated businesses, whereas women work in new businesses.

Women's participation in Haku Wiñay's activities may be more intense in areas with higher economic dynamism and more limited in areas with lower economic dynamism. This difference results from the higher opportunity costs of areas with greater economic dynamism, leading men to prefer activities they consider to be potentially more lucrative. If so, men are more likely to delegate participation in meetings and training sessions to their wives as assigned users or "in representation" of their husbands. In less dynamic areas, the opportunity costs are lower, and frequently men are still in charge of representing their households.

Díez Hurtado and Correa Aste (2018) find that women in communities participating in Haku Wiñay have a larger number of businesses and report greater satisfaction with their lives and achievements. However, the authors also find scarce to no impact in socioemotional indicators such as self-esteem, persistence, or ambition, or in indicators related to decision-making in the home.

Moving to scale by institutionalizing lessons and community structures

Haku Wiñay emerged from a desire among government officials to create a path for the economic inclusion of the rural population, to enable the poor to leverage the rising economic dynamism of Peru. In the context of the human development perspective adopted by MIDIS with its commitment to activating and multiplying the potential of low-income families, an initial diagnosis of the poverty traps of Peru's rural households revealed three interrelated factors: untapped human capital, low productivity, and lack of access to markets (Trivelli and Vargas Winstanley 2014). To address these challenges, the design of the intervention included the following strategic commitments: (1) to empower users to decide the concrete ways in which the program was to be implemented in their communities; (2) to go back to and expand the characteristics of previous successful interventions; and (3) to adopt strategic and tactical flexibility to collectively face emerging problems and ensure implementation of the intervention.

The government of Peru has implemented Haku Wiñay by leveraging previous lessons on what works in the Peruvian Andean context, in particular the value of community-based trainers. Yachachiqs are common figures in rural development and economic interventions carried out in the Peruvian Andes (Asensio 2016). They emerged in the 1980s as part of international development efforts to generate culturally relevant intervention models—that is, interventions adapted to Andean social and cultural dynamics. Since these early experiences, yachachiqs have been utilized by many other rural development interventions (run by NGOs and by the Peruvian government) to the point that they are now a standard mechanism of development interventions in the country's southern highlands. Haku Wiñay also relies on these individuals, and it has extended their work to regions where they had not previously operated. To carry out their work, yachachiqs receive training from specialists in the regional office, and in turn they are responsible for training participants and households. During the last few years, financial yachachiqs have emerged. They advise participants on the inclusive business and financial issues included in the program's fourth component.

The government of Peru has also effectively institutionalized the implementation of Haku Wiñay through the executing nuclei. Executing nuclei are not a Haku Wiñay innovation but rather an adaptation of a preexisting concept (Asensio 2019). They were created in the 1990s by the Peruvian government to facilitate the implementation of demand-driven programs. Special legislation established from the inception of the executing nuclei program allows them to directly receive funds from the Peruvian government, even when they do not have the legal status usually required. They can make financial, legal, and administrative decisions on developing business plans, opening bank accounts, hiring professionals, buying supplies, and receiving contributions from the community (such as donations of unskilled labor) and local governments. Each executing nuclei has a board consisting of four representatives elected by a general assembly in which all user households participate. They fill the positions of president, secretary, treasurer, and prosecutor. In addition to the executing nuclei, the program is further institutionalized by the Central Executing Nuclei (NEC), which channels Foncodes's resources at the district or provincial levels.

Moving to scale up through programmatic adaptations, targeting practices, and localized microstrategies

Several programmatic adaptations and adjustments have marked Haku Wiñay's successful scale-up. The Haku Wiñay pilot program was launched in June 2012 in two districts of the department of Ayacucho in the Andean region—one of the poorest departments in the country. The 1,683 households participating in the pilot program also participated in Juntos because initially Haku Wiñay and Juntos were intended to complement one another so that families receiving the conditional transfer would continue to receive government support once their children had aged out of Juntos.

In practice, limiting the Haku Wiñay intervention to recipients of the Juntos cash transfer proved impractical and detrimental, and so, as noted earlier, it was changed. The wide dispersion of the homes that received conditional transfers worked against the territorial logic of Haku Wiñay's design because it made it difficult to integrate the executing nuclei and the work of yachachiqs. Meanwhile, "negative narratives" quickly emerged among the rural populations, such as Haku Wiñay's purpose was to "replace" Juntos. Because Juntos was highly regarded by the rural population, these narratives fostered anxiety about Haku Wiñay. As a result, many potential participants refused to engage in the intervention, or they abandoned it during implementation of the pilot program. Households excluded from Haku Wiñay because they were not part of Juntos felt unfairly treated because they considered themselves to be "as poor" as their neighbors who had been included in the intervention. They felt that, in addition to the "injustice" of not receiving Juntos, they now faced the injustice of being unable to join

Haku Wiñay. These factors created an environment of suspicion and misunderstandings around Haku Wiñay, and so the notion of including only Juntos beneficiary households was abandoned.

In fact, Haku Wiñay realized that including better-off households in the community in the program would be a driver of successful livelihoods and income-generating activities. Better-off households likely already had some ongoing business, had commercial links, knew about local value chains, and could help shore up a critical volume of economic activity to allow buyers and input providers, such as veterinary support, to engage in business in poor towns.

In the end, the targeting practices allowed the entry of participants from Juntos areas, and not just Juntos-recipient households. Participating communities were selected on the basis of the presence of Juntos, but once communities were selected, participation in Haku Wiñay was open to all households wishing to be part of the program, regardless of whether they participated in Juntos. This solution—using Juntos as a proxy for identifying poor communities—prevented the problems stemming from microtargeting at the household level, which could in turn result in conflict between neighbors and accusations of favoritism. The approach also allowed Haku Wiñay to avoid being seen as a "substitute" for Juntos.

Subsequently, since 2017 the presence of Juntos has not been a central criterion in the selection of the communities where Haku Wiñay intervenes. Instead, the central criterion has become the predominance of homes with subsistence economies within each community (Apoyo Consulting 2018). Programmatically, this revision may present some drawbacks as well. The presence of Juntos is likely key to ensuring a minimal level of cash and consumption support for the poorest households, although this has not been definitively confirmed by an assessment of the real impact of an overlap with Juntos.

Tactical flexibility and the adaptation of microstrategies that local program implementers use to take into account the various rural contexts, have allowed Haku Wiñay to succeed and scale up in the widely varying regional and cultural contexts of Peru. Haku Wiñay provides those implementing the intervention in the field with significant operational autonomy and the ability to modify microstrategies (Asensio, Fernández, and Burneo 2016). These microstrategies are informed by localized experience and allow adjustments as the program is developed in each community. For example, in communities where men migrate seasonally or have other occupations, training activities are carried out with their wives, regardless of whether they are the intervention's "official" users. Other microstrategies include the use of small raffles to encourage participation in certain activities, or informal agreements with municipal officials to facilitate the use of machines or collective transportation vehicles, or the organization of fairs and festivals where the population can sell their products. This latitude for decision-making at the margins is considered essential to adapt to each community's unique characteristics and its economic and social dynamics.

In practice, Haku Wiñay, like most social programs, is a centrally designed intervention, but one that takes shape in the field through locally relevant implementation and inputs to households. Flexibility allows the intervention to be adapted locally and prevents the program from collapsing in the complicated universe of Andean communal micropolitics. The result is an intervention that evokes relatively low levels of conflict compared with other initiatives developed by MIDIS, such as Qali Warma, the national school feeding program, or Juntos.

Lessons

At present, Haku Wiñay has reached more than 246,000 households nationwide. It is well regarded by most of the population and has some noteworthy achievements, including higher agricultural production, improvements in the household conditions of rural families, and improvements in food security. Its experience with the economic inclusion of Peru's rural poor bears lessons for the field of economic inclusion at large.

Institutional lessons

Haku Wiñay leverages the know-how accumulated by previous development interventions as well as by Peruvian local populations, and it has effectively institution-alized these elements. Key community structures and established practices, including *yachachiqs*, "farmer to farmer" methodologies, executing nuclei, and business compe-titions, resulted from these previous experiences and have helped to position Haku Wiñay for success. A culture that values innovation and learning has been strength-ened, focusing on testing innovations via different projects, which are then subject to evaluation or debate by academia, international agencies, and private actors. The process has benefited Peru's development landscape and Haku Wiñay as a program.

Successful implementation of Haku Wiñay requires that implementers be sensi-tive and responsive to the heterogeneous and changing dynamics of the country's rural contexts. The skills required go beyond just technical and professional capabilities. In the years to come, Haku Wiñay and other economic inclusion interventions in Peru will likely need to select and retain personnel with the characteristics and skill sets needed to work in rural contexts that require flexibility and a capacity to make decisions on the ground. The scale-up of Haku Wiñay to date is due, at least in part, to having utilized a new generation of professionals who are from the same regions in which the program is being implemented, and so they are familiar with the local and cultural contexts. Some are also specialized in the relevant technical areas or in social development and have benefited from university training, which has given them the technical know-how and deep knowledge of social dynamics needed for such a program.

Investing in strengthening specific features of government institutional cultures is important. Scaling up economic inclusion in Peru will require institutional cultures that promote and encourage local flexibility and capabilities. It will also require institutional cultures that favor the creation of interdisciplinary teams so that knowledge in various disciplines and skills can be combined when adapting interventions to conflict-affected, heterogeneous, changing rural contexts.

Programmatic lessons

Haku Wiñay's focus on aligning its efforts with the local Andean cultural dynamics has been a significant asset, but it does make replication of efforts in other areas of Peru challenging. A significant part of Haku Wiñay's success lies in a design informed by experience accumulated over decades of rural development interventions in the Andes. Replicating this approach in other areas of Peru, with their different social dynamics or where a different history of interaction with rural development interventions has prevailed, has been difficult. As a result, Haku Wiñay has been less successful in the Peruvian northern highlands and in jungle areas (Asensio, Fernández, and Burneo 2016; Díez Hurtado and Correa Aste 2016). These societies are not familiar with the notions of yachachiqs and executing nuclei, and they lack local equivalents.

Haku Wiñay's experience demonstrates the value of a market link approach, which can contribute to economic gains by households, but also carries its own challenges and risks. Haku Wiñay attempts to link households with small rural producer markets. Without these efforts, the impact of the program is likely to be much smaller, reach fewer people, and dilute more quickly. Such interventions can gradually bring rural producers closer to markets and increase household incomes, but they come with significant costs and can distort markets. By paying users' transaction costs, Haku Wiñay may end up harming other, more dynamic autonomous producers. Required, then, is consideration of the potential systemic impact of interventions on the economic dynamics of each territory.

Increasingly, the key tenets of Haku Wiñay's theory of change—that is, the importance of rural production and the centrality of the community as a space for decision-making—are shifting, likely requiring changes in its programming approach. Haku Wiñay has adopted an approach that, at its core, regards agricultural production as the main driver of economic well-being of rural families. Many studies show, however, that increasingly rural households, especially the most dynamic ones, embrace complex income-generating strategies that no longer depend exclusively on agricultural production. Rural families also often have complex residential strategies, which involve their members moving between rural and urban spaces, temporarily or permanently. Thus Haku Wiñay's dependence on the community as a decision-making place for economic well-being is a premise that corresponds less and less with reality.

For Foncodes and MIDIS, the challenge in the coming years will be to offer economic inclusion interventions that attract an evolving rural population. Expanding secondary education in rural areas has created new expectations and abilities among the rural population, especially the younger generations. Although agricultural activities will continue to be important for many families, especially the poorest, it will be necessary to build complementary programs and promote an expansion of the Haku Wiñay menu to nonagricultural activities that reflect the evolving Peruvian rural context and take advantage of new opportunities.

References

Aldana, Úrsula, Michael Carter, Juan Sebastián Correa, and Lucía Torres Frasele. 2018. "Haku Wiñay: evaluando el efecto del programa y de la inclusión de un componente de coaching. Informe de línea de base" [Haku Wiñay: evaluating the effect of the program and the inclusion of a coaching component. Baseline report]. Institute of Peruvian Studies, Lima, and University of California, Davis.

Apoyo Consulting. 2018. "Evaluación de diseño y ejecución presupuestal de programas presupuestales 0118 'acceso a hogares rurales con economías de subsistencia a mercados locales' y 0121 'mejora de la articulación de los pequeños productores agropecuarios al mercado'" [Design and budget execution evaluation of budget programs 0118 'access to rural households with subsistence economies to local markets' and 0121 'improvement of the articulation of small agricultural producers to the market']. Paper commissioned by Ministry of Economy and Finance. Apoyo Consulting, Lima.

Asensio, Raúl. 2016. "Los nuevos incas: economía política del desarrollo rural andino en Quispicanchi (2000–2010)" [The New Incas: political economy of Andean rural development in Quispicanchi (2000–2010)]. Institute of Peruvian Studies, Lima.

Asensio, Raúl. 2019. "Haku Wiñay and the Dilemmas of Economic Inclusion in Peru." Paper commissioned by World Bank, Washington, DC.

Asensio, Raúl, Juan Fernández, and María Luisa Burneo. 2016. "Validación herramienta de género FAO para servicios de asesoramiento rural en Perú: estudio de caso Haku Wiñay" [Validation of FAO gender tool for rural advisory services in Peru: Haku Wiñay case study]. Paper commissioned by Food and Agriculture Organization. Institute of Peruvian Studies, Latin America Centre for Rural Development, Lima.

Díez Hurtado, Alejandro, and Norma Correa Aste. 2016. "Desarrollo productivo y pobreza rural. Implementación y efectos del programa Haku Wiñay" [Productive development and rural poverty. Implementation and effects of the Haku Wiñay program]. Evaluation report, Ministry of Development and Social Inclusion, Lima.

Díez Hurtado, Alejandro, and Norma Correa Aste. 2018. "Estudio cualitativo: identificando las relaciones, prácticas, aspiraciones y motivaciones conectadas a las dinámicas económicas de la comunidad en el ámbito selva (con o sin intervención del programa Noa Jayatai)" [Qualitative study: identifying the relationships, practices, aspirations and motivations connected to the economic dynamics of the community in the jungle area (with or without the intervention of the Noa Jayatai program)]. Paper commissioned by Ministry of Development and Social Inclusion. Pontifical Catholic University of Peru, Lima.

Escobal, Javier, and Carmen Ponce. 2016. "Combinando protección social con generación de oportunidades económicas: Una evaluación de los avances del Programa Haku Wiñay" [Combining social protection with economic opportunities generation: an evaluation of the progress of the Haku Wiñay Program]. Group for the Analysis of Development (GRADE), Lima.

Trivelli, Carolina, and Silvana Vargas Winstanley. 2014. "Entre el discurso y la acción: desafíos, discusiones y dilemas en el marco de la creación del Ministerio de Inclusión Social" [Between discourse and action: challenges, discussions and dilemmas in the framework of the creation of the Ministry of Social Inclusion]. Institute of Peruvian Studies, Lima.

Survey Methodology

This appendix is an overview of the methodology used in executing the survey and analyses underpinning chapters 3 and 4 of this report.

Mapping the economic inclusion program universe

The Partnership for Economic Inclusion (PEI) Landscape Survey 2020 is a comprehensive inventory of ongoing economic inclusion programs or those that are in the development pipeline. For the survey, the PEI management team (PEIMT) defined economic inclusion programs as multidimensional interventions that support and enable households to achieve sustainable livelihoods and increase their incomes and assets, while building human capital and promoting social inclusion.

To map the universe of economic inclusion programs, PEIMT reviewed the World Bank financing portfolio as well as external sources. The first stage of the World Bank portfolio scan involved manually reviewing the ongoing and pipeline programs of the Social Protection and the Jobs and Development Global Practices (listed in the World Bank Operations Portal) across all geographical regions. To determine whether a program focused on economic inclusion, PEIMT reviewed each program's development objective and the component description included in its project appraisal document (PAD) or, when a PAD was not available, its project information document (PID), project paper (PP), or project information and integrated safeguards data sheet (PSDS).

At the second stage, to validate each economic inclusion program and to speed up the mapping process, PEIMT worked with the Text and Data Analytics (TDA) team in the Development Economics (DEC) department of the World Bank. Using a predefined set of keywords,[1] the TDA team applied advanced text analytics to program summaries as well as to their PADs, PIDs, PPs, or PSDSs. They applied this technique to a sample of approximately 1,200 programs (both active and pipeline) across all geographical regions under the following Global Practices: Agriculture; Finance, Competitiveness, and Innovation; Social Protection; Jobs and Development; and Social, Urban, Rural, and Resilience.[2] The team then ranked programs based on the number of keywords found, and any program that had at least one keyword was considered an economic inclusion program.[3] In the next step, PEIMT compared the TDA-assisted selection with the manual selection for the Social Protection and the Jobs and Development Global Practices programs and found that the results were accurate in correctly excluding programs. The TDA-assisted selection, however, also included far more programs than did the manual review.

To finalize the mapping of World Bank–financed economic inclusion programs, the PEIMT team manually reviewed the TDA-assisted selection of economic inclusion programs for the remaining Global Practices. The team assessed the relevance of a program based on program summaries, the types of words identified through the TDA techniques, and the frequency with which keywords came up in the project documents. When a summary did not provide enough information, the PAD was reviewed to make a final decision. Overall, the TDA methods allowed the PEIMT to trim the number of programs for review by half, to 149 World Bank economic inclusion programs, representing 92 individual government programs in 57 countries.[4] Surveys were sent to these 92 unique identified programs, and responses were received from 77 of them. The mapping of World Bank–supported programs was updated in May 2020 through a full manual review of nearly 50 programs from the Environment and Natural Resources

TABLE A.1   **Response Rate, the PEI Landscape Survey 2020**

Project	No. of mapped projects	No. of expected responses	No. of actual responses	Survey response rate
World Bank	165	107	92	86%
External	146	139	127	91%
Total	**311**	**246**	**219**	**89%**

Source: Partnership for Economic Inclusion (PEI), World Bank.

Global Practice, which resulted in 17 additional programs for a total of 165 economic inclusion programs supported by the World Bank (table A.1).

To map projects outside of World Bank operations, PEIMT used the PEI Landscape Survey 2017 data set to identify projects that were still ongoing as well as partners, including governments, nongovernmental organizations (NGOs), regional organizations, multilaterals, and other development partners involved in economic inclusion programming. Organizations were approached to self-identify programs that met a prescribed set of criteria based on the working definition of an economic inclusion program.[5] Because the 2017 survey mostly captured nongovernmental programs, PEIMT mapped other relevant economic inclusion interventions by scanning several databases and inventories of social protection and productive inclusion programs, including the Economic Commission for Latin America and the Caribbean Non-contributory Social Protection Programmes Database and the University of Manchester's Social Assistance Explorer database[6] (GIZ 2017; IPC-IG and UNICEF 2019; SEEP Network 2018). PEIMT identified 146 projects outside of the World Bank portfolio, from which 139 responses were expected and 127 responses were received.[7]

Despite efforts to map the entire universe of economic inclusion interventions, additional programs spearheaded by some United Nations agencies, including the International Fund for Agricultural Development (IFAD) and the Food and Agriculture Organization (FAO), as well as by some NGOs, were not mapped. The majority of missing responses were from government programs (25 out of 29 missing responses) both within and outside World Bank operations. Therefore, the sample is dominated by World Bank operations and PEI partnership organizations. Because of insufficient information, it is not possible to assess whether programs not included in the survey are substantially different in nature from the surveyed programs (which included 96 government-led initiatives). Although the survey sample does not fully represent the entire universe of economic inclusion programs, by having captured responses from 219 programs in 75 countries and six geographical regions and led by more than 100 organizations, the survey still captures a sufficiently strong variation across regions and institutional setups to provide a comprehensive overview of economic inclusion programming worldwide.

The survey tool

The survey questionnaire was developed after broad consultation with World Bank partners, including the Productive Inclusion Knowledge Exchange (PIKE) group and the Atlas of Social Protection Indicators of Resilience and Equity (ASPIRE) group, and with PEI partners. Furthermore, the PEI team sent the survey questionnaire to a few programs in three countries (Malawi, Tunisia, and Zambia) to test its logic and simplify the questions as much as possible. The 44 questions in the survey were divided into eight sections that covered basic information on the program, program objectives, target beneficiaries and coverage, design and implementation features, institutional arrangements, budget and financing, research and evaluation, and additional information.

The survey was completed by staff from the lead implementing agency, implementing partners, or other organizations supporting programs.[8] It was made available in English, French, and Spanish through an online platform.[9] An offline version was provided to programs that could not complete the survey online. Each returned survey represented a unique program. Organizations that were involved in more than one economic inclusion program filled out several surveys.

The survey was administered between November 2019 and January 2020, with an update in May 2020 for programs that are a part of the Environment and Natural Resources Global Practice. This process involved reaching out to economic inclusion program representatives, soliciting survey responses, following up with emails and phone calls, and assisting with survey completion as needed.

Because data were self-reported, data quality relied primarily on respondents' knowledge of the program and understanding of the survey questions. To ensure overall quality, several quality control features were embedded in the design of the survey tool and, to further improve data accuracy, PEIMT undertook a full quality review of all of the forms, checked the completeness and consistency of survey responses during the survey data collection process, and followed up with survey respondents to request clarifications or additional information wherever data were missing or inconsistencies were found.

Analysis of survey data

The analysis presented in chapters 3 and 4 is a statistical summary of the survey results and does not attempt to draw inferences about the universe of economic inclusion programs because this is unknown. For this reason, and after internal consultations, PEIMT decided not to apply weights to the data. Additional analysis, including cross-tabulations, were performed to shed some light on the factors that may help explain differences across programs.

The PEI Landscape Survey 2020 of economic inclusion programs provides a more holistic inventory than the PEI Landscape Survey 2017 and previous editions led by the Consultative Group to Assist the Poor (CGAP). Therefore, trends across these surveys are not fully comparable (Arévalo, Kaffenberger, and de Montesquiou 2018; CGAP 2016).

The following indicators were added to the survey data to support the analysis: countries' income group, region, lending category, poverty headcount ratio at the extreme poverty line of $1.90 per day (2011 US$ at purchasing power parity, PPP), and population size (most recent data from the World Bank Open Data portal); headcount ratio using the Oxford Poverty and Human Development Initiative's Multidimensional Poverty Index (MPI); average household size (various sources); and whether a country is included in the World Bank's Classification of Fragile and Conflict-Affected Situations.[10]

PEIMT analyzed programs in terms of their primary and secondary entry points based on the principal objectives or functions of the program (see appendix D). These points are often the basis for an economic inclusion program's design. An economic inclusion program is classified according to three entry points: social safety net (SSN), livelihoods and jobs (L&J), and financial inclusion (FI). Although programs broadly fit into these three program entry points, they are diverse and often layer priorities. For that reason, secondary entry points also play an important role in the design of economic inclusion programs. To classify the entry points of each program, PEIMT assessed the program's name, development objectives, types of components included, and types of government programs linked to the economic inclusion intervention.

Analysis of coverage data

For this report, the *coverage* of a country's economic inclusion programs is considered to be the number of beneficiaries reached by all of its programs relative to the total population. The estimates delineate coverage in terms of households (direct beneficiaries) and individuals (direct plus indirect beneficiaries). The individual figure is determined by multiplying direct beneficiaries by average household size. This approach follows an accepted estimation approach across social protection programs globally (Beegle et al. 2018; Milazzo and Grosh 2008). Estimates do not account for the potential spillover and community effects of an intervention.

Of the 219 programs reporting overall, for the coverage analysis the sample is limited to 201 programs from 73 countries because 18 programs did not report the coverage numbers. Coverage estimates are likely to be biased with the likely exclusions of several programs outside of the World Bank Group, as noted earlier.

The survey asked for the number of beneficiaries currently enrolled in the respective programs. Programs could report the number of beneficiaries as the number of households or the number of individuals. To aggregate coverage data across all programs, the team calculated the total number of beneficiaries, both direct and indirect, by multiplying the number of direct beneficiaries reported by each program by the average household size in the country. Because in some programs different members of the same household are direct recipients of economic inclusion program components, in aggregating coverage figures it was not possible to distinguish between direct and indirect beneficiaries. Coverage data reported as the number of individuals thus include both direct and indirect beneficiaries. The programs for which coverage data are reported currently cover 92.5 million individuals as both direct recipients and indirect beneficiaries, which corresponds to nearly 20 million households.

Because of the tailored nature of economic inclusion programs, PEIMT considered *coverage equivalents*, defined as the number of direct plus indirect beneficiaries reached by a program relative to the total population and estimated poverty thresholds, including the national poverty line, extreme poverty line, and MPI. These equivalent measures provide important illustrations of the potential coverage of programs that have a strong focus on poverty. They also recognize a wider debate on poverty measurement thresholds (see box 4.1). Calculation of the coverage equivalent at the country level began by adding up the number of individual beneficiaries for all the programs in a given country. The number of individual beneficiaries (direct and indirect) per country was then compared with the following:

- Total population of the country. *Source:* World Bank (ID: SP.POP.TOTL).

- Poor population calculated using the total population of the country and the poverty headcount ratio at the national poverty line (percentage of population). *Source:* World Bank, Global Poverty Working Group (ID: SI.POV.NAHC).

- Poor population calculated using the total population of the country and the poverty headcount ratio at $1.90 per day (2011 US$, PPP) (extreme poverty line). *Source:* Povcalnet, World Bank (ID: SI.POV.DDAY).

- Poor population calculated using the total population of the country and the poverty headcount ratio—Multidimensional Poverty Index data. *Source:* Global MPI Databank, Oxford Poverty and Human Development Initiative.

The most recent data on poverty headcount ratio were retrieved from each country's database. In addition, population estimates were taken for the same years from the World Bank Open Data portal.

Comparing beneficiary numbers with the total population does not provide the most accurate picture of the coverage and scale of economic inclusion programs. Because a significant majority of economic inclusion programs target the poor, extreme poor, or ultrapoor populations, comparing the total number of beneficiaries with the most relevant poverty line renders a more realistic view of the coverage and scale. This finding raises a complicated question: which poverty line is the most relevant when it comes to estimating the coverage of economic inclusion programs globally? As noted earlier, the coverage analysis included in this report uses three different poverty lines:

- The national poverty line (NPL)
- Extreme poverty line—at $1.90 per day (2011 US$, PPP)
- Multidimensional Poverty Index

PEIMT selected a subsample of 20 low-income countries in Sub-Saharan Africa and compared the coverage equivalent for all three poverty lines. This analysis revealed that the number of people living below the extreme poverty line mirrors the number of poor, as defined using the NPL in these countries (figure A.1). However, comparing the NPL with the MPI reveals a different picture altogether. The MPI calculates poverty numbers beyond material income using three dimensions—health, education, and standard of living—and comprises 10 indicators. This calculation results in a significantly higher poverty headcount when compared with the NPL. Thus the coverage of economic inclusion programs is even lower for certain countries when MPI data are used (figure A.2). For example, coverage of economic inclusion programs in Ethiopia is 31 percent of the population living below the NPL and only 8 percent of the population below the MPI line.

PEIMT then compared the coverage of economic inclusion programs as a share of the poor defined using both the NPL and the extreme poverty line in upper-middle-income countries (figure A.3). The challenge in using the extreme poverty line arises in

FIGURE A.1 **Percentage of Population Living Below Extreme Poverty Line and Percentage of Population Living Below National Poverty Line, Low- and Lower-Middle-Income Countries**

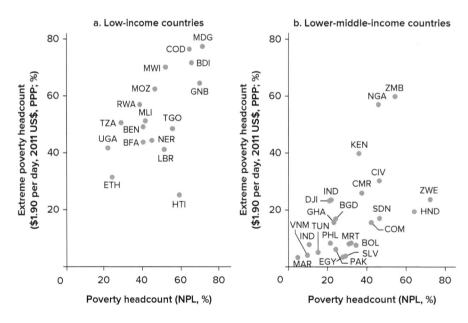

Source: Partnership for Economic Inclusion, World Bank.
Note: For country codes, see International Organization for Standardization (ISO), https://www.iso.org/obp/ui/#search. NPL = national poverty line; PPP = purchasing power parity.

FIGURE A.2 Economic Inclusion Program Coverage Equivalents, Low- and Lower-Middle-Income Countries

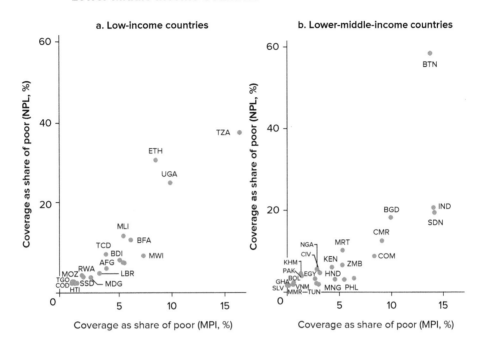

Source: Partnership for Economic Inclusion, World Bank.
Note: For country codes, see International Organization for Standardization (ISO), https://www.iso.org/obp/ui
/#search. MPI = Multidimensional Poverty Index; NPL = national poverty line; PPP = purchasing power parity.

FIGURE A.3 Economic Inclusion Program Coverage Equivalent, Upper-Middle-Income Countries

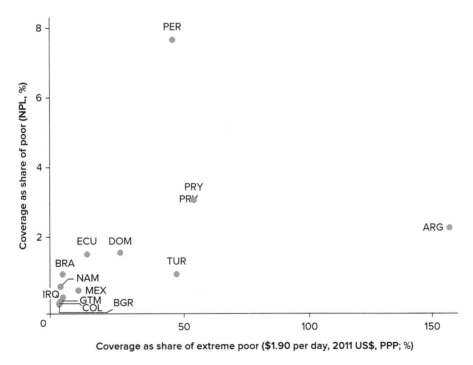

Source: Partnership for Economic Inclusion, World Bank.
Note: For country codes, see International Organization for Standardization (ISO), https://www.iso.org/obp
/ui/#search. NPL = national poverty line; PPP = purchasing power parity.

upper-middle-income countries where either the number of people living in extreme poverty is extremely low, such as in Argentina and Chile, or no people are living below the extreme poverty line, such as in Jordan and Costa Rica. Therefore, the coverage numbers reported for these countries using the extreme poverty line look very high and misleading. In some middle-income and high-income countries, higher poverty lines, such as the $3.20-a-day and $5.50-a-day poverty lines, may provide a more complete picture of the prevalence of poverty and trends in poverty reduction than the extreme poverty line (World Bank 2020). Bearing in mind all of these considerations, PEIMT chose to use the NPL as the primary unit of analysis.

Notes

1. Keywords (in italics, priority words): *inclusion; economic empowerment; safety net; access to finance;* financial access; extreme poverty; marginal; *microfinance;* microfinance institutions (MFI); *access to market;* market access; access to financing; *financial services; job creation; livelihood opportunities; job opportunities; employment opportunities;* SHG; *self-help group;* self help group; *cash transfer;* entrepreneurship opportunities; informal economy; *inclusiveness;* microinsurance; socio-economic inclusion; productive safety net; financial inclusion; *small and medium enterprise;* micro, small and medium enterprise; MSME; *SME; economic opportunity; economic inclusion; productive inclusion; financial literacy; social inclusion;* socioeconomic inclusion; *graduation; graduating; productive social safety net;* socioeconomic empowerment; WEE; women's economic empowerment; *promotion; protection and promotion; targeted;* targeting criteria; *poorest;* most vulnerable; extremely poor; *ultra-poor;* multidimensional; cash plus; *accompanying* measures; integrated package; productive package; *complimentary services; combined intervention; convergence;* integrated social safety net; asset transfer; asset grant; coaching; mentoring; hand-holding; productive grant; productive transfer; cash and care; marginalize.
2. In May 2020, PEI undertook an additional scan of projects under the Environment and Natural Resources Global Practice.
3. After applying the advanced text analytics, the TDA team distinguished between priority keywords and regular keywords. Priority keywords were deemed to be more relevant than regular keywords to economic inclusion programming.
4. The list of 92 programs excludes operations in the pipeline, additional financing projects, and other projects recently closed, which are included in the list of 149 projects.
5. Programs targeted by the survey had to be in operation and meet at least three of the following criteria: (1) they aim to increase the assets and income of participants; (2) they target the extreme poor or vulnerable people; (3) they provide an integrated package of services (that is, they are multidimensional interventions); and (4) they have a strong national commitment or vision (for example, in their policy or strategy frameworks).
6. https://dds.cepal.org/bpsnc/lpi; http://www.social-assistance.manchester.ac.uk/data/.
7. For seven programs, the PEIMT was unable to identify a focal point in either the lead implementing agency or an implementing partner to complete the survey.
8. Two research organizations provided the survey response instead of staff directly involved in implementation.
9. The online tool can be found at https://enketo.ona.io/x/#bXz0uQ9G.
10. The sources of additional indicators used to analyze survey data were the following: World Bank Open Data portal, https://data.worldbank.org/; Oxford Multidimensional Poverty Index, https://ophi.org.uk/; World Bank Classification of Fragile and Conflict-Affected Situations, https://www.worldbank.org/en/topic/fragilityconflictviolence/brief/harmonized -list-of-fragile-situations; State Statistical Committee of the Republic of Azerbaijan, https://www.stat.gov.az/source/budget_households/?lang = en; OECD Five Family Facts, https://www.oecd.org/els/family/47710686.pdf; Chile, census of population and housing results, 2017, https://www.ine.cl/docs/default-source/censo-de-poblacion-y-vivienda /publicaciones-y-anuarios/2017/publicaci%C3%B3n-de-resultados/sintesis-de-resultados -censo2017.pdf?sfvrsn = 1b2dfb06_6; Vietnam, Yearly Household Average Size Estimates, https://www.ceicdata.com/en/vietnam/household-living-standard-survey-hss-household-size /hss-household-size-hs-whole-country; CEIC Data, https://www.ceicdata.com; El Salvador,

Yearly Household Average Size Estimates, https://www.arcgis.com/home/item
.html?id = bda04062e562493290cd7f1aaeea3682; Tonga, 2011 Census of Population and
Housing, Volume 2, https://tonga-data.sprep.org/system/files/2011_CensusReportVol2
.pdf; State Committee of the Republic of Uzbekistan on Statistics, https://stat.uz/en
/435-analiticheskie-materialy-en1/2078-analysis-of-the-development-of-living-standards-and
-welfare-of-the-population-in-the-republic-of-uzbekistan; Population Estimation Survey 2014
for the 18 prewar regions of Somalia, https://somalia.unfpa.org/sites/default/files/pub-pdf
/Population-Estimation-Survey-of-Somalia-PESS-2013-2014.pdf; United Nations, Department
of Economic and Social Affairs, Population Size Estimation Tool, https://population.un.org
/Household/index.html#/countries/840; World Bank, "Challenges to Inclusive Growth:
A Poverty and Equity Assessment of Djibouti," https://openknowledge.worldbank.org/handle
/10986/33032; Democratic Republic of Congo, Demographic and Health Survey 2013–13,
https://dhsprogram.com/pubs/pdf/SR218/SR218.e.pdf; Kosovo Census 2011, https://askdata
.rks-gov.net/PXWeb/pxweb/sq/askdata/askdata__14%20Census%20population__Census%20
2011__1%20Summary%20tables/1%20census36.px/table/tableViewLayout1/?rxid – 0b4e087e
-8b00-47ba-b7cf-1ea158040712/; Tanzania 2012 Population and Housing Census, http://www
.tzdpg.or.tz/fileadmin/documents/dpg_internal/dpg_working_groups_clusters/cluster_2/water
/WSDP/Background_information/2012_Census_General_Report.pdf; Botswana Demographic
Survey 2017 (BDS), http://www.statsbots.org.bw/sites/default/files/publications/Botswana%20
Demographic%20Survey%20Report%202017.pdf; Palestine Central Bureau of Statistics,
http://www.pcbs.gov.ps/portals/_pcbs/PressRelease/Press_En_IntPopDay2018E.pdf; Pakistan
Economic Survey 2017–18, http://www.finance.gov.pk/survey/chapters_18/12-Population.pdf;
Bhutan Housing Census Report 2017, http://www.nsb.gov.bt/news/news_detail.php?id = 263;
Lebanon Average Household Size 2007, http://www.cas.gov.lb/index.php/did-you-know
-category-en/100-did-you-know-11; Tunisia Data Atlas, December 31, 2014, http://regions.ins.tn
/bxezjnb/tunisia-data-atlas-31st-december-2014; World Bank, South Sudan Poverty Profile 2015,
http://microdata.worldbank.org/index.php/catalog/2778/download/39504.

References

Arévalo, I., M. Kaffenberger, and A. de Montesquiou. 2018. *2018 State of the
Sector Synthesis Report*. Washington, DC: Partnership for Economic Inclusion,
World Bank.

Beegle, Kathleen G., Aline Coudouel, Montiel Monsalve, and Mercedes Emma. 2018.
Realizing the Full Potential of Social Safety Nets in Africa. Washington, DC:
World Bank. http://documents.worldbank.org/curated/en/657581531930611436
/Realizing-the-Full-Potential-of-Social-Safety-Nets-in-Africa.

CGAP (Consultative Group to Assist the Poor). 2016. "Status of Graduation Programs
2016." CGAP, Paris.

GIZ (Deutsche Gesellschaft für Internationale Zusammenarbeit). 2017. "Linking Social
Protection with Productive Inclusion: Innovative Approaches and Enabling Factors
for Inter-Sectoral Coordination." GIZ, Bonn.

IPC-IG (International Policy Centre for Inclusive Growth) and UNICEF (United Nations
Children's Fund). 2019. "Social Protection in Asia and the Pacific: Inventory of
Non-Contributory Programmes." IPC-IG and UNICEF, Brasília.

Milazzo, Annamaria, and Margaret Grosh. 2008. *Social Safety Nets in World Bank
Lending and Analytical Work: FY2002–2007*. Social Protection Discussion
Paper No. SP 0810. Washington, DC: World Bank. http://documents.worldbank
.org/curated/en/920421468155739339/Social-safety-nets-in-World-Bank
-lending-and-analytical-work-FY2002-2007.

SEEP Network. 2018. *State of Practice: Savings Groups and the Role of Government in
Sub-Saharan Africa*. Arlington, VA: SEEP Network.

World Bank. 2020. *Poverty and Shared Prosperity 2020: Reversals of Fortune*.
Washington, DC: World Bank. doi:10.1596/978-1-4648-1602-4.

Review of Program Impact

Methodology for literature review

This appendix describes the quantitative impact evaluations, process evaluations, and qualitative assessments used for the review of the impact evidence in chapter 5. These studies cover 80 economic inclusion programs operating in diverse contexts in 37 countries across four regions, as outlined in figure 5.1. The reviewed programs vary in terms of program typology, institutional arrangements, and size, and they include pilots, small-scale programs, and large-scale programs. Reviewed programs may be single or complementary, meaning they feature a bundle of different interventions that can be delivered by one primary agency or by more than one that work in concert. A single program provides all program components, whereas complementary programs link several programs together. The single programs reviewed are led by both nongovernmental organizations (NGOs) and governments, whereas all complementary programs are either government-led or are linked with a government program. As for typologies, the bulk of the evidence pertains to livelihoods and jobs (L&J) and less to social safety nets (SSNs). There are only four evaluations of programs for which financial inclusion (FI) is a primary objective (of these, three were experiments). As a result, the discussion in this appendix relies primarily on the first two typologies.

The following criteria were used to identify programs: (1) the program meets the definition of economic inclusion used in this report; (2) the program is operating only in developing countries—low-income countries, lower-middle-income countries, and upper-middle-income countries in four regions: Sub-Saharan Africa (SSA), South Asia (SAR), East Asia and Pacific (EAP), and Latin America and the Caribbean (LAC); and (3) the program has at least one quantitative impact evaluation or qualitative assessment, with a greater emphasis on the former.

The following programs were included in the review: (1) programs in the Partners in Economic Inclusion (PEI) Landscape Survey 2020 with an impact evaluation or qualitative assessment (the majority did not yet have an evaluation); (2) programs surveyed in the *State of the Sector Synthesis Report 2018* by PEI that had an evaluation or assessment, with a focus on large-scale programs (Arévalo, Kaffenberger, and de Montesquiou 2018); and (3) programs with evaluations listed in online research databases[1] or that had been reviewed in systematic reviews of economic inclusion programming or relevant standalone interventions such as SSN, L&J, and FI programs or that had been evaluated as part of institutional research agendas on economic inclusion.[2]

The following studies were included in the review: (1) experimental impact evaluations (individual or cluster randomized controlled trials, RCTs); (2) quasi-experimental impact evaluations (using a range of methods such as regression discontinuity design, propensity score matching, and difference-in-difference); and (3) qualitative assessments of impact. Only publicly available papers were included in the review, including published papers in peer-reviewed journals (mostly impact evaluations), working papers, reports, books, and unpublished papers available online. Primarily, the studies were published between 2009 and 2020. In the end, 108 studies met these criteria, with some programs having more than one evaluation.

The quantitative (experimental and quasi-experimental) and qualitative impact evaluations were used to examine overall impact and to assess the evidence on the bundling of interventions and heterogeneity (with one exception: there is reference to qualitative assessments on subjective well-being and empowerment). For the discussion on the drivers of impact, the impact evaluations were supplemented with nonevaluative qualitative and operational research. Treated and control participants were referred to as participants and nonparticipants, respectively. Table B.1 at the end of this appendix lists all the programs and evaluations reviewed in chapter 5, and it is followed by a bibliography of the evaluative and nonevaluative studies used.

Upcoming research pipeline

The rich research pipeline expected to yield outputs in 2020 and 2021 will respond to some critical knowledge gaps identified in chapter 5. The majority of programs in the PEI Landscape Survey 2020 have ongoing or planned impact evaluations and other research. A large number of these planned impact evaluations (85 percent) continue to focus on overall impact. However, a subset of programs (government-led and nongovernment-led) are planning more nuanced research on economic inclusion programming design, including impact at scale (25 percent), differential impact on different population groups (42 percent), bundling of interventions (41 percent combination and 10 percent sequencing), and marginal impact of specific interventions (17 percent market links and 4 percent noncognitive skills)—see figure B.1. In addition, at the time of publication of this report, BRAC has released findings from a 10-year evaluation of its program. Preliminary findings are noted in Chapter 5.[3]

In addition to this program-specific research, the following research agendas also have or will soon have useful comparable evidence on economic inclusion programming along different dimensions:

1. Ford Foundation and Consultative Group to Assist the Poor (CGAP) meta-analysis across six pilot programs in Ethiopia, Ghana, Honduras, India, Pakistan, and Peru (Banerjee et al. 2015)—completed

2. "Conditional Cash Transfer Programs and Rural Development in Latin America," International Fund for Agricultural Development (IFAD) and Center for Studies on Economic Development (CEDE) project at Universidad de los Andes examining complementary programs in Latin America and the Caribbean (Maldonado et al. 2016)—completed

3. Food and Agriculture Organization's cash-plus research on complementary SSNs and livelihood programs in Sub-Saharan Africa (FAO 2018; Soares et al. 2017; Tirivayi, Knowles, and Davis 2013)—ongoing

4. Innovations for Poverty Action (IPA) and World Bank's Sahel Adaptive Social Protection Program (SASPP) multicountry evaluation in Burkina Faso, Mauritania, Niger, and Senegal—forthcoming

5. World Bank and World Food Programme's multicountry evaluation of cash-plus programming

TABLE B.1 Reviewed Programs and Evaluative Studies (Quantitative Evaluations Only)

Country	Program	Government/NGO	Entry point	Lead implementing agency	Program components	Study	Total cost, where available (2011 US$, PPP)	Outcomes of interest analyzed (broadly defined)[a]
Afghanistan	Targeting Ultra Poor (TUP)—MISFA	Government-led	Livelihoods and jobs	Microfinance Investment Support Facility for Afghanistan (MISFA)	1. Assets 2. Consumption support 3. Skills training 4. Access to savings accounts 5. Health care services 6. Coaching	Bedoya et al. (2019)	—	Income, consumption, assets, savings, well-being, empowerment, child health, education
	WfWI 12-Month Social and Economic Empowerment Training Programme	Nongovernment-led	Livelihoods and jobs	Women for Women International	1. Consumption support 2. Skills training 3. Vocational training 4. Savings channel 5. Empowerment groups 6. Health awareness	Noble and Han (2019)	—	Income, empowerment
Argentina	Microemprendimientos Productivos (MEP)	Government-led	Livelihoods and jobs	National government	1. Grants 2. Skills training 3. Coaching	Almeida and Galasso (2010)	—	Income, employment
	Seguro de Capacitación y Empleo (SCE)	Government-led	Livelihoods and jobs	Ministry of Labour, Argentina	1. Skills training 2. Vocational training 3. Employment intermediation 4. Education support 5. Promotion of self-employment	Mourelo and Escudero (2016)	—	Employment
Bangladesh	Challenging the Frontiers of Poverty Reduction: Targeting the Ultra Poor (TUP)	Nongovernment-led	Livelihoods and jobs	BRAC	1. Enterprise development and life skills training 2. Asset transfer 3. Consumption support 4. Health subsidy 5. Community mobilization support	Bandiera et al. (2017)	$1,541	Income, consumption, assets, employment
						Ara et al. (2017)	$1,022	Income, consumption, assets, savings, employment
						Ahmed et al. (2009)		Consumption, assets, savings, education
						Emran, Robano, and Smith (2014)	—	Income, consumption, assets, savings, empowerment, overall health, education
						Raza, Das, and Misha (2012)	$275	Income, consumption, assets

(Table continues next page)

246

TABLE B.1 Reviewed Programs and Evaluative Studies (Quantitative Evaluations Only) (continued)

Country	Program	Government/NGO	Entry point	Lead implementing agency	Program components	Study	Total cost, where available (2011 US$, PPP)	Outcomes of interest analyzed (broadly defined)[a]
Bangladesh (Continued)						Krishna, Poghosyan, and Das (2012)	—	Income, assets, savings, overall health
						Misha et al. (2019)	—	Income, consumption, assets, savings
						Raza and Ara (2012)	$134	Income, consumption, assets, savings
						Bandiera et al. (2013)	$282	Income, consumption, assets, savings, employment, well-being
						Raza and Van de Poel (2016)	—	Child health
						Raza, Van de Poel, and van Ourti (2018)	—	Child health
						Asadullah and Ara (2016)	—	Income, assets, savings, employment
	Enhancing Resilience (ER+)	Nongovernment-led	Livelihoods and jobs	World Food Programme	1. Consumption support 2. Grants 3. Skills training 4. Group training 5. Women's empowerment	Hernandez et al. (2016)	—	Income, consumption, assets, savings
	Food Security for the Ultra Poor (FSUP)	Nongovernment-led	Livelihoods and jobs	World Food Programme and BRAC	1. Grants 2. Consumption support 3. Skills training	BDI (2012)	—	Income, consumption, assets, savings, empowerment, overall health
	Chars Livelihoods Programme (CLP)	Nongovernment-led	Livelihoods and jobs	UK Department for International Development (DFID)	1. Grants 2. Consumption support 3. Physical infrastructure support 4. Social development training	HTSPE (2011)	—	Income, assets, empowerment, child health

(Table continues next page)

TABLE B.1 Reviewed Programs and Evaluative Studies (Quantitative Evaluations Only) (*continued*)

Country	Program	Government/NGO	Entry point	Lead implementing agency	Program components	Study	Total cost, where available (2011 US$, PPP)	Outcomes of interest analyzed (broadly defined)[a]
Brazil	Community Development Project and Conditional Cash Transfer (BOLSA)	Government-led	Complementary	International Fund for Agricultural Development (IFAD) and national government	1. Conditional cash transfer 2. Training 3. Rural development	Costa, Helfand, and Souza (2018)	—	Income, savings
	Conditional cash transfer (BOLSA) and family farm credit program (Pronaf)	Government-led	Complementary	IFAD and national government	1. Conditional cash transfer 2. Subsidized agricultural credit	Garcia, Helfand, and Souza (2016)	—	Income
Burkina Faso	Graduation approach	Nongovernment-led	Livelihoods and jobs	Trickle Up	1. Savings 2. Skills training 3. Asset transfer 4. Coaching/mentoring	Karimli, Bose, and Kagotho (2019)	—	Income, assets, savings
							—	Child health
						Ismayilova and Karimli (2018)	$217	Child health
						Ismayilova et al. (2018); Karimli, Rost, and Ismayilova (2018)	—	Child health
	Productive transfers (cash-plus)	Nongovernment-led	Social safety net–plus	Food and Agriculture Organization (FAO)	1. Consumption support 2. Asset transfer 3. Community awareness	FAO (2016)	—	Income, assets
Burundi	Graduation model	Nongovernment-led	Livelihoods and jobs	Concern	1. Consumption support 2. Cash grants 3. Savings and internal lending community (SILC) 4. Skills training 5. Coaching 6. Health insurance	Devereux et al. (2015)	—	Income, consumption, assets, empowerment, overall health, education
Colombia	Familias em Accion and Opportunidades Rurales	Government-led	Complementary	National government	1. Conditional cash transfer 2. Cofinanced training for microentrepreneurs	Moya (2016)	—	Consumption, assets, employment, education

(Table continues next page)

TABLE B.1 Reviewed Programs and Evaluative Studies (Quantitative Evaluations Only) (continued)

Country	Program	Government/NGO	Entry point	Lead implementing agency	Program components	Study	Total cost, where available (2011 US$, PPP)	Outcomes of interest analyzed (broadly defined)[a]
Côte d'Ivoire	Projet d'insertion socio-economique pour les populations vulnérables de l'Ouest de Côte d'Ivoire (PRISE)	Nongovernment-led	Livelihoods and jobs	International Rescue Committee (IRC)	1. Grants 2. Savings 3. Credit	Premand and Marguerie (2020)	—	Income, savings, employment
	Projet d'Urgence de Création d'Emploi Jeunes et de Développement des Compétences (PEJEDEC)	Government-led	Social safety net–plus	FXB	1. Public works–plus (PWP) 2. Skills training 3. Basic entrepreneurship training 4. Wage skills training	Bertrand et al. (2017)	—	Income, consumption, savings, well-being
El Salvador	Comunidades Solidarias Rurales (CSR) and Fund for Local Development (Fondo de Inversión Social para el Desarrollo, FISDL)	Government-led	Complementary	Government	1. Conditional cash transfer 2. Agricultural field schools (for subsistence farmers) 3. Access to markets (for small and medium commercial producers)	de Sanfeliú, Ángel, and Shi (2016)	—	Income, savings, employment, empowerment
	CGAP–Ford Foundation graduation pilot	Nongovernment-led	Livelihoods and jobs	Relief Society of Tigray	1. Productive asset transfer 2. Consumption support 3. Skills training 4. Coaching 5. Access to a savings account 6. Health education	Banerjee et al. (2015)	$2,520	Income, consumption, assets, savings, well-being, empowerment, overall health
Ethiopia	Productive Safety Net Programme (PSNP), and Other Food Security Programme (OFSP), and Household Asset Building Programme (HABP)	Government-led	Complementary	Government	1. PWP 2. Cash/in-kind 3. Community-level transfers for productive asset accumulation	Gilligan, Hoddinott, and Tafesse (2009)	—	Consumption, employment, assets
						Hoddinott et al. (2012)	—	Assets
						Sabates-Wheeler and Devereux (2010)	—	Income, assets
						Berhane et al. (2014)	—	Assets, employment

(Table continues next page)

TABLE B.1 Reviewed Programs and Evaluative Studies (Quantitative Evaluations Only) *(continued)*

Country	Program	Government/NGO	Entry point	Lead implementing agency	Program components	Study	Total cost, where available (2011 US$, PPP)	Outcomes of interest analyzed (broadly defined)[a]
Ethiopia *(Continued)*	Pastoralist Areas Resilience Improvement through Market Expansion (PRIME)	Nongovernment-led	Livelihoods and jobs	Mercy Corps	1. Microfinance 2. Weather information 3. Training 4. Extension services	Sagara and Hudner (2017)	—	Assets
						Smith et al. (2019)	—	Consumption, assets, savings, employment, child health, education
	Industrial and entrepreneurial jobs	Nongovernment-led	Livelihoods and jobs	U.S. Agency for International Development (USAID)	1. Cash grants 2. Low-wage employment 3. Skills training	Blattman, Dercon, and Franklin (2019)	$450	Income, employment, overall health
	Productive Safety Net Programme (PSNP), Plus	Government-led	Complementary	USAID	1. PWP 2. Cash/in-kind 3. Community-level transfers for productive asset accumulation 4. Microfinance	Burns and Bogale (2011)	—	Income, consumption, assets, savings
Ghana	CGAP–Ford Foundation graduation pilot	Nongovernment-led	Livelihoods and jobs	Presbyterian Agricultural Services and Innovations for Poverty Action	1. Productive asset transfer 2. Consumption support 3. Skills training 4. Coaching 5. Access to a savings account 6. Health education	Banerjee et al. (2015)	$3,320	Income, consumption, assets, savings, well-being, empowerment, overall health
						Banerjee et al. (2018)	—	Income, consumption, assets, savings
Haiti	Chemen Lavi Miyò (CLM)	Nongovernment-led	Livelihoods and jobs	Fonkoze	1. Assets 2. Cash stipend 3. Village savings and loan associations (VSLA) 4. Training 5. In-kind support for housing and sanitation 6. Screening children for malnutrition 7. Village assistance committees	Roelen and Saha (2019)	—	Income, consumption, well-being, child health, overall health, education
Honduras	CGAP–Ford Foundation graduation pilot	Nongovernment-led	Livelihoods and jobs	Organización de Desarollo Empresarial Feminino, Social and Plan International	1. Productive asset transfer 2. Consumption support 3. Skills training 4. Coaching 5. Access to a savings account 6. Health education	Banerjee et al. (2015)	$1,114	Income, consumption, assets, savings, well-being, empowerment, overall health

(Table continues next page)

TABLE B.1 Reviewed Programs and Evaluative Studies (Quantitative Evaluations Only) (*continued*)

Country	Program	Government/NGO	Entry point	Lead implementing agency	Program components	Study	Total cost, where available (2011 US$, PPP)	Outcomes of interest analyzed (broadly defined)[a]
India	Targeting the Hard-Core Poor program	Nongovernment-led	Livelihoods and jobs	Bandhan	1. Productive asset transfer 2. Skills training 3. Coaching 4. Consumption support 5. Access to savings accounts 6. Health information or services	Banerjee et al. (2016)	—	Income, consumption, assets, savings, employment, well-being, empowerment, overall health
	CGAP–Ford Foundation graduation pilot	Nongovernment-led	Livelihoods and jobs	Bandhan	1. Productive asset transfer 2. Skills training 3. Coaching 4. Consumption support 5. Access to savings accounts 6. Health information or services	Banerjee et al. (2015)	$972	Income, consumption, assets, savings, well-being, empowerment, overall health
	CGAP–Ford Foundation graduation pilot	Nongovernment-led	Livelihoods and jobs	Swayam Krishi Sangam (SKS)	1. Economic package (productive asset transfer and consumption support) 2. Essential health care 3. Social development 4. Financial literacy 5. Households: training, savings accounts, health consultations, facilitation of access to government services	Bauchet, Morduch, and Ravi (2015)	$836	Income, consumption, assets, savings, employment, overall health
	Indira Kranti Patham program (NRLM)	Government-led	Livelihoods and jobs	State government, Andhra Pradesh	1. Household savings 2. Bank links 3. Community investment fund 4. Productive investments. 5 Market links	Prennushi and Gupta (2014)	—	Consumption, savings, empowerment, overall health, education
						Deininger and Liu (2013)	—	Income, consumption, assets, empowerment
	Targeting the Hard-Core Poor	Nongovernment-led	Livelihoods and jobs	Bandhan	1. Productive asset transfer 2. Training 3. Subsistence allowance 4. Coaching visits/ livestock specialist visits	Banerjee et al. (2011)	—	Income, consumption, assets, overall health
	Financial literacy and business skills	Nongovernment-led	Financial inclusion	SEWA Bank	1. Financial literacy (self-help group, SHG) 2. Business skills training	Field, Jayachandran, and Pande (20ˈ0)	—	Income, savings

(Table continues next page)

TABLE B.1 Reviewed Programs and Evaluative Studies (Quantitative Evaluations Only) (*continued*)

Country	Program	Government/NGO	Entry point	Lead implementing agency	Program components	Study	Total cost, where available (2011 US$, PPP)	Outcomes of interest analyzed (broadly defined)[a]
India (*Continued*)	SHG program	Nongovernment-led	Livelihoods and jobs	SEWA Bank	1. SHG 2. Microcredit 3. Training	Desai, Joshi, and Olofsgård (2016)	—	Income, savings
	National Rural Livelihoods Mission (NRLM)—Orissa	Government-led	Livelihoods and jobs	State government, Orissa	1. SHG 2. Microcredit 3. Training	Swain and Varghese (2014)	—	Income, assets
						Mishra (2018)	—	Employment
	Jeevika (NRLM—Bihar)	Government-led	Livelihoods and jobs	State government, Bihar	1. SHG 2. Microcredit 3. Training	Hoffman et al. (2017)	—	Consumption, assets, savings, empowerment
	NRLM (all India)	Government-led	Livelihoods and jobs	National	1. SHG 2. Microcredit 3. Training	Kochar et al. (2020)	—	Income, consumption, savings, assets, empowerment
	NRLM—Tamil Nadu	Government-led	Livelihoods and jobs	State government, Tamil Nadu	1. SHG 2. Microcredit 3. Training	Khanna, Kochhar, and Palaniswamy (2013)	—	Consumption, assets, empowerment
	Targeting the Ultra Poor	Nongovernment-led	Livelihoods and jobs	Trickle Up	1. Savings 2. Skills training 3. Grant transfer 4. Coaching/mentoring 5. Consumption support 6. Health promotion	Siahpush, Sanson, and Bombyk (2015)	—	Income, assets, savings, empowerment
Kenya	Rural Entrepreneur Access Program (REAP)	Nongovernment-led	Livelihoods and jobs	BOMA Project	1. Skills training 2. Coaching 3. Cash grants 4. Savings group	Gobin, Santos, and Toth (2016)	$274	Income, consumption, assets, savings
	Program for Rural Outreach of Financial Innovations and Technologies (PROFIT)	Nongovernment-led	Livelihoods and jobs	BOMA Project and CARE International Kenya	1. Consumption support 2. Savings support 3. Asset transfer 4. Skills training 5. Coaching 6. Health support	Sanders and Kimani (2019)	—	Income, assets, savings, empowerment, overall health, education
	Hunger Safety Net Program (HSNP); index-based livestock insurance (IBLI)	Government-led	Complementary	Government	1. Unconditional cash transfer 2. Livestock insurance	Jensen, Barrett, and Mude (2017)	$759	Income, assets, child health, education

(Table continues next page)

TABLE B.1 Reviewed Programs and Evaluative Studies (Quantitative Evaluations Only) (*continued*)

Country	Program	Government/NGO	Entry point	Lead implementing agency	Program components	Study	Total cost, where available (2011 US$, PPP)	Outcomes of interest analyzed (broadly defined)[a]
Lesotho	Child Grants Programme (CGP) and Sustainable Poverty Reduction through Income, Nutrition and Access to Government Services (SPRINGS)	Government-led	Complementary	Government	1. Unconditional cash transfer 2. Training	FAO and UNICEF (2018)	—	Income, consumption, assets, savings, education
Madagascar	FIAVOTA	Government-led	Social safety net-plus	Government	1. Unconditional cash transfer 2. Nutrition services 3. Livelihood recovery	Rakotomanana. Randrianatoancro, and Ravelosoa (2018).	—	Income, consumption, assets, employment, overall health, child health, education
Malawi	Social Cash Transfer Program (SCTP) and Farm Input Subsidy Program (FISP)	Government-led	Complementary	Government	1. Cash transfer 2. Farm input subsidy	Pace et al. (2017)	—	Income, consumption, assets
Nepal	Social Fund	Government-led	Livelihoods and jobs	Nepal Poverty Alleviation Fund (PAF)	1. Income-generating activities 2. Small-scale village and community infrastructure (INF)	Parajuli et al. (2012)	—	Consumption, child health, education
Nicaragua	Atención a Crisis +	Government-led	Social safety net-plus	Ministry of the Family, Nicaragua	1. Conditional cash transfer 2. Vocational training 3. Grants 4. Skills training	Macours, Premand, and Vakis (2012)	—	Income, consumption, assets, employment
						Macours, Schady, and Vakis (2012)	—	Overall health, education
Pakistan	CGAP–Ford Foundation graduation pilot	Nongovernment-led	Livelihoods and jobs	Pakistan Poverty Alleviation Fund (PPAF)	1. Productive asset transfer 2. Skills training 3. Coaching 4. Consumption support 5. Access to savings accounts 6. Health information or services	Banerjee et al. (2015)	$4,067	Income, consumption, assets, savings, well-being, empowerment, overall health
	PPAF Asset Transfer Program	Government-led	Livelihoods and jobs	PPAF	1. Productive asset transfer 2. Unconditional cash transfer	Rasul and Khan (2012)	—	Income, consumption, assets, savings, employment

(Table continues next page)

TABLE B.1 Reviewed Programs and Evaluative Studies (Quantitative Evaluations Only) (continued)

Country	Program	Government/NGO	Entry point	Lead implementing agency	Program components	Study	Total cost, where available (2011 US$, PPP)	Outcomes of interest analyzed (broadly defined)[a]
Papua New Guinea	Urban Youth Employment Program (UYEP)	Government-led	Social safety net-plus	Government	1. PWP 2. Training	Hoy and Naidoo (2019)	—	Employment
Paraguay	Sembrando Oportunidades Familia por Familia	Government-led	Livelihoods and jobs	Government	1. Productive asset transfer 2. Consumption support 3. Skills training 4. Access to savings accounts 5. Coaching	Maldonado et al. (2019)	—	Income, consumption, assets, savings, empowerment
Peru	CGAP–Ford Foundation graduation pilot	Nongovernment-led	Livelihoods and jobs	Asociación Arariwa and Plan International	1. Productive asset transfer 2. Skills training 3. Coaching 4. Consumption support 5. Access to savings accounts 6. Health information or services	Banerjee et al. (2015)	$34,508	Income, consumption, assets, savings, well-being, empowerment, overall health
	Juntos and Sierra Sur	Government-led	Complementary	Government	1. Consumption support 2. Agricultural credit access	Aldana, Vásquez, and Yancari (2016); Loayza (2014)	—	Assets
	Business training program	Nongovernment-led	Financial inclusion	FINCA	1. Business training 2. Technical assistance	Valdivia (2011)	—	Income, employment, empowerment
	Haku Wiñay/Juntos	Government-led	Complementary	Government	1. Skills training 2. Business grants 3. Conditional cash transfer 4. Savings	Escobal and Ponce (2016)	—	Income, consumption, assets, savings
Philippines	Kabuhayan Para sa Magulang ng Batang Manggagawa (KASAMA)	Government-led	Livelihoods and jobs	Government	1. Productive asset transfer 2. Training	Edmonds and Theoharides (2019)	—	Income, child health, education

(Table continues next page)

TABLE B.1 Reviewed Programs and Evaluative Studies (Quantitative Evaluations Only) (*continued*)

Country	Program	Government/NGO	Entry point	Lead implementing agency	Program components	Study	Total cost, where available (2011 US$, PPP)	Outcomes of interest analyzed (broadly defined)[a]
Rwanda	Grinika	Government-led	Livelihoods and jobs	Government	1. Productive asset transfer 2. Training	Argent, Augsburg, and Rasul (2014)	—	Income, assets
	Vision 2020 Umurenge Programme (VUP 2020)	Government-led	Social safety net–plus	Government	1. Public works 2. Consumption support 3. Financial services	Hartwig (2013)	—	Consumption, assets
	Graduation program	Nongovernment-led	Livelihoods and jobs	Concern Worldwide	1. Consumption support 2. Productive asset transfer 3. Savings 4. Skills training 5. Coaching	Martin and Swatton (2015)	—	Consumption, assets, savings, education
						Devereaux and Sabates (2016)	—	Consumption, assets
	Village Model	Nongovernment-led	Livelihoods and jobs	FXB	1. Grants 2. Skills training 3. Coaching 4. Food supplements 5. Health awareness	Harhay et al. (2016)	—	Assets, child health, education
South Sudan	Targeting the Ultra Poor	Nongovernment-led	Livelihoods and jobs	BRAC	1. Productive asset transfer 2. Skills training	Chowdhury et al. (2017)	—	Income, consumption, assets, savings
	Youth Business Start-Up Grant Program	Government-led	Livelihoods and jobs	Government	1. Skills training 2. Grants	Müller, Pape, and Ralston (2019)	—	Consumption, savings, well-being
Sri Lanka	Start-and-Improve Your Business (SIYB) program	Nongovernment-led	Livelihoods and jobs	International Labour Organization (ILO)	1. Business training 2. Grants	de Mel, McKenzie, and Woodruff (2014)	—	Income, employment
	Samurdhi	Government-led	Social safety net–plus	Government	1. Consumption support 2. Social insurance	Himaz (2008)	—	Child health
Tanzania	Empowerment and Livelihoods for Adolescent Girls (ELA) Programme	Nongovernment-led	Livelihoods and jobs	BRAC	1. Adolescent development centers 2. Life skills training 3. Livelihood training 4. Meetings with parents and village elders 5. Microfinance	Buehren et al. (2017)	—	Income, savings
	Tanzania Social Action Fund (TASAF)	Government-led	Social safety net–plus	Government	1. Conditional cash transfer 2. Community awareness	Evans, Holtemeyer, and Kosec. (2019)	—	Savings, overall health
						Rosas et al. (2019)	—	Consumption, savings, employment, overall health, education

(Table continues next page)

TABLE B.1 Reviewed Programs and Evaluative Studies (Quantitative Evaluations Only) (continued)

Country	Program	Government/NGO	Entry point	Lead implementing agency	Program components	Study	Total cost, where available (2011 US$, PPP)	Outcomes of interest analyzed (broadly defined)[a]
Uganda	Women's Income Generating Support (WINGS)	Nongovernment-led	Livelihoods and jobs	AVSI Foundation	1. Basic skills training 2. Cash grants 3. Supervision 4. Group formation	Blattman et al. (2016)	$1,061	Income, consumption, assets, savings, employment, empowerment, overall health
	Village Enterprise's Microenterprise program	Nongovernment-led	Livelihoods and jobs	Village Enterprise	1. Training 2. Mentorship 3. Microenterprise administration 4. Village-level savings groups 5. Cash grants	Sedlmayr, Shah, and Sulaiman (2018)	$172	Income, consumption, assets
	Empowerment and Livelihoods for Adolescent Girls (ELA)	Nongovernment-led	Livelihoods and jobs	BRAC	1. "Hard" vocational skills training; 2. "Soft" life skills training 3. A safe space to meet and socialize with other adolescent girls	Bandiera et al. (2020)	$25	Income, empowerment, overall health, education
	Youth Opportunities Program (YOP)	Government-led	Livelihoods and jobs	Government	1. Cash grants 2. Training	Blattman, Fiala, and Martinez (2014, 2018)	—	Income, assets, employment
	Asset Africa Program (Pilot)	Nongovernment-led	Financial inclusion	Local NGO	1. Conditional matching grants 2. Training	Chowa and Elliot (2011)	—	Income
	Village Model	Nongovernment-led	Livelihoods and jobs	FXB	1. Grants 2. Skills training 3. Coaching 4. Food supplements 5. Health awareness	Harhay et al. (2016)	—	Assets, child health, education
	Youth Livelihood Program (YLP)	Government-led	Livelihoods and jobs	Government	1. Credit/loan 2. Training	Bukenya et al. (2019)	—	Income, assets
Vietnam	Gender and business training	Nongovernment-led	Financial inclusion	TYM	1. Gender and business training 2. Microfinance	Vu et al. (2015)	—	Income, empowerment

Sources: Partnership for Economic Inclusion, World Bank, and the publications listed in the table.

Note: — = not available; NGO = nongovernmental organization.

a. Outcomes of interest reported in the last column are broad categories to cover a range of indicators and indexes. The review examined all indicators associated with a broad outcome category (as reported in the table) and recorded the effect size and significance levels of specific indicators. Selected key indicators within the broad outcome categories include the following in this indicative, not exhaustive, list: (1) income and revenue: monthly total household income, average monthly household income, monthly individual income, per capita annual income, total earnings, log household income, household livestock revenue, agricultural income, monthly cash earnings, sales last month; (2) consumption: consumption per capita, per capita daily food expenditure, monthly expenditure on food, total food consumption, log total consumption per capita, total consumption index; (3) assets: value of livestock, total value of household assets, value of productive asset, asset value index, total land owned, durable assets index, overall asset index, total asset holdings; (4) savings: total household savings, cash savings, proportion of households having cash savings, total saving stock, financial inclusion index, probability of savings, log savings; (5) employment: self-employment in agriculture, daily working hours, wage labor, total minutes spent on productive activities in the last day, livelihood security index, hours worked per week, business ownership, labor supply; (6) psychosocial well-being: psychological well-being index, Kessler score, stress index, self-reported happiness, member has not experienced a period of worry in last year; (7) women empowerment: z-score index measuring women's decision-making in the household, woman has major say on how to manage household finances, empowerment scale, business decision-making, autonomy in purchases (z score); (8) child health: diarrhea rate in oldest under-5 child last two weeks, weight for height (whz), height for age, wasting, child dietary diversity score, child well-being index, child immunization card up to date; (9) overall health: HIV knowledge [0–6 score], physical health index (z-score), member has not missed any days due to illness last month, overall health, self-reported health status, health knowledge and behavior index; and (10) child education: proportion of children enrolled in school, school absenteeism, child schooling index, school attendance reported, currently enrolled in school, primary enrollment rate.

FIGURE B.1 Percentage of Programs with Ongoing Impact Evaluations

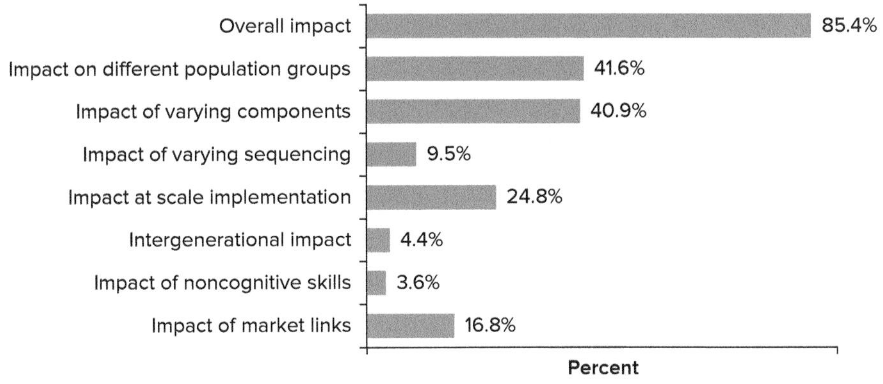

Source: PEI Landscape Survey 2020.
Note: Figure shows percentage of programs planning to conduct an impact evaluation study (N = 137).

Notes

1. Examples are the 3ie Evidence Hub (https://developmentevidence.3ieimpact.org/);
   Innovations for Poverty Action (IPA, https://www.poverty-action.org/research);
   UNICEF evaluation database (https://www.unicef.org/evaldatabase/); Campbell Library
   (https://campbellcollaboration.org/better-evidence); and Africa Agriculture for Impact
   (https://ag4impact.org/sid/socio-economic-intensification/building-human-capital
   /agricultural-extension/).
2. Examples are the Consultative Group to Assist the Poor (CGAP), Ford Foundation,
   International Fund for Agricultural Development (IFAD), Food and Agriculture Organization
   (FAO), BRAC, Institute of Development Studies (IDS), Concern Worldwide, Save the Children,
   Transfer Project, and World Bank.
3. BRAC is an international nongovernmental organization with headquarters in Bangladesh.

Bibliography

Quantitative impact evaluations

Livelihoods and jobs

Ahmed, A. U., M. Rabanni, M. Sulaiman, and N. C. Das. 2009. "The Impact of Asset
    Transfer on Livelihoods of the Ultra Poor in Bangladesh." Research Monograph
    Series No. 39, Research and Evaluation Division, BRAC, Dhaka.

Almeida, Rita K., and Emanuela Galasso. 2010. "Jump-starting Self-employment?
    Evidence for Welfare Participants in Argentina." *World Development* 38 (5): 742–55.
    https://doi.org/10.1016/j.worlddev.2009.11.018.

Ara, J., N. Das, M. Kamruzzaman, and T. Quayyum. 2017. "Walking on Two Legs:
    Credit Plus Grant Approach to Poverty Reduction." CFPR Working Paper No. 25,
    Research and Evaluation Division, BRAC, Dhaka.

Arévalo, I., M. Kaffenberger, and Aude de Montesquiou. 2018. *2018 State of the Sector
    Synthesis Report.* Washington, DC: Partnership for Economic Inclusion (PEI),
    November.

Argent, J., B. Augsburg, and I. Rasul. 2014. "Livestock Asset Transfers with and without
    Training: Evidence from Rwanda." *Journal of Economic Behavior and Organization*
    108: 19–39.

Asadullah, M. Niaz, and Jinnat Ara. 2016. "Evaluating the Long-Run Impact of an Innovative Anti-Poverty Program: Evidence Using Household Panel Data." IZA Discussion Paper No. 9749, Institute of Labor Economics (IZA), Bonn.

Bandiera, Oriana, Niklas Buehren, Robin Burgess, Markus Goldstein, Selim Gulesci, Imran Rasul, and Munshi Sulaiman. 2020. "Women's Empowerment in Action: Evidence from a Randomized Control Trial in Africa." *American Economic Journal: Applied Economics* 12 (1): 210–59.

Bandiera, Oriana, Robin Burgess, Narayan Das, Selim Gulesci, Imran Rasul, and Munshi Sulaiman. 2017. "Labor Markets and Poverty in Village Economies." *Quarterly Journal of Economics* 132 (2): 811–70.

Bandiera, Oriana, Robin Burgess, S. Gulesci, I. Rasul, and Munshi Sulaiman. 2013. "Can Entrepreneurship Programs Transform the Economic Lives of the Poor?" IZA Discussion Paper No. 7386, Institute of Labor Economics (IZA), Bonn.

Banerjee, A., E. Duflo, R. Chattopadhyay, and J. Shapiro. 2011. "Targeting the Hard-Core Poor: An Impact Assessment." https://citeseerx.ist.psu.edu/viewdoc /download?doi = 10.1.1.592.1599&rep = rep1&type = pdf.

Banerjee, A., E. Duflo, R. Chattopadhyay, and J. Shapiro. 2016. "The Long Term Impacts of a 'Graduation' Program: Evidence from West Bengal." Working paper, Abdul Latif Jameel Poverty Action Lab (J-PAL), Cambridge, MA. https://www .povertyactionlab.org/evaluation/graduating-ultra-poor-india.

Banerjee, A., E. Duflo, N. Goldberg, D. Karlan, R. Osei, W. Parienté, J. Shapiro, et al. 2015. "A Multifaceted Program Causes Lasting Progress for the Very Poor: Evidence from Six Countries." *Science* 348: 1260799.

Banerjee, A., D. Karlan, R. D. Osei, H. Trachtman, and C. Udry. 2018. "Unpacking a Multi-faceted Program to Build Sustainable Income for the Very Poor." NBER Working Paper 247271, National Bureau of Economic Research (NBER), Cambridge, MA.

Bauchet, J., J. Morduch, and S. Ravi. 2015. "Failure vs. Displacement: Why an Innovative Anti-poverty Program Showed No Net Impact in South India." *Journal of Development Economics* 116: 1–16.

BDI (BRAC Development Institute). 2012. "WFP Food Security for the Ultra Poor (FSUP)—Outcome Survey Report." Unpublished paper, BDI, Dhaka.

Bedoya, G., A. Coville, J. Haushofer, M. Isaqzadeh, and J. Shapiro. 2019. "No Household Left Behind: Afghanistan Targeting the Ultra Poor Impact Evaluation." Policy Research Working Paper 8877, World Bank, Washington, DC.

Blattman, Christopher, Stefan Dercon, and Simon Franklin. 2019. "Impacts of Industrial and Entrepreneurial Jobs on Youth: 5-year Experimental Evidence on Factory Job Offers and Cash Grants in Ethiopia." Working Paper No. 2019-65, University of Chicago.

Blattman, Christopher, Nathan Fiala, and Sebastian Martinez. 2014. "Generating Skilled Self-Employment in Developing Countries: Experimental Evidence from Uganda." *Quarterly Journal of Economics* 129: 697–752. doi:10.1093/qje/qjt057.

Blattman, Christopher, Nathan Fiala, and Sebastian Martinez. 2018. "The Long Term Impacts of Grants on Poverty: 9-Year Evidence from Uganda's Youth Opportunities Program." NBER Working Paper 24999, National Bureau of Economic Research (NBER), Cambridge, MA.

Blattman, Christopher, Eric P. Green, Julian Jamison, M. Christian Lehmann, and Jeannie Annan. 2016. "The Returns to Microenterprise Support among the Ultrapoor: A Field Experiment in Postwar Uganda." *American Economic Journal: Applied Economics* 8 (2): 35–64.

Bukenya, Badru, Saint Kizito Omala, Rogers Kasirye, and Jeanne Miranda. 2019. "Do Revolving Funds Generate Self-Employment and Increase Incomes for the

Poor? Experimental Evidence from Uganda's Youth Livelihood Programme."
3ie Grantee Final Report, International Initiative for Impact Evaluation (3ie),
New Delhi.

Burns, J., and S. Bogale. 2011. "Linking Poor Rural Households to Microfinance
and Markets in Ethiopia; Final Assessment of the PSNP Plus Project in Sekota."
Feinstein International Center, Medford, MA. https://fic.tufts.edu/publication
-item/impact-assessment-of-honey-microfinance-and-livestock-value-chain
-interventions/.

Chowa, Gina A. N., and William Elliott. 2011. "An Asset Approach to Increasing
Perceived Household Economic Stability among Families in Uganda." *Journal of
Socio-Economics* 40 (1): 81–87. https://doi.org/10.1016/j.socec.2010.02.008.

Chowdhury, Reajul, Elliott Collins, Ethan Ligon, and Munshi Sulaiman. 2017. "Valuing
Assets Provided to Low-Income Households in South Sudan." Unpublished paper.
https://static1.squarespace.com/static/58f90dbdb3db2be88860ccdc/t/5a8e67f18165
f569cb07a793/1519282162445/TUP_BRAC_SouthSudan.pdf.

Das, Narayan C., Sibbir Ahmad, Anindita Bhattacharjee, Jinnat Ara, and Abdul Bayes.
2016. "Grant vs. Credit Plus Approach to Poverty Reduction: An Evaluation of
BRAC's Experience with Ultra Poor." CFPR Working Paper No. 24, Research and
Evaluation Division, BRAC, Dhaka.

Deininger, Klaus, and Yanyan Liu. 2013. "Economic and Social Impacts of an Innovative
Self-Help Group Model in India." *World Development* 43: 149–63. doi:10.1016/j
.worlddev.2012.09.019.

de Mel, S., D. McKenzie, and C. Woodruff. 2014. "Business Training and Female
Enterprise Start-Up, Growth, and Dynamics: Experimental Evidence from
Sri Lanka." *Journal of Development Economics* 106 (C): 199–210.

Desai, Raj M., Shareen Joshi, and Anders Olofsgård. 2016. "Can the Poor Be Mobilized?
Cooperation and Public Goods in Rural India." SITE Working Paper Series 40,
Stockholm School of Economics, Stockholm Institute of Transition Economics
(SITE).

Devereux, Stephen, Keetie Roelen, Ricardo Sabates, Dimitri Stoelinga, and Arnaud
Dyevre. 2015. "Final Evaluation Report: Concern's Graduation Model Program in
Burundi." Brighton: Institute of Development Studies.

Devereux, Stephen, and Ricardo Sabates. 2016. "Final Evaluation Report: Enhancing the
Productive Capacity of Extremely Poor People in Rwanda." Concern Worldwide and
Institute of Development Studies (IDS).

Edmonds, Eric, and Caroline Theoharides. 2019. "The Short Term Impact of a
Productive Asset Transfer in Families with Child Labor: Experimental Evidence
from the Philippines." NBER Working Paper 26190, National Bureau of Economic
Research (NBER), Cambridge, MA.

Emran, M. S., V. Robano, and S. C. Smith. 2014. "Assessing the Frontiers of
Ultrapoverty Reduction: Evidence from Challenging the Frontiers of Poverty
Reduction/Targeting the Ultrapoor, An Innovative Program in Bangladesh."
Economic Development and Cultural Change 62 (2): 339–80.

Field, Erica, Seema Jayachandran, and Rohini Pande. 2010. "Do Traditional Institutions
Constrain Female Entrepreneurship? A Field Experiment on Business Training in
India." *American Economic Review Papers and Proceedings* 100 (2): 125–29.

Gobin, Vilas J., Paulo Santos, and Russell Toth. 2016. "Poverty Graduation with
Cash Transfers: A Randomized Evaluation." Monash University Department of
Economics Discussion Paper No. 23/16.

Harhay, Michael O., Mary C. Smith Fawzi, Sacha Jeanneret, Damasce`ne Ndayisaba,
William Kibaalya, Emily A. Harrison, and Dylan S. Small. 2016. "An Assessment of
the Francois-Xavier Bagnoud Poverty Alleviation Program in Rwanda and Uganda."
International Journal of Public Health 62 (1): 241–52.

Hartwig, Renate. 2013. "Short-Term Welfare Effects of Rwanda's Vision 2020 Umurenge Programme." Unpublished paper, International Institute of Social Studies, Erasmus University, Rotterdam.

Hernandez, R., A. U. Ahmed, A. Akter, N. Z. Hossain, S. Choudhury, and M. Malek. 2016. "An Evaluation of the Program on Enhancing Resilience to Natural Disasters and the Effects of Climate Change in Bangladesh." International Food Policy Research Institute (IFPRI), Dhaka.

Hoffmann, Vivian, Vijayendra Rao, Upamanyu Datta, Paromita Sanyal, Vaishnavi Surendra, and Shruti Majumdar. 2018. *Poverty and Empowerment Impacts of the Bihar Rural Livelihoods Project in India.* New Delhi: International Initiative for Impact Evaluation (3ie).

Hoffmann, Vivian, Vijayendra Rao, Vaishnavi Surendra, and Upamanyu Datta. 2017. "Relief from Usury: Impact of a Community-Based Microcredit Program in Rural India." Policy Research Working Paper 8021, World Bank, Washington, DC.

HTSPE. 2011. "Bangladesh: Independent Impact Assessment of the Chars Livelihoods Programme—Phase 1." Final report prepared for UK Department for International Development. HTSPE Limited in association with Verulam Associates.

IRC (Indochina Research and Consulting). 2012. "Impact of Program 135—Phase II through the Lens of Baseline and Endline Surveys." Phnom Penh, Cambodia.

Ismayilova, L., and L. Karimli. 2018. "Harsh Parenting and Violence against Children: A Trial with Ultra-Poor Families in Francophone West Africa." *Journal of Clinical Child and Adolescent Psychology* 53: 1–18.

Ismayilova, L., L. Karimli, J. Sanson, E. Gaveras, R. Nanema, A. Tô-Camier, and J. Chaffin. 2018. "Improving Mental Health among Ultra-Poor Children: Two-Year Outcomes of a Cluster-Randomized Trial in Burkina Faso." *Social Science and Medicine* 208: 180–89.

Karimli, L., B. Bose, and N. Kagotho. 2019. "Integrated Graduation Program and Its Effect on Women and Household Economic Well-being: Findings from a Randomised Controlled Trial in Burkina Faso." *Journal of Development Studies* 56 (7): 1–18.

Karimli, L., L. Rost, and L. Ismayilova. 2018. "Integrating Economic Strengthening and Family Coaching to Reduce Work-Related Health Hazards among Children of Poor Households: Burkina Faso." *Journal of Adolescent Health* 62 (1): S6–S14.

Khanna, Madhulika, Nishtha Kochhar, and Nethra Palaniswamy. 2013. *A Retrospective Impact Evaluation of the Tamil Nadu Empowerment and Poverty Alleviation (Pudhu Vaazhvu) Project.* World Bank and Pudhu Vaazhvu Project, Washington, DC.

Kochar, Anjini, Bidisha Barooah, Chandan Jain, Geeta Singh, Nagabhushana Closepet, Raghunathan Narayanan, Ritwik Sarkar, and Rohan Shah. 2020. "Impact Evaluation of the National Rural Livelihoods Project." Impact Evaluation Report 128. New Delhi: International Initiative for Impact Evaluation (3ie).

Krishna, Anirudh, Meri Poghosyan, and Narayan Das. 2012. "How Much Can Asset Transfers Help the Poorest? Evaluating the Results of BRAC's Ultra-poor Programme (2002–2008)." *Journal of Development Studies* 48: 254–67. doi: 10.1080/00220388.2011.621942.

Loayza, Cesar del Pozo. 2014. "Conditional Cash Transfers, Agricultural Credit and the Accumulation of Productive Assets of Rural Households in Peru." https://www.cbc.org.pe/2020/06/08/transferencias-monetarias-condicionadas-credito-agropecuario-y-la-acumulacion-de-activos-productivos-de-los-hogares-rurales-en-el-peru/.

Martin, Rosaleen, and Jenny Swatton. 2015. "Final Evaluation of the 'Unleashing the Productive Capacity of the Extreme Poor' Graduation Programme, Rwanda, 2002–2015." Concern Worldwide.

Misha, Farzana, Wameq Raza, J. Ara, and E. Poel. 2019. "How Far Does a Big Push Really Push? Long-term Effects of an Asset Transfer Program on Employment

Trajectories." *Economic Development and Cultural Change* 68 (1): 41–62. doi: 10.1086/700556.

Mishra, Abhisek. 2018. "Impact of National Rural Livelihood Mission on Livelihood Security of Rural Poor—Propensity Score Matching Approach." *SSRN Electronic Journal.* doi:10.2139/ssrn.3279277.

Mourelo, Elva López, and Verónica Escudero. 2016. "Effectiveness of Active Labour Market Tools in Conditional Cash Transfers Programmes: Evidence for Argentina." Working Paper No. 11, Research Department, International Labour Office, Geneva.

Müller, Angelika, Utz Pape, and Laura Ralston. 2019. "Broken Promises: Evaluating an Incomplete Cash Transfer Program." Working Paper No. 223, Poverty and Equity Global Practice, World Bank, Washington, DC.

Noble, Eva, and Hanna Han. 2019. "Impact Evaluation of Holistic Women's Empowerment Program on Women's Agency, Decision-Making and Economic Empowerment: Baseline Research Brief." Women for Women International, South Kivu, Democratic Republic of Congo.

Parajuli, Dilip, Gayatri Acharya, Nazmul Chaudhury, and Bishnu Bahadur Thapa. 2012. "Impact of Social Fund on the Welfare of Rural Households: Evidence from the Nepal Poverty Alleviation Fund." Policy Research Working Paper 6042, World Bank, Washington, DC.

Premand, Patrick, and Alicia Marguerie. 2020. *Résultats de l'Evaluation d'Impact du Projet d'Insertion Socio-Economique pour les populations vulnérables de l'Ouest de Côte d'Ivoire (PRISE)* [Results of the impact assessment of the Socio-Economic Integration Project for the vulnerable populations of western Côte d'Ivoire (PRISE)]. Abidjan: World Bank.

Prennushi, G., and A. Gupta. 2014. "Impacts of Andhra Pradesh Rural Poverty Reduction Program." Policy Research Working Paper 6841, World Bank, Washington, DC.

Rasul, Imran, and Adnan Khan. 2012. "Preliminary Findings: A Brief Two-Year Impact Report. Pakistan Asset Transfer Program." Centre for Economic Research in Pakistan (CERP)—Pakistan Poverty Alleviation Fund, Islamabad.

Raza, W. A., and J. Ara. 2012. "Grant Based Approach to Poverty Reduction: Evidence from Bangladesh." *OIDA International Journal of Sustainable Development* 3 (6): 37–54.

Raza, W. A., N. Das, and F. A. Misha. 2012. "Can Ultra Poverty Be Sustainably Improved? Evidence from BRAC in Bangladesh." *Journal of Development Effectiveness* 4 (2): 257–76.

Raza, Wameq A., and Ellen Van de Poel. 2016. "Impact and Spillover Effects of an Asset Transfer Programme on Malnutrition: Evidence from a Randomised Control Trial in Bangladesh." Research Monograph Series No. 64, BRAC, Dhaka.

Raza, Wameq A., Ellen Van de Poel, and Tom van Ourti. 2018. "Impact and Spillover Effects of an Asset Transfer Programme on Malnutrition: Evidence from a Randomised Control Trial in Bangladesh." *Journal of Health Economics* 62: 105–20.

Rémy, Sibomana. 2018. "Rapport final de l'évaluation d'impact des programmes Village FXB au Burundi." Fondation Roi Baudouin.

Roelen, K., and S. Devereux. 2018. "Money and the Message: The Role of Training and Coaching in Graduation Programming." *Journal of Development Studies* 55 (6): 1121–39.

Roelen, Keetie, and Amrita Saha. 2019. "Fonkoze's CLM Ultra Poverty Programme: Understanding and Improving Child Development and Child Wellbeing. Endline Report." Institute of Development Studies, University of Sussex, Brighton, U.K.

Sagara, Brad, and Dan Hudner. 2017. "Enhancing Resilience to Severe Drought: What Works? Evidence from Mercy Corps' PRIME Program in the Somali Region of Ethiopia." Mercy Corps.

Sanders, Catherine, and Francis Kimani. 2019. "PROFIT Financial Graduation: Endline Report." International Fund for Agricultural Development (IFAD), BOMA Project, and CARE International Kenya.

Sedlmayr, Richard, Anuj Shah, and Munshi Sulaiman. 2018. "Cash-Plus: Poverty Impacts of Transfer-Based Intervention Alternatives." CSAE Working Paper WPS/2017-15-2, Centre for the Study of African Economies (CSAE), Oxford, U.K.

Siahpush, A., Jo Sanson, and Matthew Bombyk. 2015. "Pathways Out of Poverty: Findings from a Quasi-Experimental Evaluation of Trickle Up's Graduation Program in India." Trickle Up, New York.

Smith, L., T. Frankenberger, K. Fox, S. Nelson, and T. Griffin. 2019. "Ethiopia Pastoralist Areas Resilience Improvement and Market Expansion (PRIME) Project Impact Evaluation: Endline Survey Report." Resilience Evaluation, Analysis and Learning (REAL) Associate Award, Washington, DC.

Swain, Ranjula Bali, and Adel Varghese. 2014. "Evaluating the Impact of Training for a National Microfinance Program: The Case of Indian Self Help Groups." *European Journal of Development Research* 26 (5): 870–85.

Valdivia, Martín. 2011. "Training or Technical Assistance? A Field Experiment to Learn What Works to Increase Managerial Capital for Female Microentrepeneurs." Grupo de Análisis para el Desarrollo, Lima.

Vu, Nhung Thi Hong, Rosine van Velzen, Robert Lensink, and Erwin Bulte. 2015. *The Impact of Gender and Business Training for Female Microfinance Clients in Vietnam. 3ie Grantee Final Report.* New Delhi: International Initiative for Impact Evaluation (3ie).

Social safety net–plus

Bertrand, M., Bruno Crépon, Alicia Marguerie, and Patrick Premand. 2017. "Contemporaneous and Post-Program Impacts of a Public Works Program: Evidence from Côte d'Ivoire." Working Paper, World Bank, Washington, DC; Abdul Latif Jameel Poverty Action Lab (J-PAL), Cambridge, MA. https://www.povertyactionlab .org/evaluation/youth-employment-and-skills-development-cote-divoire.

Buehren, Niklas, Markus Goldstein, Selim Gulesci, Munshi Sulaiman, and Venus Yam. 2017. "Evaluation of an Adolescent Development Program for Girls in Tanzania." Policy Research Working Paper 7961, World Bank, Washington, DC.

Evans, David K., Brian Holtemeyer, and Katrin Kosec. 2019. "Cash Transfers and Health: Evidence from Tanzania." *World Bank Economic Review* 33 (2): 394–412.

FAO (Food and Agriculture Organization). 2016. "Les transferts productifs (CASH +) au Niger et au Burkina Faso: Une approche innovante pour renforcer les moyens d'existence vulnérables au Sahel." FAO, Rome.

FAO (Food and Agriculture Organization). 2018. "FAO and Cash + : How to Maximize the Impacts of Cash Transfers." FAO, Rome.

Himaz, R. 2008. "Welfare Grants and Their Impact on Child Health: The Case of Sri Lanka." *World Development* 36: 1843–57.

Hoy, Christopher, and Darian Naidoo. 2019. "The Marginal Benefit of an Active Labor Market Program Relative to a Public Works Program: Evidence from Papua New Guinea." *IZA Journal of Development and Migration* 10. doi:10.2478 /izajodm-2019-0003.

Macours, Karen, Patrick Premand, and Renos Vakis. 2012. "Transfers, Diversification and Household Risk Strategies—Experimental Evidence with Lessons for Climate Change Adaptation." Policy Research Working Paper 6053, World Bank, Washington, DC.

Macours, Karen, Patrick Premand, and Renos Vakis. 2013. "Demand versus Returns? Pro-Poor Targeting of Business Grants and Vocational Skills Training." Policy Research Working Paper 6389, World Bank, Washington, DC.

Macours, Karen, Norman Schady, and Renos Vakis. 2012. "Cash Transfers, Behavioral Changes, and Cognitive Development in Early Childhood: Evidence from a Randomized Experiment." *American Economic Journal: Applied Economics* 4 (2): 247–73.

Macours, Karen, and Renos Vakis. 2014. "Changing Households' Investment Behaviour through Social Interactions with Local Leaders: Evidence from a Randomised Transfer Programme." *Economic Journal* 124 (576): 607–33. doi:10.1111/ecoj.12145.

Rakotomanana, Faly, Zo Tahiana Randrianatoandro, and Julia Rachel Ravelosoa. 2018. "Mid-term Evaluation Results: The Fiavota Program. Main Report." UNICEF, New York; World Bank, Washington, DC.

Rosas, Nina, Samantha Zaldivar, Maria Julia Granata, Gaew Lertsuridej, Nicholas Wilson, Albina Chuwa, and Rainer Kiama. 2019. "Evaluating Tanzania's Productive Social Safety Net: Findings from the Midline Survey." Washington, DC: World Bank.

Complementary social safety nets and livelihoods and jobs programs

Abramovsky, Laura, Orazio Attanasioy, Kai Barronz, Pedro Carneiro, and George Stoyek. 2015. "Challenges to Promoting Social Inclusion of the Extreme Poor: Evidence from a Large Scale Experiment in Colombia." Working Paper W14/33, Institute for Fiscal Studies, London.

Aldana, U., T. Vásquez, and J. Yancari. 2016. "Sierra Sur and Juntos: An Analysis Based on the Joint Implementation of Both Programs in Chumbivilcas, Cusco, Perú." In *Protection, Production, Promotion: Exploring Synergies between Social Protection and Productive Development in Latin America,* edited by J. H. Maldonado, R. Moreno-Sánchez, J. A. Gómez, and V. L. Jurado. Bogotá: Universidad de los Andes.

Berhane, Guush, Daniel O. Gilligan, John Hoddinott, Neha Kumar, and Alemayehu Seyoum Taffesse. 2014. "Can Social Protection Work in Africa? The Impact of Ethiopia's Productive Safety Net Programme." *Economic Development and Cultural Change* 63 (1): 1–26. doi:10.1086/677753.

Burns, John, and Solomon Bogale. 2011a. "Impact Assessment of Livestock Value Chain Interventions: Final Impact Assessment of the PSNP Plus Project in Raya Azebo." Report prepared for U.S. Agency for International Development (USAID), Washington, DC. https://fic.tufts.edu/publication-item /impact-assessment-of-livestock-value-chain-interventions/.

Burns, John, and Solomon Bogale. 2011b. "Impact Assessment of Microfinance Honey and Crop Value Chain Interventions: Final Impact Assessment of the PSNP Plus in Doba Woreda." Report prepared for U.S. Agency for International Development (USAID). https://fic.tufts.edu/publication-item /impact-assessment-of-microfinance-honey-and-crop-value-chain-interventions/.

Burns, John, and Solomon Bogale. 2011c. "Impact Assessment of Small Ruminant and Value Chain Interventions: Final Impact Assessment of the PSNP Plus Project in Dodota and Sire." Report prepared for U.S. Agency for International Development (USAID), Washington, DC. https://fic.tufts.edu/publication-item /impact-assessment-of-small-ruminant-and-value-chain-interventions/.

Burns, John, and Solomon Bogale. 2012. "Impact Assessment of Honey Microfinance and Livestock Value Chain Interventions: Final Impact Assessment of the PSNP Plus Project in Sekota." Report prepared for U.S. Agency for International Development (USAID). https://fic.tufts.edu/publication-item/impact -assessment-of-honey-microfinance-and-livestock-value-chain-interventions/.

Costa, Lorena Vieira, Steven M. Helfand, and André Portela Souza. 2018. "No Impact of Rural Development Policies? No Synergies with Conditional Cash Transfers? An Investigation of the IFAD-Supported Gavião Project in Brazil." International Fund for Agricultural Development (IFAD), Rome.

Daidone, S., B. Davis, M. Knowles, R. Pickmans, N. Pace, and S. Handa. 2017. "The Social Cash Transfer Programme and the Farm Input Subsidy Programme in Malawi: Complementary Instruments for Supporting Agricultural Transformation and Increasing Consumption and Productive Activities?" Food and Agriculture Organization (FAO), Rome.

de Sanfeliú, Margarita Beneke, Amy Ángel, and Mauricio Arturo Shi. 2016. "Conditional Cash Transfer Programs and Rural Development in El Salvador." In *Protection, Production, Promotion: Exploring Synergies between Social Protection and Productive Development in Latin America,* edited by J. H. Maldonado, R. Moreno-Sánchez, J. A. Gómez, and V. L. Jurado. Bogotá: Universidad de los Andes.

Dewbre, Josh, Silvio Daidone, Benjamin Davis, Borja Miguelez, Ousmane Niang, and Luca Pellerano. 2015. "Lesotho Child Grant Programme and Linking Food Security to Social Protection Programme: A From Protection to Production Report." Food and Agriculture Organization (FAO), Rome.

Escobal, Javier, and Carmen Ponce, eds. 2016. "Combinando protección social con generación de oportunidades económicas: Una evaluación de los avances del programa Haku Wiñay" [Combining social protection with economic opportunities generation: an evaluation of the progress of the Haku Wiñay Program]. Grupo de Análisis para el Desarrollo (GRADE), Lima.

FAO (Food and Agriculture Organization) and UNICEF (United Children's Fund). 2018. "Impact Evaluation of Lesotho's Child Grants Programme (CGP) and Sustainable Poverty Reduction through Income, Nutrition and Access to Government Services (SPRINGS) Project." FAO, Rome.

Fernández, Maria Ignacia, Maria Fernanda Leiva, Jorge Ortega, and Macarena Weason. 2016. "Synergistic Effects between Ingreso Ético Familiar and the Enterprise Support Programs in Chile, 2012–2014." In *Protection, Production, Promotion: Exploring Synergies between Social Protection and Productive Development in Latin America,* edited by J. H. Maldonado, R. Moreno-Sánchez, J. A. Gómez, and V. L. Jurado. Bogotá: Universidad de los Andes.

Garcia, F., S. M. Helfand, and A. P. Souza. 2016. "Transferencias monetarias condicionadas y políticas de desarrollo rural em Brasil: Posibles sinergias entre Bolsa Família y el Pronaf" [Conditional cash transfers and rural development policies in Brazil: possible synergies between Bolsa Família and Pronaf.] In *Protección, producción, promoción: Explorando sinergias entre protección social y fomento productivo rural en América Latina* [Protection, production, promotion: exploring synergies between social protection and productive development in Latin America], edited by J. H. Maldonado, R. Moreno-Sánchez, J. A. Gómez, and V. L. Jurado. Bogotá: Universidad de los Andes.

Gilligan, D. O., J. Hoddinott, and A. S. Tafesse. 2009. "The Impact of Ethiopia's Productive Safety Net Programme and Its Linkages." *Journal of Development Studies* 45 (10): 1684–706.

Hoddinott, John, Guush Berhane, Daniel O. Gilligan, Neha Kumar, and Alemayehu Seyoum Taffesse. 2012. "The Impact of Ethiopia's Productive Safety Net Programme and Related Transfers on Agricultural Productivity." *Journal of African Economies* 21 (5): 761–86.

Jensen, Nathaniel D., Christopher B. Barrett, and Andrew G. Mude. 2017. "Cash Transfers and Index Insurance: A Comparative Impact Analysis from Northern Kenya." *Journal of Development Economics* 129: 14–18. https://doi.org/10.1016/j.jdeveco.2017.08.002.

Maldonado, Jorge H., Viviana Leon-Jurado, John Gomez, Daniel Rodriguez, and Laura I. Villa. 2019. "The Graduation Approach for the Reduction of Extreme Poverty: Impact Evaluation of Sembrando Oportunidades Familia Por Familia in Paraguay." Documento CEDE No. 2019-19, Center for Studies on Economic Development (CEDE), Universidad de los Andes. http://dx.doi.org/10.2139/ssrn.3411131.

Moya, A. 2016. "Programas para la reducción de la pobreza rural en Colombia: Uma evaluación de las sinergias entre Oportunidades Rurales e Familias em Acción" [Programs for the reduction of rural poverty in Colombia: an evaluation of the synergies between rural opportunities and families in action]. In *Protección, producción, promoción: Explorando sinergias entre protección social y fomento productivo rural en América Latina* [Protection, production, promotion: exploring synergies between social protection and productive development in Latin America], edited by J. H. Maldonado, R. Moreno-Sánchez, J. A. Gómez, and V. L. Jurado. Bogotá: Universidad de los Andes.

Pace, N., S. Daidone, B. Davis, S. Handa, M. Knowles, and R. Pickmans. 2017. "One Plus One Can Be Greater than Two: Evaluating Synergies of Development Programmes in Malawi." *Journal of Development Studies* 54 (11): 2023–60. doi:10.1080/00220388.2017.1380794.

Sabates-Wheeler, R., and S. Devereux. 2010. "Cash Transfers and High Food Prices: Explaining Outcomes in Ethiopia's Productive Safety Net Programme." *Food Policy* 35 (4): 274–85.

Yúnez-Naude, Antonio, George Dyer-Leal, Fabiola Rivera-Ramírez, and Omar Stabridis-Arana. 2016. "The Fight against Poverty Program and Rural Development Policies in Mexico: Impact Assessments and Alternative Policies." In *Protection, Production, Promotion: Exploring Synergies between Social Protection and Productive Development in Latin America*, edited by J. H. Maldonado, R. Moreno-Sánchez, J. A. Gómez, and V. L. Jurado. Bogotá: Universidad de los Andes.

Qualitative impact evaluations

Livelihoods and jobs programs

Rocío Moreno-Sánchez, Jorge H. Maldonado, Vanesa Martínez, and Arturo Rodríguez. 2018. "Qualitative Evaluation of the Poverty-Alleviation Program Produciendo por mi Futuro in Colombia." Working Paper No. 24, Center for Studies on Economic Development (CEDE), Universidad de los Andes, Bogotá.

Social safety net–plus

Absolute Options. 2016. "Kore Lavi Haiti: Midterm Evaluation." Report prepared for CARE and U.S. Agency for International Development (USAID). https://www.careevaluations.org/wp-content/uploads/Kore-Lavi-MTE-Report-04-12-16.pdf and https://pdf.usaid.gov/pdf_docs/PA00M5HG.pdf.

Gahamanyi, Vincent, and Andrew Kettlewell. 2015. "Evaluating Graduation: Insights from the Vision 2020 Umurenge Programme in Rwanda." *IDS Bulletin* 46 (2).

ICF (International Community Foundation). 2018. "Final Performance Evaluation of the Food for Peace PAISANO Development Food Assistance Project in Guatemala." U.S. Agency for International Development (USAID), Washington, DC.

Qualitative (nonevaluative) research

The following qualitative research (in addition to the impact evaluations just cited) was used to unpack evidence on bundling of interventions and heterogeneity and to identify drivers of impact.

Acosta, P., and J. Avalos. 2018. "The Philippines Sustainable Livelihood Program: Providing and Expanding Access to Employment and Livelihood Opportunities." World Bank, Washington, DC.

Alaedini, Pooya. 2013. "Qualitative Assessment of Conditional Cash Transfer and Complementary Components under the Productive Social Safety Net Project: Institutional, Capacity, and Strategic Issues." Tanzania Social Action Fund (TASAF).

Asrudi, Tamsil Jayadi, and Wayrohi Meilvidiri. 2019. "Kelompok Usaha Bersama (KUBE) and Poverty Level Performance in Sulawesi and Kalimantan Areas." Advances in Social Science, Education, and Humanities Research Series, Vol. 383. In *Proceedings of the International Conference on Social Science 2019.* Amsterdam: Atlantis Press. https://www.atlantis-press.com/proceedings/icss-19/125927112.

Ballesteros, M., T. Ramos, J. Magtibay, A. Orbeta, G. Daval-Santos, A. J. Adona, and K. Gonzales. 2016. "Assessment of the Sustainable Livelihood Program— Employment Facilitation Process." Discussion Paper Series No. 2016-13, Philippine Institute for Development Studies, Quezon City.

Banks, Nicola. 2017. "Promoting Employment, Protecting Youth: BRAC's Empowerment and Livelihoods for Adolescent Girls Programme in Uganda and Tanzania." In *What Works for Africa's Poorest: Programs and Policies for the Extreme Poor,* edited by David Lawson, David Hulme, and Lawrence K. Ado-Kofie. Warwickshire, U.K.: Practical Action Publishers.

Berhane, Guush, John Hoddinott, Neha Kumar, Alemayehu Seyoum Taffasse, Michael Tedla Diressie, Yisehac Yohannes, Rachel Sabates-Wheeler, et al. 2013. *Evaluation of Ethiopia's Food Security Program: Documenting Progress in the Implementation of the Productive Safety Nets Programme and the Household Asset Building Programme.* Washington, DC: International Food Policy Research Institute.

CARE. 2019. *Kore Lavi Safety Net Beneficiary Resilience Assessment: Listening, Reflecting and Learning on Resilience and Food Security. Report for United States Agency for International Development (USAID).* Washington, DC: CARE.

Conroy, K., A. R. Goodman, and S. Kenward. 2010. "Lessons from the Chars Livelihoods Programme, Bangladesh (2004–2010). In *CPRC International Conference: Ten Years of "War Against Poverty": What Have We Learned since 2000 and What Should We Do 2010–2020?* Manchester, U.K.: University of Manchester

Devereux, S. 2017. "Do 'Graduation' Programmes Work for Africa's Poorest? "Chap. 11 in *What Works for Africa's Poorest: Programmes and Policies for the Extreme Poor,* edited by David Lawson, Lawrence Ado-Kofie, and David Hulme. Warwickshire, U.K.: Practical Action Publishing.

Devereux, S., and K. Roelen. 2013. "Concern Burundi Graduation Model Programme— Qualitative Baseline Report." Concern Worldwide, Bujumbura, Burundi.

Dorothee, Mukakibibi. 2017. "An Assessment of Challenges of Vision 2020 Umurenge Program on Poverty Reduction in Rwanda." *IOSR Journal of Business and Management* (IOSR-JBM) 19 (8 Ver. III): 51–56.

El-Zoghbi, M., A. de Montesquiou, with S. Hashemi. 2009. Creating Pathways for the Poorest: Early Lessons on Implementing the Graduation Model." Brief, Consultative Group to Assist the Poor (CGAP), Washington, DC.

Evans, David K., Stephanie Hausladen, Katrina Kosec, and Natasha Reese. 2014. *Community Based Conditional Cash Transfers in Tanzania: Results from a Randomized Trial.* Washington, DC: World Bank.

FAO (Food and Agriculture Organization). 2018. "FAO and Cash + : How to Maximize the Impacts of Cash Transfers." FAO, Rome.

Filipski, Mateusz, J. Edward Taylor, Getachew Ahmed Abegaz, Tadele Ferede, Alemayehu Seyoum Taffesse, and Xinshen Diao. 2017. *General Equilibrium Impact Assessment of the Productive Safety Net Program in Ethiopia.* Impact Evaluation Report No. 676. New Delhi: International Initiative for Impact Evaluation (3ie).

Goldberg, N. 2017. "What We Know about Graduation Impacts and What We Need to Find Out." *Policy in Focus* 14: 36–39.

Huda, K. 2008. "Mid-term (12 month) SKS Ultra Poor Process Evaluation." Consultative Group to Assist the Poor (CGAP) and BRAC, January.

Huda, K. 2009. "Mid-term (12 month) Trickle Up India TUP Process Evaluation." Consultative Group to Assist the Poor (CGAP)–Ford Foundation Graduation Pilot.

Huda, K. 2010. "Overcoming Extreme Poverty in India: Lessons Learnt from SKS." *IDS Bulletin* 41 (4): 31–41.

Huda, Karishma, and Anton Simanowitz. 2010. "Chemin Lavi Miyò—Final Evaluation (24 Months)." Concern Worldwide and Consultative Group to Assist the Poor (CGAP).

IDS (Innovative Development Strategies). 2011. "Assessment Survey of the PPAF's Social Safety Net—Targeting Ultra Poor Program 2011." Innovative Development Strategies (IDS) report prepared for the Pakistan Poverty Alleviation Fund, IDS, Islamabad.

Ivaschenko, Oleksiy, Darian Naidoo, David Newhouse, and Sonya Sultan. 2017. "Can Public Works Programs Reduce Youth Crime? Evidence from Papua New Guinea's Urban Youth Employment Project." *IZA Journal of Development and Migration* 7: 9.

Jawahar, V., and A. Sengupta. 2012. "SKS Ultra Poor Programme: Qualitative Assessment of Sustainability of Programme Outcomes." BDI Research Report 2, BRAC Development Institute, Dhaka.

Kabeer, Naila. 2019. "Randomized Control Trials and Qualitative Evaluations of a Multifaceted Programme for Women in Extreme Poverty: Empirical Findings and Methodological Reflections." *Journal of Human Development and Capabilities* 20 (2): 197–217. doi:10.1080/19452829.2018.1536696.

Kabeer, Naila, Karishma Huda, Sandeep Kaur, and Nicolina Lamhauge. 2012. "Productive Safety Nets for Women in Extreme Poverty: Lessons from Pilot Projects in India and Pakistan." Discussion Paper 28/12, Centre for Development Policy and Research, School of Oriental and African Studies (SOAS), University of London.

Kagin, Justin, J. Edward Taylor, Luca Pellerano, Silvio Daidone, Florian Juergens, Noemi Pace, and Marco Knowles. 2019. "Local Economy Impacts and Cost-Benefit Analysis of Social Protection and Agricultural Interventions in Malawi." Food and Agriculture Organization (FAO), International Labour Organization (ILO), and United Nations Children's Fund (UNICEF).

Karlan, Dean, and Bram Thuysbaert. 2013. "Targeting Ultra-poor Households in Honduras and Peru. NBER Working Paper 19646, National Bureau of Economic Research (NBER), Cambridge, MA.

Kenward, S., R. Blackie, and R. Islam. 2011. "Review of the CLP's Selection and Graduation Criteria, Chars Livelihoods Programme (CLP)." Bogra, Bangladesh.

Kidd, S., and D. Bailey-Athias. 2017. "The Effectiveness of the Graduation Approach: What Does the Evidence Tell Us?" *Policy in Focus* 14: 22–28.

Maldonado, J. H., R. Moreno-Sánchez, J. A. Gómez, and V. L. Jurado, eds. 2016. *Protection, Production, Promotion: Exploring Synergies between Social Protection and Productive Development in Latin America,* Bogotá: Universidad de los Andes.

Mansuri, Ghazala, and Rao Vijayendra. 2014. "Localizing Development. Does Participation Work?" *Journal of Economics* 112: 201–05. doi:10.1007/s00712-014-0394-4.

Matin, Imran, Munshi Sulaiman, and Mehnaz Rabbani. 2008. "Crafting a Graduation Pathway for the Ultra Poor: Lessons and Evidence from a BRAC Programme."

CPRC Working Paper No. 109, Chronic Poverty Research Centre (CPRC), Overseas Development Institute (ODI), London.

McIlvaine, Kassie, Corey Oser, Julianna Lindsey, and Maia Blume. 2015. "Confidence, Capacity Building and Cash: Achieving Sustained Impact for Ultra-poor Women." *IDS Bulletin* 46 (2).

Mishra, Usha, and Emmanuel J. Mtambie. 2017. "Exploring Potentials and Limits of Graduation: Tanzania's Social Action Fund." In *What Works for Africa's Poorest: Programs and Policies for the Extreme Poor,* edited by David Lawson, David Hulme, and Lawrence K. Ado-Kofie. Warwickshire, U.K.: Practical Action Publishers.

Moqueet, Nazia, and Drishty Shrestha. 2019. "Reducing Extreme Poverty in Kenya: Impact of PROFIT Financial Graduation BRAC Ultra-Poor Graduation Initiative." BRAC Ultra-Poor Graduation Initiative.

Morel, Ricardo, and Reajul Chowdhury. 2015. "Reaching the Ultra-Poor: Adapting Targeting Strategy in the Context of South Sudan." *Journal of International Development* 27 (7): 987–1011. doi:10.1002/jid.3131.

Moreno-Sánchez, Rocío, Vanesa Martínez, Jorge H. Maldonado, and Arturo Rodríguez. 2018. "Changes in Subjective Well-Being, Aspirations and Expectations in Participants of Poverty Alleviation Programs: A Qualitative Analysis of Produciendo Por Mi Futuro in Colombia." Working Paper No. 3, Center for Studies on Economic Development (CEDE), Universidad de los Andes, Bogotá.

Pavanello, Sara, Pamela Pozarny, Ana Paula De la O Campos, and Nynne Warring. 2018. "Research on Rural Women's Economic Empowerment and Social Protection: The Impacts of Rwanda's Vision 2020 Umurenge Programme (VUP)." Food and Agriculture Organization (FAO), Rome.

Pritchard, M., S. Kenward, and M. Hannan. 2015. "The Chars Livelihoods Programme in Bangladesh: Factors that Enable, Constrain and Sustain Graduation." *IDS Bulletin* 46 (2): 35–47.

Roelen, Keetie, and Carmen Leon-Himmelstine. 2019. "Graduating Out of Poverty across Generations: Unpacking Children's Well-being Trajectories in Burundi." *Children and Society* 33 (6): 507–23.

Roelen, Keetie, and Amrita Saha. 2019. "Fonkoze's CLM Ultra Poverty Programme: Understanding and Improving Child Development and Child Wellbeing. Endline Report." Institute of Development Studies, University of Sussex, Brighton, U.K.

Roelen, Keetie, and Helen Shelmerdine. 2014. "Researching the Linkages between Social Protection and Children's Care in Rwanda: The VUP and Its Effects on Child Well-Being, Care and Family Reunification." Family for Every Child, London.

Rosas, Nina, Samantha Zaldivar, and Mariana Pinzon-Caicedo. 2016. "Evaluating Tanzania's Productive Social Safety Net: Targeting Performance, Beneficiary Profile, and Other Baseline Findings." World Bank, Washington, DC.

Sabates-Wheeler, R., and S. Devereux. 2010. "Cash Transfers and High Food Prices: Explaining Outcomes in Ethiopia's Productive Safety Net Programme." *Food Policy* 35 (4): 274–85.

Sabates–Wheeler, Rachel, Stephen Devereux, and B. Guenther. 2009. "Building Synergies between Social Protection and Smallholder Agricultural Policies." Future Agricultures Consortium, IDS Working Paper No. SP01, Institute of Development Studies (IDS), University of Sussex, Brighton, U.K.

Sabates-Wheeler, R., J. Lind, and J. Hoddinott. 2013. "Implementing Social Protection in Agro-pastoralist and Pastoralist Areas: How Local Distribution Structures Moderate PSNP Outcomes in Ethiopia." *World Development* 50 (1): 1–12.

Sabates-Wheeler, R., R. Sabates, and S. Devereux. 2018. "Enabling Graduation for Whom? Identifying and Explaining Heterogeneity in Livelihood Trajectories Post-Cash Transfer Exposure." *Journal of International Development* 30: 1071–95.

Self, Vanessa, Lilly Schofield, and Md. Muzaffar Ahmed. 2018. "Graduating Out of Extreme Poverty: Who? Why and How? Evidence from Save the Children's Shiree Programme in Bangladesh." Save the Children, London.

Sengupta, Anasuya. 2012. "Pathways Out of the Productive Safety Net Programme: Lessons from Graduation Pilot in Ethiopia." BRAC Development Institute (BDI), Dhaka.

Sengupta, Anasuya. 2013. "Bandhan's Targeting the Hard Core Poor Program: A Qualitative Study on Participants' Ascent Out of Extreme Poverty." BRAC Development Institute (BDI), Dhaka.

Sheldon, Tony, ed. 2016. *Preserving the Essence, Adapting for Reach: Early Lessons from Large-Scale Implementations of the Graduation Approach.* New York: Ford Foundation.

Shoaf, Emma, and Anton Simanowitz. 2019. *Pathways to Sustained Exit from Extreme Poverty: Evidence from Fonkoze's Extreme Poverty "Graduation" Programme.* IDS report, Institute of Development Studies (IDS), University of Sussex, Brighton, U.K.

Slater, R., S. Wiggins, L. Harman, M. Ulrichs, L. Scott, M. Knowles, P. Pozarny, et al. 2016. *Strengthening Coherence between Agriculture and Social Protection: Synthesis of Seven Country Case Studies.* Rome: Food and Agriculture Organization (FAO).

Smita Premchander, Aindrila Mokkapati, and Sumit Dutta, 2018. "Innovations for Success and Scale-up: An Analysis of Bandhan's Targeting the Hard Core Poor Programme in India." *Enterprise Development and Microfinance* 29 (1): 13–31. http://dx.doi.org/10.3362/1755-1986.17-00025.

Soares, Fabio Veras, Marco Knowles, Silvio Daidone, and Nyasha Tirivayi. 2017. *Combined Effects and Synergies between Agricultural and Social Protection Interventions: What Is the Evidence So Far?* Rome: Food and Agriculture Organization (FAO).

Soares, F., and I. Orton. 2017. "Graduation: An Overview." *Policy in Focus* 14: 7–10.

Sulaiman, Munshi. 2018. "Livelihood, Cash Transfer, and Graduation Approaches: How Do They Compare in Terms of Cost, Impact, and Targeting?" In *Boosting Growth to End Hunger by 2025: The Role of Social Protection,* edited by Fleur Stephanie Wouterse and Alemayehu Seyoum Taffesse, 102–20. Washington, DC: International Food Policy Research Institute (IFPRI).

Tamyis, Ana Rosidha, Akhmad Ramadhan Fatah, Dyan Widyaningsih, Fatin Nuha Astini, Gema Satria Mayang Sedyadi, Hafiz Arfyanto, Jimmy Daniel Berlianto Oley, et al. 2020. *Strengthening Economic Opportunities for Program Keluarga Harapan Families: A Case Study of Four Districts in Java.* Jakarta: SMERU. http://smeru.or .id/en/content/strengthening-economic-opportunities-program-keluarga-harapan -families-case-study-four.

Tirivayi, N., M. Knowles, and B. Davis. 2013. *The Interaction between Social Protection and Agriculture: A Review of Evidence.* Report prepared for PtoP project, Food and Agriculture Organization (FAO), Rome.

Economic Inclusion Program Costing Survey Methodology and Analysis

Survey sample selection

The Partnership for Economic Inclusion management team (PEIMT) sought to develop a balanced portfolio of projects to complete the costing survey, thereby ensuring a sufficiently diverse sample of economic inclusion programming. The team began by selecting 28 World Bank projects for the costing survey, drawn from the 149 projects identified as economic inclusion projects from the roughly 1,200 active or pipeline World Bank projects reviewed, as described in appendix A. Selection of projects was based on a review of the following characteristics, with a view toward creating a balanced portfolio:

- Income group: low-income, lower-middle-income, or upper-middle-income

- Geographic group: South Asia, Middle East and North Africa, Africa, Latin America and the Caribbean, Europe and Central Asia, or East Asia and Pacific

- World Bank Global Practice

- Rural or urban

- Fragile context or nonfragile context

Next, PEIMT sent the costing survey to an additional 47 projects based on their expression of interest through the PEI Landscape Survey 2020.

Of the 75 projects that received the costing survey, 24 World Bank projects and 10 nongovernmental organization (NGO) projects responded. The survey was administered between November 2019 and January 2020. The analysis and follow-up consultations with program managers required two to three hours per project and were completed in February and March 2020, as detailed shortly.

Categorization by entry point

The costing data were segregated by project typology using the entry points to scale outlined in chapter 1: social safety nets (SSNs), livelihoods and jobs (L&J), and financial inclusion (FI). These typologies were reviewed and confirmed by project teams before being finalized.

Data harmonization

Programs were asked to submit costing information in local currency units (LCUs), which were expected to be easier for teams to report, or in U.S. dollars where there were issues with LCU reporting (such as where the currency's valuation was volatile). Regardless of which currency was reported, costing data were reported for different years, and so data points were deflated to 2011 U.S. dollars at purchasing power parity (PPP) values and then converted to international U.S. dollars using the formulation

$$[\text{intervention cost}(t) \div \text{CPI (2011)}] \div [\text{ICP (2011)}]$$

where ICP (2011) is the PPP conversion factor base 2011 of private consumption and CPI (2011) is the inflation for any given year in 2011 terms. Analysis of overall trends, presented in chapter 6, used this harmonized data set.

Preliminary project cost analysis and consultations

PEIMT began the costing analysis by assessing the cost structure of each project by reviewing in turn the intervention costs and project implementation costs as a percentage of the total cost. Next, the team estimated the per unit (beneficiary) U.S. dollar (2011, PPP) and LCU value of the benefits provided. This estimate included the average unit cost per beneficiary for the project as a whole, as well as that of the constituent components—size of grants and transfers, cost of skills training, coaching and mentoring, and other program components (see illustrative example in figure C.1). This preliminary analysis was then shared with the project teams for feedback, followed by calls with individual project teams to explain the calculations, gather feedback from each team, and update the analysis. In addition, PEIMT also shared the high-level findings documented in chapter 6 for review and comments, particularly as they related to the underlying projects.

Calculating the adequacy of benefits

PEIMT sought to determine the adequacy of benefits provided in a given project in order to understand the value of these benefits for beneficiaries. In the process, PEIMT developed a benchmark of sorts for other projects trying to determine their own benefit level. Adequacy was calculated by dividing the cost of a component by

FIGURE C.1 Sample Preliminary Analysis, Zambia and Côte d'Ivoire

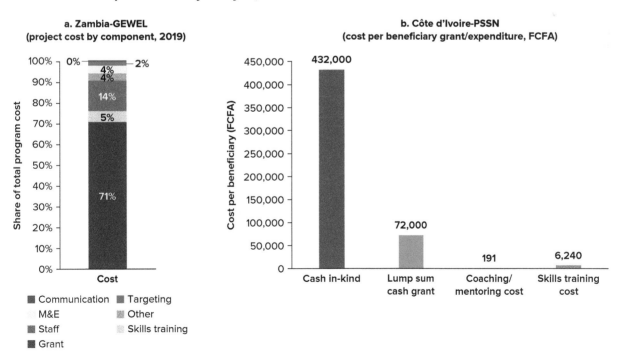

Source: PEI Quick Costing Tool 2020.

Note: See table C.1 for explanation of abbreviations following country names. FCFA = West African CFA franc; M&E = monitoring and evaluation.

the average annual per capita consumption of the poorest 20 percent of households in the relevant country.

Consumption data were obtained from the World Bank's Atlas of Social Protection Indicators of Resilience and Equity (ASPIRE) household survey data set for all the countries in the costing sample. When assessing the benefits of cash transfers and public works (provided to support consumption), PEIMT assumed that benefits were distributed across all household members as these initiatives are intended to smooth the consumption of households. On the other hand, for cash grant and asset transfers (provided to support production), it was assumed that the transfer was for production support and would benefit the household as a single unit of production with no distribution across household members. Overall, the adequacy calculations rested on a strong assumption that all the projects target beneficiaries in the bottom quintile in the respective countries.

Undertaking a qualitative analysis

Because of the varied project objectives and diverse contexts, it was important to put the cost analysis into perspective using qualitative data. For World Bank projects, PEIMT reviewed available Project Appraisal Documents and operations manuals, which provided rich information on the country and institutional context, project components, project beneficiaries, and, in some cases, economic and financial analyses. For NGO projects, PEIMT reviewed websites and process evaluation documents to gain a better understanding of the projects. In addition, project teams were asked to share any relevant documents that would help in this analysis.

Economic inclusion program costing analysis

The PEIMT costing analysis received data on 24 government and 10 NGO projects. Table C.1 is a snapshot of all the projects covered in the analysis. It shows the objectives and combinations of components in each project, demonstrating the range of projects covered in the analysis. Figure C.2 shows these projects by their cost composition.

TABLE C.1 Projects in Costing Survey: Objectives and Components

Livelihoods and jobs

Project	Country	Government/NGO	Objective/project development objective	Components
Girls' Education and Women's Empowerment and Livelihoods Project (GEWEL)	Zambia	Government	To support the government of Zambia in its efforts to increase access to livelihood support for women and access to secondary education for disadvantaged adolescent girls in extremely poor households in selected districts	1. Lump sum cash grants 2. Savings group formation 3. Coaching/mentoring 4. Life/business skills training
Programme d'actions communautaires (PAC3)	Niger	Government	To strengthen the recipient's local development planning and implementation capacities, including the capacity to respond promptly and effectively to an eligible crisis or emergency and to improve the access of the targeted population to socioeconomic services	1. Public works 2. Matching grants 3. Producer group formation 4. On-the-job training 5. Employment intermediation services 6. Local market development 7. Strengthening local institutions 8. Local resources development 9. Infrastructure development 10. Food/nutrition support
Youth Employment and Skills Development Project (YSDP)	Burkina Faso	Government	To increase access to temporary employment and skills development opportunities for out-of-school youth	1. Public works 2. Lump sum cash grants 3. Coaching/mentoring 4. Life/business skills training 5. Vocational skills training 6. Strengthening local institutions 7. Empowerment group formation 8. Local resources development
Employment Opportunities for Vulnerable Youth Project (EOVYP)	Togo	Government	To provide targeted poor and vulnerable youth in Togo with access to income-generating opportunities	1. Public works 2. Lump sum cash grants 3. Coaching/mentoring 4. Life/business skills training 5. Vocational skills training 6. On-the-job training 7. Employment intermediation services 8. Strengthening local institutions 9. Empowerment group formation
Support rural income generation of the poorest in the upper east project (SRIGP)	Ghana	Government	To assist targeted poor persons, at least 50 percent of whom should be women, to acquire business management and technical and vocational skills, as well as grant funds to start or expand their businesses	1. Lump sum cash grants 2. Coaching/mentoring 3. Life/business skills training 4. Vocational skills training 5. On-the-job training 6. Local market development
Socioeconomic inclusion in rural areas project (PISEAR)	Argentina	Government	To increase the socioeconomic inclusion of rural poor (small producers, indigenous people, and rural workers) by (1) strengthening their organizational, planning, and management capacity to achieve poverty reduction goals; (2) improving their access to community infrastructure and services; and (3) piloting a new model for developing sustainable access to markets	1. Lump sum cash grants 2. Matching grants 3. Forward links to end markets 4. Backward links to inputs markets 5. Extension services 6. Producer group formation 7. Coaching/mentoring 8. Life/business skills training 9. Orientation on good agricultural practices 10. Local market development 11. Strengthening local institutions 12. Empowerment group formation 13. Local resources development

(Table continues next page)

TABLE C.1 Projects in Costing Survey: Objectives and Components (*continued*)

Project	Country	Government/NGO	Objective/project development objective	Components
Andhra Pradesh Rural Inclusive Growth Project (APRIGP)	India	Government	To establish efficient and effective institutional platforms for the rural poor that enable them to increase household income through sustainable livelihood enhancements and improved access to financial and selected public services	1. Asset/input transfer 2. Matching grants 3. Savings group formation 4. Forward links to end markets 5. Backward links to inputs markets 6. Extension services 7. Producer group formation 8. Life/business skills training 9. Empowerment group formation
Smallholder Agricultural Production Restoration and Enhancement Project (SAPREP)	Yemen, Rep.	Government	To increase the use of productivity- and nutrition-enhancing agricultural practices by smallholders in targeted project areas	1. Public works 2. Asset/input transfer 3. Extension services 4. Life/business skills training 5. Local market development 6. Local resources development
Internally Displaced Persons Living Standards and Livelihoods Project (IDP LSLP)	Azerbaijan	Government	To improve living conditions and increase the economic self-reliance of targeted internally displaced persons	1. Asset/input transfer 2. Matching grants 3. Credit/loan programs 4. Producer group formation 5. Life/business skills training 6. Vocational skills training 7. Empowerment group formation
Transform Program	Philippines	NGO (International Care Ministries)	To address the wide range of needs faced by families living in ultrapoverty	1. Cash/in-kind transfer 2. Asset/input transfer 3. Savings group formation 4. Coaching/mentoring 5. Life/business skills training 6. Health and nutrition support
Building Resilience through Asset Creation and Enhancement (BRACE)	South Sudan	NGO (Concern)	A graduation approach designed to not only move people above a certain wealth threshold but also to facilitate a sustainable exit from extreme poverty	1. Cash/in-kind transfer 2. Extension services 3. Local resources development
Targeting the Ultra Poor	Philippines	NGO (BRAC)	To pilot the graduation approach to end extreme poverty in the Philippines	1. Cash/in-kind transfer 2. Asset/input transfer 3. Forward links to end markets 4. Backward links to inputs markets 5. Extension services 6. Coaching/mentoring 7. Life/business skills training 8. Local market development 9. Local resources development
Resilience Programming with the Graduation Model and Evidence Building for Structural Dialogues (REGRADE)	Ethiopia	NGO (Concern)	A graduation approach designed to not only move people above a certain wealth threshold but also to facilitate a sustainable exit from extreme poverty	1. Cash/in-kind transfer 2. Lump sum cash grants 3. Savings group formation 4. Forward links to end markets 5. Extension services 6. Producer group formation 7. Coaching/mentoring 8. Life/business skills training 9. Strengthening local institutions 10. Local resources development
Enabling Sustainable Graduation out of Poverty for the Extreme Poor in Southern Malawi	Malawi	NGO (Concern)	A graduation approach designed to not only move people above a certain wealth threshold but also to facilitate a sustainable exit from extreme poverty	1. Cash/in-kind transfer 2. Lump sum cash grants 3. Savings group formation 4. Forward links to end markets 5. Extension services 6. Producer group formation 7. Coaching/mentoring 8. Life/business skills training 9. Local resources development

(Table continues next page)

TABLE C.1 Projects in Costing Survey: Objectives and Components (*continued*)

Project	Country	Government/NGO	Objective/project development objective	Components
Pathways for Disability-Inclusive Graduation out of Poverty (Graduation)	Bangladesh	NGO (Humanity and Inclusion)	To advance the long-term rights and social inclusion of people with disabilities in Bangladesh	1. Cash/in-kind transfer 2. Savings group formation 3. Producer group formation 4. Coaching/mentoring 5. Life/business skills training 6. Vocational skills training 7. On-the-job training 8. Empowerment group formation
Building Disaster Resilience in Pakistan (BDRP) Program	Pakistan	NGO (Concern)	To build resilience of poor and vulnerable households and communities to climate-related natural disasters	1. Extension services 2. Life/business skills training 3. Vocational skills training
Graduating to Resilience (Graduation)	Uganda	NGO (AVSI)	To build resilience and contribute to sustainable development	1. Cash/in-kind transfer 2. Lump sum cash grants 3. Savings group formation 4. Credit/loan programs 5. Backward links to inputs markets 6. Coaching/mentoring 7. Life/business skills training
Targeting the Ultra Poor (TUP)	Bangladesh	NGO (BRAC)	To end extreme poverty	1. Asset/input transfer 2. Credit/loan programs 3. Match savings 4. Backward links to inputs markets 5. Extension services 6. Coaching/mentoring 7. Life/business skills training 8. Health care and contingency support
National Rural Livelihoods Project (NRLP)	India	Government	To establish efficient and effective institutional platforms of the rural poor that enable them to increase household income through sustainable livelihood enhancements and improved access to financial and selected public services	1. Savings group formation 2. Forward links to end markets 3. Backward links to inputs markets 4. Extension services 5. Producer group formation 6. Coaching/mentoring 7. Life/business skills training 8. Vocational skills training 9. On-the-job training 10. Employment intermediation services
Bihar Rural Livelihoods Project (JEEViKA)	India	Government	To enhance social and economic empowerment of the rural poor in Bihar	1. Savings group formation 2. Forward links to end markets 3. Backward links to inputs markets 4. Extension services 5. Producer group formation 6. Vocational skills training 7. Empowerment group formation
Graduation Model Approach (Graduation)	Ecuador	NGO (HIAS)	To protect the most vulnerable refugees, helping them to build new lives and reuniting them with their families in safety and freedom	1. Cash/in-kind transfer 2. Asset/ input transfer 3. Savings group formation 4. Credit/loan programs 5. Forward links to end markets 6. Backward links to inputs markets 7. Coaching/mentoring 8. Life/business skills training 9. Vocational skills training 10. Employment intermediation services 11. Empowerment group formation
Social safety nets				
Productive Social Safety Net (PSSN)	Côte d' Ivoire	Government	To provide cash transfers to poor households in selected regions and develop the foundations of a social safety net system	1. Cash/in-kind transfer 2. Lump sum cash grant 3. Savings group formation 4. Coaching/mentoring 5. Life/business skills training 6. Forward links to end markets 7. Backward links to inputs markets 8. Extension services 9. Producer group formation

(Table continues next page)

TABLE C.1 Projects in Costing Survey: Objectives and Components (*continued*)

Project	Country	Government/NGO	Objective/project development objective	Components
Third Northern Uganda Social Action Fund (NUSAF3)	Uganda	Government	To provide effective income support to and build the resilience of poor and vulnerable households in northern Uganda	1. Public works 2. Savings group formation 3. Strengthening local institutions 4. Empowerment group formation 5. Local resources development
Development Response to Displacement Impact Project (DRDIP)	Uganda	Government	To improve access to basic social services, expand economic opportunities, and enhance environmental management for communities hosting refugees in the targeted areas of Djibouti, Ethiopia, and Uganda	1. Savings group formation 2. Strengthening local institutions 3. Empowerment group formation 4. Local resources development
Productive Safety Net Program (PSSN) phase 4—complementary livelihoods interventions	Ethiopia	Government	To provide cash transfers to poor households in selected regions and develop the foundations of a social safety net system	1. Cash/in-kind transfer 2. Public works 3. Lump sum cash grant 4. Savings group formation 5. Credit/loan programs 6. Forward links to end markets 7. Extension services 8. Coaching/mentoring 9. Life/business skills training 10. Employment intermediation services 11. Strengthening local institutions 12. Local resources development
Social Safety Nets (SSN) Project	Cameroon	Government	To support the establishment of a basic national safety net system, including piloting targeted cash transfers and public works programs for the poorest and most vulnerable people in participating areas within the recipient's territory	1. Cash/in-kind transfer 2. Public works 3. Emergency cash transfer
National Social Safety Nets (SSN) Project	Nigeria	Government	To provide access to targeted transfers to poor and vulnerable households under an expanded national social safety net system	1. Cash/in-kind transfer 2. Lump sum cash grant 3. Savings group formation 4. Coaching/ mentoring 5. Life/business skills training
Social Safety Nets (SSN) Project	Comoros	Government	To establish the building blocks of a safety net to reach selected extreme poor and disaster-affected households through the provision of additional sources of income and nutrition services	1. Public works 2. Life/business skills training
Minimum Package for Graduation (MPG)	Rwanda	Government	To improve the effectiveness of Rwanda's social protection system, notably the flagship Vision 2020 Umurenge Programme (VUP), for targeted vulnerable groups	1. Cash/in-kind transfer 2. Public works 3. Asset/input transfer
Eastern Recovery Project (STEP)	Congo, Dem. Rep.	Government	To improve access to livelihoods and socioeconomic infrastructures in vulnerable communities in the eastern provinces	1. Public works 2. Asset/input transfer 3. Matching grants 4. Savings group formation 5. Matching savings 6. Forward links to end markets 7. Backward links to inputs markets 8. Extension services 9. Producer group formation 10. Coaching/mentoring 11. Life/business skills training 12. Vocational skills training 13. Local market development 14. Strengthening local institutions

(Table continues next page)

TABLE C.1 Projects in Costing Survey: Objectives and Components (*continued*)

Project	Country	Government/NGO	Objective/project development objective	Components
Community Savings and Investment Promotion (COMSIP)	Malawi	Government	To strengthen Malawi's social safety net delivery systems and coordination across programs	1. Lump sum cash grant 2. Asset/input transfer 3. Matching grants 4. Savings group formation 5. Forward links to end markets 6. Backward links to inputs markets 7. Extension services 8. Producer group formation 9. Coaching/mentoring 10. Life/business skills training
Support to Communes and Communities for the Expansion of Social Services (ACCESS)	Benin	Government	To improve access to decentralized basic social services and social safety nets and to strengthen the social protection system	1. Cash/in-kind transfer 2. Public works 3. Life/business skills training 4. Strengthening local institutions
Yemen Emergency Crisis Response Project (YECRP)	Yemen, Rep.	Government	To provide the most vulnerable with short-term employment and access to selected basic services and preserve the implementation capacity of two service delivery programs	1. Cash/in-kind transfer 2. Public works 3. Lump sum cash grant 4. Credit/loan programs

Source: Partnership for Economic Inclusion, World Bank.
Note: NGO = nongovernmental organization.

FIGURE C.2 **Cost Breakdown of Economic Inclusion Programs, by Region**

a. Sub-Saharan Africa, government-led

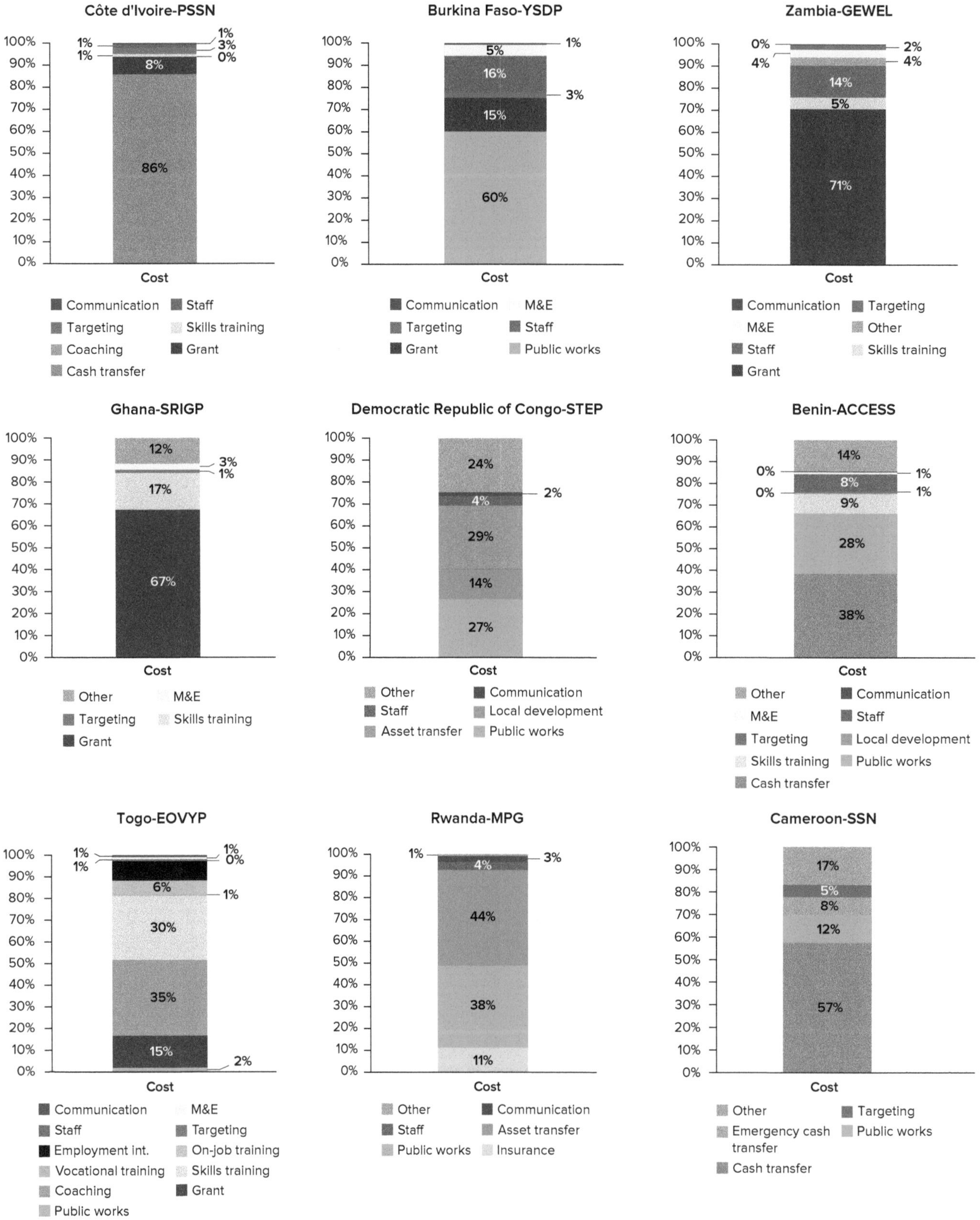
Côte d'Ivoire-PSSN
1%
1%
8%
86%
1%
3%
0%
Cost
Communication
Staff
Targeting
Skills training
Coaching
Grant
Cash transfer
Burkina Faso-YSDP
5%
16%
15%
60%
1%
3%
Cost
Communication
M&E
Targeting
Staff
Grant
Public works
Zambia-GEWEL
0%
4%
14%
5%
71%
2%
4%
Cost
Communication
Targeting
M&E
Other
Staff
Skills training
Grant
Ghana-SRIGP
12%
17%
67%
3%
1%
Cost
Other
M&E
Targeting
Skills training
Grant
Democratic Republic of Congo-STEP
24%
4%
29%
14%
27%
2%
Cost
Other
Communication
Staff
Local development
Asset transfer
Public works
Benin-ACCESS
0%
0%
14%
8%
9%
28%
38%
1%
1%
Cost
Other
Communication
M&E
Staff
Targeting
Local development
Skills training
Public works
Cash transfer
Togo-EOVYP
1%
1%
6%
30%
35%
15%
1%
0%
1%
2%
Cost
Communication
M&E
Staff
Targeting
Employment int.
On-job training
Vocational training
Skills training
Coaching
Grant
Public works
Rwanda-MPG
1%
4%
44%
38%
11%
3%
Cost
Other
Communication
Staff
Asset transfer
Public works
Insurance
Cameroon-SSN
17%
5%
8%
12%
57%
Cost
Other
Targeting
Emergency cash transfer
Public works
Cash transfer
100%
90%
80%
70%
60%
50%
40%
30%
20%
10%
0%

(Figure continues next page)

FIGURE C.2 Cost Breakdown of Economic Inclusion Programs by Region (*continued*)

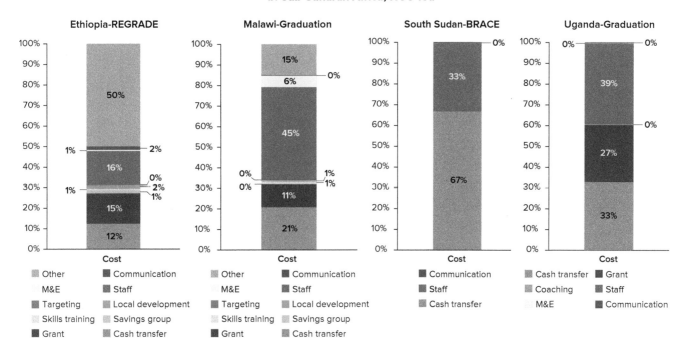

b. Sub-Saharan Africa, NGO-led

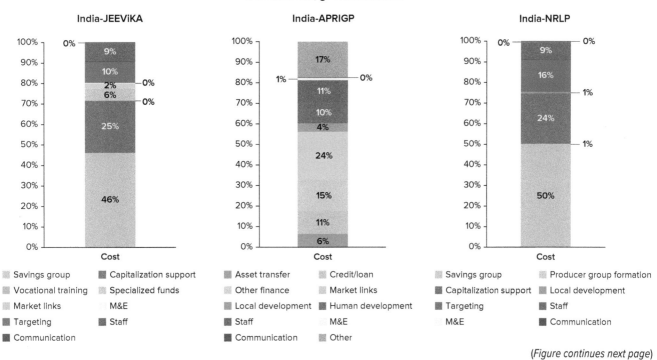

c. South Asia, government-led

(*Figure continues next page*)

FIGURE C.2 **Cost Breakdown of Economic Inclusion Programs by Region (*continued*)**

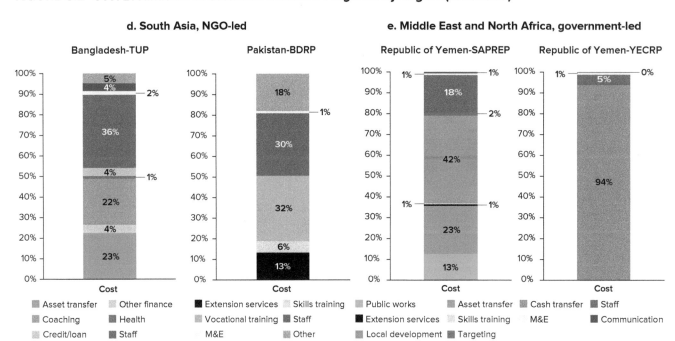

d. South Asia, NGO-led

e. Middle East and North Africa, government-led

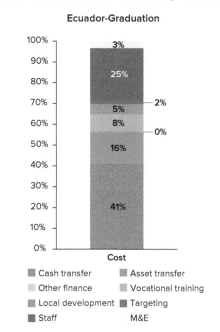

e. East Asia and Pacific, NGO-led

f. Latin America and the Caribbean, NGO-led

Source: PEI Quick Costing Tool 2020.

Note: See table C.1 for explanation of project abbreviations following country names. Employment int. = employment intermediation services; M&E = monitoring and evaluation; NGO = nongovernmental organization.

Bibliography

Balboni, Clare, Oriana Bandiera, Robin Burgess, Maitreesh Ghatak, and Anton Heil. 2020. "Why Do People Stay Poor?" STICERD Economic Organisation and Public Policy Discussion Papers Series 067, Suntory and Toyota International Centres for Economics and Related Disciplines, London School of Economics.

Bandiera, Oriana, Robin Burgess, Narayan Das, Selim Gulesci, Imran Rasul, and Munshi Sulaiman. 2013. *Can Basic Entrepreneurship Transform the Economic Lives of the Poor?* IZA Discussion Paper 7386, Institute of Labor Economics, Bonn.

Bandiera, Oriana, Robin Burgess, Narayan Das, Selim Gulesci, Imran Rasul, and Munshi Sulaiman. 2017. "Labor Markets and Poverty in Village Economies." *Quarterly Journal of Economics* 132 (2): 811–70.

Banerjee, Abhijit, Esther Duflo, Nathaneal Goldberg, Dean Karlan, Robert Osei, William Parienté, Jeremy Shapiro, Bram Thuysbaert, and Christopher Udry. 2015. "A Multifaceted Program Causes Lasting Progress for the Very Poor: Evidence from Six Countries." *Science* 348 (6236): 1260799.

Bauchet, Jonathan, Jonathan Morduch, and Shamika Ravi. 2015. "Failure vs. Displacement: Why an Innovative Anti-Poverty Program Showed No Net Impact in South India." *Journal of Development Economics* 116: 1–16.

Bedoya, Guadalupe, Aidan Coville, Johannes Haushofer, Mohammad Isaqzadeh, and Jeremy Shapiro. 2019. "No Household Left Behind: Afghanistan Targeting the Ultra-Poor Impact Evaluation." Policy Research Working Paper 8877, World Bank, Washington, DC.

Blattman, Christopher, Stefan Dercon, and Simon Franklin. 2019. "Impacts of Industrial and Entrepreneurial Jobs on Youth: Five-year Experimental Evidence on Factory Job Offers and Cash Grants in Ethiopia." Working Paper No. 2019-65, University of Chicago.

Blattman, Christopher, Nathan Fiala, and Sebastian Martinez. 2014. "Generating Skilled Self-Employment in Developing Countries: Experimental Evidence from Uganda." *Quarterly Journal of Economics* 129: 697–752. doi:10.1093/qje/qjt057.

Blattman, Christopher, Eric P. Green, Julian Jamison, M. Christian Lehmann, and Jeannie Annan. 2016. "The Returns to Microenterprise Support among the Ultrapoor: A Field Experiment in Postwar Uganda." *American Economic Journal: Applied Economics* 8 (2): 35–64.

Caldés, Natalia, David Coady, and John A. Maluccio. 2006. "The Cost of Poverty Alleviation Transfer Programs: A Comparative Analysis of Three Programs in Latin America." *World Development* 34 (5): 818–37.

Das, Narayan C., Sibbir Ahmad, Anindita Bhattacharjee, Jinnat Ara, and Abdul Bayes. 2016. "Grant versus Credit Plus Approach to Poverty Reduction: An Evaluation of BRAC's Experience with Ultra Poor." CFPR Working Paper 24, BRAC, Dhaka.

Devereux, Stephen, Keetie Roelen, Ricardo Sabates, Dimitri Stoelinga, and Arnaud Dyevre. 2015. *Final Evaluation Report: Concern's Graduation Model Program in Burundi.* Dublin: Concern Worldwide.

FAO (Food and Agriculture Organization). 2018. *FAO and Cash +: How to Maximize the Impacts of Cash Transfers.* Rome: FAO.

Gobin, Vilas J., Paulo Santos, and Russell Toth. 2016. "Poverty Graduation with Cash Transfers: A Randomized Evaluation." Economics Working Paper 23-16, Monash University, Melbourne.

Grosh, Margaret. 1994. *Administering Targeted Social Programs in Latin America: From Platitude to Practice.* Washington, DC: World Bank.

Ismayilova, Leyla, Leyla Karimli, Jo Sanson, Eleni Gaveras, Rachel Nanema, Alexice Tô-Camier, and Josh Chaffin. 2018. "Improving Mental Health among Ultra-Poor Children: Two-Year Outcomes of a Cluster-Randomized Trial in Burkina Faso." *Social Science and Medicine* 208: 180–89. doi:10.1016/j.socscimed.2018.04.022.

Kidd, Stephen, and Diloá Athias. 2019. "The Effectiveness of the Graduation Approach: What Does the Evidence Tell Us?" *Pathways' Perspectives on Social Policy in International Development* (Issue No. 27).

Maldonado, Jorge H., Rocio Moreno-Sánchez, J. A. Gómez, and V. L. Jurado, eds. 2016. *Protection, Production, Promotion: Exploring Synergies between Social Protection and Productive Development in Latin America*. Bogotá: Universidad de los Andes.

Sedlmayr, Richard, Anuj Shah, and Munshi Sulaiman. 2019. "Cash-plus: Poverty Impacts of Alternative Transfer-Based Approaches." *Journal of Development Economics* 144 (May). doi:10.1016/j.jdeveco.2019.102418.

Sheldon, Tony, ed. 2016. *Preserving the Essence, Adapting for Reach: Early Lessons from Large-Scale Implementations of the Graduation Approach*. New York: Ford Foundation.

Sulaiman, Munshi. 2018. "Livelihood, Cash Transfer, and Graduation Approaches: How Do They Compare in Terms of Cost, Impact, and Targeting?" In *Boosting Growth to End Hunger by 2025: The Role of Social Protection*, edited by Fleur Stephanie Wouterse and Alemayehu Seyoum Taffesse, 102–20. Washington, DC: International Food Policy Research Institute (IFPRI). doi:10.2499/9780896295988_08.

Tilakaratna, Ganga, and Chinthani Sooriyamudali. 2016. *Samurdhi/Divineguma Programme*. Institute of Policy Studies, Colombo, Sri Lanka.

Tiwari, Jaya, Emily Schaub, and Naziha Sultana. 2019. "Barriers to 'Last Mile' Financial Inclusion: Cases from Northern Kenya." *Development in Practice* 29 (8): 988–1000. doi:10.1080/09614524.2019.1654432.

World Bank. 2019. *Resilience through Economic Inclusion: Sahel ASP Thematic Activity–Sahel Adaptive Social Protection (SASPP)*. Concept Note, Regional Analytical Program. Washington, DC: World Bank.

Economic Inclusion Programs Mapped Globally

TABLE D.1 Economic Inclusion Programs Mapped Globally

Program	Economy	Surveyed	Lead implementing agency or agencies	Primary entry point	Secondary entry point	No. of beneficiaries (direct and indirect)
Targeting the Ultra Poor (TUP)	Afghanistan	Yes	Microfinance Investment Support Facility for Afghanistan (MISFA)	Livelihoods and jobs	Financial inclusion	32,039
Women Economic Empowerment Project	Afghanistan	Yes	Ministry of Rural Rehabilitation and Development (MRRD)	Livelihoods and jobs	Financial inclusion	957,283
Women for Women International's Empowerment Program	Afghanistan	Yes	Women for Women International	Livelihoods and jobs	Financial inclusion	79,950
The Angola (AO)—local development project	Angola	No	—	—	—	—
Enfoque de Graduación (EdG)	Argentina	Yes	Agencia Adventista de Desarrollo y Recursos Asistenciales (ADRA)	Social safety nets	Livelihoods and jobs	52
Jóvenes con Más y Mejor Trabajo (JMyMT), youth employment support project	Argentina	Yes	Ministry of Production and Labor	Livelihoods and jobs	None	288,000
Socio-Economic Inclusion in Rural Areas Project (PISEAR)	Argentina	Yes	Dirección General de Programas y Proyectos Sectoriales y Especiales (DIPROSE)	Livelihoods and jobs	Financial inclusion	25,710
Internally Displaced Persons (IDP) Living Standards and Livelihoods Project	Azerbaijan	No	—	—	—	3,000
Taking Successful Innovation to Scale—Pathways for Disability-Inclusive Graduation Out of Poverty	Bangladesh	Yes	Humanity and Inclusion	Livelihoods and jobs	Financial inclusion	10,496

(Table continues next page)

TABLE D.1 Economic Inclusion Programs Mapped Globally (continued)

Program	Economy	Surveyed	Lead implementing agency or agencies	Primary entry point	Secondary entry point	No. of beneficiaries (direct and indirect)
Empowering Women and Youth through Graduation and Financial Inclusion in Bangladesh	Bangladesh	Yes	Concern Worldwide	Livelihoods and jobs	Financial inclusion	58,110
Improving Peaceful Co-existence and Self-reliance Opportunities for Refugees and Host Community	Bangladesh	Yes	Mukti Cox's Bazar	Social safety nets	Livelihoods and jobs	11,175
Livelihood Technical Program	Bangladesh	Yes	World Vision Bangladesh	Livelihoods and jobs	Financial inclusion	199,344
Nobo Jatra–New Beginning, a five-year U.S. Agency for International Development (USAID) Food for Peace Title II Development Food Security Activity; World Vision Bangladesh	Bangladesh	Yes	World Vision Bangladesh	Livelihoods and jobs	None	31,290
Nuton Jibon Livelihood Improvement Project (NJLIP)	Bangladesh	Yes	Social Development Foundation (SDF), an organization under Ministry of Finance	Livelihoods and jobs	Financial inclusion	4,470,000
Pathways to Prosperity for Extremely Poor People (PPEPP) Project	Bangladesh	Yes	Community Development Centre (CODEC), Eco-Social Development Organisation (ESDO), Gram Bikash Kendra (GBK), Grameen Jana Unnayan Sangstha (GJUS), Nowabenki Gonomukhi Foundation (NGF), People's Oriented Program Implementation (POPI), Rangpur Dinajpur Rural Service (RDRS) Bangladesh, Self-Help and Rehabilitation Program (SHARP), Thengamara Mohila Sabuj Sangha (TMSS), UNNAYAN	Livelihoods and jobs	Social safety nets	1,000,000

(Table continues next page)

TABLE D.1 Economic Inclusion Programs Mapped Globally (continued)

Program	Economy	Surveyed	Lead implementing agency or agencies	Primary entry point	Secondary entry point	No. of beneficiaries (direct and indirect)
Self-reliance and peaceful coexistence for refugees and host communities	Bangladesh	Yes	Centre for Natural Resources Studies	Social safety nets	Livelihoods and jobs	13,410
Sustainable Coastal and Marine Fisheries	Bangladesh	Yes	Department of Fisheries, Ministry of Fisheries and Livestock	Livelihoods and jobs	None	321,840
Ultra-Poor Graduation Programme, implemented by BRAC	Bangladesh	Yes	BRAC	Livelihoods and jobs	Financial inclusion	468,957
Ultra-Poor Graduation Programme for host communities and refugee populations in Cox's Bazar	Bangladesh	Yes	BRAC	Livelihoods and jobs	Financial inclusion	9,065
Community and Local Government Basic Social Services Project (ACCESS)	Benin	Yes	Secretariat for Decentralized Community Driven Services, under oversight of Ministry of Decentralization and Local Government	Social safety nets	Livelihoods and jobs	93,420
Gazetted Forests Management Project	Benin	Yes	Ministry of Environment and Sustainable Development	Livelihoods and jobs	None	20,760
Food Security and Agriculture Productivity Project (FSAPP)	Bhutan	Yes	Department of Agriculture, Ministry of Agriculture and Forests	Livelihoods and jobs	None	33,509
Rural Economy Advancement Programme (REAP)	Bhutan	Yes	Research and Evaluation Division, Gross National Happiness Commission Secretariat	Livelihoods and jobs	Social safety nets	3,826
Economic Inclusion for Rural Families and Communities Programme (ACCESOS)	Bolivia	No	Ministry of Rural Development and Land (MDRyT)	—	—	—

(Table continues next page)

TABLE D.1 Economic Inclusion Programs Mapped Globally (continued)

Program	Economy	Surveyed	Lead implementing agency or agencies	Primary entry point	Secondary entry point	No. of beneficiaries (direct and indirect)
Improving Employability and Labor Income (Programa Mejora Empleabilidad e Ingreso Laboral, PMEIL)	Bolivia	Yes	Ministry of Planning	Livelihoods and jobs	None	11,861
Rural Alliances Project II	Bolivia	Yes	Emprendimientos Organizados para el Desarrollo Rural Autogestionario (EMPODERAR)	Livelihoods and jobs	Financial inclusion	—
Graduation program	Botswana	No	Government of Botswana	—	—	—
Acre Social and Economic Inclusion and Sustainable Development Project (PROACRE)	Brazil	Yes	Secretaria de Estado do Planejamento e Gestão (SEPLAG)	Social safety nets	Livelihoods and jobs	5,859
Bahia Sustainable Rural Development Project (Bahia Produtiva)	Brazil	Yes	Companhia de Desenvolvimento e Ação Regional (CAR)	Livelihoods and jobs	Financial inclusion	147,851
Internal Relocation Based on Job Opportunity	Brazil	Yes	Brazilian Army	Social safety nets	Livelihoods and jobs	6,620
Programme for Employment and Training of Refugees	Bulgaria	Yes	Employment Agency	Livelihoods and jobs	None	267
Delivery of Graduation in Burkina Faso	Burkina Faso	Yes	Social safety net project Burkin-Naong Sa ya (PFS-BNS) and Trickle Up	Social safety nets	Livelihoods and jobs	91,334
Inclusive Livelihoods Project for Vulnerable Women and Persons with Disabilities in Ouargaye	Burkina Faso	Yes	Ocades Caritas Tenkodogo (Diocese of Tenkodogo)	Livelihoods and jobs	Financial inclusion	1,184
Projet Filets Sociaux Burkin Naong Sa Ya (PFS/BNS)	Burkina Faso	Yes	Supervising Ministry and Ministry of Finance	Social safety nets	Financial inclusion	366,661

(Table continues next page)

TABLE D.1 Economic Inclusion Programs Mapped Globally (continued)

Program	Economy	Surveyed	Lead implementing agency or agencies	Primary entry point	Secondary entry point	No. of beneficiaries (direct and indirect)
Renforcement durable de la résilience des communautés et des ménages vulnérables à l'insécurité alimentaire et nutritionnelle de la province du Yagha dans la région du Sahel au Burkina Faso (RESA)	Burkina Faso	Yes	Humanity and Inclusion	Social safety nets	Livelihoods and jobs	21,904
Youth Employment and Skills Development Project	Burkina Faso	Yes	Ministry of Youth, Employment and Youth Entrepreneurship	Livelihoods and jobs	Social safety nets	318,703
Agro-Pastoral Productivity and Markets Development Project	Burundi	No	—	—	—	—
Burundi Landscape Restoration and Resilience Project	Burundi	Yes	Ministry of Environment, Agriculture, and Livestock—Project Coordinating Unit	Livelihoods and jobs	None	386,400
Integrated Community Development Program—FXB Village (François-Xavier Bagnoud)	Burundi	Yes	FXB International	Livelihoods and jobs	Financial inclusion	7,245
Terintambwe "Take a Step Forward"	Burundi	Yes	Concern Worldwide Burundi	Livelihoods and jobs	Financial inclusion	15,456
Livelihood Enhancement and Association of the Poor (LEAP) Project	Cambodia	Yes	Ministry of Interior	Livelihoods and jobs	Financial inclusion	75,277
Productive Assets and Livelihood Support (PALS)	Cambodia	No	World Food Programme, Ministry of Rural Development, NGOs (Mlup Baitong, Action contre la faim, World Vision International, Life with Dignity, Good Neighbours Cambodia), and Deutsche Gesellschaft für Internationale Zusammenarbeit (GIZ)	—	—	—

(Table continues next page)

TABLE D.1 Economic Inclusion Programs Mapped Globally (continued)

Program	Economy	Surveyed	Lead implementing agency or agencies	Primary entry point	Secondary entry point	No. of beneficiaries (direct and indirect)
Cameroon Social Safety Nets Project	Cameroon	Yes	Cameroon Social Safety Nets Project Implementation Unit	Social safety nets	Financial inclusion	317,378
Livestock Development Project (LDP)	Cameroon	Yes	Ministère de l'Élevage des Pêches et Industries Animales (MINEPIA)	Livelihoods and jobs	None	598,800
Refugees and Host Communities Support Project	Chad	No	—	—	—	—
Emergency Food and Livestock Crisis Response	Chad	Yes	Food and Agriculture Organization (FAO), UNICEF, and International Organization for Migration (IOM)	Social safety nets	Livelihoods and jobs	448,552
Fórmate para el Trabajo: Línea para Personas en Situación de Discapacidad (EX Más Capaz)	Chile	Yes	Servicio Nacional de Capacitación y Empleo (SENCE)	Livelihoods and jobs	None	4,650
Programa Familias	Chile	Yes	Ministry of Social Development and Family, Undersecretary of Social Services	Social safety nets	Livelihoods and jobs	382,500
Programa Mujeres Jefas de Hogar	Chile	Yes	Municipalidades de Chile	Livelihoods and jobs	Social safety nets	82,733
Integrated Community Development Program—FXB Village (Association François-Xavier Bagnoud)	China	Yes	FXB China (local CBO Bu Tuo Eyas Association)	Livelihoods and jobs	Financial inclusion	1,284
Graduation initiative for youth employability	Colombia	Yes	Government of Colombia	Livelihoods and jobs	Financial inclusion	4,410
Orinoquia Integrated Sustainable Landscapes	Colombia	Yes	World Wildlife Fund—WWF Colombia	Livelihoods and jobs	None	—

(Table continues next page)

TABLE D.1 Economic Inclusion Programs Mapped Globally (continued)

Program	Economy	Surveyed	Lead implementing agency or agencies	Primary entry point	Secondary entry point	No. of beneficiaries (direct and indirect)
Transforming My Future	Colombia	Yes	Unidad para la Atención y Reparación Integral a las Víctimas	Social safety nets	Livelihoods and jobs	441
Productive Safety Net Program	Comoros	Yes	National Agency for Design and Implementation of Projects (ANACEP)	Social safety nets	Livelihoods and jobs	22,554
Eastern Recovery Project	Congo, Dem. Rep.	Yes	Fonds Social de la RDC	Livelihoods and jobs	Social safety nets	265,000
Graduation	Congo, Dem. Rep.	Yes	Concern Worldwide	Livelihoods and jobs	Financial inclusion	5,300
Sustainable Livelihoods in the Lomako Reserve: A Conservation and Micro Enterprise Development Partnership	Congo, Dem. Rep.	Yes	African Wildlife Foundation	Livelihoods and jobs	Financial inclusion	1,272
Women for Women International's Empowerment Program	Congo, Dem. Rep.	Yes	Women for Women International	Livelihoods and jobs	Financial inclusion	35,870
Commercial Agriculture Project	Congo, Rep.	No	—	—	—	—
Empléate	Costa Rica	Yes	Ministry of Labour and Social Security, from the National Directorate of Employment	Livelihoods and jobs	Social safety nets	58,820
Livelihoods and Economic Inclusion Programme	Costa Rica	Yes	United Nations High Commissioner for Refugees (UNHCR)	Social safety nets	Livelihoods and jobs	20,068
Productive Safety Nets	Côte d'Ivoire	Yes	Safety nets project implementation unit under the Ministry of Solidarity and Social Cohesion	Social safety nets	Livelihoods and jobs	319,969

(Table continues next page)

TABLE D.1 Economic Inclusion Programs Mapped Globally *(continued)*

Program	Economy	Surveyed	Lead implementing agency or agencies	Primary entry point	Secondary entry point	No. of beneficiaries (direct and indirect)
Protection et assistance en faveur des refugies et demandeurs d'asile en Côte d'Ivoire; programme de reintegration des rapatries ivoiriens	Côte d'Ivoire	Yes	United Nations High Commissioner for Refugees (UNHCR)	Social safety nets	Livelihoods and jobs	11,748
Help Refugees Work	Cyprus	Yes	Cyprus Refugee Council (NGO) in partnership with UNHCR Cyprus	Livelihoods and jobs	None	1,020
Development Response to Displacement Impacts Project in the Horn of Africa	Djibouti	Yes	Agence Djiboutienne de Développement Social	Social safety nets	Livelihoods and jobs	6,300
Support for Women and Youth Entrepreneurship	Djibouti	Yes	Center for Leadership and Entrepreneurship, Ministry of Finance	Financial inclusion	Livelihoods and jobs	630
Progressing with Solidarity (PROSOLI), productive inclusion component of World Bank's Integrated Social Protection and Promotion Project	Dominican Republic	Yes	Social Cabinet	Social safety nets	Livelihoods and jobs	48,957
Modelo de Graduación: Estrategia de Inclusión Socio-Económica	Ecuador	Yes	HIAS Ecuador	Social safety nets	Livelihoods and jobs	56,004
Social Safety Net Project (SSN)	Ecuador	Yes	Ministry of Economic and Social Inclusion	Social safety nets	Financial inclusion	—
Bab Amal Graduation Programme	Egypt, Arab Rep.	Yes	Egyptian Human Development Association (EHDA) and Giving without Limits Association (GWLA)	Livelihoods and jobs	Financial inclusion	4,956
Self-reliance, economic empowerment, and inclusion of refugees and asylum seekers	Egypt, Arab Rep.	Yes	Catholic Relief Services, Caritas, and Refuge Egypt	Livelihoods and jobs	None	3,304

(Table continues next page)

TABLE D.1 Economic Inclusion Programs Mapped Globally *(continued)*

Program	Economy	Surveyed	Lead implementing agency or agencies	Primary entry point	Secondary entry point	No. of beneficiaries (direct and indirect)
Support to Economic Inclusion/ Empowerment Services (pilot under the Strengthening Social Safety Nets Project)	Egypt, Arab Rep.	Yes	Ministry of Social Solidarity	Social safety nets	Livelihoods and jobs	123,900
Gastromotiva	El Salvador	Yes	World Food Programme (WFP)	Livelihoods and jobs	None	485
Redes comunitarias de protección y soluciones duraderas para personas desplazadas internas, deportadas con necesidades de protección y en riesgo de desplazamiento forzado (Community protection networks and durable solutions for internally displaced persons, deportees with protection needs and persons at risk of forced displacement)	El Salvador	Yes	Plan International	Social safety nets	Livelihoods and jobs	187
JóvenES con Todo	El Salvador	No	Presidency of the Republic	—	—	—
Addressing Root Causes of Irregular Migration (ARC program)	Ethiopia	Yes	Norwegian Refugee Council	Livelihoods and jobs	None	327
Building Self-Reliance and Improving the Nutritional Status of Refugees and Host Communities in Pugnido, Gambella	Ethiopia	Yes	Concern Worldwide	Social safety nets	Livelihoods and jobs	27,831
Development response to displacement impacts project in the Horn of Africa	Ethiopia	Yes	Federal Ministry of Agriculture	Social safety nets	Livelihoods and jobs	462,360

(Table continues next page)

TABLE D.1 Economic Inclusion Programs Mapped Globally *(continued)*

Program	Economy	Surveyed	Lead implementing agency or agencies	Primary entry point	Secondary entry point	No. of beneficiaries (direct and indirect)
Emergency Nutrition Response for South Sudanese Refugees in Ethiopia (2018–20)	Ethiopia	Yes	Concern Worldwide	Social safety nets	Livelihoods and jobs	89,784
Livelihood component of Rural Productive Safety Net Program (including all phases of the program)	Ethiopia	Yes	Ministry of Agriculture	Social safety nets	Livelihoods and jobs	3,918,306
Livelihood for Resilience	Ethiopia	Yes	Cooperative for Assistance and Relief Everywhere (CARE) and Catholic Relief Services (CRS)	Social safety nets	Livelihoods and jobs	433,340
Livelihood program	Ethiopia	Yes	The Lutheran World Federation (LWF)	Livelihoods and jobs	None	692
Lowlands Livelihood Resilience Project (LLRP)	Ethiopia	Yes	Ministry of Peace	Livelihoods and jobs	Financial inclusion	—
Promoting Young Women's Livelihoods and Nutrition Project	Ethiopia	Yes	Concern Worldwide	Livelihoods and jobs	None	93,583
REGRADE (Resilience, Graduation and Evidence) Programme	Ethiopia	Yes	Concern Worldwide	Livelihoods and jobs	Social safety nets	25,821
Resilient Landscapes and Livelihoods Project	Ethiopia	Yes	Ministry of Agriculture	Livelihoods and jobs	None	1,590,450

(Table continues next page)

TABLE D.1 Economic Inclusion Programs Mapped Globally *(continued)*

Program	Economy	Surveyed	Lead implementing agency or agencies	Primary entry point	Secondary entry point	No. of beneficiaries (direct and indirect)
Urban Livelihood Programme; current project name: Job Creation for Potential Migrants	Ethiopia	Yes	Bureau of Technical and Vocational Education and Training, Bureau of Industry Development, Bureau of Labour and Social Affairs, Bureau of Job Creation and Enterprise Development, Bureau of Youth and Sport, Bureau of Women and Children Affairs, Bureau of Finance and Economy Development, sectoral associations and institutions	Livelihoods and jobs	Social safety nets	2,102
Urban Productive Safety Net Program	Ethiopia	Yes	Urban Job Creation and Food Security Agency, Ministry for Urban Development and Construction, in collaboration with Ministry of Labor and Social Affairs	Social safety nets	Financial inclusion	604,000
Comparing Livelihood Approaches for the Ultra-Poor in Ghana	Ghana	Yes	Heifer International	Livelihoods and jobs	Financial inclusion	25,582
Ghana Productive Safety Net Project	Ghana	Yes	Ministry of Local Government and Rural Development	Social safety nets	Livelihoods and jobs	24,681
Desde El Poder Local	Guatemala	Yes	Trickle Up and municipalities of Chahal, Ixcán, Nebaj, and Senahú	Livelihoods and jobs	Financial inclusion	7,816
Safety Nets and Basic Services Project	Guinea-Bissau	Yes	Project Coordination Unit, Ministry of Economy and Finance	Social safety nets	None	62,500
Building Hope and Opportunities in Haiti: An Integrated Urban Community Resilience and Conflict Mitigation Programme in Port-au-Prince, Haiti	Haiti	Yes	Concern Worldwide	Livelihoods and jobs	Financial inclusion	30,974

(Table continues next page)

TABLE D.1 Economic Inclusion Programs Mapped Globally (continued)

Program	Economy	Surveyed	Lead implementing agency or agencies	Primary entry point	Secondary entry point	No. of beneficiaries (direct and indirect)
Chemen Lavi Miyò (CLM)	Haiti	Yes	Fondasyon Kole Zepòl (Fonkoze)	Livelihoods and jobs	Financial inclusion	3,346
Support for food security, agricultural strengthening, and nutritional improvement in Grand'Anse Department (ASARANGA)	Haiti	Yes	Cooperative for Assistance and Relief Everywhere (CARE)	Social safety nets	Livelihoods and jobs	12,870
Emprendiendo una Vida Mejor (EVM, Starting Up a Better Life)	Honduras	Yes	Secretariat of Social Development and Inclusion	Social safety nets	Livelihoods and jobs	4,700
Honduras Dry Corridor Food Security Project (PROSASUR)	Honduras	Yes	Strategic Investments of Honduras, under central government	Livelihoods and jobs	None	53,640
Project on Life Improvement and Livelihood Enhancement of Conditional Cash Transfer Beneficiaries through Financial Inclusion	Honduras	Yes	Vice Ministry of Social Integration (SSIS)	Social safety nets	Financial inclusion	31,290
Andhra Pradesh Rural Inclusive Growth Project (APRIGP)	India	Yes	Society for the Elimination of Rural Poverty in Andhra Pradesh (SERP-AP)	Livelihoods and jobs	Social safety nets	1,315,858
Bihar Rural Livelihoods Project (JEEViKA-I) and Bihar Transformative Development Project (JEEViKA-II)	India	Yes	Bihar Rural Livelihoods Promotion Society (BRLPS), Rural Development Department, Government of Bihar	Livelihoods and jobs	Financial inclusion	46,614,000
Meghalaya Community-Led Landscapes Management Project (MCLLMP)	India	Yes	Meghalaya Basin Management Agency (MBMA) under Department of Planning, Government of Meghalaya	Livelihoods and jobs	None	45,700

(Table continues next page)

TABLE D.1 Economic Inclusion Programs Mapped Globally *(continued)*

Program	Economy	Surveyed	Lead implementing agency or agencies	Primary entry point	Secondary entry point	No. of beneficiaries (direct and indirect)
Intervention for Ultrapoor Households in Partnership with Odisha Livelihood Mission (OLM)	India	Yes	Lokadrusti, Self Employed Worker's Association Kendra (SEWAK), and Trickle Up	Livelihoods and jobs	Financial inclusion	4,570
Jharkhand Opportunities for Harnessing Rural Growth Project	India	Yes	Department of Rural Development, government of Jharkhand	Livelihoods and jobs	Financial inclusion	—
National Rural Livelihoods Project	India	No	—	—	—	—
North East Rural Livelihoods Project (NERLP)	India	Yes	North East Livelihood Promotion Society of the Ministry of Development of North Eastern Region, government of India	Livelihoods and jobs	Financial inclusion	1,574,589
Partnering to Scale Up Graduation with Jharkhand State Livelihood Promotion Society (JSLPS)	India	Yes	Pravah, Vedic Society, and Trickle Up	Livelihoods and jobs	Financial inclusion	19,194
State of Maharashtra's Agribusiness and Rural Transformation Project (SMART)	India	Yes	Department of Agriculture, government of Maharashtra; Maharashtra State Rural Livelihoods Mission	Livelihoods and jobs	Financial inclusion	22,850
Tamil Nadu Rural Transformation Project (TNRTP)	India	Yes	Rural Development and Panchayat Raj Department, government of Tamil Nadu	Livelihoods and jobs	Financial inclusion	1,698,303
Targeting the Hard-Core Poor Program	India	Yes	Bandhan Konnagar	Livelihoods and jobs	Financial inclusion	205,650
Tejaswini: Socioeconomic empowerment of adolescent girls and young women in Jharkhand	India	Yes	Jharkhand Women Development Society (JWDS), under Department of Women, Child Development, and Social Services (DWCDSS)	Livelihoods and jobs	None	489,973
Kelompok Usaha Bersama (KUBe)	Indonesia	Yes	Ministry of Social Affairs	Social safety nets	Livelihoods and jobs	458,603

(Table continues next page)

TABLE D.1 Economic Inclusion Programs Mapped Globally (continued)

Program	Economy	Surveyed	Lead implementing agency or agencies	Primary entry point	Secondary entry point	No. of beneficiaries (direct and indirect)
Strengthening Rights and Economies of Adat and Local Communities project	Indonesia	Yes	Samdhana Institute	Livelihoods and jobs	None	4,011
Women for Women International's Empowerment Program	Iraq	Yes	Women for Women International	Livelihoods and jobs	Financial inclusion	13,437
Rural Economic Growth and Employment Project (REGEP)	Jordan	Yes	Jordan Enterprise Development Corporation	Financial inclusion	Livelihoods and jobs	40,120
Small-Ruminant Investments and Graduating Households in Transition (SIGHT)	Jordan	Yes	Ministry of Agriculture	Social safety nets	Livelihoods and jobs	6,608
Can asset transfer or asset protection policies alter poverty dynamics in northern Kenya? A randomized controlled trial (RCT)	Kenya	Yes	BOMA Project	Livelihoods and jobs	Financial inclusion	7,644
Development Impact Bond (DIB)–Kenya	Kenya	Yes	Village Enterprise	Livelihoods and jobs	Financial inclusion	25,444
Economic Justice Program: Scaling up Graduation in West Pokot	Kenya	Yes	Village Enterprise	Livelihoods and jobs	Financial inclusion	3,276
Feed the Future (FTF) Kenya Livestock Market Systems Activity (KLMS)—Rural Entrepreneurship Access Project (REAP)	Kenya	Yes	BOMA Project	Livelihoods and jobs	Social safety nets	19,874

(Table continues next page)

TABLE D.1 Economic Inclusion Programs Mapped Globally *(continued)*

Program	Economy	Surveyed	Lead implementing agency or agencies	Primary entry point	Secondary entry point	No. of beneficiaries (direct and indirect)
Healthy food snacks for improved health and nutrition status among children and pregnant women in poor urban informal settlements in Nairobi County: An innovative public-private partnership approach	Kenya	Yes	Concern Worldwide Kenya	Livelihoods and jobs	None	582
Kenya Core Programming	Kenya	Yes	Village Enterprise	Livelihoods and jobs	Financial inclusion	213,886
Kenya Development Response to Displacement Impacts Project (KDRDIP)	Kenya	Yes	Presidency, Cabinet Affairs	Social safety nets	Livelihoods and jobs	291,200
Kenya Marine Fisheries and Socio-Economic Development (KEMFSED) Project	Kenya	Yes	Ministry of Agriculture, Livestock, Fisheries, and Cooperatives (MoALFC) with State Department for Fisheries, Aquaculture, and the Blue Economy (SDF&BE)	Livelihoods and jobs	None	—
Kenya Village Enterprise Graduation Program with Lwala Community Alliance (+ health intervention)	Kenya	Yes	Village Enterprise	Livelihoods and jobs	Financial inclusion	14,513
Kenya Youth Employment and Opportunities Project	Kenya	Yes	Ministry of Public Service Youth and Gender Affairs	Livelihoods and jobs	None	97,500
Omo Delta Program I	Kenya	Yes	Mercy Corps	Livelihoods and jobs	Financial inclusion	7,262
Rural Entrepreneur Access Project (REAP) Ongoing cohorts in northern Kenya	Kenya	Yes	BOMA Project	Livelihoods and jobs	Financial inclusion	26,645

(Table continues next page)

TABLE D.1 Economic Inclusion Programs Mapped Globally (continued)

Program	Economy	Surveyed	Lead implementing agency or agencies	Primary entry point	Secondary entry point	No. of beneficiaries (direct and indirect)
Tana River County in Kenya: Lifesaving Education and Assistance to Farmers (LEAF) Project (November 2019–January 2021)	Kenya	Yes	Concern Worldwide	Livelihoods and jobs	None	—
Omo Delta Program	Kenya	Yes	Vétérinaires sans Frontieres Germany (VSFG)	Livelihoods and jobs	Financial inclusion	8,609
U.S. Agency for International Development (USAID)–funded feed the future Kenyan livestock market systems (LMS); Expanding Economic Opportunities (EOO): Rural Entrepreneur Access Project	Kenya	Yes	Mercy Corps	Livelihoods and jobs	Financial inclusion	3,931
USAID-funded feed the future Kenyan livestock market systems (LMS); Strengthening Community Capacities for Resilience and Growth (SCCRG); Girls Improving Resilience through Livelihoods (GIRL) component	Kenya	Yes	Mercy Corps	Livelihoods and jobs	Financial inclusion	37,492
USAID-funded Nutrition in Arid and Semi-arid lands (ASALs) within an Integrated/Inclusive Resilience Initiative (NAWIRI)	Kenya	Yes	Village Enterprise	Livelihoods and jobs	Financial inclusion	2,184
Women for Women International's Empowerment Program	Kosovo	Yes	Women for Women International	Livelihoods and jobs	Financial inclusion	2,236
Emergency National Poverty Targeting Program Project	Lebanon	No	—	—	—	—

(Table continues next page)

TABLE D.1 Economic Inclusion Programs Mapped Globally (continued)

Program	Economy	Surveyed	Lead implementing agency or agencies	Primary entry point	Secondary entry point	No. of beneficiaries (direct and indirect)
Livelihood Addressing Root Causes (ARC) program	Lebanon	Yes	Agency for Technical Cooperation and Development (ACTED)	Social safety nets	Livelihoods and jobs	3,596
Livelihoods program	Lebanon	Yes	Concern Worldwide	Livelihoods and jobs	None	7,022
BRAC Liberia Ultra-Poor Graduation (UPG) Pilot Program	Liberia	Yes	BRAC Liberia	Livelihoods and jobs	Financial inclusion	3,713
Liberia Forest Sector Project	Liberia	Yes	Forest Development Authority of Liberia	Livelihoods and jobs	None	34,650
Youth Opportunities Project (YOP)	Liberia	Yes	Ministry of Youth and Sports (MYS); Liberia Agency for Community Empowerment	Livelihoods and jobs	Financial inclusion	64,028
Drought Response Program in the South of Madagascar	Madagascar	Yes	Ministry of Population, Social Protection and Promotion of Women	Social safety nets	Financial inclusion	341,550
Productive Safety Net Program	Madagascar	Yes	Ministry of Population, Social Protection and Promotion of Women	Social safety nets	Financial inclusion	160,875
Childhoods and Livelihoods Program	Malawi	Yes	Yamba Malawi	Livelihoods and jobs	Financial inclusion	2,729
Community Savings and Investment Promotion (COMSIP)	Malawi	Yes	Government of Malawi	Social safety nets	Financial inclusion	171,380
Enabling Sustainable Graduation Out of Poverty for the Extreme Poor in Southern Malawi	Malawi	Yes	Concern Worldwide	Livelihoods and jobs	Social safety nets	81,888
FUTURE (Food and Nutrition for Resilience)	Malawi	Yes	Concern Worldwide, in consortium led by United Purpose and with Save the Children	Social safety nets	Livelihoods and jobs	42,610
Drought Recovery and Resilience Project	Malawi	Yes	Ministry of Finance, Economic Planning, and Development; Department of Disaster Management Affairs	Social safety nets	Livelihoods and jobs	395,753

(Table continues next page)

TABLE D.1   Economic Inclusion Programs Mapped Globally (continued)

Program	Economy	Surveyed	Lead implementing agency or agencies	Primary entry point	Secondary entry point	No. of beneficiaries (direct and indirect)
Malawi Livelihoods Graduation Approach	Malawi	Yes	United Nations High Commissioner for Refugees (UNHCR) and Churches Action in Relief and Development (CARD)	Social safety nets	Livelihoods and jobs	2,030
Alliance pour la Résilience Communautaire (ARC)	Mali	Yes	Humanity and Inclusion, ACTED, Action contre la Faim (ACF), Danish Refugee Council (DRC), International Rescue Committee (IRC), Norwegian Refugee Council (NRC), and Solidarités International	Social safety nets	Livelihoods and jobs	116,200
Emergency Safety Nets Project "Jigisemejiri"	Mali	Yes	Project implementing unit anchored within Ministry of Finance and Economy	Social safety nets	Financial inclusion	458,990
Mali Drylands Development Project	Mali	No	—	—	—	—
Mali Reinsertion of Ex-combatants Project	Mali	Yes	Ministry of Defense and ex-combatants	Social safety nets	Livelihoods and jobs	163,842
Sustainable Landscape Management Project under the Sahel and West Africa Program in Support of the Great Green Wall Initiative (SAWAP)	Mauritania	Yes	Directorate of Nature Protection	Livelihoods and jobs	None	118,000
Co-meta. Volando Alto Program for women's empowerment	Mexico	Yes	Prosociedad	Livelihoods and jobs	Social safety nets	785
Empowering Women and Youth through Graduation and Financial Inclusion in Mexico	Mexico	Yes	Trickle Up, AMTEL Chiapas S.C., Creative Learning, Enlace Comunicación y Capacitación (CC), and Fundación Ko'ox Taani	Livelihoods and jobs	Financial inclusion	11,220
Mexico Dedicated Grant Mechanism for Indigenous People and Local Communities (IPLC) project	Mexico	Yes	Rainforest Alliance	Livelihoods and jobs	None	9,350

(Table continues next page)

TABLE D.1 Economic Inclusion Programs Mapped Globally (continued)

Program	Economy	Surveyed	Lead implementing agency or agencies	Primary entry point	Secondary entry point	No. of beneficiaries (direct and indirect)
Programa de Fomento a la Economía Social	Mexico	Yes	Instituto Nacional de la Economía Social	Livelihoods and jobs	Financial inclusion	9,956
Strengthening entrepreneurship in productive forest landscapes	Mexico	Yes	CONAFOR	Livelihoods and jobs	None	187,000
36-month Ultra Poor Graduation Model in Mongolia	Mongolia	Yes	State Labor and Social Welfare Services Agency	Livelihoods and jobs	Financial inclusion	11,520
Integrated Community Development Program	Mongolia	Yes	FXB Mongolia	Livelihoods and jobs	Financial inclusion	1,793
Programme d'Insertion Economique des Réfugiés Urbains au Maroc (PISERUMA)	Morocco	Yes	Association Marocaine d'Appui à la Promotion de la Petite Entreprise (AMAPPE)	Social safety nets	Livelihoods and jobs	1,289
Agriculture and Natural Resources Landscape Management Project	Mozambique	No	—	—	—	—
Apoio ao desenvolvimento de iniciativas de geração de rendimentos (ADIGR)	Mozambique	Yes	Instituto Nacional de Acção Social (INAS)	Social safety nets	Livelihoods and jobs	4,370
Livelihoods for Durable Solutions: Enhancing Self-Reliance in a Protracted Refugee Situation (Maratane Refugee Camp, Mozambique)	United Nations High Commissioner for Refugees (UNHCR) Graduation Approach	Mozambique	Yes	Kulima	Social safety nets	Livelihoods and jobs	1,241
Mozambique Conservation Areas for Biodiversity and Development (Mozbio)	Mozambique	Yes	Mozambique National Sustainable Development Fund (FNDS) under Ministry of Agriculture and Rural Development	Livelihoods and jobs	None	41,515
Mozambique Forest Investment Project	Mozambique	Yes	Mozambique FNDS under Ministry of Agriculture and Rural Development	Livelihoods and jobs	None	89,751

(Table continues next page)

TABLE D.1 Economic Inclusion Programs Mapped Globally *(continued)*

Program	Economy	Surveyed	Lead implementing agency or agencies	Primary entry point	Secondary entry point	No. of beneficiaries (direct and indirect)
Integrated Community Development Program—FXB Village (Association François-Xavier Bagnoud)	Myanmar	Yes	FXB Myanmar	Livelihoods and jobs	Financial inclusion	4,490
Integrated Community Development Program—FXB Village (Association François-Xavier Bagnoud)	Namibia	Yes	Hope Initiatives Southern Africa (HISA) Namibia	Livelihoods and jobs	Financial inclusion	2,192
Niger Adaptive Safety Net project	Niger	Yes	Prime Minister's Office	Social safety nets	Financial inclusion	97,680
Niger Community Action Program Phase 3	Niger	No	—	—	—	—
Niger Refugee and Host Communities Support Project	Niger	Yes	Strategy for the Development and Security of Sahelian-Saharan Areas of Niger (SDS)	Social safety nets	Livelihoods and jobs	—
Youth Employment and Productive Inclusion (PEJIP)	Niger	Yes	National Employment Agency (ANPE)	Livelihoods and jobs	None	—
Agro-Processing, Productivity Enhancement, and Livelihood Improvement Support Project (APPEALS)	Nigeria	Yes	National Coordination Office, Federal Ministry of Agriculture and Rural Development	Livelihoods and jobs	Financial inclusion	294,000
Multi-Sectoral Crisis Recovery Project for North Eastern Nigeria	Nigeria	No	—	—	—	—
Nigeria for Women Project (NFWP)	Nigeria	Yes	Ministry of Women Affairs of Nigeria	Livelihoods and jobs	None	—
Nigeria National Social Safety Net Program (NASSP)	Nigeria	Yes	National Social Safety Net Coordination Office (NASSCO) and National Cash Transfer Office (NCTO) under Ministry of Humanitarian Affairs Disaster Management and Social Development (MoHADMSD)	Social safety nets	Financial inclusion	49,000

(Table continues next page)

TABLE D.1 Economic Inclusion Programs Mapped Globally *(continued)*

Program	Economy	Surveyed	Lead implementing agency or agencies	Primary entry point	Secondary entry point	No. of beneficiaries (direct and indirect)
Nigeria: Youth Employment and Social Support Operation (YESSO)	Nigeria	Yes	State operations coordinating unit for YESSO in each participating state	Social safety nets	Livelihoods and jobs	2,427,779
Women for Women International's Empowerment Program	Nigeria	Yes	Women for Women International	Livelihoods and jobs	Financial inclusion	36,877
Benazir Income Support Programme	Pakistan	Yes	Benazir Income Support Programme	Social safety nets	Financial inclusion	488,963
Building Resilience in Pakistan Program	Pakistan	Yes	Concern Worldwide	Livelihoods and jobs	Social safety nets	33,540
National Poverty Graduation Programme (NPGP)	Pakistan	Yes	Pakistan Poverty Alleviation Fund (PPAF)	Livelihoods and jobs	Financial inclusion	64,500
Poverty Graduation for Refugees in Mansehra and Peshawar in Khyber-Pakhtunkhwa and Chaghii in Balochistan	Pakistan	Yes	Pakistan Poverty Alleviation Fund (PPAF)	Social safety nets	Livelihoods and jobs	—
Poverty Reduction through Rural Development Activities in Balochistan, Khyber-Pakhtunkhwa, and Federally Administered Tribal Areas and Neighboring Areas/Programme for Poverty Reduction (PPR)	Pakistan	Yes	Pakistan Poverty Alleviation Fund (PPAF)	Livelihoods and jobs	Financial inclusion	499,204
Panama Productive Inclusion Program in Indigenous Territories	Panama	Yes	Ministry of Social Development (MIDES)	Social safety nets	Livelihoods and jobs	4,771
Panamá Pro Joven	Panama	No	Ministry of Labor and Work Development (MITRADEL)	—	—	—

(Table continues next page)

TABLE D.1 Economic Inclusion Programs Mapped Globally *(continued)*

Program	Economy	Surveyed	Lead implementing agency or agencies	Primary entry point	Secondary entry point	No. of beneficiaries (direct and indirect)
Programa Padrino Empresario (PPE)	Panama	Yes	Ministerio de Desarrollo Social (Ministry of Social Development)	Livelihoods and jobs	None	2,378
Programa Tenonderã	Paraguay	Yes	Ministerio de Desarrollo Social (Ministry of Social Development)	Social safety nets	Livelihoods and jobs	45,948
Scaling Graduation Programs as Public Policies: Paraguay	Paraguay	Yes	Ministry of Social Development (MDS) and Ministry of Childhood and Adolescence (MINNA)	Social safety nets	Livelihoods and jobs	8,000
Acceso de Hogares Rurales con Economías de Subsistencia a Mercados Locales—Haku Wiñay/ Noa Jayatai	Peru	Yes	Fondo de Cooperación para el Desarrollo Social—Foncodes (Ministry of Social Development and Inclusion)	Livelihoods and jobs	Social safety nets	501,443
Integrated Forest Landscape Management Project in Atalaya, Ucayali	Peru	Yes	Ministry of Environment	Livelihoods and jobs	None	—
Livelihood Interventions for the Poorest Families' Transformation (LIFT)	Philippines	Yes	Local government unit of Nampicuan	Financial inclusion	Livelihoods and jobs	753
Piloting the Graduation Approach to End Extreme Poverty in the Philippines	Philippines	Yes	Department of Labor and Employment	Social safety nets	Livelihoods and jobs	5,241
Prevail	Philippines	Yes	International Care Ministries	Financial inclusion	Livelihoods and jobs	241,000
Sustainable Livelihood Programme (SLP)—various tracks, including Employment Facilitation Track and Microenterprise Development Track	Philippines	No	Department of Social Welfare and Development (DSWD)	—	—	—
Transform	Philippines	Yes	International Care Ministries	Livelihoods and jobs	Financial inclusion	142,005

(Table continues next page)

305

TABLE D.1 Economic Inclusion Programs Mapped Globally *(continued)*

Program	Economy	Surveyed	Lead implementing agency or agencies	Primary entry point	Secondary entry point	No. of beneficiaries (direct and indirect)
Social Contracts	Russian Federation	No	Ministry of Labor and Social Protection	—	—	—
Enhancing the productive capacity of the extreme poor in Rwanda and Burundi: Terintambwe "Take A Step Forward"	Rwanda	Yes	Government of Rwanda	Livelihoods and jobs	Social safety nets	9,372
Integrated Community Development Program—FXB Village (Association François-Xavier Bagnoud)	Rwanda	Yes	FXB International	Livelihoods and jobs	Financial inclusion	8,520
Socio-economic Inclusion of Refugees and Host Communities in Rwanda Project	Rwanda	No	—	—	—	—
Vision 2020 Umurenge Programme—Minimum Package of Graduation (MPG)	Rwanda	Yes	Local Administrative Entities Development Agency (LODA)	Social safety nets	Financial inclusion	76,620
Women for Women International's Empowerment Program	Rwanda	Yes	Women for Women International	Livelihoods and jobs	Financial inclusion	8,328
Emergency Income Support and Training Project (EISTP)	Sint Maarten, Netherlands (Dutch part)	Yes	Sint Maarten Training Foundation and National Recovery Program Bureau (NRPB)	Social safety nets	Livelihoods and jobs	5,640
Building Resilient Communities in Somalia (BRCiS) phase 2018–22	Somalia	Yes	Concern Worldwide	Livelihoods and jobs	None	165,200
Enhancing Durable Solutions for and Reintegration of Displacement Affected Communities in Somaliland	Somalia	Yes	World Vision	Livelihoods and jobs	Financial inclusion	1,251

(Table continues next page)

TABLE D.1 Economic Inclusion Programs Mapped Globally (continued)

Program	Economy	Surveyed	Lead implementing agency or agencies	Primary entry point	Secondary entry point	No. of beneficiaries (direct and indirect)
Somalia Inclusive Community Resilience and Gender-Based Violence (GBV) Pilot	Somalia	No	—	—	—	—
Somalia Resilience Program (SomReP)	Somalia	No	World Vision	—	—	—
Strengthening the Poorest Households' Economy and Resilience to Shocks (SPHERES)	Somalia	Yes	Concern Worldwide	Livelihoods and jobs	None	1,133
Building Resilience through Asset Creation and Enhancement (BRACE)	South Sudan	Yes	Concern Worldwide	Social safety nets	Livelihoods and jobs	119,070
Integrated Health, Nutrition, Food Security, and Livelihood Program	South Sudan	Yes	Concern Worldwide	Livelihoods and jobs	None	94,500
South Sudan Safety Net Project (SSSNP)	South Sudan	Yes	United Nations Office for Project Services (UNOPS)	Social safety nets	Financial inclusion	—
Women for Women International's Empowerment Program	South Sudan	Yes	Women for Women International	Livelihoods and jobs	Financial inclusion	1,575
National Secretariat for Persons with Disabilities Programmes	Sri Lanka	No	National Secretariat for Persons with Disabilities, Ministry of Social Empowerment and Welfare (MoSEW)	—	—	—
Social Safety Nets Project	Sri Lanka	No	—	—	—	—
Sudan Social Safety Net Project	Sudan	Yes	Ministry of Labor and Social Development and Ministry of Finance	Social safety nets	Financial inclusion	2,795,000
United Nations High Commissioner for Refugees (UNHCR) East Sudan Operation—Graduation Pilot Project	Sudan	Yes	Sudanese Red Crescent Society (SRC) and Sudanese Organization for Research and Development (SORD)	Social safety nets	Livelihoods and jobs	1,677

(Table continues next page)

TABLE D.1 Economic Inclusion Programs Mapped Globally (continued)

Program	Economy	Surveyed	Lead implementing agency or agencies	Primary entry point	Secondary entry point	No. of beneficiaries (direct and indirect)
Multisectoral resilience-building assistance to conflict-affected populations in Syria	Syrian Arab Republic	Yes	Concern Worldwide	Livelihoods and jobs	None	9,231
Tanzania Productive Social Safety Nets 2	Tanzania	Yes	Tanzania Social Action Fund (TASAF)	Social safety nets	Livelihoods and jobs	5,010,000
Transforming Household Resilience in Vulnerable Environments (THRIVE); Babati-Pamoja Project in Tanzania	Tanzania	Yes	World Vision Tanzania	Livelihoods and jobs	Financial inclusion	43,200
Employment Opportunities for Vulnerable Youth Project	Togo	Yes	National Community Development Support Agency (ANADEB)	Livelihoods and jobs	Financial inclusion	28,210
Skills and Employment for Tongans (SET) project	Tonga	Yes	Ministry of Internal Affairs and Ministry of Education and Training	Social safety nets	Livelihoods and jobs	—
Integrated Landscapes Management in Lagging Regions Project	Tunisia	Yes	Ministry of Agriculture, Water Resources, and Fisheries	Livelihoods and jobs	None	4,520
Youth Economic Inclusion Project	Tunisia	Yes	Ministry of Vocational Training and Employment (MFPE)	Livelihoods and jobs	None	—
Building Resilience through Initiatives Defining Growth Potential of Economic Solutions for Syrians (BRIDGES)	Turkey	Yes	Orange and Danish Refugee Council (DRC)	Livelihoods and jobs	None	—
Employment Support Project for Syrians under Temporary Protection and Turkish Citizens	Turkey	Yes	Ministry of Family, Labor, and Social Services and Turkish Employment Agency	Livelihoods and jobs	None	94,030
Livelihoods Innovation through Food Entrepreneurship (LIFE) Project	Turkey	No	Center for International Private Enterprise (CIPE)	—	—	—

(Table continues next page)

TABLE D.1   Economic Inclusion Programs Mapped Globally *(continued)*

Program	Economy	Surveyed	Lead implementing agency or agencies	Primary entry point	Secondary entry point	No. of beneficiaries (direct and indirect)
BRIDGE	Uganda	Yes	Mercy Corps	Livelihoods and jobs	Social safety nets	58,890
Development Food Security Activity (DFSA), Food for Peace (FFP) NUYOK Program (Graduation component)	Uganda	Yes	BOMA Project, Catholic Relief Services, and Caritas Moroto	Livelihoods and jobs	None	7,407
Development Impact Bond— Uganda	Uganda	Yes	Village Enterprise	Livelihoods and jobs	Financial inclusion	30,985
Development Response to Displacement Impacts Project	Uganda	Yes	Office of Prime Minister	Social safety nets	Livelihoods and jobs	47,261
Graduating to Resilience	Uganda	Yes	AVSI	Social safety nets	Livelihoods and jobs	29,649
Poverty Shift: Partnerships for Disability-Inclusive Ultra-Poor Graduation, Uganda	Uganda	Yes	BRAC Uganda	Livelihoods and jobs	Financial inclusion	12,231
Rakai cluster	Uganda	No	World Vision Uganda	—	—	—
Third Northern Uganda Social Action Fund (NUSAF3)	Uganda	Yes	Office of Prime Minister	Social safety nets	Livelihoods and jobs	1,873,220
Uganda Core Programming	Uganda	Yes	Village Enterprise	Livelihoods and jobs	Financial inclusion	189,263
Uganda Village Enterprise alternative livelihood program with International Institute for Environment and Development (Illegal Wildlife Trade) plus conservation intervention	Uganda	Yes	Village Enterprise	Livelihoods and jobs	Financial inclusion	2,446
Entrepreneurship Support through Business Start-up Subsidies	Uzbekistan	Yes	Ministry of Employment and Labor	Livelihoods and jobs	Financial inclusion	20,946

(Table continues next page)

TABLE D.1 Economic Inclusion Programs Mapped Globally (*continued*)

Program	Economy	Surveyed	Lead implementing agency or agencies	Primary entry point	Secondary entry point	No. of beneficiaries (direct and indirect)
Empowering Women and Youth through Graduation and Financial Inclusion in Vietnam	Vietnam	Yes	Plan International	Livelihoods and jobs	Financial inclusion	26,600
Central Highlands Poverty Reduction Project (CHPov)	Vietnam	No	—	—	—	—
Gaza Emergency Cash for Work and Self-Employment Project	West Bank and Gaza	Yes	NGO Development Center	Social safety nets	Livelihoods and jobs	33,242
Smallholder Agricultural Production Restoration and Enhancement Project	Yemen, Rep.	Yes	Food and Agriculture Organization (FAO)	Livelihoods and jobs	None	—
Girls' Education and Women's Empowerment and Livelihoods Project	Zambia	Yes	Ministry of Community Development and Social Services	Social safety nets	Livelihoods and jobs	384,750
Graduation Approach	Zambia	Yes	Caritas Czech Republic	Social safety nets	Livelihoods and jobs	2,052
Transforming Landscapes for Resilience and Development (TRALARD)	Zambia	Yes	Luapula, Muchinga, and northern provincial administrative authorities	Livelihoods and jobs	None	51,300
Innovative Solutions to Support Livelihood of Vulnerable Communities Project (ISV-COM)	Zimbabwe	Yes	GOAL Zimbabwe and World Vision	Social safety nets	Livelihoods and jobs	1,632
Self-Reliant, Resilient, and Sustainable Livelihoods	Zimbabwe	Yes	GOAL	Social safety nets	Livelihoods and jobs	2,652

Source: Partnership for Economic Inclusion, World Bank, and documents of programs listed in table.

Note: In the table, individual beneficiaries represent current direct and indirect beneficiaries. — = not available; NGO = nongovernmental organization.

Components of Economic Inclusion Programs

This appendix describes the main types and modalities of individual components of economic inclusion programs captured in the Partnership for Economic Inclusion (PEI) Landscape Survey 2020 (figure E.1). Assessing the quality and adequacy of the components provided was beyond the scope of the PEI Landscape Survey 2020 and therefore is not discussed here.

Transfers designed to smooth consumption

Economic inclusion programs often provide financial support for consumption smoothing (68 percent of all programs), in particular programs that have a social

FIGURE E.1 **Percentage of Economic Inclusion Programs, by Type of Component**

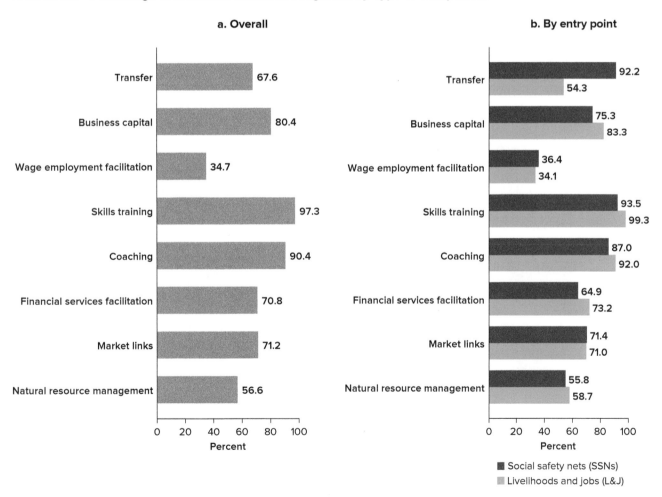

Source: Partnership for Economic Inclusion, World Bank.

Note: Panel a shows the percentages of all programs by component (N = 219). Panel b shows the percentages of programs by entry point (N = 77 SSN programs + 138 L&J programs). Financial inclusion programs are excluded due to the small subsample (four programs).

safety net (SSN) as the primary entry point (92 percent versus 54 percent of livelihoods and jobs [L&J] programs). Almost half of the programs that provide capital for consumption smoothing are existing government cash transfer programs (48 percent), and 25 percent of programs with this component are linked to an existing public works program.

Regular and predictable transfers help poor and vulnerable households meet their most pressing needs without resorting to negative coping strategies. Temporary income support can also compensate for the time program participants are not working while taking part in the program. Consumption support is mostly transferred in cash (87 percent of programs that include this component), but 30 percent of programs provide an in-kind transfer. Of the programs that include a cash transfer, 73 percent provide a direct cash transfer, whereas 32 percent provide such a transfer in exchange for work. Regardless of the type of program, most interventions rely on a single modality for the provision of the transfer (70 percent of programs that include a transfer), but differences emerge in the type of modality used by different entry points (figure E.2).

Business capital

To contribute to developing or expanding the livelihood base, most programs provide business capital for establishing or supporting small businesses (80 percent of all programs), particularly programs seeking to support income diversification (89 percent of programs with income diversification as a main objective) in order to address the financial capital constraints faced by poor and vulnerable households.

FIGURE E.2 **Percentage of Economic Inclusion Programs, by Modality of Transfer**

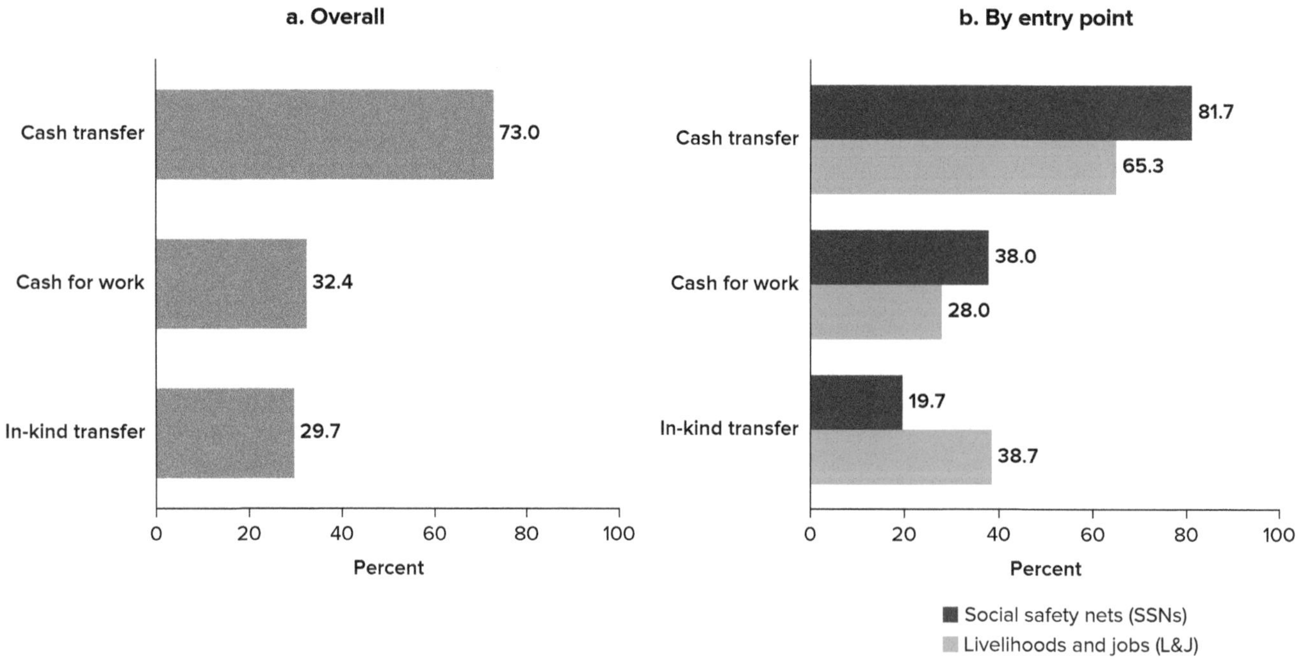

Source: Partnership for Economic Inclusion, World Bank.

Note: Panel a shows the percentages of all programs providing a transfer for consumption smoothing (N = 148). Panel b shows the percentages of programs providing a transfer for consumption smoothing by entry point (N = 71 SSN programs + 75 L&J programs). Financial inclusion programs are excluded due to the small subsample (two programs). Programs may use more than one transfer modality.

Business capital can take the form of cash grants (71 percent), in-kind grants and asset transfers (44 percent), matching grants (17 percent), and soft loans—credit with favorable conditions (17 percent)—or other forms of support such as coupons or market rate credit (5 percent). Some programs combine multiple forms of business capital (figure E.3). More nongovernment-led programs provide business capital than government-led programs (85 percent versus 76 percent). The costing exercise outlined in chapter 6 reveals that the average grant size of programs is $381 (2011 US$ at purchasing power parity, PPP) and is similar for government-led and nongovernment-led projects ($387 and $369, respectively). The average cost of business capital in nongovernment-led programs ($232) is higher than in government-led programs ($182).

The overall costs in programs led by nongovernment institutions are relatively evenly spread across multiple components. But in a majority of government-led programs, the cost is primarily driven by either a consumption support component or a business capital component.

Cash-based capital (offered by 85 percent of programs providing business capital) is more commonly provided, mostly as grants, than in-kind (asset) transfers (figure E.3).

Wage employment facilitation

About a third of programs facilitate access to wage employment opportunities (35 percent of all programs). Forty-five government-led programs in 30 countries facilitate access to wage employment, 40 percent of which build on an existing

FIGURE E.3 **Percentage of Economic Inclusion Programs, by Modality of Business Capital**

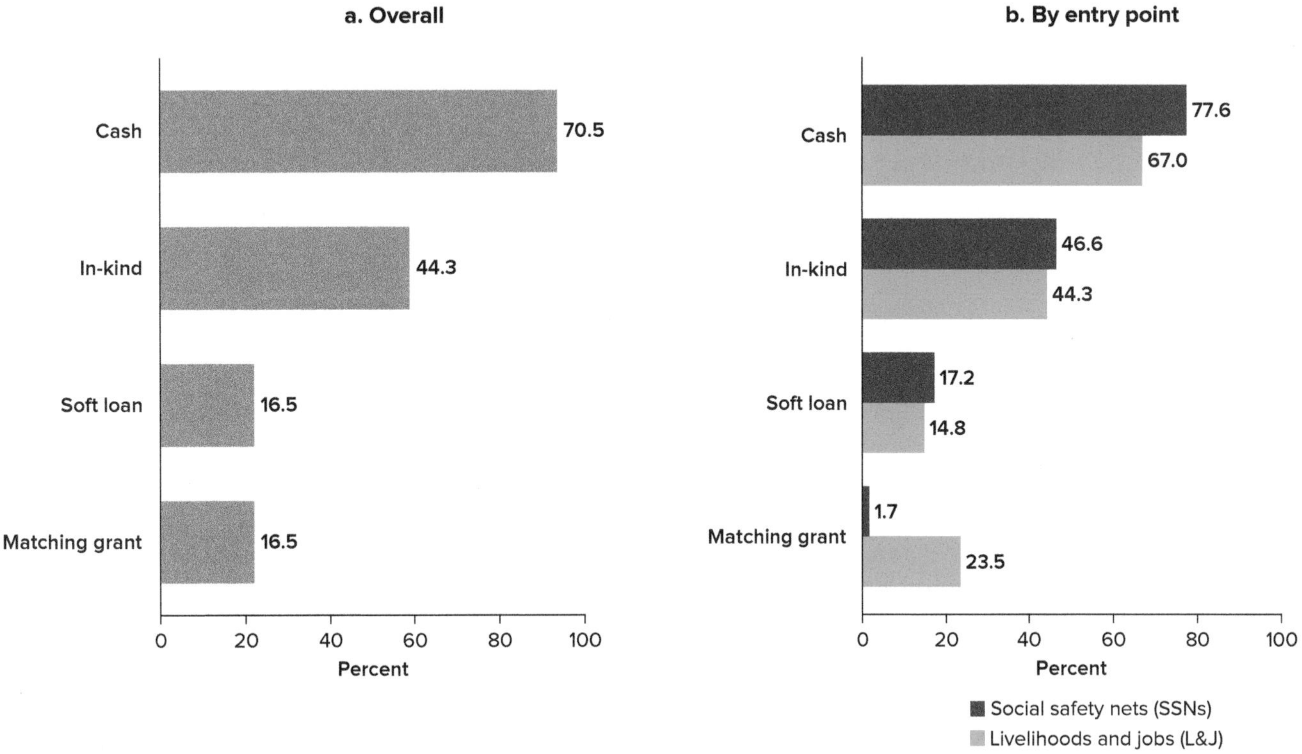

a. Overall

Modality	Percent
Cash	70.5
In-kind	44.3
Soft loan	16.5
Matching grant	16.5

b. By entry point

Modality	Social safety nets (SSNs)	Livelihoods and jobs (L&J)
Cash	77.6	67.0
In-kind	46.6	44.3
Soft loan	17.2	14.8
Matching grant	1.7	23.5

■ Social safety nets (SSNs)
■ Livelihoods and jobs (L&J)

Source: Partnership for Economic Inclusion, World Bank.

Note: Panel a shows the percentages of all programs providing business capital (N = 173). Panel b shows the percentages of programs providing seed capital by entry point (N = 58 SSN programs + 115 L&J programs). Financial inclusion programs are excluded due to the small subsample (three programs). Programs may use more than one modality to transfer business capital.

FIGURE E.4 **Percentage of Economic Inclusion Programs, by Type of Wage Facilitation**

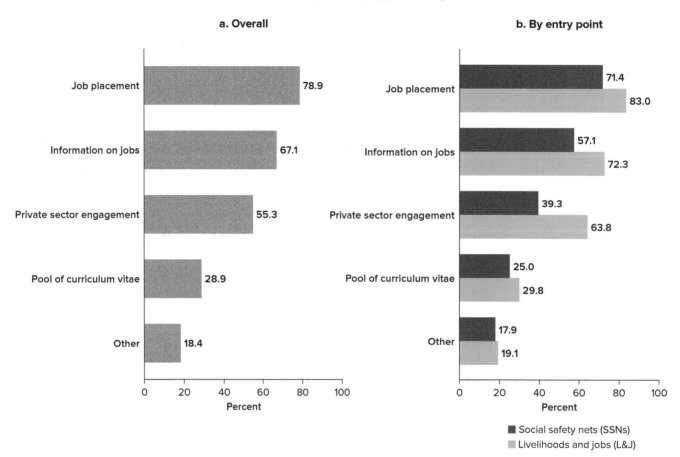

Source: Partnership for Economic Inclusion, World Bank.

Note: Panel a shows the percentages of all programs facilitating access to wage employment (N = 76). Panel b shows the percentages of programs facilitating access to wage employment by entry point (N = 28 SSN programs + 47 L&J programs). Financial inclusion programs are excluded due to the small subsample (one program). Programs may use more than one type of intervention to facilitate access to wage employment.

government labor intermediation program. Twenty-seven percent of government-led programs that facilitate access to wage employment build on active labor market programs.

Most programs facilitating access to wage employment opportunities (93 percent), both government- and nongovernment-led, link with potential employers to achieve better participant outcomes. Most common, programs help beneficiaries to obtain internships, traineeships, and apprenticeships (figure E.4), after or as part of the skills training course(s) in order to increase the relevance of new skills and reduce beneficiaries' time outside of the labor market. About a third of programs supporting wage employment establish a pool of curriculum vitae (CVs) from which enterprises can identify job candidates. Of those programs creating a CV pool, 82 percent also engage with the private sector to increase the effectiveness of the CV pool.

Skills training

To address the specific needs of targeted groups, economic inclusion programs provide different types of training, including on entrepreneurship and business management, financial literacy, and technical, vocational, and life skills (figure E.5). Some programs

FIGURE E.5 **Percentage of Economic Inclusion Programs, by Type of Skills Training**

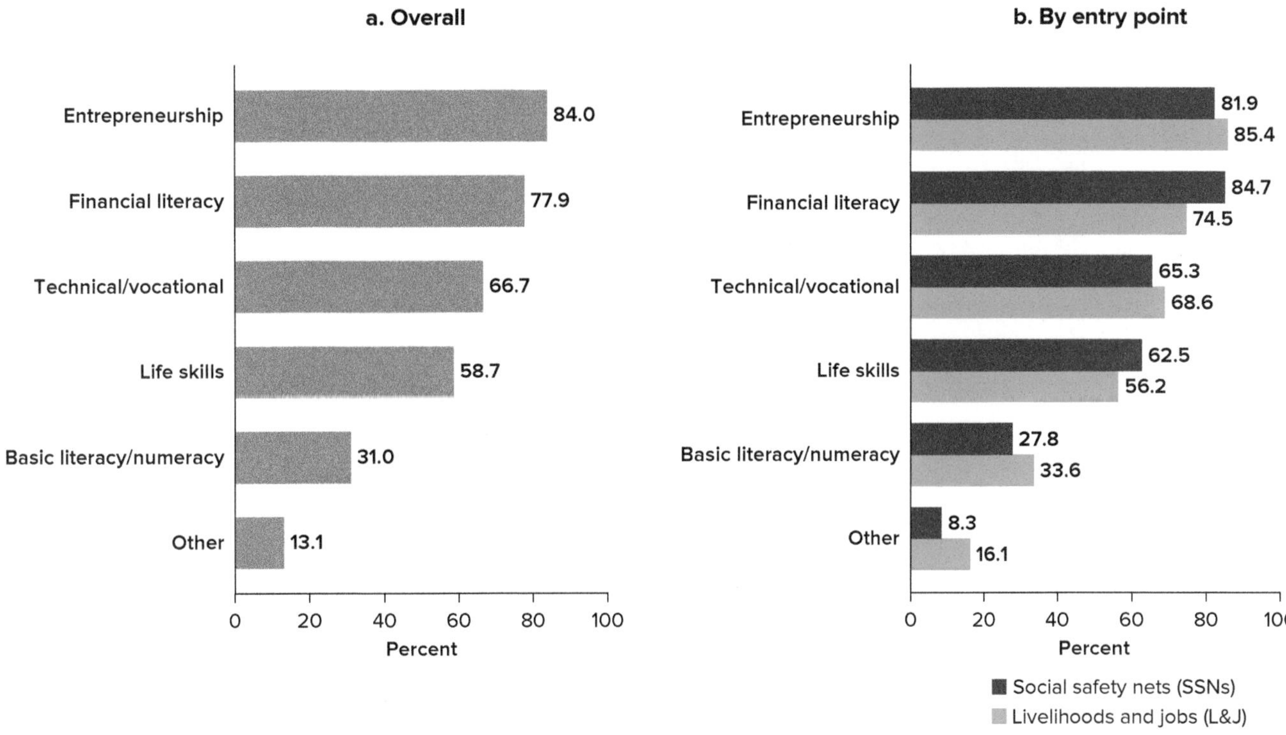

a. Overall / b. By entry point

■ Social safety nets (SSNs)
■ Livelihoods and jobs (L&J)

Source: Partnership for Economic Inclusion, World Bank.

Note: Panel a shows the percentages of all programs providing skills training (N = 213). Panel b shows the percentages of programs providing skills training by entry point (N = 72 SSN programs + 137 L&J programs). Financial inclusion programs are excluded due to the small subsample (4 programs). Programs may deliver more than one type of training.

focus on one type of training (8 percent of programs with training), most often technical or vocational, while others seek to expand participants' skills with a broader suite of training opportunities. For example, entrepreneurship training is usually combined with financial literacy training to increase business management skills more broadly (71 percent of programs providing training), particularly if program participants receive financial support for establishing or developing businesses (79 percent versus 35 percent for programs that do not provide business capital).

Coaching

Defined as informal guidance provided in an informal way, coaching is used by programs to build soft skills, support self-confidence, provide emotional support, and foster changes in attitudes and social norms. Ninety percent of all programs include coaching, most of which provide coaching related to the livelihood (84 percent), particularly business development. Coaching on business development during the "ideation phase" can enable participants to identify and act on business challenges and opportunities and help match livelihoods to individual circumstances and market contexts.[1] Counseling on job placement is not widely used because far fewer programs facilitate access to wage employment.

Economic inclusion programs also use coaching to address the social and psychosocial barriers to economic inclusion and to improve the overall quality of life for beneficiaries (68 percent of programs with coaching). Coaching may include topics on social issues affecting the family and community (such as child marriage and

FIGURE E.6 **Percentage of Economic Inclusion Programs, by Type of Coaching**

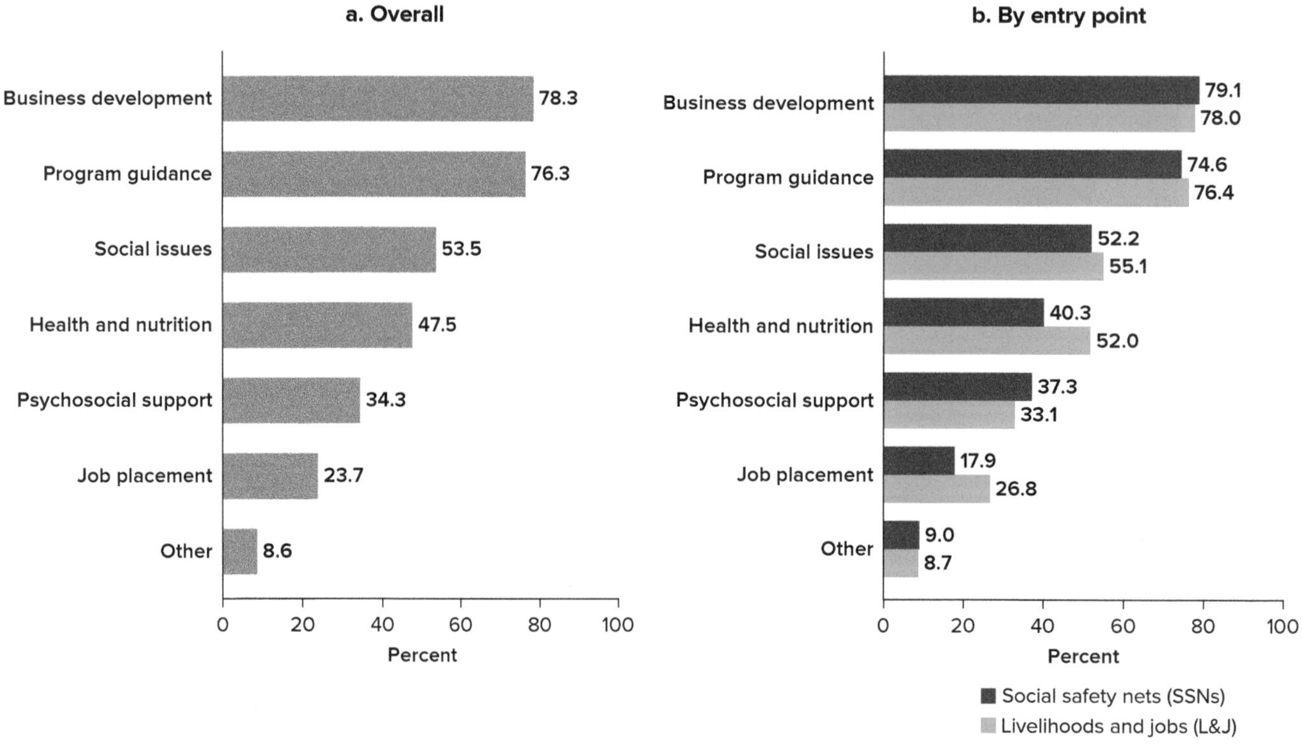

a. Overall

Business development	78.3
Program guidance	76.3
Social issues	53.5
Health and nutrition	47.5
Psychosocial support	34.3
Job placement	23.7
Other	8.6

b. By entry point

	Social safety nets (SSNs)	Livelihoods and jobs (L&J)
Business development	79.1	78.0
Program guidance	74.6	76.4
Social issues	52.2	55.1
Health and nutrition	40.3	52.0
Psychosocial support	37.3	33.1
Job placement	17.9	26.8
Other	9.0	8.7

Source: Partnership for Economic Inclusion, World Bank.

Note: Panel a shows the percentages of all programs providing coaching (N = 198). Panel b shows the percentages of programs providing coaching by entry point (N = 67 SSN programs + 127 L&J programs). Financial inclusion programs are excluded due to the small subsample (four programs). Programs may include more than one type of coaching.

intrahousehold dynamics), psychosocial support, and health and nutrition guidance (figure E.6). This type of coaching is more prevalent among programs working with vulnerable groups, such as the ultrapoor and the extreme poor populations, than programs not specifically targeting these groups.

Financial services facilitation

Seventy-one percent of all programs facilitate access to financial services. Most programs facilitate access to savings (87 percent of programs facilitating access to financial services), credit (78 percent), or both (66 percent); see figure E.7. Building savings is particularly important in programs serving households that fall in the extreme poor category. They are more vulnerable to shocks and have fewer means of growing their businesses than less poor households.

Insurance, such as index, crop, or livestock, can help households reduce risk exposure and cope with shocks. However, there is limited availability of appropriate insurance products and limited uptake by poor and vulnerable households (El-Zoghbi, Holle, and Soursourian 2019). Moreover, the number of economic inclusion programs facilitating access to insurance products is low (18 percent of programs facilitating access to financial services).

FIGURE E.7 **Percentage of Economic Inclusion Programs, by Type of Financial Service**

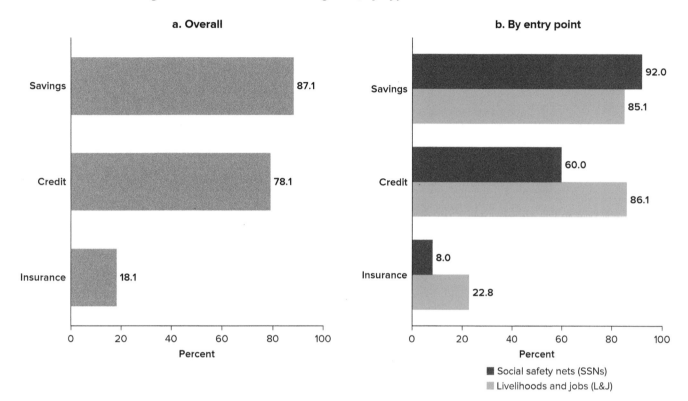

Source: Partnership for Economic Inclusion, World Bank.

Note: Panel a shows the percentages of all programs facilitating access to finance (N = 155). Panel b shows the percentages of programs facilitating access to finance by entry point (N = 50 SSN programs + 101 L&J programs). Financial inclusion programs are excluded due to the small subsample (four programs). Programs may facilitate access to more than one type of financial service.

Market access facilitation

Seventy-one percent of all programs facilitate integration into markets for program participants. Programs that facilitate market access follow a mix of market integration strategies (figure E.8). Facilitating access to inputs, technology, and capital can further address households' constraints. Establishing new or developing existing producer organizations (POs) can help strengthen the position of and increase market access for small producers.

POs can further support market integration by, for example, facilitating access to improved inputs, technology, and key market players. Compared with other programs, programs that develop POs tend to facilitate more access to improved inputs (84 percent versus 46 percent); access to technology (85 percent versus 30 percent); links to service providers (76 percent versus 58 percent); links to national, regional, and local markets (76 percent versus 51 percent); and links to international markets (24 percent versus 5 percent).[2]

FIGURE E.8 Percentage of Economic Inclusion Programs, by Type of Market Facilitation

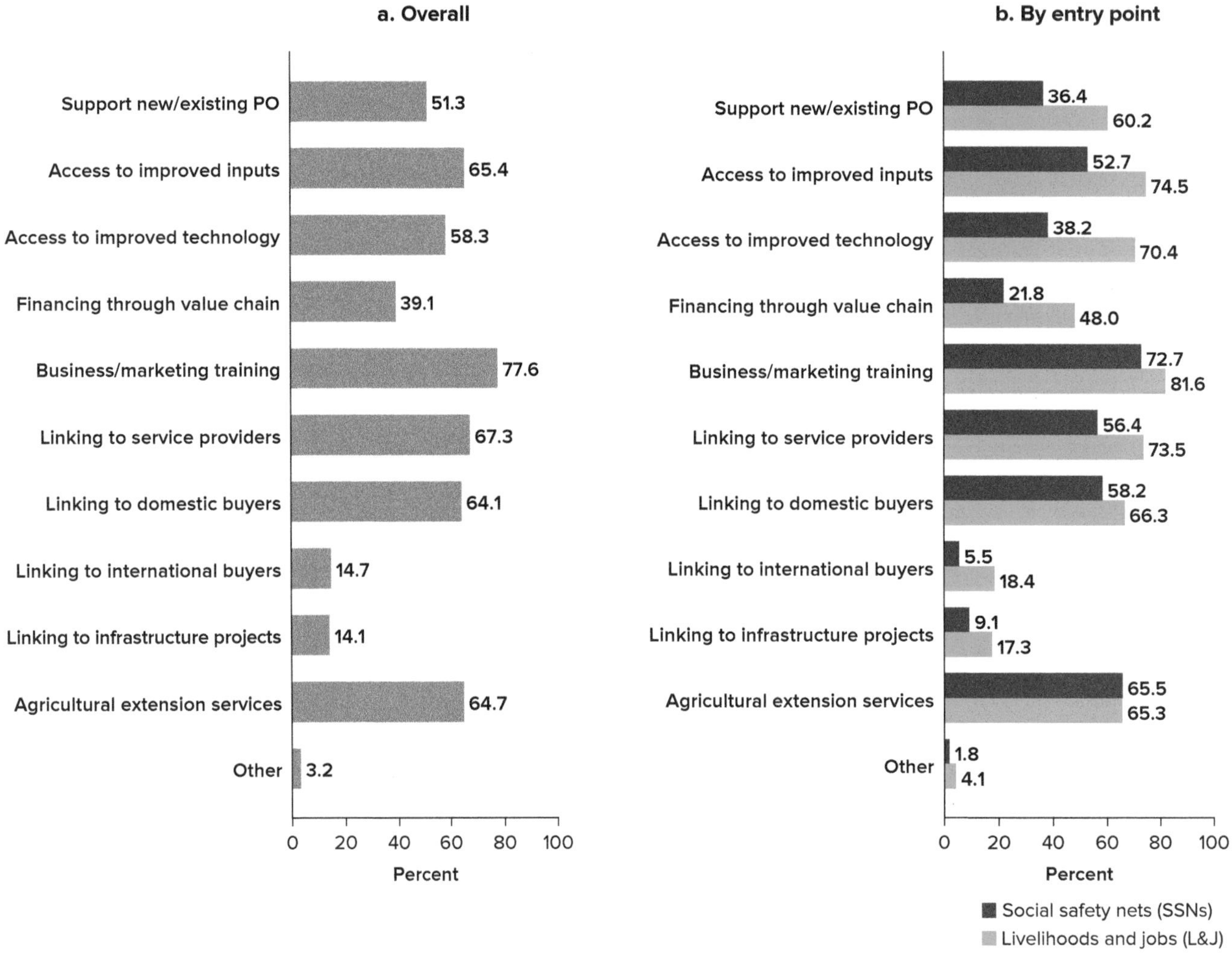

a. Overall

	Percent
Support new/existing PO	51.3
Access to improved inputs	65.4
Access to improved technology	58.3
Financing through value chain	39.1
Business/marketing training	77.6
Linking to service providers	67.3
Linking to domestic buyers	64.1
Linking to international buyers	14.7
Linking to infrastructure projects	14.1
Agricultural extension services	64.7
Other	3.2

b. By entry point

	Social safety nets (SSNs)	Livelihoods and jobs (L&J)
Support new/existing PO	36.4	60.2
Access to improved inputs	52.7	74.5
Access to improved technology	38.2	70.4
Financing through value chain	21.8	48.0
Business/marketing training	72.7	81.6
Linking to service providers	56.4	73.5
Linking to domestic buyers	58.2	66.3
Linking to international buyers	5.5	18.4
Linking to infrastructure projects	9.1	17.3
Agricultural extension services	65.5	65.3
Other	1.8	4.1

Source: Partnership for Economic Inclusion, World Bank.

Note: Panel a shows the percentages of all programs facilitating access to markets (N = 156). Panel b shows the percentages of programs facilitating access to markets by entry point (N = 55 SSN programs + 98 L&J programs). Financial inclusion programs are excluded due to the small subsample (three programs). Programs may include more than one type of intervention to facilitate access to markets. PO = producer organization.

Natural resource management and climate change adaptation

Fifty-seven percent of economic inclusion programs include interventions that support the sustainable management of natural resources or climate change adaptation, or both, as a way of protecting and enhancing the livelihood base of program beneficiaries. Interventions include water management and land tenure systems (figure E.9), with a higher percentage of L&J than SSN programs focusing on improved forest management practices and smart agriculture.

FIGURE E.9 **Percentage of Economic Inclusion Programs, by Type of Natural Resource Management or Climate Change Adaptation Intervention**

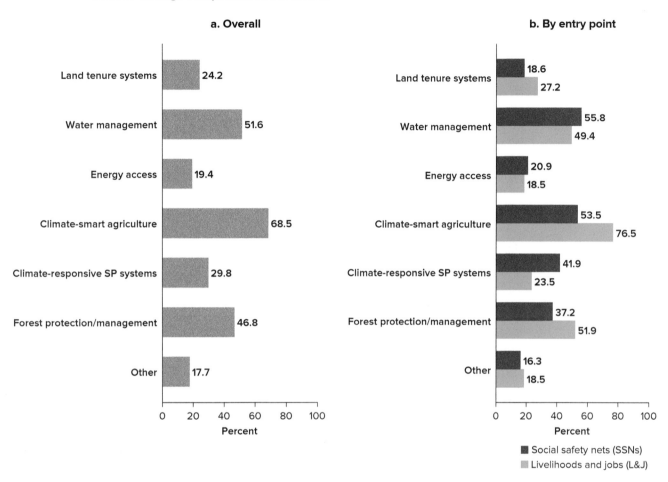

a. Overall

	Percent
Land tenure systems	24.2
Water management	51.6
Energy access	19.4
Climate-smart agriculture	68.5
Climate-responsive SP systems	29.8
Forest protection/management	46.8
Other	17.7

b. By entry point

	Social safety nets (SSNs)	Livelihoods and jobs (L&J)
Land tenure systems	18.6	27.2
Water management	55.8	49.4
Energy access	20.9	18.5
Climate-smart agriculture	53.5	76.5
Climate-responsive SP systems	41.9	23.5
Forest protection/management	37.2	51.9
Other	16.3	18.5

■ Social safety nets (SSNs)
■ Livelihoods and jobs (L&J)

Source: Partnership for Economic Inclusion, World Bank.

Note: Panel a shows the percentages of all programs supporting natural resource management or climate change adaptation or both (N = 124). Panel b shows the percentages of these programs by entry point (N = 43 SSN programs + 81 L&J programs). Financial inclusion programs are excluded from this analysis because they are few in number. Programs may include more than one type of intervention. SP = social protection.

Notes

1. Evaluations of programs in Paraguay and Colombia reveal that participants find the business plan process empowering because it increases their knowledge and self-confidence about their enterprise choice (CADEP 2017; Moreno-Sánchez et al. 2018; Escobal and Ponce 2016).
2. All differences are statistically significant at 1 percent, with the exception of the difference in the links with service providers, which is significant at 5 percent.

References

CADEP (Centro de Análisis y Difusión de la Economía Paraguaya). 2017. "Evaluación de proceso del programa Sembrando Oportunidades Familia por Familia" [Process evaluation of the Sembrando Oportunidades Family by Family program]. CADEP, Paraguay.

El-Zoghbi, Mayada, Nina Holle, and Matthew Soursourian. 2019. "Emerging Evidence on Financial Inclusion: Moving from Black and White to Color." Consultative Group to Assist the Poor (CGAP) Focus Note, World Bank, Washington, DC.

Escobal, Javier, and Carmen Ponce. 2016. "Combinando protección social con generación de oportunidades económicas: Una evaluación de los avances del Programa Haku Wiñay" [Combining social protection with the generation of economic opportunities: An evaluation of the progress of the Haku Wiñay program]. Grupo de Análisis para el Desarrollo, Lima.

Moreno-Sánchez, Rocío, Jorge H. Maldonado, Vanesa Martínez, and Arturo Rodríguez. 2018. "Qualitative evaluation of the Poverty-Alleviation Program Produciendo por mi Futuro in Colombia." CEDE Working Paper No. 24, Center for Studies on Economic Development (CEDE), Universidad de los Andes, Colombia.

Glossary

adequacy. In this report, the calculation of whether a grant amount, cash transfer amount, cost of asset transfer, and public works wage received by a beneficiary is sufficient to meet average consumption needs of the poorest households in the respective countries. Adequacy is calculated by dividing the per beneficiary cost of a component by the average annual per capita consumption rate for the bottom 20 percent of households in the relevant country.

agency. The capacity of individuals to act independently and to make their own free choices.

antipoverty program. Program designed or directed to reduce or abolish poverty. Term is used in this report to describe large-scale government programs.

community structure. Community-based entity that can be mobilized within the purview of a program intervention or, if existing, be utilized by a program intervention. Examples include informal community savings and credit groups, local governance groups, formalized producer organizations, demographic groups (women's cooperatives, youth groups), or activity groups (sports, religious, interests).

complementary/single program. An economic inclusion program package that features a bundle of coordinated interventions. In a complementary program, several programs are linked together to provide all program components, whereas in a single program, one program provides all program components.

Consultative Group to Assist the Poor (CGAP)–Ford Foundation Graduation Program. A program that, between 2006 and 2014, partnered with local organizations and governments to launch 10 pilot projects in eight countries. A robust learning and evaluation agenda, including qualitative research and randomized controlled evaluations, or both, was embedded in all the pilot sites.

convergence/program convergence. When the components of two or more existing, discrete programs serve the same group of beneficiaries.

coverage. The total number of beneficiaries reached by a program or a combination of programs relative to the total population.

coverage equivalent. The total number of beneficiaries reached by a program or combination of programs relative to specific poverty measures. This report considers three measures: the national poverty line, extreme poverty line, and Multidimensional Poverty Index.

delivery system. In social protection systems, the system used to implement social protection (including labor) benefits and services, including the implementation phases and processes along the delivery chain, main actors (people and institutions), and enabling factors (communications, information systems, and technology).

dosage. The amount of capital required for adequate transfers. In this report, *dosage* may refer to a threshold below which programs are deemed to lack the type of impact necessary to meet the objectives set forth by the program.

economic inclusion. The gradual integration of individuals and households into broader economic and community development processes. This integration is achieved by addressing the multiple constraints or structural barriers faced by the poor at different levels. Examples of levels are the household (such as human and physical capacity), the community (such as social norms), the local economy (such as access to markets and services), and across formal institutions (such as access to political and administrative structures). Throughout the report, these constraints are viewed as simultaneous and often nonseparable. They are viewed as most intensively affecting extreme poor and vulnerable groups.

economic inclusion program. A bundle of coordinated, multidimensional interventions that support individuals, households, and communities in their efforts to increase their incomes and assets. Economic inclusion programs therefore aim to facilitate the dual goals of strengthening both the resilience of and opportunities for individuals and households who are poor. These goals are met through strengthening community and local economy links. The term *economic inclusion* is sometimes used interchangeably with the term *productive inclusion*.

extreme poor. See *poverty level.*

fast climber. See also *slow climber.* Participants who are experiencing positive changes during the program and who are on an upward trajectory during the program and after program exit and manage to sustain those changes afterward.

financial inclusion. One of the three program entry points defined in the report. Support is provided through the use of savings groups, formal banking services, microcredit, government-to-person (G2P) payments, digital payments, and other means that have the potential to improve resilience and opportunities for the extreme poor and vulnerable, particularly women.

fragility, conflict, and violence (FCV). World Bank classification of countries with high institutional and social fragility and of countries affected by violent conflict.

functional scale-up. Increasing the scope of an activity, where initially a program starts with a single focus but then layers or links additional multisectoral interventions.

International Bank for Reconstruction and Development (IBRD). One of the two organizations comprising the World Bank (see also **International Development Association**). IBRD provides loans and advice to middle-income and credit-worthy poor countries. IBRD and IDA share the same staff and headquarters and evaluate projects with the same rigorous standards.

International Development Association (IDA). One of the two organizations comprising the World Bank (also see **International Bank for Reconstruction and Development**). IDA helps the world's poorest countries. Overseen by 173 shareholder nations, it aims to reduce poverty by providing loans (called "credits") and grants for programs that boost economic growth, reduce inequalities, and improve people's living conditions.

livelihoods and jobs. One of the three program entry points defined in the report. For the poorest and most vulnerable, access to employment tends to be informal, risky, and often limited by constraints to the labor supply—human capital (such as education, skills, and networks)—and labor demand—the business environment (such as access to finance, infrastructure, technology, and markets). An increasing number of livelihood and job programs are focusing on removing barriers that prevent the extreme poor and vulnerable (such as poor households in rural or urban areas, youth, refugees, and women) from participating in the local economy and in higher-productivity jobs.

Multidimensional Poverty Index (MPI). A measure of the prevalence of poverty based on indicators that go beyond monetary metrics and span three dimensions: health, education, and standard of living. The MPI is overseen by the Oxford Poverty and Human Development Initiative at the University of Oxford.

nongovernmental organization (NGO). An organization that is neither part of a government nor a conventional profit-maximizing business. Although some NGOs may accept funding from governments or work in collaboration with government agencies, an NGO is by definition not itself a governmental entity.

nongovernment-led. Programs led by institutions other than governments.

opportunity. The capacity of households in economic inclusion programs to capture and capitalize on investments that improve human capital outcomes and that they would otherwise miss.

poverty level.
    poor. Persons whose consumption is below the national poverty line, as defined by the government. Or those who, because of their personal or community characteristics, face barriers in accessing opportunities to earn sustainable livelihoods and have elevated risks of being or staying in poverty or being socially marginalized.

    extreme poor. Persons whose consumption is below $1.90 per day (2011 US$ at purchasing power parity, PPP) and who can work on a sustained basis. Also defined as the bottom 50 percent of the poor population in a country or those unable to meet basic needs.

    ultrapoor. Persons whose consumption is below $0.95 per day (2011 US$, PPP). Also defined as those experiencing the severest forms of deprivation such as being persistently hungry or lacking sources of income.

    other vulnerable. Other groups that do not meet any of the previous criteria such as those just above the poverty line or groups marginalized irrespective of their poverty level.

purchasing power parity (PPP). The number of units of a country's currency required to buy the same amount of goods and services in the domestic market as a U.S. dollar would buy in the United States.

randomized controlled trial (RCT). A program evaluation in which participants and nonparticipants are deemed to be statistically comparable and in which participants are randomly allocated to receive a given intervention. By monitoring outcomes in both groups, an RCT reveals the differences that can be attributed to a specific program intervention.

resilience. The strengthened ability of a household to manage risk and respond to and cope with sudden shocks that are likely to overwhelm them.

rotating savings and credit association (ROSCA). A group of individuals who meet regularly in order to save and borrow together.

scale-up or scale. The process by which a program is established, expanded, or adapted under real-world conditions into broader national policy and programming. Scale-up often builds on the success of programs shown to be effective on a small scale or under controlled conditions. Scale-up may also be driven without prior piloting and testing, and often in response to a political decision or directive.

Scale-up is is not just about coverage—the number of beneficiaries served by the program in relation to the total population of the country—but also about quality—the quality of impact and sustainability of coverage, as well as processes of change and adaptation. Economic inclusion at scale therefore considers the programmatic and institutional mechanics required to embed programs at the national level through large-scale antipoverty programs, led by governments with clear alignment with national strategies, partnership development, and underlying political economy considerations.

self-help program. A savings-and-credit group consisting of women and men who meet regularly and undertake financial savings and internal loans from the group's common funds. Self-help groups can be federated, with each group represented in a federation structure that can serve as a platform for economic inclusion, linking the poorest to the formal banking system and enabling a range of services, including insurance, credit counseling, sound financial practice orientation, as well as digital and mobile banking.

single/complementary program. Economic inclusion program packages feature a bundle of different interventions that can be delivered either by one primary organization or by more than one, working in concert. In single programs, one program provides all program components, whereas complementary programs link several programs together.

slow climber. See also *fast climber.* A participant who may only gradually begin to experience positive changes during the program.

social protection. Social protection and labor systems, policies, and programs that help individuals and societies manage risk and volatility and protect them from poverty and destitution by means of instruments that improve equity, resilience, and opportunity.

social safety net or safety net. One of the three program entry points defined in the report. Noncontributory transfer programs target in some manner the poor and those vulnerable to poverty and shocks. Social safety nets can include cash, in-kind transfers, social pensions, public works, and school feeding programs aimed at poor and vulnerable households. It is analogous to the U.S. term *welfare* and the European term *social assistance.*

social safety net–plus (SSN-plus). A term together with *cash-plus* gaining prominence as countries expand the coverage and financing of safety net programs, in particular cash transfers. The "plus" indicates the potential to complement cash with additional inputs, service components, or links to *external services.*

ultrapoor. See *poverty level.*

vulnerable group. See *poverty level.*